MEMORIALS
OF
OLD CHELSEA

MEMORIALS
OF
OLD CHELSEA

BY
ALFRED BEAVER

WITH A NEW PREFACE
BY
PATRICIA MEARA, A.L.A.
Chelsea Reference Librarian, Royal Borough
of Kensington and Chelsea Public Libraries

Republished S. R. Publishers Ltd., 1971
First published Elliot Stock,
London, 1892

ISBN 0 85409 710 4

Reprinted by Scolar Press Ltd.,
Menston, Yorkshire, U.K.

PREFACE

In the eighty year since Alfred Beaver was writing Chelsea has altered in many ways particularly in the kind and number of people living here. When Beaver wrote the population was over 74,000 but it has now fallen to about 40,000 due largely to redevelopment. The nineteenth century inhabitants, though including those distinguished in art and literature, were predominantly artisans living in workmen's cottages. Many of these cottages, picturesque but insanitary, have been demolished and replaced by various trust buildings and by council and private housing; the remaining cottages, now modernised command high prices and their occupants may be associated with the theatre, films and television. Redevelopment is still taking place and at present a large new housing complex, designed by Eric Lyons, is replacing the Victorian housing built on the site of Cremorne Gardens in West Cheslea.

A conspicuous change was made to the view of the waterfront in 1910 when Crosby Hall, a house originally in the City of London and once owned by Sir Thomas More, was rebuilt on part of the garden of his Chelsea house for the British Federation of University Women. The second world war caused further alterations in Chelsea, the worst loss historically being the bombing of the Old Church now restored and with the majority of its monuments replaced. The houses between the church and Crosby Hall were also destroyed and Roper's Garden now occupies the site. The east wing of the Royal Hospital was bombed in both world wars but was restored each time and a new infirmary has been built for the Pensioners. On a site to the west of the Royal Hospital is a new building for the National Army Museum which is due to be opened in 1972.

Many visitors to Chelsea arrive by underground at Sloane Square station, also bombed and subsequently rebuilt. Next to the station is the Royal Court Theatre, called the Court Theatre when Beaver was writing, which was restored to use as a live theatre in 1952 and became the home of "the angry young men" of the decade and remains an important part of the English theatre. On the opposite side of the square is Peter Jones department store, rebuilt in 1936 and still among the best modern buildings in London. The square has an attractive fountain, designed by Sir Gilbert Ledward, which was placed there in 1953.

There have been changes too in the administration of Chelsea. The old parish vestry was replaced by a Borough Council in 1900 when Chelsea became a Metropolitan Borough; at the same time the detached portion of the parish at Kensal was split between Kensington and Paddington and a tidying up of boundaries transferred Chelsea Barracks to Westminster. Then in 1965 Chelsea was merged with the neighbouring Royal Borough of Kensington to form the Royal Borough of Kensington and Chelsea.

Chelsea's name at present is widely known for differing reasons. The football fan knows the Chelsea Football Club, whose ground in fact is in neighbouring Fulham; the gardener thinks of the Royal Horticultural Society's annual flower show held for many years in the grounds of the Royal Hospital; and to young people it means the fashions of King's Road, whose village high street atmosphere has gone as the local grocers, greengrocers, butchers and fishmongers have given way to ever more fantastically named boutiques, although comparatively few major alterations have been made to the buildings apart from the many new shop fronts. Only The Royal Military Asylum, now known as the Duke of York's Barracks and the various garden squares off King's Road continue to provide a welcome expanse of green. Despite the changes of the twentieth century, only the more obvious of which have been mentioned above, Chelsea still retains a lot of its old character and Beaver's history remains an interesting and worthwhile work.

Patricia Meara.

CARLYLE'S HOUSE IN CHEYNE ROW.

Memorials
of Old Chelsea:

A NEW HISTORY OF THE VILLAGE
OF PALACES.

BY

ALFRED BEAVER.

WITH NUMEROUS ILLUSTRATIONS BY THE AUTHOR.

LONDON:
ELLIOT STOCK, 62, PATERNOSTER ROW, E.C.
1892.

I DEDICATE THESE PAGES TO MY

EXCELLENT FRIEND,

JOHN SCOTT, B.A.,

AS SOME

SLIGHT EXPRESSION OF

MY ESTEEM AND GOOD WISHES.

PREFACE.

A PLACE of such exceptional interest as Chelsea has naturally had many historians, among whom may be mentioned Bowack, 1705, slight but useful for contemporary details; Rev. Daniel Lysons, M.A., 1795 (supplement, 1799), accurate and full of research; Hughson, 1809; Nightingale; Brewer and Norris, 1815; Thomas Faulkner, 1809, second edition, 1829, to whom we must all own a heavy debt; Bryan, 1869, who continues the record, though very imperfectly; Isabella Burt, 1875; Rev. A. L'Estrange, 1879, who treats the biographical side in a very interesting manner; and Dr. Martin, 1887, who gives a sympathetic and picturesquely written sketch.

But notwithstanding this array of authors, which might well deter other aspirants in the same field, it has been felt by many that a new history of Chelsea, covering the whole ground, including the latest researches, and amply illustrated, was a want distinctly felt by those who take an interest in this fascinating subject; and when it was suggested by some old Chelsea residents that I should undertake the task, I bent myself to it with alacrity.

So great is the mass of material available, that though I have kept as strictly as possible to the title, 'Memorials of *Old* Chelsea,' yet it has been necessary to discard much interesting matter, because well known, in order to include other matter previously unedited or not given due prominence. This course necessarily involves a certain incongruity of treatment, giving an apparently undue importance in some cases to certain persons and incidents. A work of this class, however, is valuable, rather for its research and historic accuracy than for its literary style; and to ensure this accuracy, as far as may be, I have summoned to my aid 'a cloud of witnesses,' and allowed them to speak for themselves.

With regard to the meagre treatment of recent history, which may be disappointing to some (particularly local readers), as the necessity of it was to myself, I must plead the difficulty of space. Two bulky volumes would barely have sufficed had this part been written in any detail. Early in the course of my work I found it would be necessary to limit the field of treatment, and therefore it was that the present title was chosen.

I cannot close this preface without expressing my thanks to several gentlemen who have assisted me in the progress of this work, particularly to the Right Hon. Sir Charles Dilke, Bart., Right Hon. L. H. Courtney, M.P., Dr. J. S. Phené, F.S.A., Mr. Walter Rye, Mr. R. F. Sketchley, M.A., Mr. C. J. Quinn, Mr. J. R. S. Clifford, Mr. C. D. Sherborn, Mr. John Scott, B.A., Mr. J. C. Feret, F.R.Hist.S., Mr. W. Lovell, Mr. G. P. Boyce, R.W.S., and Mr. David Hodge.

CHELSEA,
May, 1892.

CHELSEA IN 1738, FROM A PRINT BY THOMAS PREIST, OF CHELSEA.

MEMORIALS OF OLD CHELSEA.

HISTORICAL INTRODUCTION.

THE History of England, unlike that of certain Continental States, has been made by the whole people, and not merely by a small privileged class. Gentle and simple have played their parts in its development. Naturally, therefore, it teems with stirring deeds and memorable events, whose results have been great and momentous, and whose influence to-day is far-reaching and widespread. In such a country the local record of almost any part of it must needs be interesting and valuable to the modern historian, and if to none other, at least to its own inhabitants. This is eminently the case with Chelsea : for many years the Chelsea folk have been distinguished for their pride in their home and its story—a pride which has been sympathetically recognised even by visitors from the other side of the world. Chelsea, however, has more than a mere local interest : it has historical associations that belong to the nation—of patriots and martyrs, poets and artists, kings, queens, and statesmen, aristocrats and soldiers ; awakening the most varied thoughts and feelings of pride and joy, or of shame and sorrow. Every street and corner, almost every foot of ground, is historic. Few parts of London or of our country are so rich in varied and charming memories. But with all this wealth of association there is little or nothing that is lurid or exciting in its records. The peaceful village that stood by the water's edge has not (in modern times, at least) been the scene of any of the battles, plots, and insurrections that crowd so thickly, and often so uselessly, the blood-stained pages of our history. The interest of Chelsea lies very largely in the records of its illustrious inhabitants, a long line of whom, reaching back to the Middle Ages, connects us, often intimately, with many of the events that have influenced the making of our nation. The stately homes of these famous men and women gave to Chelsea the exalted title of the 'Village of Palaces,' which it has borne time out of mind.

London is growing with alarming rapidity: the huge desert of bricks and mortar, steadily, yet swiftly, spreading on every side, is burying in oblivion alike the quiet hamlet and the storied mansion—obliterating even the natural landmarks of what were once its rural suburbs. Chelsea has not escaped; it has suffered sadly in both respects. No longer can we say with the authors of ' The Beauties of England and Wales,' writing as late as 1815, ' The hand of recent speculation has been denied access to certain favoured spots,' or speak of the elegant villas 'adorned by a fine spread of home scenery.' The great houses which gave Chelsea its fame have all but disappeared, and the quaint old streets, or ' rows,' as so many of them were called, will soon have disappeared too. Where is the West Bourne, a wood-skirted trout-stream of olden days, or even the little rivulet on the western boundary? The one is now a sewer ; a railroad occupies the bed of the other. Gone, too, is the belt of open land which fringed the little village—the Lots, the Lammas Lands, the famous Meads, and the Common with its pond. Labyrinths of narrow, squalid streets now cover its ancient fields and gardens.

At the present time the wave of destruction is once more at the full : now it is a landlord (or perhaps a vestry) intent on what are called ' improvements '; now a tradesman with no thought but for the increase of business ; now a tenant whose hazy ideas of taste bid him rebuild his house in the fashion that happens to prevail. These care nought for the poetry of life ; they see nothing but dirt in the stain of time ; and if they cannot scrape or paint or plaster the invaluable bequests of the past—relics of the best works of our fathers—will ruthlessly destroy them, leaving not even a trace, and barely a name, to remind some curious searcher of the all but forgotten associations of the past.

Nevertheless, the shadow of bygone days still lingers here and there on Chelsea ; the once delightful place has not entirely lost its old character; the nobly-proportioned Hospital, with its beautiful grounds, and the hoary old church, with its wealth of monuments, still remain to give an old-world air to the place; and there are yet enough old-fashioned houses—' mellowed by the stealing hours of time ' to the tints so dear to the artistic sense—to show us what the place once was, and to save it from that modern hideousness (begotten of the stern conflict for life thrust upon us by our modern competitive system), which marks, almost universally, the London suburb.

It may be well to notice here that there are or were other Chelseas than that in Middlesex. In the thirteenth and fourteenth centuries we have frequent notices of a Chelse in Hertfordshire; we find Chebbeseye, in Worcestershire, called Chelsheye in the Taxation of Pope Nicholas; in the reign of Edward I., and afterwards in that of Henry VII., we read of a Chelsea Manor in Staffordshire; Cholsey in Berkshire is written Cealsea in the time of Henry III., Chelseie in the Nonæ Roll, and frequently Chelsey in Tudor times; at the commencement of the Great Rebellion, before Charles I. had raised his standard at Newark, we find a body of soldiers mustered at Chelsey Wood, somewhere in the north, and perhaps identical with Midelchelseye in Yorkshire, where a certain Milo de Stapelton acquired land in the reign of Edward I. Selsey, however, which Norden calls Chelsey, was, so far as I have observed, never properly so called. In Saxon times it was Selesegh—'the isle of seals.' There are also two Chelseas in America, one in New England, founded probably by planters who went over with one of the Gorges' expeditions in 1622, and another in Vermont, also possibly founded by emigrants from the old Chelsea in Middlesex.

The situation of Chelsea in Middlesex is a pleasant and healthy one; it stands on an angle of the river, with a wide straight reach, stretching some two miles to the east. Its gravel soil, rising gradually from the river bank, was the first land, westward of London, fairly above its waters. Its nearness to the capital, its healthy air, and the convenience of the water-highway were among the causes of its early selection as an aristocratic suburb.

The origin of place-names is always a matter of interest, and not unfrequently sheds a ray of light upon the darkness of early times. The labours of modern students of language have developed philology into a science, by the light of which the vague guesses of the older (and not unfrequently the modern) writers often appear ridiculous; but notwithstanding this the etymology of Chelsea is still a matter of dispute.

Let us examine the conjectures first. The least plausible is that which, judging from the amount of space given to it, emphasized by the use of capitals and italics, seems to have particularly pleased the fancy of Faulkner (second edition, vol. i., pp. 4, 5). This is founded on the spelling Chelcheya or Chelchey, which has, for the purpose, a sufficient resemblance to Chaulchée, an old form of *Chausée*, middle English *Causey*, modern Causeway. We might find some sort of justification for this in the fact that, as the great part of Chelsea had been brought under cultivation when Domesday Book was compiled (1085-86), there must have been some sort of embankment to the low-lying lands in those days. Whitaker, moreover, has asserted that the

Thames, east and west of London, was embanked by the Romans. But there is no evidence, not even a tradition, of so ancient a causeway in Chelsea; and the name Chelchey, which occurs only in Norman-French documents, is evidently a softened form of an older name, in which the final c of the first syllable is hard. The name Cealchythe, or Celchyth, is certainly Saxon, and it is to this language we must look for its derivation.

Bosworth, in his 'Anglo-Saxon Dictionary,' derives Chelsea from Ceoles-ige, 'the place of ships,' which at first sight seems plausible enough, but it was necessary to invent a spelling which does not exist. It may be noticed that this is the actual derivation of Cholsey in Berkshire, as recognised by Bosworth's recent editor, Mr. T. N. Toller, M.A., who, however, also retains it as the derivation of Chelsea in Middlesex, which is certainly incorrect, as will presently be shown.

Camden found the origin of the name in the beds of sand in the river; Leland and Somner wanted to make it Shelfsey, 'from the shelves of sand near it.' It is quite certain that these did then exist; we find the 'shelves of sand' spoken of in a church record, 1631 ('Scudamore Papers;' B.M., n. 11,056, f. 292). Norden develops the idea, and says in his 'Speculum Britannica' :

> 'So-called of the nature of the place, whose strand is like the chesel, which the sea casteth up of sand and pebble-stones; therof called Cheselsey, briefly Chelsey, as is Chelsey, in Sussex, north (*sic*) of Chichester, which stands upon the very edge of the sea, as this Chelsey on the Thamise.'

Chelsey sands were proverbial as far back as the days of James I. Ben Jonson in 'The Forest' mentions 'the sands of Chelsey Fields.' An etymology that is supported by the geology of the place is certainly very tempting, and finds several followers in the present day. Its derivation would thus be the Anglo-Saxon *ceosl*, pebble, and *ey*, shoreland, and the name would thus mean the 'pebbly shore or eyot.' If this were the correct view, our numerous records would certainly supply us with some intermediate forms, such as that invented by Norden. Not only are these lacking, but we have instead a series of forms which directs us to another source altogether. To ignore these is to put on one side our most reliable source of information, and the comparison of such names as Chelsfield, Chesilhampton, Chelsil Beach, etc., depends entirely upon the modern forms, Chelsey and Chelsea.

The only safe way of ascertaining the origin of a place-name is to trace its historical descent. The form Chelsea is quite modern; its use began very early in the eighteenth century (French ambassadors misspelled it so even in the seventeenth century), though Chelsey is found some fifty years later. This latter spelling came into use in the sixteenth century—1531 is, perhaps, the earliest date at which it has been noted, although Chelshey and Chelchea occur in Norman-French documents as mentioned above, and Chelseia is found, though most unaccountably, as early as 1189. These serve to show how soon the Normans began to soften the hard final *c* of the Saxon name. In Tudor times we have it written Chelcheth, Chelseth, Chelshith, Chelsith (so More wrote it), Chelsyth, Chelsehith, and Chelscithe. Chelchith occurs anno 20 Edward IV.; Chelcheth in 4 Henry IV.; Chelchehith from 1302 to 1378; Chelcheth in 1291; Chelched in the Domesday Book; Cealchylle, or perhaps Cealchyde (the reading is doubtful), in Edward the Confessor's charter; Celchyth in 996 under Athelred the Unready; Celchyð in 899, when Alfred the Great was nearing his end; Celchiðe in 801, under Coenwulf of Mercia; and Celchyð, under Offa, in 785 (the old-standing dispute upon the site of this place is dealt with later on). In the Domesday Book we find two forms given: the one, Chelched, is apparently intended for Chelchyd or Chelchythe; while the other, Cercehede, indicates the difficulty that a Norman scribe, unacquainted with the Saxon tongue, might be expected to have with Saxon names. A large number of names, where there can be no doubt as to identity, are similarly mangled in this valuable compilation; for example, Putney, originally Potten, or Putten heath, appears as Putelei.

Newcourt, in a more etymological spirit than his predecessors, conjectured from the early forms of the name with which he was acquainted that it was derived from the Anglo-Saxon *ceald*, cold, and *hyth*, or *hyd*, wharf or haven, signifying, therefore, 'cold harbour.' This, he says, 'agrees very well to the situation of this place, it standing bleak and open to the Thames, where it is wide.' This guess is certainly ingenious, and as to the latter syllable, Newcourt was undoubtedly correct; but with regard to the former, his conjecture fails, for the same reason as Norden's—that history supplies us with no forms to warrant its acceptance.

The spelling in Edward's charter, Cealchylle, if that be the correct reading, is undoubtedly a clerical error for Cealchythe, the spelling used in the Saxon Chronicle. There is little or no doubt that this is the original spelling of the name Chelsea in its uncorrupted or unabbreviated form, and from it we must find the derivation. With our present information it admits of but one explanation, and evidently signifies 'chalk wharf' or 'haven,' and as no chalk is found anywhere in the neighbourhood, we may explain it either, as Lysons suggests, a place at which chalk for building or other purpose was landed (from Kent and Essex, or the opposite county, Surrey, where it abounds), from very early, and possibly Roman times, or a wharf built of chalk and flints. In support of this, it must not be forgotten that such a haven or dock did exist at

Chelsea, from time immemorial; that the remains of a causeway leading to a ford, constructed of chalk stones, still exist; and that the most ancient part of the church (although this does not carry us back very far) is built of chalk.

Chelsea was thus one of the series of Thames havens, some of which still retain the latter part of their names almost in ancient form, such as Queen-

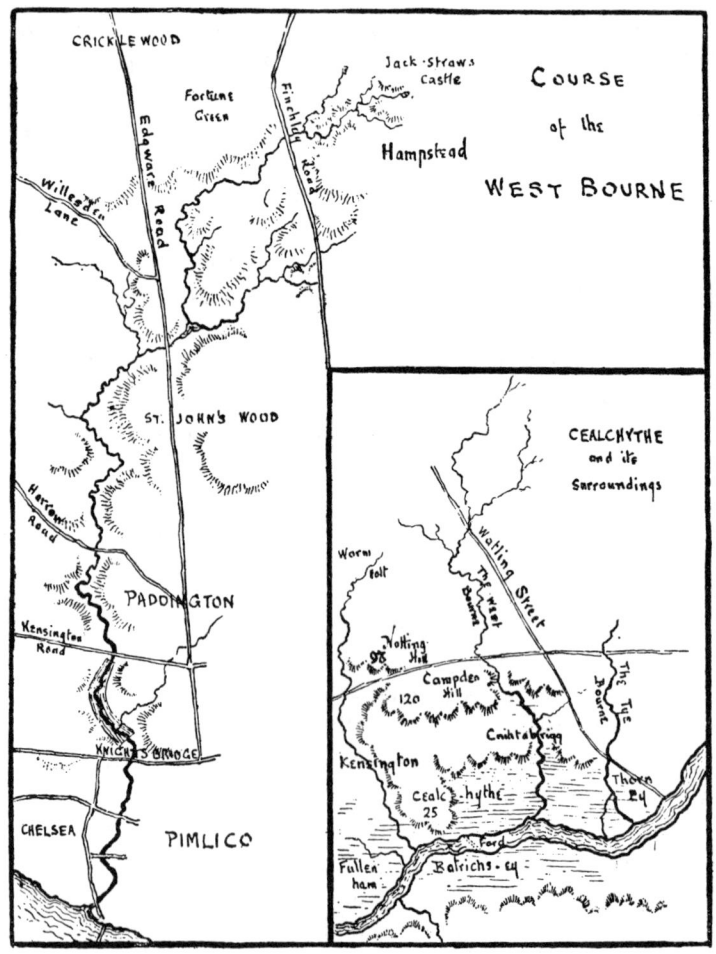

hithe, Rotherhithe, Garlickhithe, and Greenhithe, while others, like Lambeth and Erith, have been arrested in the process of corruption. In Stepney, originally Stebonhythe, we have a name which has suffered similar curtailments to Cealchythe.

In the remote period which preceded the Saxon Conquest, Chelsea was the southern end of a narrow tongue of land (averaging twenty-five feet above the level of high tides), which extended through Kensington to the higher lands round Campden Hill (one hundred and twenty feet high) ; it was covered with heath and scrub, having on the north-east a dense wood, and on the east and west a morass, which was flooded with every tide. It was the home of the wild ox, the wolf, the boar, and the red deer, whose bones (with others of earlier date, such as the hyæna and elk) have been found in various spots round about. Its marshes swarmed with wild-fowl ; even in the memory of some yet alive the adjacent ' Five Fields,' now Pimlico, was a favourite spot for snipe-shooting, and the name of the neighbouring parish of Fulham, anciently Fullenham, is believed to mean ' the abode of fowls.' The human inhabitants of pre-Saxon Chelsea were a few casual families of the Trinobantes, a Celtic tribe that had crossed the narrow Dover strait in their wanderings westwards, and who had their fortress at Llyn Dyn, 'the hill by the pool,' destined in after-days, as London, to become the centre of the world.

On the west was the rivulet known since the eighteenth century as Batter-sea Bridge Creek, rising in Wormholt (now Wormwood) Scrubs, north-west of Notting Hill. In 1828 it was made navigable for barges as far as Kensington ; but all beyond Stanley Bridge has since been drained, and the bed now forms the roadway of the West London Extension Railway. On the east was the Westbourne, which took its rise in the ponds on Hampstead Heath, near Jack Straw's Castle. It passed through Kilburn, receiving on its way the waters of another streamlet, the Kil or Cold Bourne ; thence, by the notorious Bagnigge Wells, and so into Hyde Park. There it widened into several ponds, which, by the direction of Queen Caroline, whose taste in landscape-gardening is well known, were formed into the Serpentine and Long Water. This, with the tiny streamlet at the southern end, is all that remains to mark the course of the ancient stream, and this even is now supplied from another source. From Hyde Park it passed under the Knightsbridge (the origin of which Mr. Loftie would find in Neytesbridge, from the Manor of Neyte), through wooded shades, with a pleasant pathway along its bank (where Lowndes Square now stands), under Blandel (afterwards Bloody) Bridge and Stone Bridge, and so into the Thames near Ranelagh Gardens. The narrow passage between the Nell Gwynne Tavern and Chelsea Barracks occupies the site of part of its course. In January, 1809, the Westbourne overflowed its banks, causing considerable damage, and forming a lake of some size, across which visitors to the Bun-house had to be ferried. The Thames also overflowed at the western end of the parish, and worshippers at the old church had to be conveyed thither in

2

boats. As the neighbourhood developed, the 'rapid Rhone,' as the boys of Chelsea called the once pleasant stream, became, like the old Fleet River, little better than an open sewer (a fate which afterwards overtook the noble Thames itself), whirling along an unlovely burden of festering refuse. Part of it was open as late as 1854, but is now drained into the Ranelagh Sewer, which passes over the underground railway at Sloane Square; its name survives in

The Westbourne
at Knightsbridge.

Westbourne Park, Paddington, and in Westbourne Street, near Eaton Square, where Bloody Bridge stood.

The Westbourne and the other streams which take their rise in the uplands of Hampstead have been important factors in determining the character of the soil of this neighbourhood. During the last three centuries, too, they were the chief source of the water supply of the western suburbs of London. In 1620 James I. granted to Thomas Day, of Chelsea, license to convey the waters within Hyde Park and elsewhere—that is, those of the Westbourne—

to the City of Westminster. A grant of similar purport was made to Thomas Hawes, of Westminster, by Charles II. in 1663.

Many finds of ancient British weapons, implements, and other relics have been made in and about Chelsea—at Kensington, St. James's Park, Battersea, Wandsworth, etc. Among the objects discovered at Kensington, some of which are preserved in the British Museum, were fragments of knives, gouges, a large button or boss from a shield, together with several lumps of metal, which had lain there, all these long centuries, among the rough metal and the cinders, in the very place where the manufacture had been carried on. A

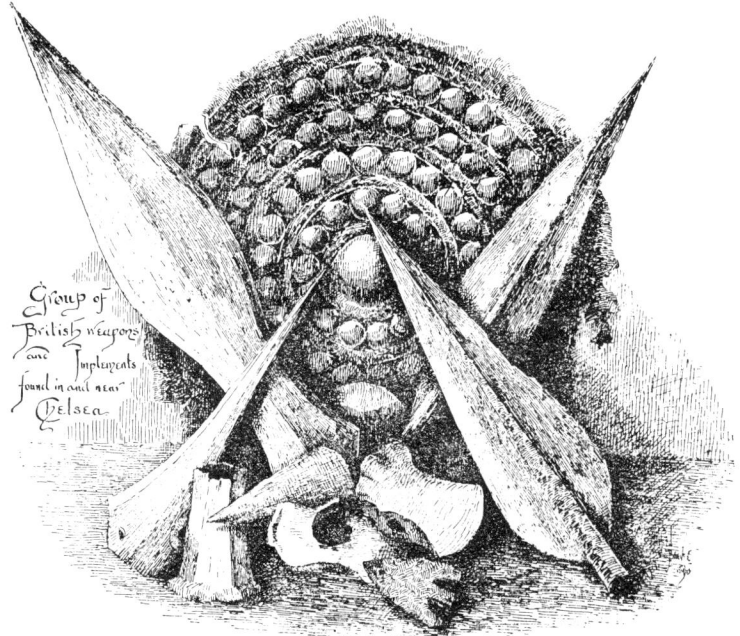

Group of British weapons and Implements found in and near Chelsea

large portion of an ancient caldron, made of hammered copper-plates, riveted together, was found off the Middlesex shore, near the Chelsea Suspension Bridge. Hence we are justified in assuming that the district generally was inhabited by the Britons, while the high antiquity of man's presence in this neighbourhood is shown by a few finds of palæolithic celts, etc. The many objects found in the Thames between Battersea and Chelsea, mostly in the near neighbourhood of a ford, which existed here until comparatively recent times, seems to imply that this ford was well known and used in those early times; and the heavy preponderance of weapons—swords, sheaths, daggers, and spearheads—almost forces on us the suggestion of a contested passage of the river by some large body of armed men.

Some have supposed that Chelsea was the spot at which Cæsar crossed the Thames with his victorious legions in pursuit of the flying Britons. They argue that as Llyn Dyn was the most important town in South Britain, it would naturally be the point towards which the Britons would retreat, the more especially as the width of the river and the extensive marshes gave it many elements of safety. The Romans, too, would be likely to cross at a point as near to this fortress as was possible, and on this consideration Chelsea has its claim.

The modern discovery of the ford was due to the painstaking research of Maitland, author of the 'History of London.' The account of the passage of the Thames by the army under Claudius, as related by Dion Cassius, had moved him to look for a ford nearer to London than Chertsey. He says:

> 'I discovered that the greatest marshes on that (the Surrey) side, before the embankment of the said river, reached from Wandsworth in the west to Woolwich in the east. Then sounding the said river (at several neap tides) from the first of these places to London Bridge, I discovered a ford (on the 18th of September, anno 1732) about ninety feet west of the south-west angle of Chelsea College Garden; whose channel, in a right line from the north-east to the south-west, was no more than four feet seven inches deep; where, the day before, it blowing hard from the west, my waterman assured me that the water was then above a foot lower; and it is probable that at such tides, before the course of the river was obstructed, either by banks or bridges, it must have been considerably shallower' (ed. 1756, vol. i., p. 8).

Sir Richard Phillips, writing of this ford in 1820, says:

> 'I have surveyed it more than once. At ordinary low tide a shoal of gravel, not three feet deep, and broad enough for ten men to walk abreast, extends across the river, except on the Surrey side, where it has been deepened by raising ballast. Indeed, the causeway from the south bank may yet be traced at low water; so that this was doubtless a ford to the peaceful Britons, across which the British army retreated before the Romans, and across which they were doubtless followed by Cæsar and the legions.'

This matter was mentioned by Major Lambert, F.S.A., in an address to the members of the London and Middlesex Archæological Society, in July, 1887:

> 'Old people,' he said, 'could remember when the "Draw Dock" existed, that boys used at low water to wade out at this part for a long distance, the water scarcely reaching to their knees. This showed the shallowness of the river here, and gave support to the probability of Cæsar having crossed here.'

Maitland, however, was wrong in supposing Chelsea to have been the only ford near London; there were, at least, two others between this place and the City—one crossing from Milford Lane, and the other at York Stairs; while Bagford, who relates the passage with all the circumstance of an eye-witness, fixes it at Dowgate. A very strong point in favour of Chelsea is the fact that its distance from Ritupiæ exactly agrees with that given by Cæsar, whereas the site above Shepperton, chosen by Dr. Stukeley, is some seventeen miles more distant.

That a fierce fight between the Britons and the invaders took place at Chelsea is beyond all question. When the foundations of Chelsea Suspension Bridge were being laid in 1856, the workmen discovered (on the Middlesex shore, and extending to the middle of the river) large numbers of human crania of two types, with bronze and iron weapons and other relics. Most of the crania were of the long oval type characteristic of the Celtic race, and mingled with them were others certainly of the Roman type. All were of a deep ebony black from their long burial in the bed of the river. Weapons undoubtedly British, such as the *cleddyv*, or leaf-shaped sword, were lying with others as undoubtedly Roman. Some of the discoveries were of great antiquarian interest, *e.g.*, a beautifully finished *ysgwyd*, or Celtic shield, one of the finest that have been found, and now preserved in the British Museum ; a *caliga*, or shoe worn by the rank and file of the Roman army ; a worked piece of limestone, pierced at one end, apparently belonging to a flail-like weapon, the use of which has survived even to the present day in the wilder parts of the Caucasus. Besides these were many other swords, spearheads, daggers, etc. Casual finds of similar weapons have been made along the opposite (Surrey) bank, and at the mouth of the Wandle. The inference seems quite clear. The Romans, having passed the river, were met by the British in the water, as they had been at Deal. There they fell, side by side with their relentless foe, and there their bones and weapons have lain, as many doubtless still lie, for nearly two thousand years, to be accidentally discovered in these latter days. There is an old tradition that Cæsar's passage of the Thames was fiercely contested, that the fight was ended by sending across an elephant, and that at the sight of this monster, strange and terrible in their eyes, the Britons fled in dismay. Whether the struggle which took place at Chelsea was during Cæsar's invasion, on the later occasion by Claudius, or during some unrecorded passage, of course we cannot determine ; but the fact of there having been such a fight, which is beyond doubt, coupled with the correspondence of the distance of Chelsea ford from Ritupiæ with the estimate of Cæsar himself, renders the conjecture that this famous passage occurred at Chelsea much more probable than has appeared heretofore.

There is no evidence of any Roman settlement in Chelsea, although tokens of their presence have been found in the immediate neighbourhood. The remains of a temple have been unearthed at Westminster, and a Roman burial-place was found at Battersea Fields, now the park, from which a leaden coffin, still containing the skeleton embedded in lime, was exhumed at the end of the eighteenth century. Dr. Pettigrew had a number of Roman pipes from the same neighbourhood.

Little or nothing is known of the origin of the Middle Saxons, beyond what may be inferred from their name. They have no place in the chronicle of the Conquest, and they have no record as a kingdom; it is probable, therefore, that they were merely a branch of the great East Saxon family. They were few in number, a handful here and there, settled along the water-courses and along the tracks of the Roman roads. One such family, the Kensingas or Chenesingas, it may be, founded Kensington, and possibly an offshoot of this family first settled at Chelsea and made it their hythe or port. The sparseness of the population of this part of Middlesex is shown by the fact that when the county was divided, the largest hundred was Ossulstone, in which Chelsea is situated. The neighbourhood was thickly wooded. Even as late as the time of Henry II., as FitzStephen tells us, London, on the west, was surrounded by 'an immense forest, in which were densely-wooded thickets, the coverts of game, stags, fallow-deer, boars, and wild bulls.' Much of this forest remained until Stuart times, and we may trace it in such names as Wormholt, Kingsholt, etc.

In the days of Offa, King of the Mercians, we have many references to a place called Celchyth, which I believe to be identical with Chelsea in Middlesex. If it be so, then Chelsea, during the Mercian supremacy, as the scene of several important councils, and probably a royal residence, was (as it is called in several charters), a celebrated place. The identity of Chelsea with the place so frequently mentioned in the documents of this reign has been much questioned, and several of the highest authorities have hesitated about it. Kemble in his ' Codex Diplomaticus,' and Thorpe in his ' Diplomatarium,' left it an open question; and so, apparently, does Birch in his ' Cartularum Saxonicum.' Several other sites have been named for it. Usher and Gibson placed it at Kulcheth in South Lancashire, which was included in Offa's dominions; Sprüner so marked it in his Atlas; and Mr. W. Basevi Sanders, in one of the ' Reports of the Deputy-Keeper of the Records,' still holds to this opinion. Ingram, in his index to the Saxon Chronicle, fixed it at Challock in Kent; Bosworth, in his ' Anglo-Saxon Dictionary,' agrees with this, and so does Toller, his reviser. The improbability of Ingram's attribution becomes apparent, when we find that in 824 Challock was written *Cealfa locan*, and in 833 *Cealf-locan*, *i.e.*, ' the place of calves,' a name quite distinct from Cealchythe. Finally, Mr. Loftie, in his recent ' History of London,' asserts that Cealchythe was higher up the river, in Oxfordshire, a statement for which he gives no authority.

Michael Alford (otherwise Griffith) was, perhaps, the first to identify

Celchyth with Chelsea in Middlesex (see his 'Fides Regia Britannica,' 1663, vol. ii., p. 647). To my mind, all the probabilities tend in this direction; and if we carefully consider the several points mentioned in the charters, and compare the spellings of the name at the different dates, we need have little or no doubt upon it.

England in the eighth century was emerging from a state of chaos. For nearly three hundred years the various Saxon, Anglian, and Jutish tribes who had forsaken 'the windy nesses and lone fenlands' of their older home, to settle in our smiling land, had waged one long struggle for mastery, first with the Britons and then with one another. The political history of each tribe is a long chronicle of internecine strife; of triumphant victories alternating with crushing defeats; of a temporary supremacy gained through the personal qualities of a leader only to be lost again under a new combination of circumstances. Such was the state of England when Offa mounted the Mercian throne in 757.

It was the dream of Offa's life to form a united England under his overlordship, and with this object in view he had annexed Kent to his dominions. Middlesex had been added by his predecessor Æthelbald, as we may infer from a grant of lands at Geddings 'in provincia Midelsexorum' by this King to Withred and Ansith. We find a grant of lands on the Medway by Offa to the Bishop of Rochester as early as 764. The conquest of Kent was destined to give the Mercians much trouble. The tendency to rebellion, natural in a conquered people, was eagerly fomented at the Court of Charlemagne, and this condition of affairs would give Chelsea, with its ford, a strategic importance that so experienced a warrior as Offa would be little likely to neglect. The ease with which the river could be passed at this point placed Chelsea within a day's march of the very heart of Kent. There was another reason which would weigh with Offa and his council in making Chelsea one of the seats of government of the Mercian kingdom. Its position made it a very convenient meeting-place; the broad highway of the Thames rendered access easy from east and west, and the convergence of the great military roads towards London facilitated the approach from north and south. London, it may be conceded, would have been still more convenient; but there is not sufficient proof that this fortress was under Offa's control. If we turn to the several charters signed or endorsed at Celchyth, we shall find that the subject-matters refer, almost without exception, to the southern portion of England—that is, to localities surrounding Chelsea —and never to the more distant north and west. None of these considerations can be urged in favour of any other site which has been suggested.

The story of this period is not easy to tell in any case: besides the scarcity of matter, we have to reckon with imperfect and untrustworthy documents, with conflicting dates and statements. Some element of supposition is therefore unavoidable, but by a careful collation of all the available authorities, it is possible to arrange a fairly connected account of the events of the time, so far as Chelsea is connected with them.

During the struggle with Kent, referred to above, the Archbishop of Canterbury, Jaenbryht (Jambert or Lambert, as it is variously written), naturally sided with his own countrymen; he was even charged with having invited Charlemagne to send a force hither against Offa, promising to open a passage for him, and to assist him generally in the enterprise. To punish the Archbishop, and probably, also, to give additional dignity to the Mercian kingdom, Offa determined to establish a second archbishopric at Lichfield. The 'Saxon Chronicle' records that a contentious synod was held at Cealchythe in 785, when Jaenbryht was deprived of some portion of his province, and Ecgferth, eldest son of Offa—a prince in whom he had great hopes—was solemnly hallowed as the king's successor. Here are the words of the Chronicle:

> 'Her wæs geflitfullic sinoþ at Cealchyþe, and Iaenbryht Ærcebisceop forlet summe dæl his bisceopdomes, and from Offan kyninge Hygebryht wæs gecoren and Ecgferþ to cyninge gehalgod.'

Ecgferth shared the government with his father until the latter's death in 795, but himself died four months later. The fact of his coronation seems to prove that the meeting was a witenagemòt, or State council—the Parliament of Saxon times—and not a Church synod. The accuracy of the Chronicle with regard to the date is witnessed by a charter of Offa granting lands at Ioccham and Perhamstede in Kent to the thegn Ealdbeorht and his sister Selethryth. This charter is inscribed—'Actum anno dominicæ incarnationis DCCLXXXV. in synodali conventu in loco ubi nominatur Celchyð.' Florence of Worcester (died 1118) says, 'In loco qui lingua Anglorum Cealchythe dicitur litigiosa facta est synodus.' Henry of Huntingdon (early twelfth century) spells the name *Cealchide*. Roger de Wendover (died May 6, 1237) says, 'Tenuerunt autem concilium apud *Chalchuthe*,' and Richard de Cirencester (died 1400-1) spells it in the same way. The three last named use the spelling commonly in vogue for Chelsea in their own day, whence it would appear that the Chroniclers had no doubt about the identity of Cealchythe.

For the consummation of Offa's project with regard to Lichfield, the consent of the Pope, though not indispensable, was still highly desirable, and this Offa secured by means not only unworthy, but unpatriotic. First, on behalf of himself and his successors (as we learn from a letter of Leo III. to Coenwulf, who had refused to be bound by his predecessors), he promised an annual sum of 365 mancuses to the Church of St. Peter at Rome, towards the support of the poor and the lights used in the church. Thus arose Romescot, or Peter's Pence. The mancus was estimated by Akerman as equal to half a sovereign in weight, its exchange value then being, of course, many times more than an equal weight at the present day. Secondly, Offa, in all matters ecclesiastical, voluntarily submitted to the authority of the Pope, and thus brought about the first papal interference with the affairs of the Saxon Church, since Gregory sent Augustine and his monks to evangelize the Angli. George (miscalled Gregory by Spelman and his followers), Bishop of Ostia, and Theophylact, Bishop of Todi, came to England with the character of Legates. The report of their mission has been printed by the Magdeburg Centuriators, and though they give no account of their manuscript, which has not yet been identified, it bears ample internal evidence of authenticity. From this report we learn that one of the Legates travelled into Northumberland and there received the submission of King Oswald and all his clergy, and that subsequently they presented his Holiness's letters to Offa and Keniulph (King of East Anglia). Offa was present at the council held at Calcuith, *i.e.*, Cealchythe of the Chronicle, or Celchyð of the charters. This was probably in 787, but the date is variously given by different authorities.

The holding of this synod was one of the most memorable incidents in the history of the Saxon Church. Twenty important canons were drawn up and agreed to, and they shed much light upon the character of the people and the state of the nation. Among them were the following : strict adherence to the decisions of the Council of Nice ordered ; two provincial synods to be held every year ; priests and deacons not to be ordained without sufficient testimonials of probity and ability ; clergymen taking part in conspiracies to be expelled the holy society (this seems to have been specially aimed at Jaenbryht) ; ministers of justice enjoined not to favour litigants for their quality or wealth ; marriages within prohibited degrees condemned ; payment of tithes urged ; usury and the use of unjust weights and measures condemned. Among the more curious of the resolutions we may notice these : the clergy not to perform divine service without stockings ; illegitimate issue, particularly the children of nuns, debarred from inheritance ; heathenish customs, especially deforming the body with superstitious marks or scars, forbidden. There is nothing, however, about the freeing of slaves, as has been occasionally asserted.

As we have several other documents (hereafter cited) dated from Celchyth, extending over a considerable period, chiefly during the Mercian supremacy, it becomes highly probable that Offa and his successors had a residence here, and that Chelsea was one of the seats of government of the Mercian kingdom. If we could feel sure that Kyngesbyrig and Kyngesholt, frequently mentioned in connection with Chelsea, were in the near neighbourhood, we should be tempted to look for the origin of these names in this circumstance.

In 788, by a grant dated from Celchyth, Offa bestowed lands at Duningcland in Kent to the thegn Osberht his minister. This is evidence of another gemòt, or council, held at Celchyth.

In the following year a pontifical council was held at 'the famous place which is called Celchyð,' when a suit of inheritance between Heathored, Bishop of Worcester, and Wulfheard, son of Cussa, was decided. Grants for the enlargement of the monastery at Rochester were also signed. Mutual confirmation of the holding of this synod is obtained from the Cartularies of Worcester and Rochester.

In Matthew Paris ('Chron. Maj.,' vol. vi.) we have mention of another synod at Celchyth in 793, at which grants of land were made to the Abbey of St. Albans, which Offa had recently built on the site where the supposed remains of England's protomartyr were discovered. From internal evidence Professor Stubbs considers this charter to be probably spurious; but it is interesting to find the phrase 'in loco celebri qui dicitur Celchyth,' closely corresponding to that in the charter already quoted. This charter, though apparently forged, was several times confirmed by the monarchs after the Conquest, and in the fourth year of Henry VI. we find the phrase 'in loco celebri vocat' Celchid'' still preserved. Two other grants of land to this abbey, purporting to have been signed at a public synod at Celchyth in 796, under Ecgferth, are considered by the same authority to be almost certainly forgeries. Although the matter contained in these charters is probably worthless from a historical point of view, yet the forgers would surely aim at investing their productions with an air of historical truth, and we thus get additional evidence of the celebrity of Chelsea in those days.

There is good evidence of a 'synodal council' having been held at Celchyth in 799, at which an agreement was made between Coenwulf, King of the Mercians (successor of Ecgferth), and Wiothun, Bishop of Selesegh. Another charter of the same date contains a grant of land by the same King to Abbot Balthun. It is dated from Colleshyl (usually supposed to be Coleshill in Berkshire), and is marked by Kemble as spurious. If we might suppose Colleshyl (as suggested by Hadden and Stubbs) to be a transcriber's error for Celchyth, the probability of its authenticity would be greater. It is particularly interesting, as it mentions the conclusion of peace between Wessex and Mercia.

Another document upon the agreement with the Bishop of Selesegh mentioned above, records a synod at Celchithe in 801, and although it is of questionable authenticity, yet a 'synodal council' does appear to have been held at Cælichyth, from the endorsement of an old charter of Offa (767) granting lands in Middlesex to the venerable Stidberht; moreover, the proceedings of this synod were confirmed at the Council of Cloveshoe in 825.

The Abingdon charter of 815, professing to have been signed at a synod held at Celchyth, is misdated 811, and is almost certainly a forgery; but in the year 815 there met 'in loco qui dicitur Celichyth,' a council of the Bishops of the Province of Canterbury (the archbishopric of Lichfield had been abolished by Coenwulf in the third year of his reign), almost equal in importance to the legatine council of 787. Eleven important canons were agreed to, among which were the following: Every church was to have the saint to whom it was dedicated set forth on the wall, on board, or on the altar (the reading leaves us in doubt whether an effigy or the name alone was intended, otherwise this would be an important indication of the state of the arts at this period); uniformity in doctrine and practice was recommended; Scotchmen were prohibited from performing any part of the sacerdotal office (perhaps because the memory of Aidan—the great Celtic missionary from Iona, who founded the religious colony at Lindisfarne—had not yet died out in the north, and the submission to the See of Rome was not so universal as in the south); Bishops, Abbots, etc., were forbidden to alienate the lands of religious houses; and secular persons were forbidden to have the government of or residence in monasteries. The acts of this council are to be read in full in MS. Cott., Vesp. A. xiv., ff. 147-151; they are incorrectly given in Spelman and Wilkins.

We are tempted to speculate where these important Church congresses were held in Chelsea. The mere fact of their being held implies a building of some sort in Chelsea of considerable extent. There is no record of the discovery of any remains which would serve to locate the spot; but down to the time of Henry VIII. a field in the south-eastern part of the parish was known as Gospelle Shott, an undoubted Saxon name, which seems to suggest some religious origin.

Collier, in his 'Ecclesiastical History' (vol. i., p. 357), asserts that in 824, in the reign of Bernulph, King of Mercia, another council was held at Calcuith, when a controversy between Heabert, Bishop of Worcester, and the monks of Berkeley was considered. This is an error, as the council in question was held at Cloveshoe (*i.e.*, Cliffe, near Rochester), and adjourned to Thorney Abbey.

At the date of this council Mercia was no longer the great power it had been under Offa and Coenwulf. Distracted by civil contentions, the Mercians had been easily defeated by Ecgberht of Wessex at Ellandune ; the East Anglians rose in revolt, and Bernulph and his successor, Ludeca, both fell in two great defeats at their hands. In 827 Mercia submitted to Ecgberht, who became over-lord of all the English kingdoms, and thus the dream of Offa was realized by his chief opponents. Whatever importance Cealchythe had possessed in the days of Mercian supremacy as the key to Kent would now be lost, and, indeed, we hear nothing more of it until the end of the ninth century, when King Alfred, Archbishop Plegomund, and Æthelred, Duke of Mercia, met at Celchyth to discuss the rebuilding of London. The authenticity of this charter from the Wessex Register is recognised by Dr. Pauli, author of the best life of Alfred yet written.

Nearly another century elapses before anything more is heard of Cealchythe —in 996, in the reign of Æthelred, when the Mercian Earls, taking advantage of the weakness of the King, were once more struggling for Mercian independence. A charter granted to the Abbey of St. Albans this year purports to have been signed at Celchyth in public synod. Its authenticity is not questioned by Kemble.

Nearly two hundred years before a terrible enemy had swooped down upon the English shores ; the same narrow fiords of Scandinavia, and the same sandy shores of Jutland and Denmark, from which our Saxon fathers had emerged for their career of conquest, now poured forth their hosts of Norse pirates. Their long black ships, with snake-like motion, were seen gliding along the English shore, filling the breasts of the coast-dwellers with a dread that was only too well founded. Their first descent was made in 787, and for a century onward the land was filled with murder and rapine and nameless horrors. The winter following the peace of Wedmore (878), by which at last Alfred secured peace for his people, a Danish force sailed up the Thames, and encamped at Fulham. The moat now surrounding the Bishop's palace is supposed to mark the site, but more probably it was farther westward, between the palace and the Crabtree Tavern. With our knowledge of the usual proceedings of these terrible foes, it is unlikely that Celchyth would have escaped scathless ; but, unfortunately, I can find no record of the place, either then or during the Danish rule.

In 1042, the English, sickened with the brutalities of Harold and Harthacnut, chose Edward (surnamed the ' Confessor '), son of the redeless Æthelred, for their King. A singular halo of sanctity surrounds the memory of this last of the English Kings, and the act in his life which connects his name with that of Chelsea was one of piety. A certain Thurstan was the Governor of Edward's palace at Westminster, and to him the King had granted a manor

CHELSEA REACH, 1823 (AFTER GIRTIN).

in Cealchythe. After holding the lands for some time, Thurstan bestowed them on the Abbey of Westminster, and Edward confirmed the gift by a charter. This charter is addressed to ' Robert the Bishop and to Osgod Clapa and Ulfus, Viscounts, and to all my thegns and faithful friends in Middlesex.' It was in the house of this Osgod Clapa, at Lambeth, that Harthacnut, the brutal son of a wise father, ' died at his drink.' The charter goes on, ' I make known unto you that I will and consent that Holy Peter, and the fathers and brothers of Westminster, for their support, may possess that manor which is in Cealchylle [Cealchyde, Cealchyðe], and all things by right thereunto belonging, with lands and with water, with wood and with field, with meadow and with pasture land, with food for swine, with the fruits, and with all the emoluments, as fully and as freely as Thurstan, the governor of my palace, first held them of me, and afterwards gave them to that sacred place. Which gift I indeed confirm to them again ; grant that, moreover, they may have the privilege of holding a court to try causes, and settle disputes between vassals and villeins, with the power of fining transgressors and calumniators, and of mitigating such fines ; also, that they may have, in selling and buying goods, an immunity from toll, with the privilege of possessing the whole offspring of their slaves, the power also of bringing to justice and punishing thieves taken in the act of thieving, on their lands, with the liberty of committing fugitives, and all other rights which in any manor thereout may arise ; besides, together with this manor (as a free gift) every third tree and every third horse-load of fruits grown in the neighbouring wood of Kyngesbyrig, which, as in ancient times, was confirmed by law.' This charter is now in the British Museum (MSS. Cott., Faust. A. III., f. 108 b.) ; it is written in the Saxon language, and, after the Norman fashion, is sealed with a waxen seal, suspended by a silken cord, and inscribed ' The seal of Edward, King of England,' on both sides. On each side, too, is the effigy of the King ; the figure on the front holds a cross in the right hand and a globe in the left, while above is a dove.

The appurtenances of the manor are sufficiently defined in this charter. A manor has been described as ' the unit of tenure under the feudal system,' and it was essentially a Norman feature ; but Laveleye, in his ' Primitive Property,' has pointed out that the old Saxon mark or march had, even in the tenth century, been transformed into the manor, although the term had not then come into use. The privilege of holding a court, mentioned in the charter, was that afterwards known as the Court Baron, and incident to the manor itself. It would be interesting to find the origin of the ancient rights of the abbey in the woods of Kyngesbyrig, but I have searched in vain on this point. All previous writers have identified this Kyngesbyrig with the modern

Knightsbridge, at the north-eastern boundary of the parish, but Mr. Loftie, in his recent history of Kensington, confidently asserts that Kingsbury-next-Neasdon is intended, and that this ancient gift to the monks of Westminster accounts for Chelsea's possessions at Kensal Town. This is a point which will require some further consideration in our later pages. It is to be noted that this charter mentions 'a manor in Chelsea,' not 'the manor of Chelsea,' a phrase which implies that the whole district called Cealchythe was not included in the grant; and this becomes apparent from a later document.

England was then nearing one of the great turning-points of its history. In 1066 William the Norman utterly defeated Harold at the battle of Senlac, near Hastings, and by this one fell blow, followed by skilful diplomacy, and aided by faction and intrigue among his foes, he easily became King of the English. Two years later the relentless severity with which he crushed the National Revolt gave him the title of the 'Conqueror.' In parcelling out the land among his followers he paid but little heed to the rights of property as they then existed. 'Stark he was,' says the Saxon Chronicle, 'to men that withstood him. So harsh and cruel was he that none dared resist his will.' But he was 'mild to them that loved God;' thus he respected Thurstan's gift to the Abbey of Westminster, and confirmed the Confessor's charter by a special enactment of his own, dated at Westminster, in which it is called 'land at Chelchea,' and thus the abbots of Westminster remained in possession of a large part of Chelsea until the time of Stephen.

Domesday Book was probably commenced about the year 1085 and finished in 1086, and from it we learn all that we know of Chelsea at this time. It is evident that there were, as Lysons suggested, two manors in Chelsea in the days of the Confessor. Edward de Sarisberie held the manor of Chelched or Cercehede in Ossulston Hundred, which, in King Edward's time, had been held by Wluuene, one of his vassals, who 'might sell it to whom he would.' It is impossible to identify this Wluuene, as there are several of that name mentioned in Domesday Book; but his Norman successor was a man of considerable importance in his time. He was the younger son of Walter de Eureux, Earl of Rosmar, and held lands in Surrey, Hampshire, Dorsetshire, Somersetshire, Buckinghamshire, Oxfordshire, Middlesex, and Wiltshire; and as he was Sheriff of the last-named county, he not improbably derived his surname from a residence at its chief town, Salisbury. He was not undistinguished in warfare, for at the terrible battle of Breneville, in Normandy, he bore the standard of Henry I. The family of such a man naturally contracted some important alliances; thus, his daughter Maud married the second Humphrey de Bohun, and his grand-daughter Ela married William Longespée, son of Henry II. His manor in Chelsea was but two hides in extent, and was valued at nine pounds.

The hide and other land measurements varied in size at different periods, and also in different parts of the country, apparently according to the quality of the land ; but assuming the hide to have been one hundred and twenty acres, according to several ancient authorities, Edward de Sarisberie's holding would have contained about two hundred and forty acres, while the whole of Chelsea (excluding Kensal Town) measures something over six hundred acres. The entry describes the manor in the following terms : ' There is land for five plough-teams. One hide is in demesne, and there are now two plough-teams there. The villeins have one plough, and two ploughs might yet be made. There are two villeins of two virgates, and four villeins of half a virgate each ; and three borders of five acres each, and three bondmen. Meadow for two ploughs. Pasture for the cattle of the village. Pannage for sixty hogs.'

Pannage for so many hogs is the usual way of expressing the amount of forest land in any district. The ' pasture for the cattle of the village ' was not improbably that piece of open pasture which, under the name of Chelsea Common, retained its original use down to the present century.

The system of cultivation then in use was entirely different from that which now prevails. Land was sub-let to the villein, borders, etc., by the lords in small half-acre strips scattered over the manor. A collection of these strips was called a virgate or yard-land. The normal virgate contained about thirty acres, and the normal hide consisted of four virgates. The size of the hide, however, as already mentioned, varied very considerably in different localities, and ranged from 120 to 240 acres.

Mr. Seebohm traces this curious system to the ancient days when our Saxon ancestors, like those of all Aryan nations, lived in communities in a state of serfdom, and cultivated the land on a system of co-aration. Remnants of it still survive in Wales, Scotland, and Ireland, and traces of the system can still be observed in those parts of England where no Enclosure Act has swept them away. The Common pasture and the Lots were survivals of it in Chelsea, and the King's Road was formed out of the headland or farm-road which gave access to the fields.

The remaining portion of Chelsea—that which had been Thurstan's—was, as we have seen, the property of the Abbots of Westminster, and it is very probable that it is this portion which is described in the following extract from Domesday Book :

' In the village where the Church of St. Peter (*i.e.*, Westminster Abbey) is situated, the Abbot holds thirteen hides and a half.

' In the same village, Bainiard holds there three hides of the Abbot. There is land for two plough-teams, and they are there in the demesne and one cottage. Pannage for one hundred hogs. Pasture for the cattle. There are four arpents of vineyard newly planted. Its whole value is sixty shillings, when received twenty shillings, in King Edward's time six pounds. This land belonged and belongs to the Church of St. Peter.'

This Bainiard held other property in Middlesex, and has been thought to be identical with the person who gave his name to Baynard's Castle. Assuming the same acreage as before for the hide, Bainiard's holding amounted to three hundred and sixty acres, which, with that held by Edward de Sarisberie, would about equal the whole extent of Chelsea proper. The newly-planted vineyard was probably laid out—in accordance with an ancient custom of the Church—on the occasion of the endowment of the abbey with the lands in question. Until the middle of the eighteenth century there existed another vineyard at Kensington, of nearly the same age as that of Chelsea; and it is said that the wine it produced was esteemed by the inhabitants as being similar to that of Burgundy.

From the details in Domesday Book we can form an estimate of the very small population that then inhabited Chelsea. Thus, on Edward de Sarisberie's manor there were two substantial farmers of sixty acres each, four small farmers with fifteen acres each, three small cultivators with five acres each, and three bondmen. Supposing each of them to have been married, and allowing an average of three children to each couple, it follows that the population of this manor was something considerably less than a hundred, while Bainiard's holding had scarcely more than a score. As the former is the more valuable, and also the more cultivated portion, it is reasonable to suppose that it was situated in the more elevated, or western, portion, and that Bainiard's land lay to the east.

In after-years we only hear of one manor in Chelsea, whence it follows that they were at some period united, probably before the enactment of the Statute of Quid Emptores, 1290; but we have no record to fix the date. From the Conquest to the days of Henry VII. the history of Chelsea is very obscure, a few disconnected facts only having been preserved. No feudal lord built a frowning castle at Chelsea, no band of pious monks here found a retreat, and we thus lack two of the most fruitful sources of information. Right onward till the time of Henry VIII. Chelsea was, there is no doubt, entirely occupied in farming, the most uneventful of all careers, peaceful and useful, but leaving no mark on history.

In the days of King Stephen, Gervace, a natural son of the King, was Abbot

4

of Westminster—a grasping and not over-scrupulous man, who is recorded to have greatly impoverished the abbey by grants to his poor relations and dependents. Among these grants was that of Chelchithe to his mother Dameta, ' to be held in fee with the village and appurtenances, land and water, to hold it peaceably and honourably, with all privileges, at a yearly rental of four pounds.' In return for this grant Dameta gave the Church the sum of forty shillings and a pall to the value of one hundred shillings. Stephen died in 1135, and shortly afterwards the manor was still in the possession of Dameta.

When Richard of the Lion Heart was King, the manor, or some portion of it, seems to have been leased to one William de Bocland, as, in the last year of this reign, 1198-99, we find in the Rotuli Curiæ Regis (Rolls and Records of the Court held before the King's Justiciars) a note of a cause between him and the Abbey of Westminster concerning the manor of Cheliseia, Middlesex. This spelling of the name is very puzzling, but seems certainly to refer to our Chelsea.

There is also in this roll a note of a cause tried in the first year of King John, between Gerard de Chalchell (Chelsea?) and Ailward Juvenis and others concerning the former's right in the common pasture in Kingesbirig. Perhaps in this Ailward Juvenis we may see an ancestor of William le Jeune, whom we shall find mentioned in the Hundred Roll.

Several notices of Chelsea in the reign of Edward I. are found. This King was in the Holy Land when Henry III. died, and did not arrive in England until nearly the end of the second year of his reign. One of his earliest acts was to cause an account of all the landed estates in the country to be drawn up, in order to prevent the numerous frauds on the revenue which had become possible by the turbulence of the previous reign. This account is preserved in the Rotuli Hundredorum, from which we obtain the following list of tenants in capite and in antient demesne in the Hundred of Ossulston in which Chelsea is situated : Bartholomew Campeneys, Robert Purcel, William le Jeune, Martin de Iseldene (Islington), Roger de la Hale (possibly the ancestor of Richard de Heyle, of whom we shall hear presently), John at Wodeton, Roger de Nortfolk, John Jon, Gerin' le Lingedrap, John de la Hall, Alan' le Feron, Robert le Cupre.

In the Patent Rolls for the year 4 Edward I. (1276-77), we read of the appointment of Master Roger de Seyton and Solomon de Rochester to take the certification arraigned by Walter Pipard and Juliana his wife against William West, William le Cirograffer, Peter de ——, and Laurence de Septem Fontibus, touching some lands in Chilteheth, Middlesex (m. 5d. 79). Ralph de Septem Fontibus was witness to a grant of lands in Fulham in 1270, and forty-six years later we hear of a certain Bartholomew de Septem Fontibus in connection with the manor of Chelsea.

In 1288 Pope Nicholas IV. granted the tenths, which had been paid to the See of Rome for many years, to Edward I. for a period of six years, towards the cost of a crusade. The record (completed about 1291) is most important, because all taxes were regulated by this valuation until the survey in the twenty-sixth year of Henry VIII. In the temporalities of the archdeaconry of Middlesex, under the head of Property of the Convent of Westminster, we find :

'In Chelcheth for lands and customs ... ... £4 3s. 0d.'

Again, in the Taxation of the Spiritualities of the Archdeaconries of London and Westminster :

'Church of Chelcheth ... ... £8 13s. 4d.'

How the convent at Westminster came to have any possessions in Chelsea after they had been aliened by Gervace is shown by the reply to a writ of Quo Warranto issued in the twenty-second year of the same reign (1294-95) to Walter of Wenlock, Abbot of Westminster. This writ inquires ' by what authority he claims to hold the pleas of the Crown, to have free warren, a market, a fair, toll, a gallows, the chattels of persons condemned, and of runaways, the right of imprisonment, and similar privileges, including the appointment of a coroner in Eye, Knythbrigg, Chelceheth, Braynford, Padyngton, Hamstede, and Westburn,' etc., etc. He replied that these places were members of the town of Westminster, that Henry III. had granted to God and the Church of St. Peter of Westminster, and the monks therein, all his tenements, and had commanded that they hold them with all their liberties and free customs, etc.; and he produced the charter to that effect.

We get the names of other early inhabitants of Chelsea from the Abstract of the Roll of the Originalia in the Court of the Exchequer in the thirtieth year of Edward I., when John le Heymong de Chelcheheth and Cecilia his wife recovered possession of two acres of land in Chelchehethe and the moiety of a messuage thereto belonging from the wife of William Lundreys and others.

In the office of the Treasurer's Remembrancer is a manuscript entitled ' Nomina Villarum '—' A Booke of the Citties, Burroughs, Villages and Hundreds, their names and who were the Lords of every Mannor throughout all the Counties of England, from the year of our Lord 1316 to 1559.' There is a rough transcript in the Harleian Collection at the British Museum, n. 6281,

4—2

and on fol. 127 b we have this entry (undated)—' Chelcheth : Her. Barthi. de Sept. fontibȝ,' *i.e.*, 'the heirs of Bartholomew de Septem Fontibus,' doubtless a connection of the Lawrence already mentioned, but nothing further is known of him. In the reign of the weak and foolish Edward II., we first hear of a rector of Chelsea, a certain Sir Robert de Staundone, who was Rector in 1314-15. He was succeeded by Roger de Berners, who had the King's letters patent (Pat., 9 E. II., p. 2) in 1316. This Roger in 1324 was appointed one of the Bishop of London's proctors before the justices of the King's Bench in cases of clergy accused ; he was therefore a man of some eminence.

In 1341, the fourteenth year of Edward III., a Parliament was held at Westminster, when it was enacted that 'in consideration of the grants, releases, and pardons, of the chattels of felons and fugitives, and many other things underwritten, which the King had granted to the prelates, earls, barons, and all the commons of his realm, for the ease of them perpetually to endure, the said prelates, etc., willingly of one assent and good-will, having regard to the will that the King their liege-lord hath toward them, and to the great travaile he hath made and sustained, as well in his wars of Scotland as against the ports of France, etc., etc., have granted to him the ninth lamb, the ninth fleece, and the ninth sheaf, to be taken by two years then next to come. And of cities and boroughs the very ninth part of all their goods and chattels, to be taken and levied by lawful and reasonable tax, by the same two years,' etc. Parishes were assessed at Pope Nicholas' Valor, and the tax-roll drawn up takes note of any difference in the value, and accounts for it. Chelchehuth was then valued at £6 13s. 4d., being forty shillings less than in 1291, because there were now thirty acres of arable land and two of meadow belonging to the Church as glebe, thirty acres of meadow as tithe, and one hundred acres of land lying unoccupied. The commissioners account for the reduced sum received from John le Hert, Walter Pikard, and Thomas Est. From this record it has been inferred that Chelsea had no church previous to the allotment of the glebe, but we have just seen that a church is mentioned in the Taxation of Pope Nicholas.

From the heirs of Bartholomew the manor passed (perhaps by marriage) to Richard de Heyle (or Hyde). From an inquisitio post mortem taken in the eighteenth year of Edward III. (1345), we find that Robert de Wodehous, Archdeacon of Richmond, held certain possessions in the neighbourhood for John, Archbishop of Canterbury. These included lands and tenements in Willesdon, Kyngesholt, Chelchiche, 'a tenement called Forestars Land,' West Tyborne, and Fulham. In this document, Richard de Heyle is styled Lord of Chelsith. Twenty-three years later this same Richard leased the whole of his manor (valued in the following year at £25 6s. 6¾d.), except Kingsholt and Westbourne, to the Abbey of Westminster. In exchange he was to have a residence in the abbey, twenty pounds a year, two white loaves and two flagons of ale daily, and a robe of esquire's silk yearly, which does not seem to have been at all an unworldly bargain on his part. The King's license for this lease is preserved among the records of the Dean and Chapter, and from the Abstract Roll of the Exchequer Court, before quoted, we read that in the forty-first year of Edward III., the Abbot of Westminster gave half a marc for license to acquire the manor of Chelcheheth from Richard de Heyle, of Chelcheheth, for the whole of his life.

In this same year, 1368, the abbey appointed two rectors in succession, viz., William Palmer and John Basset. From this it appears that the abbey acquired the advowson of the church about the same time as the lease of the manor. This the abbey held until the reign of Henry VIII. Previous to 1368 the living had been in the gift of the King.

The Lawrence Chapel in the old church, evidently, from its architecture, dates from this century. From its name some have supposed that it indicates the period at which the family of Lawrence first settled in Chelsea, but there is evidence that this family were of Chelmarsh previous to the reign of Elizabeth.

There is ground for believing that the great Beauchamp family had a long connection with this place. In Dugdale's 'Baronage' (vol. i., p. 232) we read in the life of Thomas Beauchamp, Earl of Warwick—a famous soldier who was in the van at Cressy and Poictiers—that :

'His testament bears date at Chelchench (id est Chelsey juxta Westminster) on Tuesday 6 Sept., Anno 1369 (43 Edward III.).'

This is quoted from the Whitlesey Register, f. 510. Sir N. H. Nicholas, is his 'Testamenta Vetusta,' gives the name as Chelchesch, and adopts Dugdale's identification of this place with Chelsea in Middlesex. But it must not be forgotten that this family was connected with Cheddesley-Beauchamp, in Worcestershire, and that this name was also written Shelsley and in other ways, similar to the variants of Chelchithe. In the Patent Roll, anno 5 Edward I. (m. 11d. [6]), we have the record of a dispute between Geoffrey de Chedesley-Beauchamp and Hugo de Bello-Campo (the Latinized form of Beauchamp), concerning a tenement in this place. On the other hand, Dugdale, in his 'History of Warwickshire' (p. 766), gives extracts from the will of Lord Beauchamp of Powyk, dated April 9, 1475, which shows that he was then living at Chelchith, in the county of Middlesex ; and Lysons, who quotes the Patent Roll, anno 2 Richard III. (p. 2, Sept. 14), says that a house and premises which had belonged to Richard Beauchamp, Bishop of Salisbury, were granted to Elizabeth, relict of Thomas Mowbray, Duke of Norfolk (1485), at a yearly rental of one red rose.

From 'The Calendar of Inquisitiones Post Mortem,' published by the Record Commissioners in 1828, it appears that Richard de Bello Campo, Earl of Warwick, who died in 1439, possessed a tenement called 'The Lord Lyle's Place,' in Fulham. This was undoubtedly the small manor containing lands in both Chelsea and Fulham which had belonged to Warenne de Insula, but it had not long been in the hands of the Beauchamp family at the above date.

In the Calendar of Patent Rolls we find this entry among the 'Prima Patent' de anno 4° Regis Henrici Quarti' (1403-4): 'Exemplificatio petitionis et responsis pro decano S. Martini London' pro terris in Fulham et Chelcheth.' From Faulkner's 'History of Fulham' (p. 444) we learn that in 1403 Henry, Earl of Northumberland, gave a small manor in the parishes of Fulham and Chelsea, consisting of some rents of assize, a messuage, a toft, a cottage, sixty acres of arable land, and four of meadow, to the Dean and Chapter of St. Martin-le-Grand, in exchange for a house in Aldersgate Street. This estate was afterwards known as the manor of Sandford, by a corruption of which we have now Stamford Bridge, called Standford Bridge in Faulkner's time. This Earl of Northumberland was the father of the famous Hotspur, and himself one of the bitterest foes of Henry IV., who had displaced the weakling Richard II. Five years after the transaction related above he fell in the battle of Bramham Moor, near Tadcaster, a rebel to the last.

By the time that the youthful Richard II. mounted the throne in 1377, a great revolution in the social system had been silently effected. The slave-tillers of the Saxon era had gradually become peasant proprietors (from whom arose the class of copyholders), and were no longer in the power of the lord. But there were still serfs who belonged strictly to the land, and whom the lord of the manor could sell 'with their litters' or families, if he were so disposed; and the peasant proprietors—the villeins, the cottars, and bordars—were still bound to cultivate the demesne or home-farm for the lord. Many causes operated towards this gradual freeing of the tiller, *e.g.*, the commutation of service by a money-payment, shown by such words as 'malt-silver,' 'wood-silver,' 'larder-silver,' and the like; and the scarcity of labour after the terrible scourge known as the Black Death (1349). Then came reaction: the land-owners made desperate efforts to bind the labourers once more to the soil, but the tillers stubbornly resisted, and at length the struggle culminated in the great Peasant Revolt (1377-81), which spread through the south, east, and midlands, and was headed by such men as John Ball and Wat Tyler, of Kent; Jack Straw, of Essex; William Grindecobbe, of St. Albans; and Littester, of Norwich. The revolt at the moment of apparent success was suppressed partly by the precocious wisdom and fair promises of the young King. Alas! no sooner was the point gained than (as usual) these promises were ruthlessly broken. That the men of Chelsea played their part in this memorable social rebellion is shown by the fact that among those exempted from pardon by Parliament was one John Knot, of Chelchuth.

It is possible that Robert Howard, an ancestor of the Lord of Effingham, had a house in Chelsea in this reign. In the Parliament Roll for 1378, we have the petition of Aleise de Nevill', which sets forth that John Brewes and other ill-doers broke into her mansion at London, abducted Margerie de Nerford, grand-daughter of the said Aleise, and carried her to the palace of the Bishop of Norwich. Here they were met by Mons. Robert Howard, who carried the hapless Margerie by water to Chelchehith, and subsequently into the country, where he detained her in secret places, etc.

Lysons has copied one or two items from the court rolls of the manor during this reign, which serve to illustrate the manners and customs of the time. Thus in the eleventh year the wife of Philip Wells was fined sixpence for being a garrulatrix, or common babbler; and in the sixteenth year Florence North, brewster, was presented at the court leet for not putting up a sign.

Simon Bayle is said to have been the lessee of the manor-house in 1455. From the inquisitio post mortem held on the possessions of William Essex in the twentieth year of Edward IV. (1481), we learn that he died possessed of lands and manors in 'Kynsyngton, Brompton, Knyghtbridge, Fulham, Westburne, and Chelchith.' Ten years later William, Marquis of Berkeley, left a house in Chelsea to John Whiting and his heirs.

Henceforward the history of Chelsea becomes fuller and clearer, and the details must be left to after-pages, to be treated in their proper places. Henry VII. came to the throne in 1485, and during his reign the manor came into the possession of the famous Sir Reginald Bray. In 1520 was built at Chelsea a great house for one whose life adds the greatest lustre to the parish— Sir Thomas More, a man most noble and lovable, brave, wise, generous, upright and meek. So many memories gather round his life in Chelsea— memories of Henry VIII., a strange mixture of brutality and refinement; of the famous German painter, Hans Holbein; of the learned Erasmus; of Bishop Fisher; of Heywood the poet; of Tunstall, and of many others—that to exhaust them all would in itself require a volume.

In his frequent visits to More at Chelsea the King seems to have been charmed with the clear air and convenient situation of the healthy place. Lord Sandys (from whom some would derive, though quite improbably, the name of Sands End in Fulham) had married a niece of Sir Reginald Bray, and by some means, which cannot clearly be made out, came into the possession of the manor, for which the King offered to exchange Mottisfont, near Romsey. This was in 1536. Lord Sandys would doubtless feel that a wish from such a King was equal to a command, and it may be that he himself was not averse to the exchange, as he had considerable interest in the neighbouring town of Basingstoke. The exchange was therefore effected, and the Hampshire property is still held by the descendants of Lord Sandys, the present representative being Sir Charles Mills. On coming into possession, Henry built a new palace eastward of the site of Albert Bridge, and adjacent to that of Cheyne Walk, where one of the old houses, recently pulled down, bore the name of Manor House in memory of it.

Chelsea is indirectly connected with the shameful divorce proceedings by which Henry rid himself of his first wife, Katherine of Aragon; for it was in the choir of the old church, then called All Saints', that John Olyver, D.D., produced the King's commission to John, Bishop of London, to act as his proctor, the same Bishop who, in the same year, 1531, at More's house, condemned the heretic John Tewkesbury to the fagot. The State Papers, from which this information is derived, are not always strictly accurate in details, *e.g.*, in the grant of More's house to Sir William Pawlet, Chelseheth is described as being in Surrey, and it may be that there is an error in the record just mentioned, and that the Bishop's own church, All Saints', Fulham, is meant. Chelsea, however, is the place given. It must be remembered that All Saints' is the original dedication of the church; it is so given in the 'Liber Regis' (Henry VIII., anno 16), and as it is the Bishop's own certificate that gives us the information, an error in the name of the place is not probable. Henry seems to have passed a large portion of his time at Chelsea this year, for many of his grants and warrants are dated from this place. This being so, it is remarkable that no mention of Chelsea is to be found in the Privy Purse payments. The name Charsaye or Charteseye occurs therein several times, and Nicholas identifies it with Chelsea; but it is quite certain that Chertsey, in Surrey, where Henry often resided, is the place intended by the scribe.

If we may trust a passage in 'Wriothesley's Chronicle,' Chelsea was still more intimately associated with another of Henry's marriages:

'1536. Also the 20th daie of Maie [the day after the ill-fated Anne Boleyn went to the block] the King was married secretlie at Chelsey in Middlesex, to one Jane Seymor, daughter to Sir John Seymor, Knight, in the Countie of Wilshire, etc.'

Charles Wriothesley, who wrote this chronicle, was Windsor herald, and the work (after the eleventh year of Henry VIII.) bears internal evidence of being contemporaneous with the events described.

From the same authority we learn that Chelsea was not without some share in the iconoclastic doings that followed Henry's renunciation of the authority of the Pope.

> '1538. Allso this yere, in the moneth of July, the images of Our Lady of Wallsingham and Ipswich were brought up to London, with all the jewelles that honge about them, at the Kinges Commaundement, and divers other images, both in England and Wales, that were used for common pilgrimages, because the people should use noe more idolatry unto them, and they were burnt at Chelsey by my Lord Privie Seale' (Cromwell).

Among the 'divers other images' then burned were Penrise of Islington and St. John of Ossulston. The latter was also called 'Mrs. John Shome,' and his special virtue was that he had shut the devil up in a boot!

Other famous men lived in the Village of Palaces in this reign. Hugh, Bishop of Exeter, who died December 16th, 1518, bequeathed 'such houses, lands, etc., lying in Chelsea,' which he had 'bought of Reynold Braye,' to Corpus Christi College, 'to have and to hold to the same college for ever, by the ordinance of my Lord of Winchester' (MSS. Lansdowne, 949). In 1536 Thomas Howard, Duke of Norfolk, writes to Cromwell from Chelsea: 'When I sent last night for my servant, Robert Knyvet, for the matter you know of, I learnt he was sick, and since my arrival here, I have heard that Dr. Augustine and Dr. Wotton thinks it the Sickness, and recommend bleeding. To-morrow I shall be certain, and if it is the Sickness I shall defer my departure into Norfolk. As I will remove to the Bishop of London's house at Fulham, I have sent away my servants who lodged in the new lodgings where he lies; the rest being in the house at the water's side are in no danger.' From the account of the funeral of Robert Ratcliffe, first Earl of Sussex and Lord High Chamberlain, preserved in the Heralds' Office, we learn that he died at Chelsea on November 26, 1542. The residence of the Earls of Shrewsbury at Shrewsbury House, which stood between the sites of Cheyne Row and Oakley Street, dates from this reign or earlier.

A fire which occurred at Chelsea in 1553 was sufficiently important for Henry Machyn, citizen and merchant tailor, to chronicle in his diary, which extends from 1550 to 1563. He writes: 'The sam day [xix of August] was a gret feyre at Chelsay [beyond] Westmynster, and ther was dyvers howsses brent, [and] dyvers barnes with corne brent, to the nombur . . . .' Unfortunately the manuscript, which is in the Cottonian Collection, was injured by the fire that destroyed so many valuable records and injured so many others, and the rest of the reference is indecipherable. Such accidents as that mentioned by

5

the chronicler were much more frequent in those days than in our own. Some years previously John Williamson, writing to Cromwell on September 5, 1529, mentions another fire at Chelsea : ' Sir Thomas More's barns at Chelsey are burnt, full of corn, with more of his neighbours'.'

After the judicial murder of Sir Thomas More, his house was occupied by a long succession of noble, or at least titled, persons, until at last it was demolished, very barbarously we cannot help thinking, by Sir Hans Sloane. In the century following More's death the interest of Chelsea is mainly centred in the new manor-house, for there lived Katherine Parr, Princess Elizabeth, the Lady Anne of Cleves, the unfortunate Lady Jane Grey, the scheming Lord Admiral Seymour, and the brave Lord Howard, created Earl of Nottingham.

During the Tudor period other great houses rose up in Chelsea, such as Sir Arthur Gorge's house, where Milman Street now stands; and Stanley House, still standing as rebuilt in the seventeenth century. That there were others of less importance we may infer from the residence of Fletcher, Bishop of London ; Thomas Hungerford, of a famous Wiltshire family ; Sir Edmund Burton ; Lord Robert Stapleton ; John Townshend, esquire ; Richard Gervoise, etc., all persons of consequence in their time. Chelsea was, in fact, rapidly becoming the aristocratic suburb of the period, as the Strand had been in earlier days. But apart from its great houses, Chelsea in Queen Elizabeth's reign was still an insignificant village. We can form an idea of its size at this period from a chantry roll of the first year of Edward VI.'s reign, from which it appears that the number of communicants was only seventy-five, less than in any other parish in the county. Several years later the baptisms averaged only a fraction above five per annum.

During the reign of ' Good Queen Bess ' England went striding ahead in every direction. The astuteness of her policy is shown, above everything else, by her wise choice of Ministers. No such famous Council was ever gathered as that which advised Queen Elizabeth. Chelsea counts two of its members among its residents : William Pawlet, Marquis of Winchester, and the great Lord Burleigh. Another diplomatist of the time, Anthony Bacon, friend of the Earl of Essex, also came to Chelsea in 1594, and stayed here for about a year. In the latter half of this reign English literature shone with a wondrous light, and although Chelsea had no very direct connection with this great renascence, yet it is not altogether without its associations. On January 18, 1562, was acted the first English tragedy—' Gorboduc ' (published in 1571 as ' Ferrex and Porrex '), by Norton and Thomas Sackville, Lord Buckhurst. The latter was frequently at Chelsea, where his sister, Lady Dacre, lived, in the house that had been More's. The tragedy, however, could not have been written there, as Dr. Martin conjectures, for the Dacres did not take the house until 1572. Spenser, 'the poets' poet,' whose 'Faerie Queene' is perhaps the sweetest poetry in our language, was also often at Chelsea, visiting his friend, Sir Arthur Gorges, himself a literary man, celebrated in several of Spenser's poems. John Fletcher—of the Fletcher and Beaumont partnership —was doubtless often at Chelsea, if he did not live there. His parents lived there : his father was a benefactor to the parish, and his mother lies buried in the old church. The famous Sir Francis Bacon, Lord Verulam, was another visitor to Chelsea.

Explorers and buccaneers were carrying their bold exploits into the most distant parts of the world. Hardened by these enterprises and ennobled by the patriotism that surely comes to the land risen from blood and turmoil into peace and progress, a hastily improvised English fleet in 1588 easily defeated and drove to utter destruction the 'invincible' Armada, which four years before had gathered at the mouth of the Tagus. The leader of this famous deed, the tercentenary of which has just been celebrated, was another Chelsea man— Charles, Lord Howard of Effingham, afterwards Earl of Nottingham.

The year previous saw the execution of the unfortunate but intriguing Mary Queen of Scots. Two Chelsea men besides Burleigh were closely connected with this tragedy—the Earl of Warwick was one of the two judges at Fotheringhay, and the Earl of Shrewsbury, who for several years had been her keeper, was, with the Earl of Kent, appointed to see the death-warrant carried out.

Towards the end of the sixteenth century there lived two brothers named Inglebert or Engilbert, engineers, who had invented certain engines of war, which, according to their own account, were to effect a great advance in military science. In a paper of observations, dated March 3, 1597, they say:

'If for want of water or otherwise, we should not be able to come within a mile of a town, yet we could shoot a certain shot, as well by night as day, which would fall into all parts of the town, burst and blow up the houses in such terrible sort, that it would not be possible for anyone to live there; and being but a small time plied with this kind of shot, the terror of it would be so great that, for the safety of their lives, and that of their wives and children, they would be fain to sue to their assailants for mercy. If we should come near the town, sconce, or citadel, we should send from mortars shot of such bigness that nothing would be able to resist their violence, and every such shot would discharge, every way round about, above 2,000 musket-shots, with such force that everyone of them would be death to man and horse. If necessitated

5—2

to go into battle, and we should be far off, we might use the shot out of the ordnance, if near out of the bombards and mortar-pieces, which in a moment would overthrow them, tear in pieces, and so shatter them that they would be unable to withstand.'

Three years previously the attention of the Government had been drawn to these inventions, and in a memorial of 'things necessary to be put into execution' we find noted 'a view to be had of certain engines, made by Inglebert and his brother, where they are, and how they may be made.' It is possible that Chelsea was the scene of their manufacture, for on May 9, 1594, we find a warrant to pay Ursula Smith, a widow, forty-nine pounds ten shillings for two years and a quarter rent of her house at Chelsea, 'used for making her Majesty's engines.'

Under James I. Chelsea acquired a new interest, for here was commenced, but never completed, the college for the study of polemical divinity, which Laud afterwards nicknamed 'Controversy College.' What was built of it was removed in 1682, after a most unprosperous career, to make way for the present military hospital; but the old name of Chelsea College clung to the new establishment and still obtains among the inmates and many of the people of Chelsea, while its grounds are generally known as the College Gardens. Through this college many famous theologians and controversialists are connected with Chelsea.

The Chelsea fishery, first heard of in this reign, was the subject of continual dispute. About 1606-7 the Thames fishermen complained to the Lord Mayor that the Lord High Admiral (the Earl of Nottingham) had permitted the Chelsea men to fish for salmon, and Chelsea, they said, had 'never before been allowed for fishing.' The Lord Mayor, therefore, requested the Admiral to withdraw his warrant. This does not appear to have been done, and in 1607 one Bennett Joy 'was tried at law and condemned to forfeit some portion of his goods for unlawful fishing at Chelsea.' The troubles were revived some seven years later, when another attempt was made to suppress the Chelsea fishery. The Admiral complained in 1614 that the Water-bailiff had molested the fishermen of Chelsea, whom he (the Admiral) had allowed to fish there, 'as had been used time out of mind.'

About 1664 Sir Walter St. John resigned all his rights in the Thames salmon fishery between Chelsea and Lambeth to the Chelsea fishermen. The limits of the fishery were 'Upper Lindsey Place above "The Feathers"' on the west, and York Place Creek on the east. The Chelsea fishermen began to fish on May 30, 1664, and by the following Saturday had taken 172 pounds of salmon, which they sold to the Duchess of Ormond, Lord Cheyne, Squire

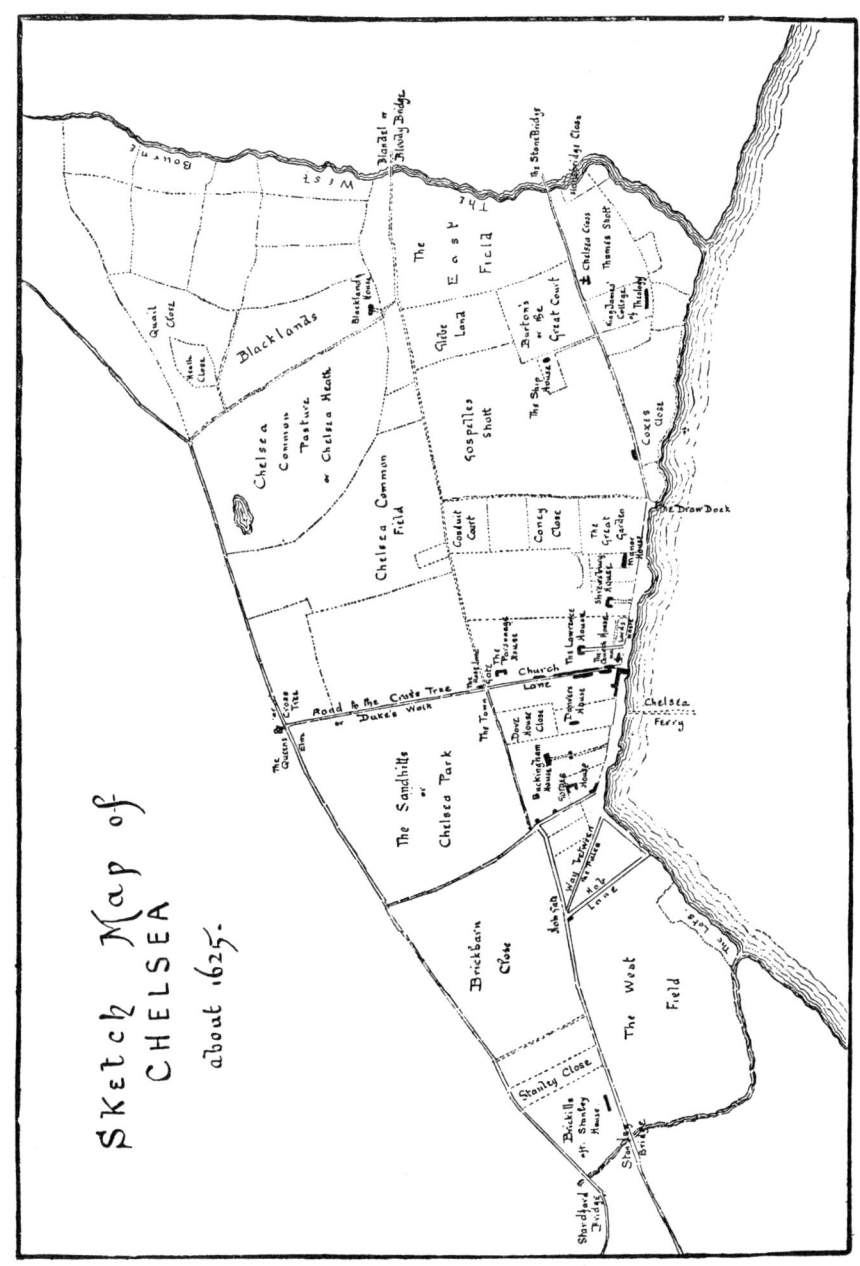

Sketch Map of CHELSEA about 1625.

Alston, and several fishmongers, at prices varying from fourteen-pence to eighteen-pence per pound.

The salmon fishery at Putney was carried on as late as 1792, when Lysons says it was 'not very productive, but the fish are of a very good quality and sell for a high price.' The late Mr. Frank Buckland attempted to reintroduce the salmon into the Thames, but without success. This is the more remarkable because, as Sir Charles Dilke has remarked, they still ascend the Liffey and the Tyne, much dirtier streams than the Thames.

Bryan, who wrote in 1869, says: ' In my earlier days two or three fishermen earned a scanty living by selling the fish they caught, and a few lovers of angling also occasionally pulled up some very fine roach and dace, in the prime season, at Battersea Bridge.' Upon this point, John Hassell, the water-colour artist, has a word to say in his ' Excursions on the Thames,' 1828 : ' Upon the last two hours of ebb-tide, and the first hour of the flood, there may be had very good fishing at the starlings of this bridge, close by the foot of the bridge, on the Chelsea side ; there live several fishermen, who provide boats and attend parties that are desirous of the sport. . . . The best station for sport is to moor about the fourth, fifth, and sixth arches from the Surrey side of the bridge, taking care to fish in the eddy of the tide. Roach, dace, gudgeon, eels, and sometimes barbel, are caught here.' A flounders fishery is still carried on off Chelsea Hospital.

Chelsea had game to preserve in James I.'s time. In 1623 a certain Robert Stacey was appointed to keep the game near Westminster, viz., at Chelsea, Kensington, Islington, etc.

Healthy and open as the place was in Stuart times, it did not escape that deadly scourge, the Plague, engendered by the narrow streets, bad drainage and unclean habits of the city. In 1625, when one thousand a day were dying in London, hither came Dr. Donne, Dean of St. Paul's, to stay with his friends at Danvers House. Others, acting on the same idea, spread the disease all around, so that, in Donne's own quaint words, ' it was no good manners to go to any other place,' and Chelsea became so ' infamous ' that he ' no longer went to Court.' According to the burial register, twenty-two people out of its small population died during this visitation. Almost annually came this dread Plague, causing terrible distress among the people. The great inconvenience to the Court led to Sir Theodore Mayerne, David Bethune, and Matthew Lister, the King's physicians-in-ordinary, being appointed in 1631 to inquire into the best means of preventing the pest. This report was, by the King's direction, presented to the Council. Among various suggestions for improved sanitation, they recommended the establishment of four or five hospitals, ' one distinguished above the rest, to be established at Chelsey, near the College of Controversy, or towards Paddington, by the side of the stream which runs in that district.' This recommendation, at least as regards Chelsea, was not carried out, but the college itself was little more than a pest-house on one or two occasions.

The dreadful condition of the homeless poor in these times is well known. The following ' short and simple annals of the poor' from the Chelsea parish registers tell their own sad tale, and present a sharp and painful contrast to the picture suggested by the pompous title ' The Village of Palaces ':

' 1594. Alice Griffith, a poor washerwoman, buried 2 Februarie from Mr. Holbourn's barn.
Ann, a poor woman, buried from a stable.
.' 1603. George, a poor boy, died in the Lordship's yard, buried 2 Marcii.
' 1609. William Gulley buried out of the Earl of Lincoln's stable, 14 August.
William Morgan, a poore man, died in a straw house, buried Oct. 1.
' 1613. Jana, a poore woman, buried out of a barne, Dec. 25.
A poor woman found dead at the Earl of Lincoln's.
Another in the Lordship's barn, buried the same day.
"Fielde," a poor man child, found in the East Field of Chelsey, baptized Oct. 13.
' 1639. "Chelsey," a child born in the West Fields, baptized Feb. 1.'

The nearness of Chelsea to the city and to Westminster rendered the village peculiarly subject to infection by the passage of travellers to and from these places, especially in the hurried flights of the fear-stricken. That the inhabitants were fully conscious of this danger is shown by a proclamation issued on May 20, 1630, a rough draft of which is found among the Scudamore papers. It sets forth that—

' Wee, whose names are underwritten, have thought fitt to signify and declare to all and any the Inhabitants of this Parish, that First, if any Uictualler, Tavern^r, or Ale-housekeep^r shall, through heedlesse enterteyninge of Strangers, or otherwise, induce or bring in the said dangerous Sicknesse, or that they be not careful to prevent it, by a faire course and respectful Cariage of themselves, and causing it in others, wee shall euermore ioyne to suppresse such Uictuallers, Tavern^{rs}, or Alehousekeep^{rs} for ever hauing licence thereunto within this Parish; and if any other Inhabitant or Householder shall give offence in y^t Nature, wee shall likewise ioyne to bring on him or her a punishm^t answer-able and due for such an offence and priudice; and if ye Constable, Churchwardens, and Ouerseers do not use their diligence, and perfourme their duty in due course and paynes, and ye purpose herein expressed, wee shall likewise endeauo^r to effect their punishm^t according to ye meritt of such offence. On thother side, when it shall please God to let us see and find His blessing on this place, wth health and safety, through their general meanes and endeauo^{rs}, wee shall be induced to afford, out of o^r owne purses, and oth^{r}wise such gratificacon and requital for any man's suffering and paynes taking, as wee doubt not shall giue them all good comfort.'

Evelyn gives us a picture of the distresses and dangers of the times. ' London,' he says, ' and its infected skirts was every man's province, which had I deserted or not personally supplied, multitudes of poor sick and wounded seamen of our own, and prisoners of the Dutch, must inevitably have perished. Two of my marshalls employed at Leeds Castle [in Kent] and Chelsey prison, who had frequent intercourse with me, died of the Plague, and one had come to me with the tokens upon him.' This was, of course, in the time of Charles II., when there was certainly a pest-house in Chelsea. In the lost parish registers the following notice occurred :

> ' 1667. Spent upon measuring the pest-house ...   .   £0   5s.   od.
>   Oct. 12. Payed Jas. Gould for the pest-house in full ...   £1 10s.   od.'

The smallness of these sums implies that it was for some repairs that the money was paid, but no earlier notice of this house has been preserved. Faulkner suggests that it stood upon the Common Land, and that the premises were afterwards converted into the Chelsea almshouses, which appear upon Hamilton's survey map, corrected to the year 1717.

Chelsea on several occasions during the Stuart period was the residence of foreign Ambassadors. Many of the despatches of M. de Puysieulx, Ambassador from France, are dated from ' Chelsea ' and ' Chelsey ' from April to July, 1609. In the Colonial State Papers is a letter (November ? 1622) from Edward Conway to his Excellency (the Marquis of Buckingham), giving an account of an interview at Chelsey between the Lord Treasurer and the State Ambassadors, at which Conway was present, when there was 'a civil, temperate, and effectual debatement of the several points raised,' too long to trouble his Excellency with.

In the register of burials we find :

> ' 1631. Thomas, servant to the Dutch Ambassador, March 16.'

The Marquis de Senecterre dates some of his despatches from Chelsea in 1635. Two years later the affairs of the Palatinate were under consideration, and the Conde d'Onato e Villa Mediana—' a very gallant gentleman, but some-what hasty '—was named English Ambassador from Spain. He came to London in 1637, and his letters are dated from Chelsea, as is also a copy in Secretary Windebank's handwriting (preserved among the Clarendon papers in the Bodleian Library) of the preliminaries of the treaty. It begins :

> ' April $\frac{3}{13}$, 1637. Commencement du Traité entre l'Ambassadeur d'Espagne et Francois Windebank à Chelsea,'

and proposes, on the part of the Spanish Ambassador, to join in quieting France, and either to adopt the secret treaty, or to agree on the consideration in lands or money to be given for the restitution of the Lower Palatinate. The Conde d'Onato remained at Chelsea until March, 1638-39, when he was recalled, and in the year following was made a grandee.

Chelsea had already begun to lose some of its open lands. In the Domestic State Papers (Car. I., vol. cxciii., No. 55) is a report of the Justices of the Peace of the County of Middlesex (1631) as to 'several recent inclosures in the East and West Field of Chelsey, submitted to the Council as offences against the Statute 35 Elizabeth' (forbidding inclosures within three miles of London), 'or as ill-examples, inducing oppression of the King's subjects.' No doubt the inclosure of four acres of Lammas Land by Lady Elizabeth Gorges and her daughter Lady Lane (Madam Dudley Gorges), on the payment of twenty shillings a year, was one of these 'ill-examples.' The Lammas Lands were near the site of the present Park Walk; by their inclosure the parishioners lost the right of common-pasture during four months of the year, and the sum, small as it was, does not appear to have been ever paid.

During the death-struggle for liberty, Chelsea does not make a very great figure. While John Hampden was making his noble stand against the principle involved in the impost of ship-money, some of the Chelsea people— Margaret, Countess of Nottingham; Elizabeth, Countess of Devonshire; Edward, Lord Gorges; Sir John Danvers and Sir John Lawrence, with others—were protesting against the amount levied on Chelsea (it being at a rate four times greater than that of other taxes), but taking care to state that their complaint was only against the amount, and not against the tax itself. The Sheriffs replied that the unusual rate was 'in respect of persons of honour and quality who had summer houses there, but land and property else-where'—an interesting side-light upon the administration of justice in this time of tyranny. This was not the whole of the trouble, however. In the year following (1638), Sir John Lawrence, Nicholas Harman, and Sir John Abeale drew up another petition, stating that, by appointment of the High Constable, they had lately made a 'ratement' for ship-money, according to every man's estate. They had rated themselves and some few others at a higher proportion, in order to spare the minister and some of weak estate. The Sheriffs, however, who were strangers to the place, at the instigation of some 'factious spirits,' had struck out the names of several persons of quality, and abated others, throwing the whole of these abatements upon the petitioners, the Countess of Devon and Sir John Fearne. They prayed that the first rate might be confirmed, but with what success is not recorded.

Meantime the storm was gathering. A great part had been played through-out the struggle by a Chelsea resident, John Pym, the eloquent and resolute Somersetshire squire—'King Pym,' as the Cavaliers fitly styled him. Nothing could avert a struggle but the submission either of the King or the Commons, and at length the King took the irrevocable step of raising his standard at Nottingham, on August 23, 1642.

6

In 1643 the Common Council of London, alarmed by the near approach of the royal forces, ordered London to be fortified. Besides the rampart thrown round the city itself, a number of detached forts and earthworks were constructed in the surrounding districts. These included several in the neighbourhood of Chelsea : a large fort with batteries at Hyde Park Corner, a court of guard at Chelsea turnpike, by the Queen's Elm in Fulham Road, a small redoubt and battery on Constitution Hill, a battery and breastwork at Tothill Fields, etc. A frigate, the *Notre Dame*, had been sent by the Commis-

FORT AT HYDE PARK CORNER.

sioners of the Admiralty, in November, 1642, to ride off Chelsea, for the guard of the river above London Bridge. Many a skirmish which has not found its way into history took place in the neighbourhood of Chelsea, and they have left traces all round its boundaries. A helmet, breastplate, and some swords, all of this time, were discovered when Lowndes Square was laid out ; in 1840 many human remains, horse-trappings, and shoes, with coins of the time of Charles I., were found at Albert Gate, and other relics have been unearthed in Grosvenor Place and the Five Fields (Pimlico).

Clarendon, in his 'History of the Rebellion' (book x., section 114), tells us that in August, 1647, when the King was a prisoner at Hampton Court:

> 'The army of horse, foot, and cannon marched through the city, . . . over London Bridge into Southwark, and so to those quarters to which they were assigned. . . . The general's [Fairfax's] head-quarters were at Chelsy, and the rest of the army quartered between Hampton Court and London, that the king might be well looked to ; and the council of officers and agitators sat constantly and formally at Fulham and Chelsy, to provide that no other settlement should be made for the government of the kingdom than what they should well approve.'

Several of the prominent figures in this great struggle were connected with Chelsea. Edward, Earl of Manchester, who at first took the country's side, and played a distinguished part at Marston Moor, was one of these. Among the Duke of Manchester's MSS. is a letter, dated July 21, 1624, from R. Willis to Sir Nathaniel Rich, requesting the latter to go to Chelsea, 'to speak with my Lord.' He was then known as Viscount Mandeville, and two years later was summoned to the House of Peers as Lord Kimbolton. He succeeded to his father's title in 1642. Sir Nathaniel Rich was brother-in-law to Lord Mandeville. That the Earl of Manchester was living at Chelsea in 1644 we find from another letter from Henry Ireton, addressed to him at Chelsea on September 13 of that year. Again, in the 'Perfect Summary of Every Day's Proceedings in Parliament' for August 19, 1647, we have:

> 'This day the lords sat not, some of them purposing to dine at the Earl of Manchester's house at Chelsea.'

As to the situation of the house there is no record. Another distinguished Parliamentary General, the Earl of Essex, is said to have lived in Church Place; Commissioners Lisle and Bulstrode Whitelock successively occupied Buckingham House, which, in 1650, had been used as a barrack for the Parliamentary soldiers, 'it being very convenient to the service on which they were employed.'

On the other hand, Sir Arthur Gorges was distinguished for his steady loyalty to the failing cause. Another Chelsea Royalist was Sir Richard Hastings, who was assessed by the Committee for the Advance of Money on May 25, 1646, at £600. Two months later, when it was proved that he was a delinquent (that is, had levied war on the Parliament), it was ordered that his horses at Chelsea should be seized and brought away, and he himself apprehended and brought up in custody to pay his assessment.

In after-years the gallant and accomplished Prince Rupert, whose headlong courage more often injured the royal cause than otherwise, lived in Chelsea, where he had a 'glass house' for his experiments near the ruins of the Theological College.

The King was executed on January 30, 1649; Sir John Danvers of Chelsea was among those who had signed the death-warrant.   He is styled by Echard ' one of the most inveterate of the King's judges,' and certainly he has obtained a very large share of Royalist abuse.   Another Chelsea resident, Sir William Monson, Lord Castlemaine, was also accessory to the trial, and lived to bear the punishment for his part in it.   Following this tragedy, the infant Common-wealth was surrounded with dangers, and before the close of the year was at war with its former allies, the Scotch.   But the genius of the Republican soldiers, animated as they were with a religious fervour that sanctified their every act, led them on through all dangers to victory, and hundreds of Scotch prisoners were hurried southward.   Many of them were lodged in Controversy College, which now came to be called Chelsea Prison.   Among the prisoners who were shut up there during the next two or three years were James White, Marshal of the Scotch army at Worcester, and James Wemyss, General of Artillery, etc.

No one of the Continental Powers showed such hostility to the Common-wealth as the Protestant Dutch States.   In retaliation, a Navigation Act was passed, which aimed at destroying their carrying trade.   Upon this the States General sent over Ambassadors to treat for peace.   These were lodged at Chelsea.   While negotiations were pending between the two countries, the Dutch fleet, under Van Tromp, opened fire upon Blake before Dover.   The public indignation rose to fever-heat, and the Government felt constrained to send a guard, consisting of four files of musketeers and twenty horse, to Chelsea, for the protection of the Ambassadors.   War, however, was inevitable, and once more Chelsea College became crowded with prisoners.

So favoured a resort did Chelsea become with the gay, witty, and profligate frequenters of the Court of Charles II., that the Merry Monarch, as one of the saddest figures in our history is so inaptly styled, is reported to have named Chelsea Reach 'Hyde Park on the Thames.'   Before the advent of steamers, tugs, and launches, Chelsea Reach was well known as a place for two or three hours' pleasant sailing.   Charles II. was often at Chelsea ; on more than one occasion he was feasted and entertained by the Earl of Radnor ; and it was off Chelsea that Charles was bathing when the notorious Colonel Blood lay hidden among the reeds of the Battersea shore, awaiting an opportunity to shoot him. The Thames, not yet degenerated into a common sewer, was then a sweet and clear stream, and Chelsea was a favourite bathing-place for many years after-wards.   There still lives in Chelsea an old lady whose grandfather made a comfortable living by taking bathers out to the favoured spots.

In 1661 the Count d'Estrades came to England, as Ambassador from Louis XIV., to negotiate the cession of Dunkirk.   He resided at ' Chelsé,

Londres,' in 1661 and 1662, as may be gathered from the dates on his despatches, which have been published. This discreditable bargain, which naturally excited much indignation at the time, was at length concluded for £40,000. In the following year De Lubienitz, the Swedish resident at Hamburg, appears to have stayed at Chelsea. Letters from him to Count Wrangel, dated hence in September, 1662, are preserved in the Castle of Skokloster.

In 1664 the old quarrel with the Dutch was revived, this time upon disagreements with regard to the Guinea coast. The Ambassador Van Gogh came to England, and was lodged at Chelsea ; his fortnightly despatches are nearly all dated from this place between August 1664 and August 1665. He remained at Chelsea some little time after this, as appears from a letter among the Graham MSS., from Patrick Vaus to A. Slingsby, dated Oxford, December 15, 1615, in which Vaus says : ' The Dutch Ambassador had a private audience on Thursday, and took leave of his Majesty on Thursday last, and posted home to Chelsey.' It was during this war that Admiral de Ruijter made the famous observation of the English, equally true of both nations : ' They may be killed, but they cannot be beaten.'

It appears that the Spanish Ambassador also stayed at Chelsea this year. In the parish register was entered :

'Payed the ringers when his Majesty dined at the Spanish Ambassador's, 10s. od.'

This was the Ambassador d'Ognaté, at whose request two prisoners in Chelsea College — dwellers in Flanders, and subjects of the King of Spain — were released.

In 1678 all England was startled by the pretended revelation of a Popish plot, in which Titus Oates and Bedloe played such infamous parts. Chelsea did not escape the general perturbation, as the Bishop of Winchester was accused of harbouring arms for a rebellion in his palace there.

Up to these days the village, or town as it was beginning to be called, had nestled round the riverside church, with an outlier at Little Chelsea. Its baptisms, averging only some forty a year, would give it a population of about one thousand. Beyond the village were farm lands, nursery grounds, meadows, and the common ; through these an ancient baulk, or headland, separating the fields, extended across Bloody Bridge. During Charles II.'s reign this track was widened and converted into a private road for the King's use.

The fame of the Chelsea nurseries and gardens dates from this time, and in this, as with so many other industries, we owe its importance in some degree to foreign persecution, and the consequent immigration of its victims. The revocation of the Edict of Nantes drove many Frenchmen to England, and among them many gardeners, some of whom settled at Chelsea. The older nurseries have long been driven out by the growth of the town, but their works live after them. Dr. Martin, in one of his pleasant articles on Old Chelsea, observes :

'Although Butterfly Alley, sought by sauntering swells, is gone, King's Road is still countrified by its florists ; their famous wistarias grow on the Hospital walls and climb the houses of Cheyne Walk ; you still find their fig-trees in private gardens, their vines on old-fashioned trellises ; they make Chelsea streets all green and golden with their varied creepers through summer and through autumn.'

Far back in the first half of the sixteenth century Sir Thomas More's garden had been the delight of all who saw it, though gardening must have then been in a very rudimentary condition. Early in the seventeenth century James I. is said to have planted a mulberry garden in the 'great garden' where Cheyne Walk now stands ; and Sir John Danvers laid out the grounds of Danvers House in the Italian taste (1618-1620), one of the earliest specimens, if not the earliest, of that style in this country. We may form an idea of their appearance from the Italian gardens at Hampton Court, which have descended to us, almost unaltered, from this time. Towards the end of the century the gardens at the Manor-house, with waterworks by Winstanley, the Dutch gardens at Ranelagh House, and those of the Royal Hospital, which retained their original form until the present century, became famous. More important than any of these was the planning of the Apothecaries' Garden in Paradise Row, which has the special interest of being the first public botanic garden established in this country, and is still put to its original use. Gerarde's herb-garden at Holborn, and Tradescant's at Lambeth, though established earlier, were private, and have long ceased to exist.

With the increase of buildings, the old agricultural character of the place, of course, rapidly disappeared. When Lysons wrote his 'Environs of London,' in 1795, he said :

'It is computed that there are now only 130 acres of pasture and meadow, and about 170 of arable, the greater part of which is occupied by market gardeners.'

An interesting note on the agricultural position of the parish at the beginning of the present century is given in Faulkner's first edition of the 'History of Chelsea' (1810). He says :

'The barley grown in the parishes of Chelsea, Fulham, and Chiswick has been for many years distinguished for its good quality, and is much sought after for its seed. But of late years very little corn has been sold in this parish, as the gardeners find it much more advantageous to apply their grounds exclusively to the rearing of vegetables and flowers for the London markets ; and it is computed that one half of the vegetables sold in Covent Garden Market are raised in Chelsea and the adjoining parishes of Fulham, Kensington, and Chiswick.'

Until recently Little's Nursery held its ground in the older portion of the King's Road, linking the present with the past ; and the names of Veitch, Bull, and Wimsett give Chelsea, though no longer rural, a celebrity throughout the horticultural world.

In the latter half of the seventeenth century Chelsea became more famous as a fashionable suburb than it had been at any time previous. The manor was now in the possession of Charles Cheyne, who was created Viscount Newhaven, and the list of aristocratic residents is so long that it would be tedious here to recite the whole of them : among them were the second Duke of Buckingham, the Earl of Radnor, the Marquis of Wharton, the Earl of Ranelagh, the Duke of St. Albans, the Earl of Pelham, the Earl of Sandwich, the Duchess of Hamilton, the Duchess of Ormond, the Duchess of Mazarine, the Earl of Bristol, the Duke of Beaufort, the Earl of Lindsey, etc.   Queen's House, in Cheyne Walk, derives its name from the supposed residence of Charles II.'s neglected Queen, Catherine of Braganza.

The famous Hospital, 'Chelsea's glorious pile,' as Rogers called it, dates from this time, having risen from the ruins of the old Theological College beween 1682 and 1690, and has since been the chief feature of the place.

Chelsea was growing rapidly.   Dr. King, 'the antiquarian Rector,' tells us in his MS., which has never been published, but is still preserved at the rectory, that in 1717, the year in which he wrote, the parish contained about three hundred and fifty houses, and that the number was continually increasing.   Fifty years previously there had been less than forty.   We get an idea of the appearance of Chelsea in 1738 from the print of Thomas Preist, a Chelsea man, who lived ' near the Ferry.'   By 1780 the number of houses had increased to more than seven hundred ; and in the twelve years following an additional six hundred were built.

The village had always been famous for its healthiness, and we constantly come across notices of people visiting it for convalescence.   Thus, in 1599, Rowland Whyte writes to Sir Robert Sydney how ' the gallant Earle of Essex,' being in ill-health, had ' gone to Chelsey, where he purposed to be sicke.'   In 1639 Henry, Earl of Danby, came to stay at Danvers House, on account of ' the malady which assaulted him in his old age.'   Edward Montagu, Earl of Sandwich, took a lodging at Chelsea in 1663, 'to take the ayre,' and there stayed for some time, though his mode of life, as described by Pepys, was calculated to undo any good which ' the ayre ' might have done him.   Four years later Henry Middiman, writing to Sir George Cooke, says : ' The Duke of Cambridge is removed to Chelsea, eats what he likes, and seems better.' Swift, in his journal to Stella, April 24, 1711, writes : ' I design in two days, if

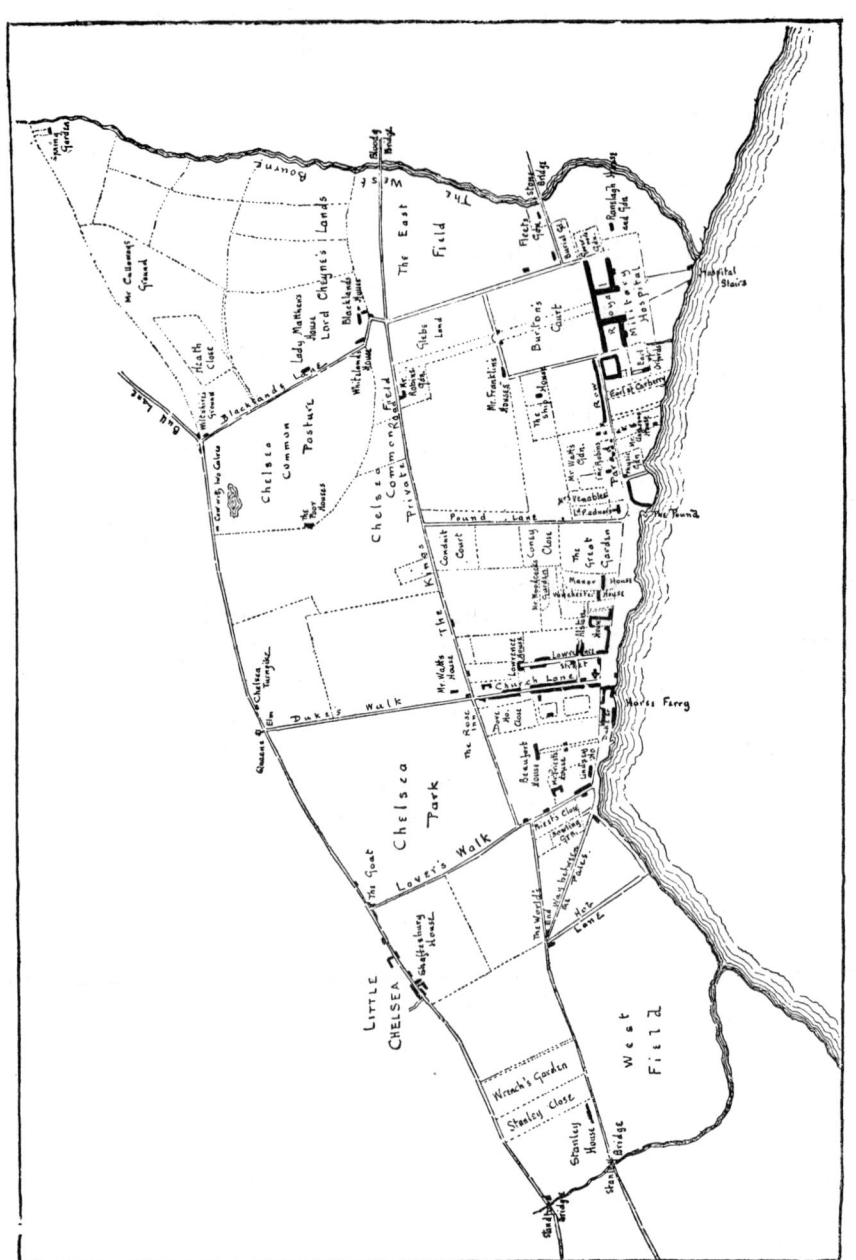

SKETCH MAP OF CHELSEA EARLY IN 18TH CENTURY.

possible, to go to lodge at Chelsea for the air, and put myself under the necessity of walking to and from London every day.' Dr. King's MS. contains a note that ' No village in the vicinity of London contributes more to the ease and recovery of asthmatical and consumptive persons.' It was on this account that Smollett came to Monmouth House in 1749, hoping for the recovery of his only daughter. That the Consumption Hospital, and recently its important enlargement, were built in this neighbourhood is a proof that this reputation has endured even to the present day. Madame d'Arblay, speaking of her father, Dr. Burney, coming to Chelsea, says : ' Chelsea air is even proverbially salubrious, Drs. Arbuthnot, Sloane, Mede, Cadogan, Farquar, etc., having given it a medical celebrity in making it their chosen residence.'

It was the healthy air, probably, that made Chelsea in the eighteenth century a favourite place for private and other schools. In the previous century, 1636, when Sir Francis Kynaston wished to move his Museum Minervæ from London, on account of the plague, he sought to obtain Chelsea College for it, but, being foiled in this, he carried it to Little Chelsea. Bowack, writing in 1705, mentions that both Blacklands House and Henry VIII.'s Manor-house were then occupied as ladies' schools. In 1729 Mary Astell, with Lady Elizabeth Hastings and other ladies, founded and endowed the school for daughters of pensioners in the Hospital, out of which the present celebrated asylum has grown. A Mr. Glover apparently kept a well-known school for dancing and deportment at Chelsea in those days, for in ' The Birth and Education of Genius,' written in 1751, by the Rev. Mr. Cawthorn (Master of Tunbridge School), we read :

'But all your more majestic charms,
*   *   *   *   *
Were form'd by Glover's skilful glance
At Chelsea.'

In 1770 Mr. Lewis Lochee established his military academy at Little Chelsea, with grounds laid out as a fortification ; and seven years afterwards a naval academy was established at Ormond House. Later on Monmouth House and Gough House were both used as schools ; Miss Landon, with several others who became famous, were educated at 22, Hans Place ; and in 1825 the first school for reformation in London—' The School of Discipline '—was founded by Mrs. Elizabeth Fry in Paradise Row.

In the eighteenth century Chelsea still retained its reputation as a fashionable quarter, and included among its residents such various people as the Earl of Shaftesbury—author of the ' Characteristics,' Count Zinzendorf the Moravian, the Duchess of Monmouth, the Cadogans of Oakley, etc. But

7

during this period Chelsea acquires greater interest from its scientific, literary, artistic, and political residents than from its 'fashionable people.' In the first half of this century 'Radical Chelsea,' as it afterwards came to be called, in curious contrast to its early cognomen, was a nest of Whigs, counting among its residents Sir Robert Walpole, Wharton, Sir John Cope, Shaftesbury, Steele, Addison, Stepney, etc. Some of these are exhibited in an interesting picture supposed to be painted by Sir Godfrey Kneller. It is described as 'A Scene in Christopher Catt's House, Chelsea Walk : Steele, Lord Orford, Addison, and his stepson, little Lord Warwick, Sir Godfrey Kneller, and others at tea.' The Tory side, however, was well represented in the person of Dr. Atterbury, whose Jacobite leanings earned for him an exile. Among the MSS. of the Marquis of Townsend is an informer's letter, dated March 5, 1715, conveying intelligence of a secret Jacobite assembly. No names are given, nor is the place of meeting specified ; but the presumption is that it was not unconnected with Atterbury, as the writer gives his address as ' Matthew Price, Callico Officer att Mr. E. Grafton's, by the Horse Ferry at Chelsea.' No less than five Presidents of the Royal Society have had connection with Chelsea, viz., the Earl of Carberry, Robert Boyle, Sir Joseph Banks, Sir Christopher Wren, and Sir Hans Sloane. Here, too, lived Ranby and Cheselden, the surgeons ; Miller and Pettiver, the botanists ; Gay, the poet ; Bishop Hoadley and his son, Dr. Hoadley ; Hamilton, Collet, and Reinagle, painters ; Wilton, the sculptor ; Hall and Dixon, engravers, and many more.

Chelsea now became very celebrated as a holiday-resort and place of entertainment. Gay, in his ' Epistle to Pulteny,' speaks of the popularity of Chelsea Meads in spring-time :

' Chelsea's meads o'erhear perfidious vows.'

The home of the Earl of Ranelagh, with its beautiful grounds, had become the rival of Vauxhall, and all society flocked to its Rotunda, its water-gardens, its masquerades, ridottos, bals paré, and the idle promenades so sharply satirized by Bloomfield. Don Saltero's coffee-house, dating from 1695, or earlier, was one of the chosen lounges of the literati of the day—Johnson, Addison, Steele, and the whole of that brilliant circle came hither to be barbered, to sip their coffee, gossip over the news, and inspect the odds and ends of the ' knackatory,' or museum. Chelsea had a theatre as early as 1705. Among the MSS. of Sir H. Verney, Bart., is a letter from Ralph Palmer to his nephew, Lord Fermanagh. It is dated from Little Chelsey, December 3, 1705, and in it he says : ' My Lord Wharton's great stable in Church Lane, Chelsey, is converted into a playhouse, where we have all been to see great things, a fine scaramouch, etc., performed by the Duke of Southampton's servants.' But the stable was only probably put to this use for a short time, as we do not hear of this 'playhouse' again.

Chelsea Bun - house, just over the boundary, was patronized by royalty, and at festival times was frequented by almost incredible numbers of holiday-folk; it, too, had its museum and gardens, and dotted over the parish and its confines were numerous taverns with their tea-gardens, grottos, and arbours, such as the World's End (celebrated in Congreve's comedy); the Swan, where Pepys came to divert himself; the Dwarf's, in Chelsea Fields, kept by 'the un-paralleled John Coan,' Stromboli House, a sort of Ranelagh for the tiers état; the Black Lion, etc.

Chelsea also began to show an activity in more important directions than the entertainment of loungers and holiday-makers; famous waterworks, since removed to Sunbury, were established at the eastern end of the parish, near Ranelagh, in 1722—the company had a reservoir in Hyde Park, where the sunken flower-garden with its fountain now stands, and its memory is preserved in the name of Engine Street, near at hand. Still more famous was the china factory in Lawrence Street, whose productions rivalled the finest efforts of Dresden and Vincennes, and were eagerly purchased by dealers as they were finished, and to-day are competed for by collectors all over the world. A silk-manufactory was started in Chelsea Park, and at first showed some promise of success. Crowds of sightseers were attracted by this novelty, but the experiment failed after a trial of a year or two. One Le Blon, a French-man, afterwards started a tapestry-factory on the same ground, but his conduct in a previous enterprise gave the public no confidence in him, and this venture failed also. Several paper-factories were started, and at the west end was Janeway's foundry, where bells and heavy siege guns were cast. An enterprise of another sort was the laboratory of Michael Arne, son of the famous musician, built at Chelsea, about 1767, to carry on his experiments for the dis-covery of the philosopher's stone.

Though Chelsea had now grown into a town, and had largely lost the delightful rural character which had so long been its charm, its surroundings were still dangerous to the traveller. Knightsbridge had long had an unenvi-able reputation for highwaymen. When Lowndes Square was laid out, various relics, such as staves and handcuffs, telling of struggles between the law and the outlaw, were found. The Five Fields, 'where robbers lie in wait,' as the *Spectator* puts it, had also a bad character for footpads. Steele, we know, pre-ferred on one occasion to lie at Chelsea for the night rather than brave the dangers of the road. Bloody Bridge had borne its ominous name since the days of Elizabeth, and seems to have gained it from the number of crimes committed in its neighbourhood, though some regard it as merely a corruption of the older name—Blandel Bridge.

It is a matter of common knowledge that the keepers of taverns and ale-houses of the more disreputable class were often in league with the ' knights of the road,' and gave them information as to whether travellers were worth powder and shot or not ; but it is very unusual to find clergymen mixed up in such transactions. However, in the Coffin MSS. at Portledge, in Devonshire, is a letter dated January 30, 1691-92, which states that ' one Parson Smith, Reader or Lecturer of Chelsey, was yesterday committed (by the Lord Chief Justice Holt), being accused for being concerned in many robberies and assisting highwaymen.'

On October 22, 1706, Ralph Palmer, of Little Chelsea, writing to Lord Fermanagh, at Little Claydon, says : ' There is a great housebreaking all about London, and at Great Chelsea two watchmen last week were almost killed by four rogues, who had taken off a casement at Dr. King's.'

So dangerous was the district that, in 1715, the Government, in response to a representation from the inhabitants, ordered a patrol of the more able-bodied of the Hospital pensioners to watch the roads between Chelsea and St. James's. Later on it was found necessary to increase the number of this guard, and fifty privates and six non-commissioned officers were appointed to patrol the district, half on each alternate night. Visitors returning from Ranelagh or going to Kensington would wait until a sufficient body was formed for mutual protection, and then proceed, escorted by guides, who carried lanterns suspended from long poles. The King's Road itself, then mainly occupied by florists and market-gardeners, was frequently the scene of disgraceful outrages. The people of Chelsea were fully aware that this evil notoriety was harmful to the prosperity of the rising town, and took some steps to remedy the bad state of affairs. In the Additional MSS. of the British Museum (No. 15,609, f. 21), we find the following proclamation, dated November 21, 1753 :

'The Inhabitants of the Parish of Chelsea, being desirous to prevent, as far as in them lies, any Robberies or Felonies being committed in the said Parish, do hereby give Notice, that they have enter'd into a Subscription, for a Reward, for the discovery of Robberies or Felonies, and have therefore, paid into the Hands of Mr. Edward Anderson, of Chelsea, aforesaid, as Treasurer, a sum of Money to answer the several purpses hereafter mentioned ; to such Person or Persons who shall, during the space of one whole Year from the Date hereof, apprehend or take any Offender or Offenders as are hereinafter described, the several and respective Rewards hereafter mentioned, in fourteen Days after Conviction, over and above what such Person or Persons may be entitled unto by such Apprehending and Conviction by any Law now in Being.

'For every Highwayman or Foot Pad who shall commit any Robbery within the said Parish (except that part of the Parish and Road leading from London to Harrow-on-the-Hill, which belongs to the said Parish) the sum of Ten Pounds.

'For every person who shall break into the Dwelling House of any Subscriber, or send any Incendiary Letter to any Subscriber, the sum of Ten Pounds.

'For every Person who shall steal any Horse, Mare or Colt, or other Cattle, belonging to a Subscriber, or commit a Theft or Robbery in any of their Out-houses, the sum of Five Pounds.

'For every Person who shall commit any Theft or Robbery in any Garden, Garden Grounds or Fields, Orchard, Court Yard, Back-Side or Fish Pond, or any Barge or Craft lying ashore, belonging to any of the Subscribers, or shall steal any of their Fruit, Poultry, Fish, Linnen, Lead, Iron, Gates, or Gate-Hinges, Pales, or Fences, the sum of Forty Shillings,' etc.

CHELSEA IN 1809.

Notwithstanding this and the efforts of the patrol, the neighbourhood, at night-time, was decidedly unsafe for the solitary traveller, even down to the present century.

The destruction of the famous old Chelsea began in the eighteenth century. Danvers House was the first to go, in 1716; Beaufort House followed in 1740—after some years of neglect; Henry VIII.'s Manor-house did not long survive Sloane's death in 1753. After a break of fifty years the work of demolition began again. Ranelagh House and the Rotunda were pulled down soon after the closing of the gardens in 1803; the ancient home of the Shrewsburys—degraded to a paper-stainer's—in 1813;

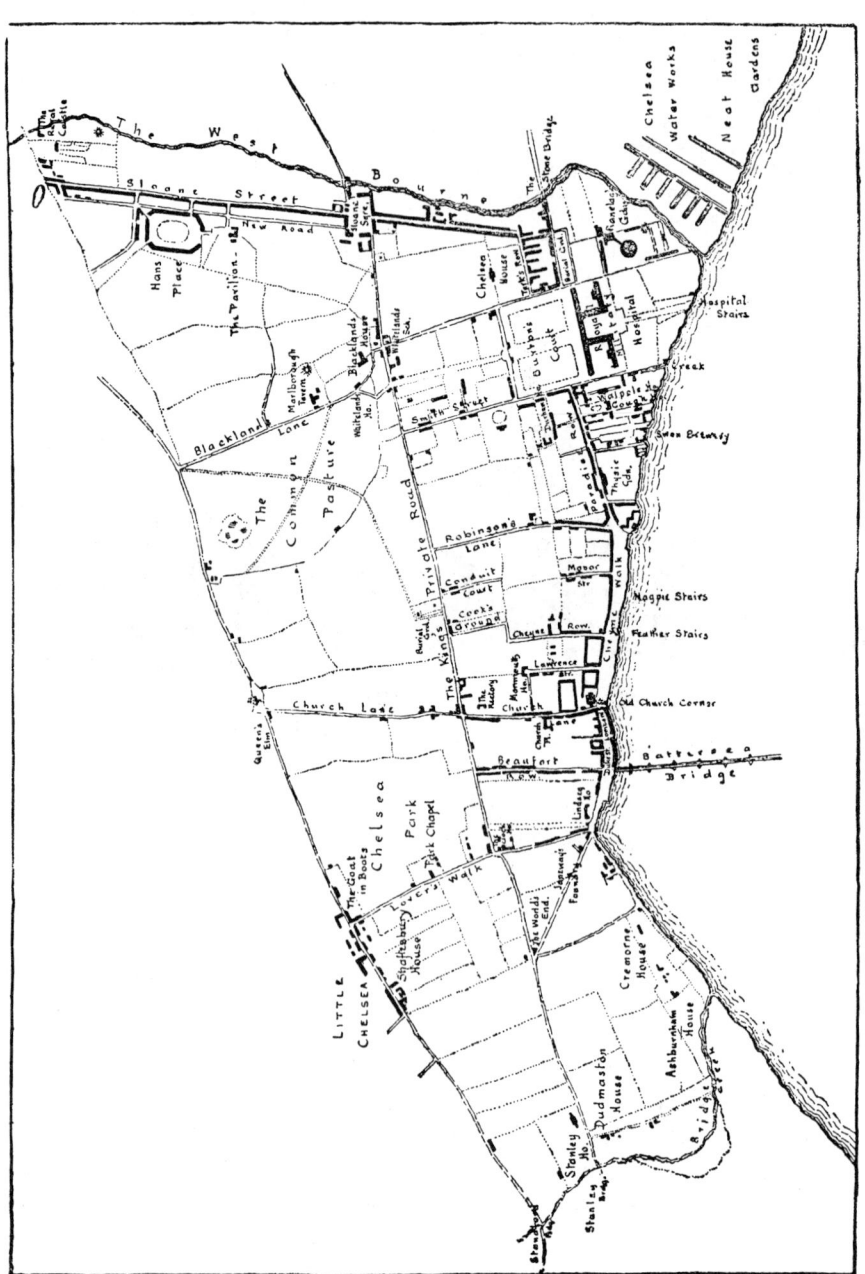

SKETCH MAP OF CHELSEA AT END OF 18TH CENTURY.

Winchester House disappeared about 1830; the Lawrence House, latterly called Monmouth House—a dilapidated wreck—in 1833-34; and Church Place in 1840-42.

How long, in spite of destruction and an invading population, Chelsea retained some last remnants of its old village character, is witnessed by Leigh Hunt, who lived here from 1832 to 1840. In his 'Autobiography,' speaking of the quiet of the place, he says: 'I got to like the very cries in the street, for making me the more aware of it by the contrast. I fancied they were unlike the cries in other quarters of the suburbs, and that they retained something of the old quaintness and melodiousness which procured them the reputation of having been composed by Purcell and others. Nor is this unlikely, when it is considered how fond these masters were of sporting with their art, and setting the most trivial words to music in their glees and catches. The primitive cries of cowslips, primroses, and hot cross-buns seem never to have quitted this sequestered region. They were like daisies in a bit of surviving field. . . . This sense of quiet and repose may have been increased by an early association of Chelsea with something out of the pale, nay, remote.'

We have still surviving several of the notable houses of the older time. The rectory house was built by Paulet in the reign of Queen Elizabeth; Stanley House, as rebuilt at the end of the seventeenth century, is now the residence of the principals of St. Mark's College; Lindsey House, partly refronted and cut up into several tenements, is known as Lindsey Row; Gough House, largely added to, is the Victoria Hospital for Children; Walpole House, with a story added, is part of the Infirmary of the Royal Hospital; Whiteland's House is part of the wall-paper factory of Messrs. Scott, Cuthbertson and Co.; the Duchess of Mazarine's little house (until 1890 the School of Discipline) and several adjacent houses are still standing, though the hand of the destroyer has been busy at the western end; at the riverside end of Milman Street are several weather-beaten houses about three hundred years old; one or two others verging upon two hundred years in old Duke Street and at the end of Danvers Street have just been destroyed, but some later terraces, with a quaint old-world air upon them, still hold out against the prevailing spirit of renovation in Cheyne Walk, Cheyne Row, King's Road, St. Leonard's Terrace, and elsewhere.

The old Chelsea of which we have been speaking possessed many elements of the picturesque which have not been neglected by our artists. The Rotunda at Ranelagh was painted by Canaletti, and the Gardens by Hogarth; De Cort, of Antwerp, painted Cremorne Villa; Girtin made a mezzotint of Chelsea Reach; Turner sketched from the top of the little house in Upper Lindsey

Row; De Wint sketched Cheyne Walk, and there is a distant view of St. Luke's Church by him in the South Kensington Museum; Pether and several others painted the Hospital; Cotman painted the old bridge, and Etty the park-lands above it; Wilkie laid the scene of one of his most famous pictures in Turk's Row; John Varley, Edmund Dorrell, and James Stark each sketched much in the neighbourhood. In our own day its picturesque qualities have not altogether disappeared, and have found even more exponents than in the past; the old pensioners are a perennial source of inspiration. Whistler has painted and etched many subjects here in the neighbourhood of the old bridge; Cecil Lawson made several pictures from his windows in Cheyne Walk; Seymour Haden has etched Lindsey Row; Mrs. Allingham has painted an interesting picture of the old pensioners' gardens; Tristram Ellis has pointed out the pictorial qualities of the district in his 'Sketching Grounds within the London Cab Radius;' Birket Foster, J. C. East, C. E. Holloway, C. J. Lewis, and many others, have recently found important subjects on the water side.

It would be beyond the scope of this work to enter into the history of the present century in any detail; but in dismissing it, we may observe that Chelsea has, down to the present day, maintained its distinction as a home of famous men—Brunel and Bramah among engineers; Turner, Martin, Maclise, Holman Hunt, Rossetti, Cecil Lawson, Herkomer, and Whistler among painters; J. B. Philip, Nelson McLean, and Fontana among sculptors; Paul Bedford, Wright, and Mrs. Mellon of the actor's craft; Sir Charles Dilke, John Morley and the Marquis of Ripon among statesmen; and Carlyle, George Eliot, W. B. Scott, and Justin McCarthy among authors, are but a few of the many notable people who have made their home in Chelsea during the present century. Within recent years, too, the place has been resuming something of its old character of a village of palaces. The noble embankment, which swept away so much that was old and picturesque, if also insanitary (qualities which, unfortunately, often go together), was the forerunner of many 'improvements.' Many dingy and squalid streets have disappeared; stately squares and terraces are taking their places, so that an absentee of twenty years wonders what has become of the Chelsea of his boyhood.

THE OLD CHURCH.

I N olden times when Chelsea was a village, it was grouped round its riverside church. This spot is thus the fittest starting-point for an antiquarian ramble, and as portions of the church are by far the oldest specimens of building now remaining in the parish, it shall receive first attention.

From the importance of Chelsea in early ecclesiastical history, and the probability of there having been a royal residence here during the Mercian supremacy, we would naturally expect to find some record of a church dating back to Saxon times. None is to be found, however, nor is any endowment for a priest mentioned in Domesday Book, and though ' Ecclesia de Chelcheth ' is found in the taxation of Pope Nicholas (1291), and is valued at £8 13s. 4d., no Rector is heard of until the reign of Edward II.

The oldest portions now standing are the chancel and the north chantry or chapel. The main fabric of the latter, as shown by the form of the Gothic windows, now almost bricked up, dates from the early part of the fourteenth century. It is known as the Lawrence Chapel, from the family in whose possession it was for about a century and a half. It is generally supposed to have been the manor-chapel, built by one of the early lords of the manor, to have passed with the manor into the hands of Henry VIII., and to have been granted by him, with the old manor-house, to the Lawrences. No chapel, how-ever, is mentioned in Lord Sandys' grant of the manor to Henry VIII. in 1536, nor in a Particular of the Manor drawn up in 1544, nor in any of the manorial grants and assignments ; and I can find no better reason for supposing the Lawrence house to be identical with or on the site of the old manor-house

8

than the fact that it was near the *Lordship* Yard (originally the site of the manor-barns and stables) and a vacant piece of land (now occupied by Carlyle Mansions) called the *Lord's* Waste, and that these names were supposed to indicate the near neighbourhood of the old manor-house. This is a point, however, that will be further discussed in its place.

The chapel does not appear to have belonged to the manor or to have been

THE LAWRENCE CHAPEL, CHELSEA OLD CHURCH.

used for burial in the time of the Brays, who were laid ' in the myddest of the hyghe chauncelle.' Had the chapel then belonged to the manor, it is most probable that the Brays would have been buried there. No monuments, however, earlier than that of Thomas Lawrence, 1593, is to be found there. I conclude, therefore, that this chapel was never attached to the manor, but

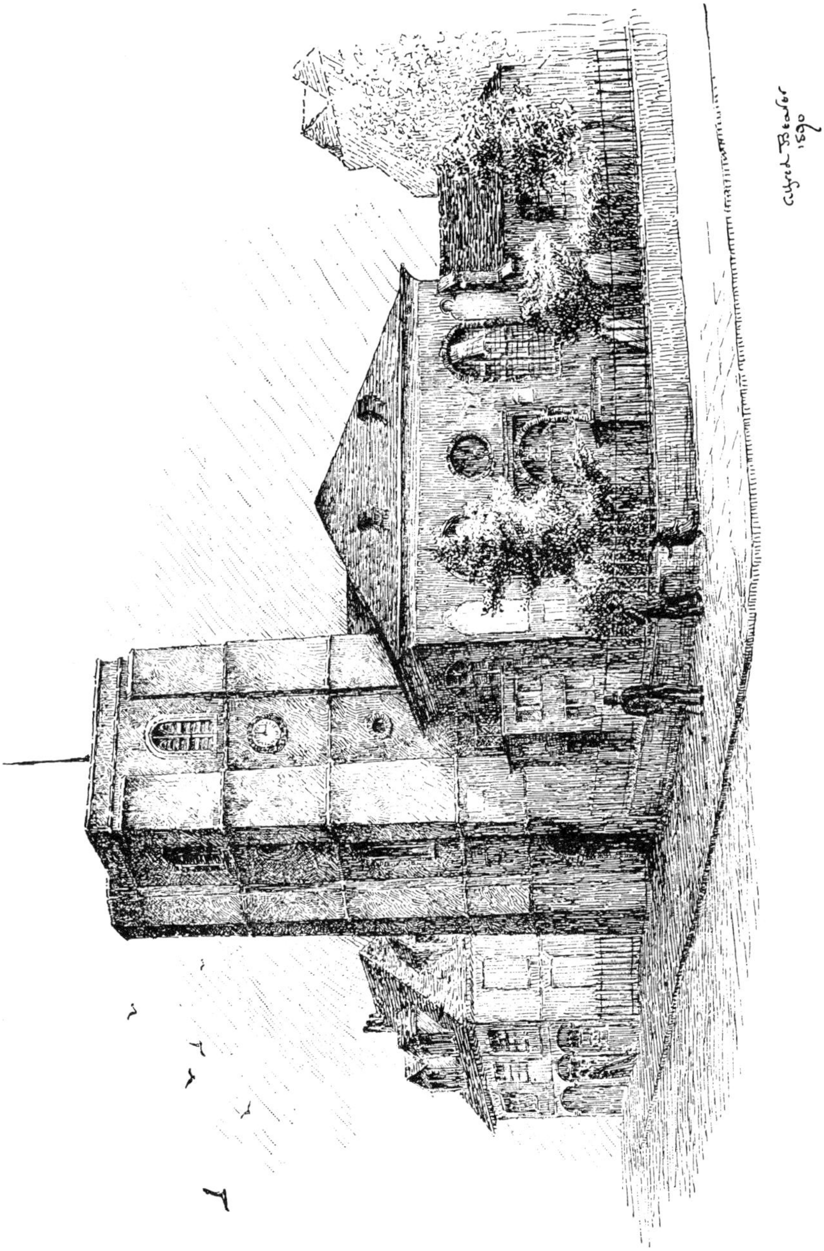

THE OLD CHURCH AT CHELSEA, 1890.

first became private property when Thomas Lawrence purchased some property in Chelsea, and built a house near the church late in the sixteenth century. Having thus become a private chapel, it escaped subsequent restorations,—particularly that of 1667, when such extensive alterations were made in the other parts of the church—and still retains some of its ancient features. The window at the east end, however, is of the same date as those of the main fabric, and the pier of the arch is inscribed, 'This pier was rebuilt in the year 1784.' It is still in private hands. In the eighteenth century a Mr. Offley bequeathed it to Colonel Needham, from whom it was bought by Mr. Lewer, with the east side of Lawrence Street. It now belongs to Mr. Charles Rawlings, whose aunt, Mrs. Rawlings, was a member of the Lewer Family.

In 1860 Mr. Burnell, the architect of the repairs then undertaken, placed before the Archæological Association the remains of an old painted window, about 20 inches in width, representing St. Osyth, which had been found bricked up in one of the windows of this chapel. It appeared to have been intentionally smashed and smeared with mortar.

The Rev. H. R. Davies, M.A., incumbent of the church, describing the reparations carried out under his care, in a paper read before the Middlesex Archæological Association, 1887, says:

'From the determined manner in which we found the piscina and aumbry blocked and plastered up, and a niche in the north chapel, *where probably a statuette of the Virgin might have given the title of the Lady Chapel,* it would seem that Protestant zeal was at fever-heat in Chelsea.'

The suggestion in this passage which I have italicised is highly probable.

In the early part of the sixteenth century the More Chapel, on the southeast, was added. The period of its building has been accurately fixed by the date, 1528, carved on the arch between the chapel and the chancel. The ornaments on the capitals of the arch have been minutely explained as references to the Catholic ritual, but those on the east are in reality emblems obscurely allusive to the builder of the chapel. The ' Moor's head,' the Chancellor's well-known crest, appears among them, and the same shields as may be seen on the tomb. When Lysons wrote his 'Environs of London,' the carvings were so thickly buried in whitewash that that very careful observer could only describe them in general terms; but in 1833, after the church had undergone a thorough cleansing and repair, they were completely exposed, and John Gough Nichols was able to give a minute description of them in the *Gentleman's Magazine.* Though the carvings have necessarily suffered from time, this arch is, from an architectural point of view, one of

SIR THOMAS MORE'S MONUMENT.

the most interesting things in the church. Apart from the interest which attaches to any relic of Sir Thomas More, it marks the birth of a new development in art decoration in this country, for it is one of our earliest examples of the Italian workmanship imported and fostered by Henry VIII. Various speculations have been made as to the carver: Torrigiano has been named; but, as he died in 1522, this is impossible. They have been attributed also to Holbein, who was an excellent decorative designer, as many of his drawings prove; but these capitals are manifestly in the Italian taste. The King had several Italian artists in his employ at that date. Thus in 1527, engaged in building a banqueting-hall at Greenwich, were

'Italian painters, Vincent Vulp and Ellys Carmyan at xx^s the week.'
'Italian painters and gilders, Nicholas Florentine and Domyngo at xvj^d day and night.'

These men, described as painters, were of the class of decorative artists, and capable of carving, moulding, and decorative work generally, and Nicholas Florentine is found seven years later engaged with Benedetto da Majano on a figure of St. James. But besides these there was engaged at Greenwich John de Mayne or Demyauns, described as an 'Italyan gravour' (sculptor). Any one of these would be a likely designer for this arch; for we find from the Royal Accounts that Hans Holbein was working with them, and could have introduced them to More's notice. The western capital, it may be noticed, is much inferior in workmanship to the other, and is therefore set down as English.

The chapel is 15 feet wide and 20 long, but was formerly longer: the Rev. Mr. Davies tells us that when sinking a chamber for the warming apparatus, the chalk-block foundations of the west wall were discovered, nearly on the spot where the pillars of the present gallery stand; and he believes that there was originally another arch corresponding to the one now existing. This would account for the early description of the chapel as an aisle. The change took place during the enlargement of 1667, when the aisles were lengthened to their present size. The western arch of the nave of the old building is still standing, with the organ built in and around it.

Remains of a stained glass window were also found bricked up in this chapel in 1858. These windows may have been hidden to escape the ravages of the notorious Dowsing, or some other agent of the extreme Puritan party, employed by Parliament in 1643-44 to destroy 'superstitious' pictures and carvings in churches.

The More Chapel was private property until quite recently, and went with the house which More had built, until Sir Arthur Gorges sold the latter to

Lord Treasurer Cranfield, when he reserved the chapel for his own use. In 1664 Gorges' house and the chapel were sold by Sir Arthur's son to Mr. Thomas Pritchard, from whom they passed to Sir Francis Milman, Bart., M.D.; towards the eighteenth century the chapel belonged to a Mr. Flight, afterwards to Mr. Mann, of Paradise Row, and lastly to Mr. Crew, of Cheyne Walk, from whose executors it was acquired for the church, at a price of £100, the present incumbent having raised subscriptions to that amount.

In the sixth year of the reign of Edward VI. (1552), a jury was appointed to make a return to the King's commissioners of all the 'goods, plate, ornaments, jewells, and bills' belonging to the church. Faulkner has printed the entire inventory, a long list of chalices, crosses, masers, altar-cloths, candlesticks, books and vestments. Many of them were sold, and amongst the purchasers we find Thomas Hungerford, gent., Walter Harborde, gent., and Sir Edmund Burton. Between the first drawing up of the inventory in the third year of Edward VI., and the report of the jury in the sixth, the church had been broken into and various things, duly set forth in the report, stolen. Many of the objects mentioned in this inventory were probably gifts of Sir Thomas More, for we are told that the parish church 'had all ornaments belonging thereunto abundantly supplied at his charge, and he bestowed thereon much plate, often speaking these words, " Good men give it, and bad men take it away." '

The parish registers were commenced in 1559, and the first volume, a small folio, bound in vellum, is, for the most part, beautifully written. It begins with this memorandum :

> 'A Booke begun in the House of God for Regestringe of all Christenynges, Marages, and Burialls within the Parish of Chelsey, provided for that purpose by J. Tomkins and Thomas Saunders, Churchwardens, the 19 daye of Februarie, 1559.'

There are some unfortunate omissions, especially during the Commonwealth period ; but on the whole the register is fully and accurately kept.

Among the Scudamore Papers (vol. xvi., f. 292) is the rough draught, probably in the handwriting of George Hamden, Rector, and dated 1631, of

> 'Articles and consideracons, to be enlarged or altered according as it may seeme requisite, for ye advancemt and perfecting of ye pious worke of enlarging and repayring the church at Chelsey.'

These reparations consisted chiefly of the repewing of the church, and making the doors, windows, etc., 'soe perfect as that neither cold in Winter or Heat in Somer may ouermuch annoy ye parishionrs when they shall be together.' They included also the reconstruction of the ' Wharfe before ye pound places ' at the cost of Sir John Lawrence and his tenants ; of the vault from ' Sr Edward Powell's house, wch now passeth under ye wharfe '; and of the ' abatinge of ye grounds in a falling manner towards yᵉ Thames,' at the expense of ' Sʳ Edw. Powell, Sʳ Jo. Dãvers, Mr. Rich. Wringhurst, etc., residing upon yᵉ Towne Lande.' The cost of the general repairs was to be met by a levy upon the inhabitants 'according to yᵉ proporčons of his or their Seats or Roomes,' and ' if any some upon anyone be unpaid by yᵉ space of one month, it may be lawful for yᵉ Churchwardⁿˢ to consigne give and appoint yᵉ seaterooms of such persons to other persons to hold and enjoy as aforesaid.' It is gratifying to find as a special article

'That great respect be had to yᵉ monumᵗˢ or graues of yᵉ deceased at yᵉ enlargemᵗ or reforming soe yᵗ if necessity require yᵉ stirring of any of them, it may be their re-edificacon rather than destruccon,'

and it would have been well had all subsequent restorations been carried out in a like spirit.

Bowack, quoting from a paper in the Manorial Records, entitled ' A Disposition of the pues in Chelsey Church,' tells us that

'In the year 1667, the old church, which was much decayed, being too small to contain the congregation, grown large by the vast increase of buildings, about that time in the town, it was agreed by the parishioners that part of it should be demolished, and that such alterations and additions should be made as were necessary for decent accommodation. Accordingly the shattered tower and west end of the church were pulled down, and the north and south aisles carried several yards towards the west, by two brick walls, being in all about 80 feet from the ground. The walls of the church were raised, the windows enlarged, the old parts beautified, the inside new pewed, the churchyard considerably raised, and enclosed with a high wall of brick ; and most of this done at the voluntary charge of the inhabitants, and the whole roof, lead, timber, etc., at the sole cost of Lady Jane Cheyne. The church was furnished with all the requisite ornaments, and the steeple with a good ring of six bells, by the bounty of the inhabitants.'

It is probably this restoration which is alluded to in another draught of articles preserved among the Scudamore Papers, which begins :

'Forasmuch as yᵉ small parish of Chelsey hath of late years bin greatly increased by the buildings, resort and residence of divers great and noble personnages, etc., whereby the church is become too little for the parishioners : by which means also many of the Ancient Inhabitants and their families are too comonly put from their seats, and in a sort excluded from such right and place to serue God in this church, as is very requisite, or wᶜʰ their predecessors enioyed ; it is humbly desired that the same church may bee speedily enlarged and substantially repaired. Wherefore the present Churchwardens especially, as also any Noble, Good, and Charitable persons are hereby moued and appoynted to inuite a contribucon from one an other as well wᵗʰin as wᵗʰout the Parish.'

The wharf is also mentioned in this document :

'as it wilbe most necessary in yᵉ first place for the receaving and placing of yᵉ stone and timber and materialls neere yᵉ worke, we will it be requisite to enlarge the wharf before yᵉ said church, amply to receaue the same, wᶜʰ will proue a bountiful addicon and convenience both to yᵉ Church and Parishionʳˢ and Strangʳˢ, who for passage and accesse will have a great ease and benefit thereby.'

The following note was copied by Lord Cheyne from the parish registers under date 1669-70 :

> 'The sum of 580*l.* 12*s.* 10*d.* was collected by voluntary contributions of the principal inhabitants for the rebuilding of the church.'

Dr. Baldwin Hamey was a very liberal contributor : he gave to the value of £530, out of which the great bell was purchased. Dr. King has preserved the inscription :

> 'D. Lucæ Medico Evangelico Baldwiney Hamey Philevangelicus Medicus, M.D.'

The tower, with its 'cupola' or steeple, was finished about 1679, and was reckoned to be one of the highest pieces of brickwork in the country. A recently restored inscription tells us that it was repaired in 1704. Its walls were originally battlemented, as shown in several old views, and the height to the top of the battlements was 90 feet. Upon this was the Ashburnham bell-tower, very similar in design to those at Battersea and Wandsworth, and the top of its vane was 113 feet from the ground.

In 1748 some of the inhabitants were seriously alarmed by the shaking of the tower when the bells were rung ; a committee was appointed to investigate, but the surveyor employed reported that there was no cause for alarm, there being no more shaking than was usual where there was a peal of bells. The turret, however, required bracing. In 1756 it was found that one of the bells was cracked, and the parishioners met in vestry to consider the question of recasting the whole peal. This was decided on, but not until 1761, or five years afterwards, was sufficient money subscribed for the purpose. The steeple was then reported to be very sound, and the bells were recast by Thomas Janeway—whose foundry is commemorated in Foundry Place, World's End Passage—at a cost of £104 10*s.* 10*d.*

When the new church was building in 1821, the safety of this tower was once more in question, and it was finally decided that it was dangerous to ring the old bells there. Accordingly, 'the good ring of six bells' was melted down to contribute towards the peal to be cast for the new church.

In 1698 Mr. Thomas Hill and Mr. John Clarkson built the south gallery, in the place, it is supposed, of the rood-screen, removed during the Reformation. This they built at their own expense, 'upon condition of having the power of seating such persons as they shall think fit for one turn'—possibly one 'term' is meant—'and then the gallery to return to the use of the parish.' In 1745 we find from a vestry minute that it was agreed to allow the Rector £6 per annum in lieu of the gallery to be taken down.

Mr. Bryan says : 'The original altar-piece was very plain, formed by an obtuse arch, ornamented slightly with foliage, etc. In the centre was painted the Decalogue, while the north side displayed the Camp of Israel, and the south side Moses on the Mount, receiving the Tables of the Law.' What he means by the 'original' altar-piece is not clear, and the one he describes is hardly 'very plain,' being much more elaborate than that which now exists. Probably he means that of 1667, as his description indicates a common type of the Stuart period. In 1740 a Mr. Stewart (there was a thoroughfare called Stewart's Grove leading from Cale Street to Fulham Road) bequeathed £100 ' to be applied towards making a handsome altar-piece in the parish church of

CHELSEA OLD CHURCH IN 1760. (AFTER CHATELAIN.)

Chelsea, as soon as that part of the church shall be rebuilt, or repaired fit for it ; and in the meantime, and until such altar-piece can conveniently be made, my will is that the said sum of £100 remain in the hands of my executors.' The church authorities do not appear to have ever availed themselves of this bequest.

To the Supplement of the *Gentleman's Magazine,* 1832, Faulkner communicated an account of the repairs that were effected in that year. The pavement was relaid ; the pews lowered and newly arranged ; the pulpit removed from the wall of Sir Thomas More's chapel, and placed in the middle aisle, near

PULPIT AND CANOPY FORMERLY IN CHELSEA OLD CHURCH.

the lower chancel. But the chief alteration was the removal of another un-
sightly gallery placed across the chancel, obscuring the light, and partly hiding
More's monument. On this occasion the whitewash was removed from the
capitals already described, and in digging up the floor of the More Chapel, the
brasses missing from the Gorges' tomb were found.

Some old brass chandeliers, which formerly hung in the nave, have disappeared. They were given to the church by Mr. T. Franklin and his wife in

THE CHAINED BOOKS IN CHELSEA OLD CHURCH.

1693. (Franklin's Row faces the east side of Burton's Court.) What became
of these chandeliers is not recorded; the probability is that they vanished
during some process of restoration, to be sold as old brass.

Besides the fine series of tombs, several interesting relics are to be seen in
this church—among them, a little wooden figure of St. Luke, evidently of some
age, which formerly stood on the apex of the canopy of the pulpit; it was
afterwards fixed in an out-of-the-way place on the ledge of the buttress of the
More Chapel. The Rev. R. H. Davies, who throughout his incumbency has
shown a most reverent care for his venerable charge and all it contains,

brought the figure into its present position in 1886, and Mr. Wilson, a young Chelsea artist, made and gave the tastefully carved bracket on which it stands.

More interesting than this is the oaken bookcase and reading-desk, with six folio volumes chained to it, standing against the south wall. 'Six great bowkes beside the Bible' are mentioned in the inventory of 1552, but none of those now preserved are of so early a date. They are copies of the 'Vinegar Bible' (Basket, Oxford, 1717), lacking its title-page ; the 'Common Prayer' (1723) ; the 'Homilies' (Oxford, 1683, with the autograph of J. Trelawney) ; and the 'Book of Martyrs' (vols. i. and iii., London, 1684). They formerly stood at the west end of the north aisle, near the old font. This vivid symbol of the days when books were scarce, and learning itself as carefully chained as these volumes are, is not uncommon in the remote village churches of our land, but this in Chelsea is the only example in or near London, and it is fortunate that it has been so carefully preserved to the present day.

Another interesting relic is seen on entering the porch. This is the Ashburnham bell, originally hung in the steeple, but taken down for safety in 1807 (or 8). Near it hangs a board, on which is painted the following account of its history :

'This bell was given to the old Parish Church of Chelsea by the Hon. Wm. Ashburnham in the year 1679. It was a grateful offering on his part to commemorate his escape from drowning in the Thames, into which he had wandered during a dark night of the above year, and from which he was saved by hearing the clock of this church strike nine. Many changes in the church have taken place since then, and this bell having long remained unused and nearly forgotten, it is here preserved as an interesting Chelsea antiquity, having been removed from the clock tower and placed in the present position by order of the church trustees, and under the direction of

> A. Gerald Blunt, M.A., Rector,
> R. Henry Davies, B.A., Incumbent of the Church,
> T. B. Diplock, M.D., } Churchwardens.
> G. W. Richards,

March, 1862.'

There is another, and manifestly more probable, version of the story. According to this, Ashburnham was returning from Lambeth by boat ; when off Chelsea a dense fog came on, but the striking of the church clock enabled him to judge of his situation and row for the shore. Subsequently it was found that, if he had drifted much farther, his boat would have been upset, and he, in all probability, drowned. Hence his gratitude.

Besides giving the bell, a sum of money was left that it might be rung every evening during the winter months, in case any similar accident should happen. The bellringer received the princely stipend of five shillings for attending every evening during the season at nine o'clock. Faulkner remembered an old man that had rung the bell for many years.

A later relic but not without interest, is found inside the church. Some of the banners which hang from the roof of the nave were presented to the Chelsea, or Queen's Royal Volunteers by Queen Charlotte, and are believed to have been designed by her in 1804; one, at least, is supposed to be her own needlework. Their presentation took place in the Rotunda at Ranelagh, and the ceremony will be described in the account of that place. On the disbandment of the volunteers, the banners were hung in the church, where they have since remained, and are now in a very tattered condition.

Many of the writers who have mentioned the old church at Chelsea have spoken of its ugliness, some going so far as to say that only the mellowness of age redeems it from absolute hideousness. But taste has changed in the last two or three decades; we now look upon this class of architecture with very different eyes. Chelsea Old Church is plain and unpretentious in every particular, but there is a beauty in humility very soothing to those who will look at it aright: the various additions at wide intervals have given it a certain incongruity, but they also reveal the story of its building, and carry with them a host of associations that I, for one, would not lose for the smartest brand-new building all the learning of to-day could produce. It possesses, too, by reason of this same incongruity, all those quaintnesses so essential to the picturesque, which make such buildings equally charming to the artist and the antiquarian. Its massive weather-beaten steeple, which has stood like

> 'A tower of strength
> Four-square to all the winds that blow,'

gives the keynote to all views of Chelsea, and its air of hoary antiquity impresses every passer-by.

The old church of Chelsea is famous for its crowd of monuments; no other parish church anywhere in the suburbs of London is so wealthy in this respect. But here, as in so many other places, there has been much ruthless work among the objects, which, above all other earthly things, should surely be held sacred. There is no monument earlier than the sixteenth century. This absence seems to indicate that some very sweeping changes were effected during that period, otherwise something, surely, would have been saved. Weever found nothing worth recording but the Bray, More, and Northumberland tombs in his ' Funeral Monuments,' published in 1631, and destruction has gone on since that time. Monuments perfect in the eighteenth century have been sadly mutilated, or have entirely disappeared. Yet, all this notwithstanding, there is much left for us to preserve with reverence.

The oldest monument now existing is undoubtedly that of the Brays. It is an altar-tomb, much defaced, set in the north wall of the chancel. Originally it was adorned with brasses of Lord Edmund Bray and his son, Lord John Bray, but these have gone. The inscriptions, also, have disappeared, but, fortunately, were in part copied by Weever :

> 'Of your charitie pray for the soul of Edmund Bray, knt., Lord Bray, cosin and heir to Sir Reginald Bray, Knight of the Garter.'

He was the son of John, and nephew of Sir Reginald Bray, and died in 1539, when he was brought to Chelsea, to be laid by his father and his brother Reginald (not to be confused with the uncle, who is buried in the chapel he built at Windsor). The monument was at first placed in the middle of the

THE BRAY MONUMENT, CHELSEA OLD CHURCH.

high chancel, but removed to its present position in 1857. Near, in the floor, is a stone, with the brass gone, apparently that of John Scarburgh, Rector of Chelsea (d. 1433). The brasses of this and the Bray tomb are figured in Faulkner. The Bray vault is near the present font.

We have no account of the interments of the elder Brays, but there is a long and very interesting account of the burial of Lord John Bray, son of Edmund, preserved in the Heralds' College, which has been printed at length by Faulkner. There is another account by an eye-witness, Henry Machyn ; it is little known, and, being short, it may be given here :

> '1557. The xxiij day of November was cared from Blake-freres to Temes syd, and ther wher rede to grett barges, covered with blake and armes hangyng for my Lord Bray, and so by water to Chelsey, to be beryed by his father, with iiij haroldes of armes, and a

standard and a baner of armes, and ij baners of emages, borne by ij haroldes of armes in ther cott armurs, and so many nobull men mornurs in blake, and xvj pore men had new gownes, and a xvj greet torchys, ij whytt branchys, and iiij grett tapurs, and a cott armur, elmett, target, sword and mantylles and a dosen of skochyons ; and after messe, and ther wher mony prestes and clerkes, and the diner at ys plasse at Blake-freres, and so they cum bake from Chelsey to dener.'

The next in point of date, and highest of all in interest, is the monument to Sir Thomas More. It is an altar-tomb, set against the south wall of the chancel, erected by More himself in 1532. The Tudor arch has a cornice ornamented with foliage, with his crest—the Moor's head—in the centre. The spandrils, decorated with vine-branches, bear the shields of himself and his two wives, the first of whom is here buried.

'Thomas Morvs vrbe Londinensi familia non celebri sed honesta natvs in literis vtcvnq versatvs ; qvvm et cavsas aliqvot annos ivvenis egisset in foro et in vrbe sva, pro shirevo ivs dixisset ; ab invictissmo Rege Henrico octavo (qui viri Regum omnivm gloria privs inavdita contigit, vt Fidei defensor qvalem et gladio se et calamo vere præstitit, merito vocaretvr) adscitvs in Avlam est, delectvsq; in concilivm et creatvs Eqves, Proqvæstor primv, post cancellarivs Lancastriæ, tandem Angliæ miro principis favore factvs est sed interim in pvblico Regni senatv lectv est orator popvli præterea Legatv Regis nonnvnqva fvit, alias alibi, postremo vero Cameraci comes et collega ivnctvs principi Legationis, Cvthberto Tvnstallo tvm Londinensi, mox Dvnelmensi Episcopo qvo viro vix habet orbis hodie qvicqvam ervditivs, prvdentivs, melivs. Ibi inter svmmos orbis Christiani Monarchas rvrsvs refecta fœdera, redditamq; mvndo div desideratam pacem, et lætis-simvs vidit, et Legatvs interfvit.

'"Qvam svperi Pacem firment faxentq; perennem."

'In hoc officiorvm vel honorvm cvrsv qvvm ita vertaretvr vt neq; Princeps optimvs operam eivs improbaret neq; nobilibvs esset invisvs nec inivcvndvs popvlo, fvribvs avtem et, Homicidis molestvs. Pater eivs tandem Joannes Morvs Eqves et in evm ivdicvm ordinem a Principe cooptatvs qui Regivs Confessvs vocatvr ; homo civilis, svavis, innocens, mitis, misercors, æqvvs et integer, annis qvidem gravis, sed corpore plvsqvam pro ætate vivido, postqvam, eo prodvctam sibi vitam vidit, vt filivm viderit Angliæ Cancellarivm, satis in terra iam se moratvm ratvs, libens emigravit in cœlvm. At filivs defvncto patri cvi qvamdiv svperarat, comparatvs et ivvenis vocari consveverat, et ipse qvoq; sibi videbatvr amissvm iam Patrem reqvirens et æditos ex se liberos qvatvor, ac nepotes vndecim respiciens apvd animvm svvm cæpit persenescere. Avxit hvnc affectvm animi svbsecvta statim velvt adpetentis seni signvm, pectoris valitvdo deterior. Itaq; mortalivm harvm rervm satvr, qvam rem à pvero pene semper optaverat vt vltimos aliqvot vitæ svæ annos obtineret liberos, qvibvs hvivs vitæ negotiis pavlatim se sedvcens futvræ possit immortalitatem meditari ; eam rem tandem (si cæptis annvat Devs) indvlgentissimi Principis incomparabili beneficio, resignatis honoribvs impetravit : Atq; hoc Sepvlchrvm sibi, qvod mortis evm nvnqvam cessantis adrepere qvotidie com-monefaceret transeatis huc prioris vxoris ossibvs extrvendvm cvravit. Qvod ne svperstis frvstra sibi fecerit. Neve ingrventem trepidvs mortem horreat, sed desiderio Christi libens, oppetat, mortemq; vt sibi non omnino mortem, sed ianvam vitæ fælicioris inveniat precibvs evm piis Lector optime spirantem, præcor, defvnctvmq; pro seqvere.'

The following is the inscription to More's first wife :

'Clara Thomæ iacet hic Ioanna Vxorcula Mori
Qui tumulum Aliciæ hunc destino quiq; mihi
Vna mihi dedit hoc coniuncta virentibus annis
Me vocet vt puer et trina puella Patrem
Altera priuiquis (qua gloria rara Noverca est)
Tam pia quam gnatis vix fuit vlla svis

Altera sic mecum vixit, sic altera viuit
Charior insertum est hæc sit an illa fuit
O ! simul O iuncta peteramus viuere nos tres
Quam bene si factum religioq; sinant
Ét societ tumulus, societ nos obsecro cœlum
Sic Mors non potuit quod dare vita dabit.'

This epitaph, written by More himself, is on a black marble tablet, and has been twice recut. When Weever visited the church, some time anterior to 1631, he found the inscription so much effaced that it was 'hardly to be

CHAPEL BUILT BY SIR THOMAS MORE.

read.' Sir John Lawrence, in repairing it, caused the word 'hæreticisque' (given in Weever's copy) to be omitted, and a blank now stands in its place. More had classed heretics with thieves and murderers, but thought had naturally undergone a great change by Sir John's time, and he regarded its retention as dishonourable to the memory of an otherwise great and good man.

Erasmus criticised its introduction, and in one of his epistles to the scholar of Rotterdam, More warmly defends himself on its employment.

Aubrey gives an inaccurate account of the restoration. He says:

'Near the middle of the south wall . . . was some slight monument erected, which being worne by time, about 1644, Sir John Lawrence, of Chelsey, at his own proper costs and chardges, built to his memory, a handsome one, with the inscription of marble.'

The monument, however, is so entirely in the Tudor taste, that there can be no doubt that the one now existing is the actual one erected by More himself. For many years it was partly concealed by the gallery staircase, already mentioned. This was entirely removed in 1832, and the monument thoroughly repaired by 'Mr. J. Faulkner, statuary, of Chelsea,' who, Thomas Faulkner says, 'accomplished his difficult task with much skill in imitating and preserving the antique style of the various mouldings, frieze foliage, etc., so that the whole monument now displays a uniform appearance and harmony, equally creditable to the artist who performed the work, as to the committee who superintended it.' The opportunity was taken to examine the slab, in the hope that the original epitaph might be found on the back. This back, however, was found to be in a rough condition, the front only having been polished. A slight drawing of this monument, made in 1620, is preserved among the Harleian MSS.

It has been asserted by Weever, Anthony à Wood, and Aubrey, that More's headless body was removed from the chapel in the Tower, and re-buried at Chelsea. 'This is certain,' says Weever, but gives no authority; and it was possibly a tradition he had heard at Chelsea on his visit during the rectorate of George Hamden. Wood and Aubrey probably copied from Weever, as have many others since. Neither Stapleton (who wrote in 1583, and was well acquainted with the family), nor Cresacre More (great-grandson of Sir Thomas), nor even Roper (his son-in-law), mentions this circumstance, and it is incredible that they did not know it, or, that knowing, they did not attach importance to it. The probability, therefore, is wholly against this re-burial at Chelsea. The trunk almost certainly lies in the Tower Chapel, side by side with that of Fisher, which had been exhumed at Barking for burial with More, as he himself had desired. The vault in Chelsea Church is quite empty now.

Another circumstance which weighs against Weever's statement is the fact that the head is buried elsewhere—in the Roper family vault in St. Dunstan's Church, Canterbury (Aubrey erroneously says in the cathedral). Had the body been buried in Chelsea, we cannot help thinking his daughter would have caused the head to be placed with it.

A romantic story has been told to account for Margaret Roper's possession of her father's head.   Passing one day under London Bridge, on which it was exposed, she exclaimed, 'That head hath many a time lain in my lap, and would to God that it would fall into my lap as I pass under !'   The story says that 'it did fall into her lap, and is now preserved.'   But Stapleton is probably correct in saying that she obtained it by bribing the executioners or gaolers.   He tells us also that ' she most carefully preserved it with aromatic substances as long as she lived.'   Isabella Burt and others have said that she was imprisoned for this bribery, but this is another unauthenticated statement. The head was seen and drawn in 1715, and Mr. Burnell made a copy of this drawing, which he exhibited at a meeting of the Archæological Association in 1866.   The vault at St. Dunstan's was accidentally opened in 1835, when the Rev. J. B. Bruce saw it, 'in the niche in the wall, in a leaden box, something in the shape of a bee-hive, open in the front, and with an iron grating before it ' (these words are identical with those of Gostling, in his ' History of Canterbury,' 1744), ' in the place where it was seen many years ago.'   The vault was again opened a few years since, on the occasion of a visit by the Kent Archæological Society, when the Rev. J. G. Hoare described it as ' fast decaying.' Margaret Roper is believed to have kept the head in the wooden box, which is religiously preserved at Baynard's Park, Surrey, the residence of Mr. Thurlow.

At the first festival of the Chelsea Martyrs, More and Larke, celebrated at St. Mary's, Cadogan Street, in May, 1888, Father Morris exhibited a mournful relic of the great Chancellor.   It was one of the vertebræ of his neck, formerly in the possession of Father Thomas More, Provincial of the Society of Jesus in England, and the last male descendant of the martyr.   Father More gave it to his sister, a nun of Louvain, in Belgium, from whom it was obtained by Father Morris.

Previous to the alterations of 1667, More's chapel contained three magnificent monuments.   One, the Dacre monument, is now in the south aisle, but the time-worn remains of the Duchess of Northumberland's still stand against its north wall.   It consists of an altar-tomb, with a canopy supported by five pillars under an arched recess, and is beautiful in its decay. The back of the recess is divided into three compartments, richly designed. That on the east still displays the effigies on brass of the Duchess and her daughters, but those of her sons have disappeared, as have, also, all but one of the shields from the quatrefoils on the faces of the tomb.

' Here lyeth yᵉ right noble and exellent prynces Lady Iane Gvyldeford late dvches of Northᵛberland davghter and sole heyre vnto yᵉ right honorable Sʳ Edward Gvildeford knight Lord Wardeyn of yᵉ Fyve Portes yᵉ which Sʳ Edward was sonne to yᵉ Right Honorable Sʳ Richard Gvyldeford some tyme knight and companion of yᵉ most noble ordre of yᵉ gartor and yᵉ said dvches was wyfe to the right high and mighty prince

John Dvdley late Dvke of Northv̄berland and by whome she had yssew xiii children that is to wete viii sonnes and v Davghters and after she had lyved xlvi years she departed this transitory world at her maner of Chelse yᵉ xxii daye of Janvary in yᵉ second yere of yᵉ reigne of our sovereyne lady Qvene Mary the first and in Aᵒ MDLV on whose sovle IESV have Mʳcy.'

Before the Duchess died, she wrote a quaint will with her own hand on a small slip of paper, in which occurs the following injunction :

'My will is earnestly and effectually, that little solemnities be made for me, for I had euer have a thousand folde my debtes to be paide, and the poore to be given unto, than anye pompe to be shewed upon my wretched carkes ; therefore to the wormes will I goe, as I have afore wrytten in all poyntes, as you will answer yt afore God ; and you breke any one jot of it, your wills hereafter may chance be as well broken.'

She had seen too much of the vanity of earthly pomp during her chequered life to care for any in death; her family, however, paid little regard to her injunctions, and her funeral is always quoted as one of the most imposing that has ever taken place in Chelsea. Citizen Machyn went to see it, and gives us the following account :

'1554[-5]. The j day of February was buried the Duchess of Northumberland at Chelsey, where she lived, with a goodly herse of wax and pensils, and escocheons, ij baners of armes, and iiij baners of images, and many mornurs, and with ij haroldes of armes. Ther was a mageste and the valens, and vj dosen of torchys and ij whyt branches, and all the chyrche hangyd with blake and armes, and a canepe borne over her to the chyrche.'

Near is the stone of 'Catherine, Countess of Huntington, 2ᵈ daughter of John late Duke of Northumberland, dyed without Yssue May yᵉ 2ᵈ 1620 aged 72 and is below Inter'd by her Mother.'

Between the north aisle and the lower chancel is a large arched monument about 10 feet high, ornamented with carvings of roses, branches and flutings. This was erected to the memory of Richard Gervoise, son of the Sheriff of London, who 'died 16ᵒ die Feb Aᵒ Dni 1563 Ætatis suæ 27 1563.'

The monument of Thomas Hungerford stands in the upper chancel, and contains the effigies of himself and two sons in armour, kneeling on one side, with his wife and daughter on the other. The inscription tells us nearly all we know of this old Chelsea resident :

'Here lieth the bodies of Thomas Hvngerford of Chelsey, in the Covntie of Midd, Esqvier, the second sonne of Robert Hvngerford thelder of Cadname in the Covnty of Wilth, Esqvier, which hath served King Henry the viii in the rometh of a Gentlemā pencioner, and was with his Maᵗⁱᵉ at the wining of Bologne, and King Edward the vi, at Mvsselbrovghe field, besides Qvene Mary and Qvene Elizabeth in their affaires, being of thadge of lxx yeres, who had to wife Vrsvla Maidenhead, the davghter of the Lady Sands. Anno Domne 1587.'

The Lawrence monuments are placed in the chapel which bears their name. On the north wall is that of Thomas Lawrence (d. 1593), the earliest of this family to be found here. On the right are the effigies of his three sons, facing those of his wife and six daughters, all kneeling. On the cushion on which his wife kneels are the figures of two infants. The epitaph ends :

'Thus Thomas Laurence spekes to tymes ensoing,
That Death is sure, and Tyme is past reneving.'

This monument, designed in the touching spirit of pious humility, so characteristic of the older English artists, is that of which Henry Kingsley (in his 'Hilliers and the Burtons') makes James Burton say :

'I always loved that monument better than any in Chelsea Old Church. 'Tis a good example of a mural monument of that time they say ; but they have never seen it on a wild autumn afternoon, when the sun streams in on it from the south-west, lights it up for an instant, and then sends one long ray quivering up the wall to the roof, and dies.'

Sir John Lawrence (d. 1638)—the second son represented in the previous monument—has an ornamental black tablet on the east wall, with a satirical inscription, bad in taste, but containing much truth :

'When bad men dye and turn to their last sleep,
What stir the poets and engravers keep,
By a feigned skill to pile them up a name,
With terms of Good and Just outlasting fame ;
Alas ! poor men, such most have need of stone
And Epitaphs ; the good, indeed, lack none,
Their own true works enough do give of glory
Unto their names, which will survive all story ;
Such was the man lies here, who doth partake
Of verse and stone—but 'tis for fashion's sake.'

One of the daughters of Thomas Lawrence, Sarah, who married Richard Colvile, of Newton, in the Isle of Ely, has a monument on the same wall, with a curious effigy representing a female figure in a winding-sheet rising from a tomb. She died in 1631. The monument is the work of the brothers Christmas.

In the floor is an inscription to Henry, Sir John Lawrence's youngest son.

The most beautiful monument in this church is that to Lord and Lady Dacre, against the wall of the south aisle. It is a very fine example of the rather too gorgeous taste which succeeded the purity and severity of the older times. The white marble effigies lie on a sarcophagus under an arch supported by Corinthian columns, with an obelisk on either side. It is most richly decorated with various marbles and mosaics, and elaborately gilded. According to the will of Lady Dacre, it was erected in Sir Thomas More's Chapel; it was placed in its present position after the rebuilding in 1667. Lady Dacre bequeathed to the parish of Chelsea two presentations, for a man and a woman, to Emanuel Hospital, after foundation, in Westminster, on the condition that this monument was kept in repair, and it is to this fact that we

owe its present perfect state.   In the parish register, April 11, 1696, was
entered :

'To Thomas Burt, for cleansing Lady Dacre's tomb   ...   ...   *ol. 5s. od.*'

In 1823 the sum of £80 was spent upon it, and it was redecorated again, about

THE DACRE TOMB.

1868, at a similar expense under the direction of J. B. Philip, R.A., the sculptor,
who was a resident in Chelsea.   There is a small model of this tomb at
Emanuel Hospital, and a drawing by Trotter in the British Museum.

At the east end of the south aisle is the interesting monument (composed of various coloured marbles) to Sir Robert Stanley. Three large urns bear medallions of Sir Robert and two of his children, and between them stand figures of Justice and Fortitude. Sir Robert, the second son of the 'Earle of Darbie,' according to the inscription, died in 1632. This inscription is very fulsome, even for an epitaph; but that to his two children is in better taste, with an adroit reference to the family arms:

> 'The Eagle death found where the Infants lay.
> And in his talons bore their souls to Heaven.
> Let no profane hand their reliques sever,
> But as they lye, so let them rest for ever.'

Sir Robert's funeral helmet, painted and gilded with the crest of the eagle and child, still hangs above the monument. J. G. Nicholls, writing to the *Gentleman's Magazine* in 1832, noticed that the monument then was 'in a lamentable state of dilapidation, and must speedily fall down if not repaired.' The church had no funds for the purpose, and it seemed as if the family took no interest in it. Years after, however, it was cleaned and restored by the late Earl of Derby.

A square slab on the south wall near the communion-table bears an inscription to the memory of Elizabeth, Marquise de Cugnac, daughter of Sir Theodore Mayerne, and wife of a Protestant immigrant; she died in 1653 at the early age of twenty years.

A black marble slab on the north wall of More's Chapel records the death of Arthur Gorges in 1668. A fulsome epitaph says that he had 'all the Gorges' soules in one,' and ends:

> 'Live Arthur, by the spirit of thy fame,
> Chelsey itself must dy before thy name.'

The monument to Sir Arthur Gorges (d. 1625), the friend of Spenser, seems to have been in good preservation in 1705, when Bowack wrote his account of Chelsea. When the floor was dug up in 1832, brasses, with the effigies of Sir Arthur and Lady Gorges and their children, were recovered, and placed upon the western pier of the arch.

Against the wall of the north aisle is a large imposing monument that cannot fail to attract attention of the visitor entering the church. This is the monument erected to the memory of Lady Jane Cheyne—a semicircular temple with Corinthian columns of scagliola, over a black marble sarcophagus, on which is a life-size recumbent figure of Lady Cheyne.

Among the Cheyne papers preserved with the Bridgwater MSS. are many documents relating to this monument. Among them we have the original

THE STANLEY MONUMENT IN CHELSEA CHURCH.

draught, by Charles Cheyne, of the inscription to be sent to Dr. Adam Littleton to be put into Latin, and with it is the doctor's version. There is also a paper of instructions for the making of the family vault, besides thirteen.letters from Edward Altham at Rome concerning the carving of the figure in white Carrara marble at a cost of 700 crowns, or £200 sterling. The sculptor's name, however, does not appear to be mentioned. The figure has been attributed to Bernini, the best artist of the Italian period of decadence, and probably correctly. It is a good specimen of his work. The whole monument is said to have cost about £500.

On the sarcophagus is the memorial of her husband, Charles Cheyne, first Viscount Newhaven, who died in 1698, and at the entrance to the family vault is the following inscription:

'Charles Cheyne, Esq., Lord of this Manor of Chelsea, which was purchased by the rich dower of his wife, the Lady Jane Cheyne, eldest daughter of William, Duke of Newcastle, not long deceased, and for his own use, when he shall die. It was consecrated the 3rd day of November, 1669. I beseech thee, Almighty God, that she may quietly rest here till the resurrection of all flesh. Amen.'

Near this monument is a marble tablet to Richard Guildford (d. 1680), and his two wives. There is another to Dr. Littleton (d. 1694) on the north wall of the lower chancel; and a small monument to Sir William Milman (d. 1713) near that of the Duchess of Northumberland.

Outside the church there are also some monuments of interest. To Dr. Chamberlayne, the founder of the charity at the Parish Schools, there is a large slab on the south wall facing the river. The inscription includes a pun, 'Novem liberos genuit, sex libros composuit '—Nine children he begot, six books he wrote—and the following very odd statement:

'He was so studious of doing good to all men, and especially to posterity, that he ordered some of his books, covered with wax, to be buried with him, which may be of use in times to come. God preserve thee, O traveller! Go, and imitate him.'

No books were found in the vault when it was examined in 1791. They had either been removed in 1737, or had rotted away.

There are other memorials of the Chamberlayne family here; especially notable is that to his daughter Anne—casta virago—who, in 1690, fought for six hours against the French in a fireship. His son John Chamberlayne also has a tablet.

The inscriptions on the Chamberlayne monuments have been recently (1890) recut under the supervision of the Society for Preserving the Memorials of the Dead.

At the south-east corner is the monument to Sir Hans Sloane, a canopy with four pillars covering a white marble urn entwined by serpents. It was designed

THE CHEYNE TOMB IN CHELSEA OLD CHURCH.

by Wilton the sculptor, to whose two daughters there is a bas-relief on the east wall, and to his niece a slab on the left of the western entrance.

The obelisk near the east entrance was erected by the fellows of the Linnean and Horticultural Societies in 1815, to the memory of Philip Miller, 'the Prince of Gardeners,' who died in 1781. Near it is a flat stone with the inscription, now worn out, to the memory of Woodfall (d. 1815), the printer of the letters of Junius.

Besides those above mentioned, we may observe the memorials of Humphrey

SIR HANS SLOANE'S MONUMENT.

Peshall (d. 1650), a curiosity, for it is probably the smallest in the world, being a brass no larger than a visiting-card; Dr. Baldwin Hamey ('restored by the Royal College of Physicians of London, A.D. 1880, in grateful remembrance of their benefactor'); Ralph Palmer, of Little Chelsea; Mrs. Ann Banks (d. 1759); Henry Powell, 'a great friend to the widow and fatherless;' Henry Raper (d. 1823); Sydenham Teast Edwards, F.L.S. (d. 1819); the Rev. John Rush (d. 1855), etc. It is well known, however, that others, who played a more or less conspicuous part in their day, were buried here, of whom no memorial can now be found. Among these may be noted Thomas Shadwell, Poet Laureate, whose funeral sermon was preached by Dr. Nicholas Brady (associated with Nahum Tate, Shadwell's successor to the Laureateship, in a metrical version of the Psalms); Mossop the actor, whose funeral was one of the grandest seen in Chelsea; Jean Antoine Cavallier, the brave leader of the Camisards in their heroic struggle against the revocation of the Edict of Nantes, who ended his days in London in 1740; and another French Protestant, Captain Rieutort, who fought at Landen and Gibraltar, and died at Chelsea in 1726.

A complete list of all inscriptions will be found in Appendix II.

THE RECTORY AND THE GLEBE.

In 1327, the thirty-first year of Edward III., the rectory was rated at 13 marks; and in the reign of Henry VIII., in the Liber Regis, at £13 6s. 8d.; tithes, £1 6s. 8d. Where the rectory-house originally stood we have no means of knowing. In the time of Elizabeth, when Robert Richardson was rector, the parsonage-house, with 14 acres, 22 perches of land, stood to the west of Sir Thomas More's house (then held by the Marquis of Winchester). This land is described as bounded by the West Field on the north and west, and the Thames on the south. There were also belonging to the glebe 3 acres of land in the East Field, between 'the lands of the Manor of Chelsea, called Gospell Shott,' on the east, and the lands of Thomas Hungerford on the west, having the 'common field' on the north. To the south of this were 9 acres more belonging to the rectory. All these lands were exchanged by Richardson with the Marquis of Winchester in 1566 for one close of land of nearly 3 acres, on which a house with appurtenances had recently been built, with another close of arable land, about 18 acres in extent, adjoining it. The boundaries of the latter were: a parcel of the manor, then in the tenure of Stephen Claybroke, on the east, the common field on the north, and the Queen's Manor of Chelsea on the south. These are the lands which have since constituted the church glebe and the house that which is still the rectory.

In the year following, the lands thus obtained from Richardson (long afterwards known as Parsonage Close), together with a farm-house and 130 acres of land in various parts of Chelsea and Kensington, were leased by the Marquis of Winchester to Nicholas Holborne, of Chelsay, gent., and Katherin his wife, at the yearly rent of £13 6s. 8d. On Hamilton's Survey, Parsonage Close was marked as occupied by a Mr. Priest, who kept a school in Chelsea, and whose name frequently occurs in the parish records.

In 1650 it was reported to Parliament that the parsonage-house at Chelsea, with 20 acres of glebe, was valued at £60, and the tithes at another £60. Forty-four years later, the glebe was let for £51 19s.; the tithes produced £123 9s; and the rent of the seats in the chancel £7; or a total of £182 12s. (The lecturer then received the burial fees.) After an interval of another thirty years (that is, in 1723), the living was worth £380 per annum, made up as follows: the glebe was let for £132 10s. 6d.; the tithes, £108; the chancel seats, in consequence of the enlargement of the church, £18 14s.; burial fees, etc., £120 15s. 6d. These figures indicate very distinctly the extraordinary growth of the place.

In 1766, the sixth year of George III., an Act was passed to enable the rector to let off portions of the church lands for building purposes, provided that the rectory-house and pleasure-grounds were not interfered with.

From the schedule annexed to the Chelsea Rectory Act, 1825, we learn that at that time leases had been granted to the extent of 28 acres, 6 perches. The oldest was that of 4 acres, 1 rood, 29 perches, leased to Jane Grignion (a connection of the celebrated Madame de Grignion), May 13, 1794; the situation is not described, but is that occupied by St. Leonard's Terrace, and the lease is still held by the descendants of Jane Grignion. The White Stiles (the site of Royal Avenue), containing 2 roods, 15 poles, was rented annually by the Royal Military Hospital.

Another Chelsea Rectory Act was obtained in 1870, which empowered the leasing of the whole of the kitchen garden. Glebe Place, part of Bramerton Street and the adjacent shops in the King's Road were then built.

LAWRENCE STREET.

Adjacent to the church is one of the oldest thoroughfares in the parish, called Laurence or Lawrence Street, in memory of a family long connected with Chelsea. There is little about it now to recall the olden time, but at a lodging-house opposite Justice Walk we may observe a large porch, bearing a close resemblance to that of Monmouth House (the home of Smollett, demolished in 1835); and in the passage leading to Augusta Court there is a vaulted ceiling of much earlier time than the surrounding buildings.

Lordship Place, leading from Lawrence Street into Cheyne Row (celebrated as the residence of Thomas Carlyle, 'the sage of Chelsea') was formerly called Lordship Yard, and marks the site of the manor barns and stables. This appears from the following memorandum (Cadogan Records) :

> 'Charles Cheyne, Esq., leased to Elizabeth Preston a piece of garden ground, having the backway in the Lordship Yard, leading to the houses of Lady Lawrence on the north, and on the south the way by the Thames, for forty-five years, at the annual rental of £4. Elizabeth Preston allowed Charles Cheyne to take down and carry away the old barn and stable standing thereon.'

This must have been in 1662, for the memorandum goes on :

> 'Thomas Kender assigned the lease to William, Lord Newhaven, 4th Nov., 1707.'

Here in early times stood the cage, the stocks and the ducking-stool. They are referred to in a presentment of the Court Leet and Court Baron, 1682 :

> 'We present that the cage and stocks as they now stand [by the church and near the river-side] are a public nuisance, both to the church and passengers, and that they would much more conveniently stand in the Lordship Yard, being the place where they stood formerly. And it is prayed that the Lord of the Manor would order the same.'

In another verdict of the Court Leet (1705) we find Lord Cheyne was 'amerced' for not repairing the cage and stocks, and not erecting a new 'ducking-stool.'

The cage or watch-house (shown as a low square building in several old views of Chelsea) appears to have been occasionally used as a casual ward. In the Parish Books, 1697, we have :

> 'Payd for a truss of straw to put in the cage for a poor woman to lye on, and gave her twopence ...   . 8d.'

THE LAWRENCE HOUSE.

The Lawrence or Monmouth House stood, as we have seen, to the north of Lordship Yard. The Lawrence Chapel, which belongs to this property, is sometimes called the Manor Chapel, and from this circumstance, apparently, it has been generally assumed that the Lawrence House stood on the site of the original manor-house. This may be so, but, as I have attempted to show in the account of the old church, there is no real foundation for the belief that there was a manor chapel; and I can find no other circumstance beyond the name, Lordship Yard, that would serve to locate the manor-house. It must not be forgotten, too, that Dr. King says the house which was Sir Reginald Bray's stood 'at the Arch wch is now built into several Tenements,' but this will be further treated in another place.

The date when Sir Reginald Bray came into possession of the manor is not known. He had been an ardent supporter of the Earl of Richmond's claim to the throne, and it has been generally assumed that Chelsea was granted to him, with other broad acres, by Henry VIII. in return for services rendered.

By his will, dated August 4, 1503, Sir Reginald bequeathed the profits of sundry of his manors, including Chelchyth in Middlesex, to his wife during her life, and on her death to his nephews, sons of John Bray, if they married his wards, Agnes and Elizabeth, daughters and heirs of Henry Lovell. It has been noted in the Introduction that Bray had sold part of his manor of Chelsea to Hugh Oldham, Bishop of Exeter; the remaining portion, which should have come to Edmond or John, Lords Bray, passed, with other manors, by an arrangement between Sir William Sandys and Dame Margery, his wife, on the one part, and Edmund Bray on the other, into the possession of the first named. This was on May 6, 1510

MONMOUTH HOUSE.

In 1519 he leased to Thomas Heyle of London for forty years 'all those houses, gardens, orchards, pastures, groves and curtilages situate between the walls, etc., of the manor, except the barns, granary, common pound, great court, etc.' (Particular of the Manor, 1544). Sir W. Sandys was raised to the peerage in 1523, as Lord Sandys. His connection with the manor of Chelsea ended in 1536, when he exchanged it with Henry VIII. for lands at Mottisfont, in Hampshire. The king's grant to Sandys is dated July 14 of the same year. Thomas Heyle's tenancy would terminate, and the property pass to the crown, in 1559, in which year 'a messuage in Chelsay' was granted by

Queen Mary to Francis Englefield, Esq. (Mem. et Orig., 5 pars orig., An. 4 et 5 Phil. et Mar., rot. 30). The coincidence of dates suggests the proba-bility that this messuage was the house occupied by Heyle. There was another house belonging to the manor, called 'Long House,' on the common field, which was leased to one John Paterson, or Patynson, at a rent of 13s. 4d. per annum (Particular, u.s.). We also find that the great barn was let to John Chamberlayne (perhaps an ancestor of Dr. Chamberlayne), a granary to Patenson, and a small barn and stable to Henry Greaterake (whose name, under the form of Greatorex, is still to be found in Chelsea), etc.

It is possible that the house built by the Lawrences was on the site of that occupied by Thomas Heyle, and that this older building was the manor-house; but on this point we have no information at all. The first Lawrence that we find connected with Chelsea was Thomas Lawrence, goldsmith, of London, but we do not know how he obtained the Chelsea property, nor the date of his coming. In the Harleian MSS., No. 6,583, is an abstract of the rental of Chelsea Manor, 1544, and 'Mr. Tho. Lawrence, Esquire,' appears upon it. This name, however, is not in the original document (see MSS. Lansdowne, No. 2, art. v.), and is apparently an addition in later ink, perhaps merely to indicate the owner of the document.

Faulkner, in the second edition of his 'History of Chelsea,' 1829, printed a number of genealogical details, which he had obtained from a document pur-porting to be the pedigree of the Lawrences of Gloucestershire. It was several feet long, and entitled 'A Curious Pedigree copied from an Ancient Manuscript.' On the publication of these details a witty letter appeared in the *Gentleman's Magazine* from the pen of Sir James Lawrence, author of 'An Essay on the Nobility of the British Gentry.' Sir James unsparingly ridiculed the 'pedigree,' and plainly declared it to have been the fabrication of Isaac Lawrence of Chelsea, who had married Grissell, a daughter of Sir John Lawrence, the first of the name. Faulkner, in reply, asserted the genuineness of the document, but neither offered evidence in its favour, nor refuted the criticisms of Sir James; this leaves us no option but to reject it, and rank it with the many similar forgeries which have misled antiquarians and genealogists.

From the Chelsea Burial Register we learn that 'Thomas Larrance de civitate Londini,' goldsmith, died on Sunday, October 28, 1593, and was buried the day following—'in a chappell appropriat to his familie at Chelsey in Com. Middlesex' (Pedigree of Lawrence of Chelsea and Iver, in the Visitation of Bucks, 1634). This Thomas, according to the Lilly MS., Harl. 1096, was the son of Thomas Lawrence 'of Chelmarsh, juxta Bridgenorth, co. Salop,' and grandson of another Thomas, of the same place. His 'house at Chelsey, with all grounds, orchards, gardens, etc.,' he bequeathed to his wife (Martha, daughter of Anthony Cage, of London, salter), over to his son Thomas in tail, over to his son John in tail. The eldest son, Thomas, died (aged 20) in the same year as his father, and probably before him.

The second son, John, was knighted by James I., at Royston, on January 16, 1609-10 (Metcalfe, ' Book of Knights,' 1885, p. 161), and became a baronet in 1628. He died ten years later. It was his son and heir—another John—who restored the inscription on More's monument, but Faulkner was wrong in identifying him with the Lord Mayor of London who made such noble exertions during the great plague, for the latter bore different arms, and was of Flemish extraction.

One Rigep Dandulo, a Turk, who had made the acquaintance of Sir John's son at Smyrna, was a frequent visitor to the Lawrence House in 1657, where his conversion to the Christian faith was brought about. This affair seems to have caused some excitement at the time, and an account of it was written by Dr. Warmstry. This book, published in 1658, is dedicated ' To the Right Honourable the Countess of Dorset, the Honourable Lord Gorge, and the Worshipful Philip Warwick, Esq., Witnesses at the Baptism of Signior Dandulo the Convert.' Dr. Warmstry was an inhabitant of Chelsea, as he himself tells us :

> ' A while after he [the Turk] came again to the Lady Lawrence, of Chelsey, at whose house I happily found him when I came thither one evening to do those observances which I owe unto that worthy Lady (by whose favour I enjoy an habitation as her Tenant in the Towne of Chelsey).'

The worthy lady in question was May, the second daughter of Sir Thomas Hempson, of Taplow; and was buried at Chelsea in 1664; the date of her husband's death is not known, but he was alive in 1676. His son Thomas was the last to hold the title, and died in 1714, without heirs, his two children, Anne and Thomas (or John) having died previously. It is stated in Burke's ' Extinct Baronetcies ' (p. 300) that he emigrated to Maryland about 1700, after having spent all his estate. He has been identified with Sir Thomas Lawrence, who was Secretary of Maryland in 1696; but this secretary is reported to have died in 1712, while Sir Thomas of Chelsea was buried in the old church on April 25, 1714.

Lady Lawrence appears to have then let her Chelsea house to Ann, Duchess of Monmouth, who came to reside in it in the same year; and we find no later record of the Lawrence family in Chelsea, except that on November 2, 1723, Ann, Lady Lawrence, was buried in the old church.

The Lawrence House now became ' Monmouth House,' or, as it was sometimes called, ' The Great House.' Dr. Johnson tells us that the witty John

12

Gay was for some time secretary to the Duchess. His familiarity with Chelsea (he mentions the place several times in his poems) makes it probable that he came with the Duchess to Monmouth House; but if so, his Chelsea life could not have lasted more than a few weeks, as we find him writing to Swift on June 8, 1714: 'I am quite off from the Duchess of Monmouth's.' Dr. Arbuthnot, too, in a letter of about the same date, mentions that Gay had lost the favour of the Duchess.

In 1716 Princess Caroline of Anspach (afterwards Queen of England) visited the Duchess at Chelsea, and the parish registers record that six shillings were paid to the ringers on that occasion. The Duchess stood high in the Princess's favour. Lady Cowper (Lady of the Bedchamber), who retails some of her gossip in her Diary, has the following note upon her, under date 1716:

'The Duches of Monmouth used often to be there [Hampton Court]; the princess loved her mightily, and certainly no woman of her years ever deserved it so well. She had all the life and fire of youth, and it was marvellous to see that the many afflictions she had suffered had not touched her wit and good nature, but at upwards of threescore she had both in their full perfection.'

The afflictions referred to were doubtless the Duke's neglect of her and his tragic end, after his rebellion and defeat at Sedgmoor. His death, however, could have touched her but lightly, as she married Lord Cornwallis shortly afterwards.

The Duchess died in 1732, and the next known tenant is Dr. Tobias Smollett, who came to Chelsea in 1749, for the benefit, as is said, of his daughter and only child. She was consumptive, and died in 1763. In this house Smollett wrote 'Sir Launcelot Greaves,' 'Ferdinand, Count Fathom,' the completion of 'Hume's History of England,' the translation of 'Don Quixote,' and much else. A famous scene in 'Humphrey Clinker' is believed to set forth a phase of his life at Chelsea, and one of the figures in 'Roderick Random,' Strap the Barber, portrays the character of William Lewis, a bookbinder, who was Smollett's companion during his journey from Scotland to London. By the advice of the novelist, Lewis took a house in Lombard Street (now part of Cheyne Walk), where he settled and, in 1785, died. Faulkner knew his widow well, and vouches for the accuracy of this statement.

Smollett lived a very quiet life at Chelsea, taking little or no part in the busy whirl of society, but amongst his friends and visitors were Johnson, Garrick, Laurence Sterne, John Wilkes (of the *North Briton*), and John Hunter, the famous anatomist, who lived not far off, at Earl's Court. Smollett had the faculty of overspending his income, and his life at Monmouth House was by no means a happy one. Among the Morrison MSS. is a letter from him to Dr. Macaulay, dated from Chelsea, November 16, 1754, in which he expresses his deep mortification at not being able to pay a sum of money he owed Macaulay. 'Never,' he says, 'was I so much harassed by duns as now.' In a letter to his friend, Dr. John Moore, of Glasgow, dated from Chelsea, December 11, 1755, he pictures his retired life :

'Far from being used to the great as you imagine, I have neither interest nor acquaintance with any person whose countenance or favour could be of advantage to myself or my friends. I live in the shade of obscurity, neglecting and neglected, and spending my vacant hours among a set of honest phlegmatic Englishmen, whom I cultivate for their integrity of heart and simplicity of manners. I have not spoken to a nobleman for some years, and those I once had the honour of knowing were such as had very little interest of their own, or very little consideration for me.'

PORTRAIT OF SMOLLETT.

In another letter, Chelsea, May 12, 1757, he particularly mentions one of those 'honest phlegmatic Englishmen':

'The bearer, Captain Robert Mann, is my neighbour in Chelsea, and I recommend him to your friendship and acquaintance as a brave, experienced officer, and an honest tar in whom there is no guile. . . . My friend Bob has been round the world with Anson, and proved in fourteen or fifteen sea engagements, during which he behaved with remarkable gallantry ; but his good nature is equal to his courage, and, indeed, he is the most inoffensive man alive. If you want to know how I spend my time in this retreat, he can satisfy you in that particular, for he has been my club companion these seven long years.'

12—2

The family of the Manns was well known and respected in Chelsea for several generations.

He alludes to his Chelsea friends again, in a letter to Mr. Alexander Reid, a surgeon, of Chelsea, dated from Boulogne, August 3, 1763 :

> 'Your obliging letter was doubly acceptable, both from the entertainment I received from it, and as it convinced me that I am still remembered by old friends in Chelsea. Indeed, I cannot help respecting Chelsea as a second native place, notwithstanding the irreparable misfortunes which happened to me while I resided in it : I mean the loss of my health, and that which was dearer to me than health itself, my darling child, whom I cannot yet remember with any degree of composure.'

Smollett returned to England in 1765, 'no more than the mere skeleton of what he once was,' and, again retiring into exile, died at Leghorn in 1771, where a kinsman erected a tall column to his memory. A short time before his death he had written a jesting letter to Hunter offering his 'poor carcase in a box,' to be placed among his 'rarities.'

In 1815, Monmouth House, or part of it, was occupied as a boarding-school by Mrs. Pilsbury ; it afterwards fell into Chancery, and eventually, being in a very ruinous condition, was ordered to be removed. About one third of it had already been removed by its last tenant, one Anderson, when the site was finally cleared in 1835.

Monmouth House was drawn and etched in 1835 by R. Schnebbelie, a careful topographical draughtsman, whose pencil has preserved for us the outward appearance of many of the features of Old London and its suburbs. The house was evidently not very old, but built in the late Elizabethan style, and therefore probably erected by Thomas Lawrence some time previous to 1593. Nothing appears to remain of it but the porch, already mentioned, of the common lodging-house, which stands close to the site of the mansion.

THE PORCELAIN WORKS.

On the site of 'The Prince of Wales'—a little tavern at the corner of Justice Walk—and the adjacent houses, stood the porcelain factory which has done more for the fame of Chelsea than anything else connected with it. None of these buildings now remain ; they were demolished when the manufacture was discontinued, and, unfortunately, no view of them can be found.

Mr. Timbs, in an article in the *Leisure Hour* (October 1, 1867), says :

> 'We remember to have seen one of a set of three Chelsea vases, painted with a view of the manufactory ;'

but I do not know of the existence of such a vase myself, though I have carefully noted several hundred specimens during the last few years. There is in

GROUP OF CHELSEA CHINA.

an interleaved copy of Faulkner, at the Chelsea Public Library, an autograph letter of the author, containing a rough sketch of the south part of the premises, taken from a drawing then in Faulkner's possession.

The furnaces, however, are still intact, and can be seen in the gloomy, rat-infested cellars of 'The Prince of Wales.' J. T. Smith, in his 'Nollekens and his Times,' makes Panton Betew, a dealer in works of art, say that the Chelsea factory stood 'upon the site of Lord Dartrey's House, just beyond the bridge '—a curious mistake, for Betew was a resident in Chelsea. This mistake was afterwards copied into Cunningham's 'Lives of British Artists,' and also without comment into Llewellyn Jewitt's otherwise careful and accurate articles on Chelsea Porcelain.

Notwithstanding the labours of Marryat, Jewitt, and Chaffers, the origin of these works is still obscure, and there is much conflict of opinion upon it. In Forster's notes to the Stowe Catalogue it is stated that ' Martin Lister mentions a manufacture at Chelsea as early as 1698, comparing its productions with those of St. Cloud, near Paris.' Whether this had any connection with that afterwards so famous is not clear; the probability is that Dwight's Factory at Fulham was intended by the writer. Miss Meteyard, the biographer of the Wedgwoods, however, says that 'some Venetians' established a porcelain manufactory at Chelsea at the end of the seventeenth century, and that a few years afterwards the Brothers Elers, who had, at first, settled at Burslem, came to Chelsea 'after encountering opposition and passing through vicissitudes of fortune.' This writer has no doubt that the Elers ' contributed towards preparing the way to the eminence which the Chelsea porcelain attained half a century afterwards.'

I have not been able to find Miss Meteyard's authority for connecting the Chelsea Elers with the porcelain manufacture. Peter Elers, of an ancient German barony, migrated to this country on the accession of George I. His only son, Peter, settled at Chelsea, where he acquired considerable property, but lost heavily over the South Sea and other schemes. George and Carew Elers, son and grandson of the second Peter, were both buried at Chelsea, the former in 1784, and the latter in 1821, but the family has no longer any connection with the place.

Mr. Chaffers thinks the conjecture that the first Chelsea workmen were Venetians to be highly probable. In gilding and painting, Chelsea ware is similar to the Venetian, and both are marked with an anchor. He further says that some specimens of the Cozzi fabrique (at Venice) are so similar to the Chelsea ware, both in paste and decoration, that they can scarcely be distinguished.

On the other hand, we have the statement that the factory was established by Francis, first Earl and Marquis of Hertford, who, it may be remembered, was born at Chelsea, in Lindsey House. He travelled on the Continent from 1736 to 1739, and is said to have brought over some workmen from Dresden, with a quantity of Saxony clay, and to have started them at work in what was afterwards Cheyne Walk, Chelsea. This is given in Marryat's 'History of Pottery and Porcelain,' on the authority of Mr. O. Morgan, who had unfortunately forgotten the source of his information, and it is at present unconfirmed.

Mr. Chaffers does not think that the Chelsea factory was established before 1745, and quotes the following from Shaw's 'History of the Staffordshire Potteries':

'Carlos Simpson was born at Chelsea, to which place his father, Aaron Simpson, went in 1747, along with Thomas Lawton, slip-maker, Samuel Parr, turner, Richard Weir, fireman, and John Astbury, painter, all of Hot Lane ; Carlos Wedgwood, of the Stocks, a good thrower, Thomas Ward and several others of Burslem, to work at the Chelsea china factory. They soon ascertained that they were the principal workmen, on whose exertions all the excellence of the porcelain must depend ; they then resolved to commence business on their own account at Chelsea, and were in some degree successful ; but at length, owing to disagreement among themselves, they abandoned it and returned to Burslem.'

This, however, apparently refers to some other factory than the Porcelain Works, as Burslem had no workmen capable of making porcelain.

Mr. Chaffers quotes yet another account of the early years of the Chelsea factory—that of a workman named Mason:

'I think the Chelsea china manufactory began about 1748, or 1749. I went to work about 1751. It was carried on by the Duke of Cumberland [died 1765] and Sir Everard Fawkener [died 1758], and the sole management was entrusted to a foreigner of the name of Sprimont—report says at a salary of a guinea a' day, with a certain allowance for apprentices and other emoluments. [A beautiful little bust of the Duke of Cumberland in white glazed porcelain was modelled at Chelsea. Examples are to be seen at the British and Geological Museums.] I think Sir Everard died about 1755, much reduced in circumstances, when Mr. Sprimont became sole proprietor, and, having amassed a fortune, he travelled about England, and the manufactory was shut up about two years, for he would neither let nor carry it on himself.'

In an advertisement of the year 1757, this absence is attributed to illness:

'The public is hereby acquainted that the Chelsea porcelain manufacture has been very much retarded by the sickness of Mr. Sprimont ; nevertheless, several curious things have been finished, and are now exposed to sale at the warehouses in Piccadilly.'

It would appear that English porcelain had obtained considerable celebrity before 1745, for about that time a certain French company, desiring to obtain exclusive privileges for a manufactory at Vincennes, urged that the works recently established in England would be the means of taking considerable sums of money from France, as their productions appeared more beautiful than those of Saxony, from the nature of the composition. Such a description could only apply to Bow and Chelsea ware.

From an advertisement in the *Public Advertiser* for December 17, 1754, we learn that among the objects then being produced at Chelsea were various 'porcelain toys,' such as 'snuff-boxes, smelling-bottles and trinkets for watches (mounted in gold and unmounted), in various beautiful shapes, of an elegant design, and curiously painted in enamel, a large parcell of knife-hafts, etc.'

Hanway, writing in 1750-51, notices with great satisfaction that 'the manufactures of Bow, Chelsea and Stepney have made such considerable progress.' Chelsea china is also mentioned in terms of approval in the *London Magazine*, 1753, Rouquet's 'Present State of the Arts,' 1755, and Campbell's 'London Tradesman,' 1757. The proprietor of the Chelsea works does not appear to have been so thoroughly satisfied. In the Lansdowne MSS., No. 289, f. 21, is a paper entitled 'The Cause of the Undertaker of the Chelsea Manufacture of Porcelain Ware.' This 'undertaker' has been supposed to be Sprimont's successor, but from internal evidence it is apparent that the manuscript was written shortly after 1752. It is therefore the work of Sprimont himself, and sets forth the difficulties experienced by stress of foreign competition. It may be noticed that throughout the writer takes to himself the whole credit of the Chelsea establishments :

> 'Several attempts have likewise been made here ; few have made any progress, and the chief endeavours at Bow have been towards making a more ordinary kind of ware for common use. This undertaker [referring to himself], a silversmith by profession, from a casual acquaintance with a chymist who had some knowledge that way, was tempted to make a trial, which, upon the progress he made, he was encouraged to pursue with great labour and expense ; and as the town and some of the best judges expressed their approbation of the essays he produced of his skill, he found means to engage some assistance. The manufacture was then put upon a more extensive footing, and he had the encouragement of the public to a very great degree, so that the last winter he sold to the value of more than £3,500, which is a great deal, considering the thing is new, and is of so great extent, that it has been beyond the reach of his industry to produce such complete assortments as were required in a variety of ways. This has been a great spur to his industry, so that, notwithstanding some discouragements, the ground-plot of the manufacture has gone on still increasing.
> 'The discouragements, besides the immense difficulties in every step towards the improvement of the art, have been from the introduction of considerable quantities of Dresden porcelain. . . .
> 'The manufacture in England has been carried on so far by great labour and at a large expense : it is in many points to the full as good as the Dresden, and the late Duke of Orleans [died 1752] told Col. Yorke that the metal or earth had been tried in his furnace, and was found to be the best made in Europe. It is now daily improving, and already employs at least one hundred hands, and there is a nursery of one hundred lads taken from the parishes and charity schools, and bred to designing and painting—arts very much wanted here, and which are the greatest use in our silk and painted linen manufactures.'

The writer then speaks of the evasion of duty on large quantities of imported

Dresden, and asks that the law should be strictly enforced. He goes on to say :

'A few samples of seizures would put a stop to this, and which cannot be difficult, as all Dresden china has a sure mark to distinguish it by ; but if this commerce is permitted to go on, the match between a crowned head and private people must be very unequal, and the possessors of the foreign manufacture will at any time, by the sacrifice of a few thousand pounds, have it in their power to ruin any undertaking of this kind here. This must be the case at present with the Chelsea manufacture, unless the Administration will be pleased to interpose and enjoin, in the proper place, a strict attention to the execution of the laws.'

This appeal does not appear to have had any result; probably the Administration considered that a factory that was doing a business of £3,500 a year, and ' still increasing,' did not stand in need of any assistance.

An advertisement of a sale of Chelsea porcelain in 1759 mentions ' compleat services of plates and dishes, tureens, sauceboats, etc.,' ' elegant epargnes for desarts,' figures, ' branches with the best flowers,' a chandelier, etc.

Sprimont offered the factory for sale in 1764, as announced in the following advertisement :

'To be sold by auction, by Mr. Burnsall, on the premises, some time in March next [1764], at the Chelsea Porcelain Manufactory. Everything in general belonging to it, and all the remaining unfinished pieces, glazed and unglazed ; some imperfect enamelled ditto of the useful and ornamental, all the materials, the valuable and extensive variety of fine models in wax, in brass and in lead ; all the plaster moulds, and others, the mills, kilns and iron presses ; together with all the fixtures of the different warehouses ; likewise all the outbuildings, etc., etc. And as Mr. Sprimont, the sole possessor of this rare porcelain secret, is advised to go to the German Spaw, all his genuine household furniture, etc., will be sold at the same time.'

It was this announcement, doubtless, which led M. Grosley to say (in his ' Tour to London,' 1765) that the Chelsea factory had just fallen. It is not clear that Sprimont succeeded in selling the factory, but the presumption is that he at least retired from the active management, and was succeeded by a Mr. James Cox. That he did not immediately give up his house at Chelsea appears from the following receipt, discovered by Mr. Llewellyn Jewitt :

'Sept. 5th, 1770.—Rec^d of Mr. Sproemont, by the hands of Mr. Morgan, Twelve Pounds for Half a Year's Rent, due for a House at Chalsa at Lady Day, 1770. I say Rec^d by Me, Thos. Bush, Executor to the late Mr. Chas. Ross, 12l.'

In March of the following year, Mr. Christie, of Pall Mall, advertised the sale of the pictures of Mr. Nicholas Sprimont, ' the late proprietor of the Chelsea porcelain manufactory, who is retired into the country, brought from his late houses in Richmond and Chelsea.'

The tone of this announcement seems to indicate that Sprimont had retained an interest in the factory until it was again offered for sale in 1769, when the following advertisement appeared in the newspapers :

'To all proprietors of porcelane manufacture and others : there is to be sold at the Chelsea manufactory, by order of the proprietor (having recently left off making the same), everything in general belonging to it, etc. . . . For further particulars enquire of Mr. Thomas at the said manufactory.'

This advertisement attracted the attention of Josiah Wedgwood, who wrote to his partner, Thomas Beilby :

> 'The Chelsea moulds, models, etc., are to be sold, but I'll enclose you the advertisement—there's an immense amount of fine things.'

He also wrote to his clerk, Mr. William Cox :

> 'Pray enquire of Mr. Thomas whether they are determined to sell less than the whole of the models, etc., together ; if so, I do not think it would suit me to purchase. I should be glad if you could send me any further particulars of the things at Chelsea.'

Wedgwood did not become the purchaser. From the following receipt obtained by Mr. Jewitt, we learn that the Chelsea works were taken over by Duesbury, of Derby :

> 'Recd. London, 5th Feby, 1770, of Mr. Wm. Duesbury, Four Hundred Pounds, in part of the purchase of the Chelsea Porcelaine Manufactory, and its Apurtenances and lease thereof, which I promise to assign over to him on or before the 8th instant, James Cox.'

It is known, however, that Duesbury had been working the factory since August in the preceding year. Francis Thomas, mentioned in the advertisement, was manager under both Sprimont and Cox ; he died on January 6, 1770, and there is a slab to his memory in the pavement of the old church. He was succeeded by Richard Barton.

Among the workmen employed at Chelsea during Duesbury's time were : Mr. Boreman, or Bowman, the chief painter of landscapes, at 5s. 3d. per day ; Wollams, 4s. 6d. a day ; Snowden and Jinks, 3s. 6d. a day ; and O'Niell. The last-named, who painted birds, insects, flowers, landscapes and miniatures, gives his address as 'Lawrence Street, near the Church, Chelsea,' in the Catalogue of the Incorporated Society of Artists, 1772. Barton appears to have been the chief modeller (at 3s. 6d. a day), and Robert Boyer, Roberts, Piggott and Inglefield the firemen.

Various artists of eminence have been named in connection with these works. Panton Betew, according to J. T. Smith, asserted that Sir James Thornhill designed for them, and mentions a set of plates by him at Strawberry Hill, from Mrs. Hogarth's sale. These Walpole describes as 'twelve earthen plates in blue and white delf, painted with the twelve signs of the zodiac, by Sir James Thornhill, in 1711.' Delft ware was not made at the Chelsea factory at any period of its career, as far as is known, and Mr. Chaffers thinks it most probable that these plates were made at Lambeth. The elder Nollekens, according to his son, painted for the Chelsea works ; P. F. Ferg (d. 1740) and Paul Sandley as painters, with Nollekens and Bacon as modellers, have a reputed connection with them.

Mr. Duesbury's stock from Chelsea was offered for sale at Christie's in May, 1779, without reserve, 'the leases of the premises being expir'd.' It is certain, however, that the works were carried on until 1784, when the buildings were pulled down, and all the property of value removed to Derby. This date is obtained from a letter addressed by Robert Boyer (one of the workmen mentioned above) to Mr. Duesbury:

'Lawrence Strt., Chelsea, Feb. 18, 1784.—Sir, I Wright to Inform yow how we are pretty forward in the pulling Down of the buildings at Chelsea. I think a little better than a fortnight they will be all down to the ground and cleared of the premises, wich I shall be glad to my Hart, for I am tired of it.'

From what follows, it is clear that he had been working at Chelsea up to that date. Further on he says:

'I wish yow will lett me no if yow will have the mold of the Large figur of Britannia sent to the Ware hous or Broake.'

This figure was one of the most famous of the Chelsea productions. Several copies are still in existence. Mr. Jewitt mentions one in the Bateman collection.

Thus came to an end the most famous of all the English porcelain works, whose productions still hold the market as the rivals of the finest specimens of Dresden and Sèvres. Its success was followed by the establishment of many other factories in various parts of the country, which it supplied with models and workmen. During its career it had received royal patronage from George II., George III. and the Duke of Cumberland. The first-named, taking example from several German princes, is said to have greatly aided the Chelsea factory, importing models, materials and workmen from Saxony. Walpole, writing to Sir Horace Mann (March 4, 1763), mentions an elaborate service of Chelsea porcelain—'dishes and plates without number, an epergne, candlestick, salt-cellars, sauce-boats, tea and coffee equipages'—sent by the King (George III.) and Queen of England to the Duke of Mecklenburg, which cost £1,200. Walpole was not pleased with the taste displayed in this set, for he goes on to say, 'I cannot boast of our taste; the forms were neither new, beautiful, nor various. Yet Sprimont, the manufacturer, is a Frenchman. It seems their taste will not bear transplanting.' It is probably the same set which is referred to in Watkin's 'Life of Queen Charlotte':

'I beheld with admiration a complete service of Chelsea china porcelain, rich and beautiful in fancy beyond expression. I really never saw any Dresden porcelain near so fine.'

An interesting episode in the history of the works is the attempt of Dr. Johnson, 'the great Cham of Literature,' to improve the manufacture. The portly person of the doctor, attended by a quaint old-fashioned housekeeper bearing a basket of provisions, must have been a familiar sight in Cheyne

Walk. The proprietors allowed the worthy doctor to have access to every part of the factory except the mixing-room. So earnest was he, that on one occasion he delivered a lecture to the workmen; but his secret, whatever it was, he kept to himself. All his experiments were failures, and resulted in nothing but injury to his eyesight, which, much to his annoyance, Reynolds has perpetuated in one of his best portraits. As a memento of his efforts, the proprietors presented him with a complete service of their ware. This subsequently became the property of Mrs. Piozzi, whose former husband, Thrale the brewer, was one of Johnson's best friends. Her collection was sold in 1816, when Johnson's service was bought by Lord Holland, and is still preserved among the many treasures of that stately English home, Holland House.

The fine artistic qualities of Chelsea porcelain will always ensure it a high place in the estimation of collectors, but it does not now command the extravagant prices that it did some years ago. Thus, two splendid pairs of oviform vases, with covers, painted with scenes representing the seasons, after Boucher, were bought in at the Earl of Dudley's sale (1886) for 2,000 guineas the pair. The four vases had cost the Earl nearly £10,000. One of them, painted with the figure of a bagpiper, had been presented by Dr. J. Garnier to the Foundling Hospital, and had remained there until 1868, when it was purchased by the Earl of Dudley. At the same sale, a tea-service, previously in the Earl of Lonsdale's collection, was sold for 850 guineas.

Among the first efforts of the factory were imitations of Nankin blue and white; they are painted with great delicacy, and closely in imitation of the Chinese porcelain. Specimens of 'early Chelsea blue and white' are mentioned in Walpole's Strawberry Hill Catalogue. They bear no mark, and experts recognise them only by their general characteristics. In the British Museum are two quaint milk-jugs, with goats and a bee in relief. One of these is marked 'Chelsea, 1745,' with a triangle. These jugs, therefore, must be regarded as two of the earliest products of Sprimont's factory, and the interesting signature has helped Mr. Franks and Mr. Chaffers to conclude what they had long suspected, that the triangular mark usually assigned to Bow must be given to Chelsea.

The distinguishing mark of Chelsea china is of course the well-known anchor. The best specimens bear it in burnished gold, sometimes in an oval; the inferior qualities have it painted on the glaze, in red, brown, or purple, occasionally with a cross added. It is not safe, however, for collectors to rely entirely upon this mark, for the anchor has been used at Savona, Sceaux-Penthièvre, Gustafsberg, Popplesdorf, Venice, Longport, Worcester, Middlesborough, and Bow, as well as in various examples which cannot be identified with a particular pottery. Collectors, therefore, should be well acquainted with the paste and the character of the design and execution.

There are now ample opportunities in London for the study of this beautiful ware. At the South Kensington Museum some lovely vases and other pieces are included in the munificent bequest of Mr. John Jones. There are many interesting specimens of all classes in the valuable gift of Mr. and Mrs.

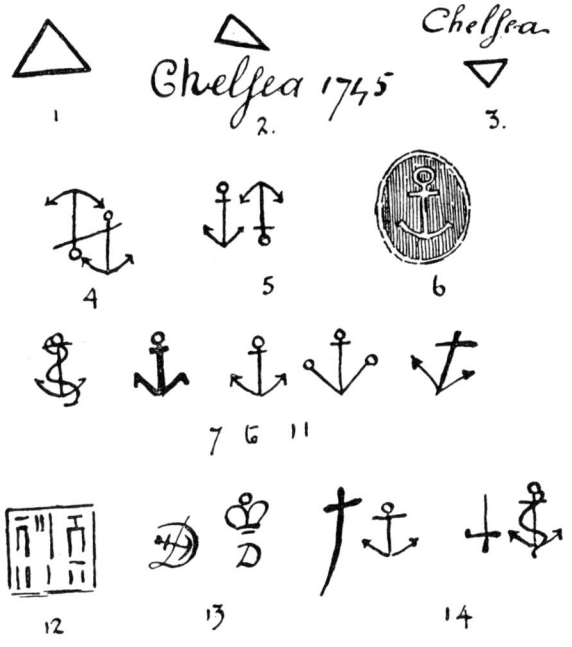

MARKS ON CHELSEA CHINA.

1-3. Early marks on goats-head milk-jugs. 4, 5. Marks on early pieces of best quality. 6. Mark in relief on a copy of Palissy's 'La Nourrice.' 7-11. Varieties of the common signature. 12. Imitation of Chinese mark on cup in British Museum. 13. Marks on Chelsea-Derby. 14. Marks on pieces variously attributed to Bow and Chelsea.

Schrieber, besides others collected by the Museum authorities. There is another large collection at the British Museum (mainly the gift of Mr. A. W. Franks), which is so varied as to form almost a history of the undertaking; and finally, several interesting examples may be seen at the Geological Museum, in Jermyn Street.

In 1842 the site of the factory was let on a building lease, and in digging for the foundations of the new houses, a great quantity of the waste of the factory was found, and among it many specimens of the ware in various stages of finish. Faulkner preserved a number of these, and wrote an account of the discovery for the *Illustrated Polytechnic Review*, 1843. (See also some MS. letters in Mr. Mayer's copy of the ' History of Chelsea.')

CHURCH STREET.

It is but a few yards from Lawrence Street into Church Street; the way lies through a narrow alley—Justice Walk. This squalid passage was once a pleasant thoroughfare, planted with an avenue of lime-trees. Its name, said to have been taken from the adjacent residence of a magistrate, is not a new one, as we find H. Hemsley, an artist, gives his address as ' Justice Walk, Chelsea,' in 1813. The large building in the middle of the Walk is a Wesleyan Chapel, built in 1841.

Church Street was formerly called Church Lane, and in width is little more than a lane now, narrow and crooked, with traces of its olden character yet remaining at the waterside end.

Sir Charles Dilke has called this thoroughfare ' one of the most famous streets in the world,' and having regard to its many celebrated inhabitants, it undoubtedly has some claim to honour. In early times it was the only road in Chelsea leading northward from the river, the upper portion (towards the Fulham Road) being known as the ' Road to the Cross Tree,' or ' Queen's Elm.'

At the south end of Church Street was a large house, extending across Lombard Street to the river bank. This, presumably, was Sir Edward Powell's House, already mentioned in connection with the repair of the church. It was the scene of some violent proceedings during the Commonwealth.

The evidence given before the House of Lords in the cause of Levingstone against the Countess of Stirling and others, in June, 1660, affords a curious illustration of the inadequate protection of private individuals, and the secluded character of Chelsea, at that date.

In September, 1651, Lady Mary Powell, wife of Sir Edward, but separated from him for many years, lay dying at her house at Chelsea. On September 3, Lady Powell's niece, a Mrs. Anne Levingstone, came with her husband, Thomas, and several followers, to the house, and forcibly attempted to take possession ; two of Lady Powell's servants armed themselves, one with a halbert and the other with a pitchfork, and finally succeeded in ejecting the intruders, Sir John Danvers and Lord Commissioner Lisle interfering to quell the riot. The invaders left Chelsea the next day, but returned on the fifth, 'accompanied by Sir Edward Powell, Mr. Hinson *alias* Powell, and a band of armed men in coaches, whom they had collected in the interval—butchers, fencers, and others well experienced in arms. They then got possession of the house, turned out all the servants, and had them arrested and imprisoned in feigned actions, refusing bail; the doors and windows of the house were secured with bars, chains and shutters, a window that looked upon a neighbouring garden was barred up, and the owner of the garden forbidden to allow anyone to attempt to communicate with Lady Powell; regular watches were kept, and sentries posted by the armed party in the house as if it had been a garrison, while Lady Powell's relations and friends were not allowed to see her.' Poor Lady Powell died on October 6, without issue. She had been forced to acknowledge a fine of her estate which settled it upon Mr. and Mrs. Levingstone, though the rightful heirs were the grandchildren of Sir Peter Vanlore, Bart. (In the Chelsea Register we find this record, 'The ritte worshipful Lady Wanlore was buried the last day of April, 1636.') The matter came before Parliament in 1657, and a report of the debate is given in Thomas Burton's Parliamentary Diary, under date May 2, 1657. Most of those implicated in this disgraceful affair were afterwards punished for riot and perjury, but it was not until eleven years after, and then only by a special Act of Parliament, that the true heirs were enabled to recover their property.

The house apparently belonged to Sir William Powell, of Fulham, in later years, and is mentioned in the verdict of the Court Leet, 1679:

> 'We present Sir William Powell, of Fulham, knt., for an encroachment in Church Lane, for erecting three stacks of chimneys, each stack jetting about 10 inches [and he is amerced] . . . *ol. 2s. od.*'

Dr. King, it will be remembered, says that in his time the house at the arch was built into several tenements, the reason, perhaps, for the erection of these three stacks of chimneys.

Here it has been supposed, lived Dr. Francis Atterbury, the famous Jacobite bishop, whose plottings and unguarded avowals gained him an exile, in which he died. He was certainly living in Chelsea as early as 1685, when he was fined £6 for not keeping his portion of the river wall in repair. This fact seems to indicate that the house was at the extreme south end of the lane. The Rev. Mr. Norwood, a former curate of St. Luke's, Chelsea, however, suggests that Atterbury had leased the rectory from Dr. King, who, it is known, did not live there. I do not find that King mentions this circumstance, and Dr. King did not come to Chelsea until 1692. The point, therefore, must remain undecided.

Atterbury had been educated at Westminster School under Dr. Busby, of whom Sir Roger de Coverley had so high an opinion. Possibly it was during his pupilage there that he became acquainted with Chelsea. In Folkestone Williams' Memoir we read of his love of rambling about the neighbourhood with some of his schoolfellows, such as Rowe, the future dramatist, Prior, the future poet, and the sons of John Dryden. Another fellow-pupil was Jonathan Trelawney, who, as Bishop of Winchester, afterwards came to live near him at Chelsea. To Trelawney he owed many favours; by him he was collated to the Archdeaconry of Totnes, and afterwards to a prebend in the cathedral. Atter-

PORTRAIT OF ATTERBURY.

bury acknowledges these favours in the following letter, dated from Chelsea, June 26, 1711 :

> 'I return my humble thanks to your lordship for the venison, but more for your Lord-ship's kind intention of seeing me at my house. I beg your lordship to believe that I am, and ever will be while I live, the same faithful and grateful servant to your lordship that I was at the time when you conferred the greatest favours upon me. Those early obligations, my Lord, can never be forgotten by me, and, if Providence shall dispose of me, so as to put it anyways in my power to return them to your Lordship, or your family, I shall look upon that as one of the most pleasing circumstances of my preferment.'

He was also well acquainted with the Earl Shaftesbury, author of 'The Characteristics,' who came to Little Chelsea in 1698, and with Mary Astell, the educationalist, who lived in Paradise Row.

He corresponded with ' James III.'—the old Pretender—as ' Robert Young,' and many of his letters and reports to the leading Jacobites are printed in Nichol's ' Epistolary Correspondence,' Williams' ' Memoir,' and Dalrymple's ' Tracts.' The last note I have found connecting him with Chelsea is a letter to Swift, dated thence April 21, 1713, congratulating him on his preferment.

For a few weeks in 1711 Atterbury had for a neighbour the caustic Dean, who came to Chelsea for the benefit of the air. He was not unacquainted with the place, for he had visited it several times in the previous year, when he came to dine with Addison in his ' retirement.' The lodging he took was ' just over against Dr. Atterbury's house,' and he paid no less than six shillings a week ' for one silly room with confounded coarse sheets and an awkward bed !' He says that he should not like the place any the better for the neighbourhood of Atterbury, but, apparently, was very glad to partake of his hospitality. All this with other minutiæ he records in his ' Journal to Stella.' Unfortunately the particulars he enters are not very important nor interesting. He tells us, how-ever, of the ' sweet scent of the flowery meads ' in Chelsea, though we note with regret that ' the haymaking nymphs are perfect drabs, nothing so clean and pretty as further in the country.' Two of his letters from Chelsea are printed in Scott's edition of his works.

PETYT SCHOOL.

Next to the Church stood Petyt's School, one of the oldest educational buildings in Chelsea. It was built by William Petyt, who lived near. He was ' Keeper of the Records of our Sovereign Lady Queen Anne within her Majesty's Tower of London,' and a law writer of some repute in his day. The piece of ground on which the school is built is, and was, parish property. On it stood an old house, built early in the seventeenth century for a church house. In Lord Cheyne's notes from the parish register, as quoted by Faulkner, we read :

' Mem. Towards the latter end of the Book, a record of the use of the money given by Edward Page to the Poor, being 10*l.* to continue, with the help of which Dr. Richard Warde, Parson, did build the house called the church house, 1603, which now yieldeth to the use of the poor, xxvj*s.* viij*d.* yearly, besides a dwelling for the clerke.'

The house is also mentioned in 1618 and 1647, and in Dr. King's MSS., we have the following :

' The clerk's house and yard, 46 feet long and 17 broad, was a piece of waste adjoining to the church, and thought to be part thereof ; but, by consent of the Lord of the Manor, the Earl of Nottingham, about 60 years before, was built by Mr. Ward, Rector of Chelsey, by 10*l.* given by Bishop Fletcher, the Bishop of London, and the rest he dis-bursed himself for the clerk's habitation and school-house.'

14

In the Register of Burials we have recorded the death of the first master of the school that preceded Petyt's:

1608, March 26 —' Richard Eryth, our poore Schoolmaster.'

PETYT SCHOOL, 1829.

From the Marriage Register we obtain the following:

1656, May 28.—'James Irish, of Chelsey, in the County of Middlesex, Schoolmaster, is this present day sworne and approved Parish Register there, by me Sir John Thorowgood, of Kensington, in the said County, knt., one of the Justices of the Peace of this Countie, according to the tenor of an Act of Parliament of the 24th of August, 1653, intituled An Act touching Marriages and the Registringe thereof, and also touching Births and Burials.'

About 1705 the Vestry authorized William Petyt to rebuild and refurnish the school, and agreed that when it was finished, it should and ' ought to be repaired, maintained, and upheld by and at the costs and charges of the said parish for ever.' Petyt rebuilt the school accordingly, ' out of respect to the Parish and Town of Chelsea, and in Charity to the poor children thereof, at his own costs and charges.' How small the village then was (though it had grown considerably), we may judge from the size of the building (only 28 feet by 26 feet) which was then considered sufficient for this purpose. It contained ' one Vestry-room wherein the affairs of the parish are to be considered and settled,' and also ' one upper room for lodgings for the schoolmaster.'

Petyt's gift to the parish was suitably acknowledged at a Vestry held on March 25, 1707, when it was again declared that the school should be maintained by the parish, but with the important addition, ' and by other Charities and gifts already, or hereafter to be, given for or towards the same.' These gifts, which were by no means inconsiderable, have now entirely disappeared.

On April 15, 1707, the Vestry attempted to obtain a fixed and certain endowment for the school, by passing the following resolution :

'Whereas there is a charity school newly erected, etc., we the ancient Parishioners of the said Parish, at our Parish Vestry or Parish Meeting, do make it our request to the gentlemen and others who have a right of common in Chelsea Common, that they will be pleased that the said common may be enclosed for the Clothing, Educating and Binding them out Apprentices, to some honest trade or calling ; and that Doctor King, our Rector, and one of the Churchwardens of the Parish do apply themselves to the Rt. Hon. Lord Cheyne, and the several proprietors of the right of Common, and agree with them for their several rights for the good and charitable use above mentioned ; and that we will stand by what agreement they shall make.'

Nothing came of this resolution.

In the Additional MSS., at the British Museum, No. 15,609, we have a very interesting paper, a copy of the original, entitled ' Orders made at a Public Vestry or Meeting of the Parishioners and Inhabitants of the Parish of Chelsey within the County of Midd^x, this first day of December, Anno Dni., 1707, touching the Charity School there lately erected to be observed from time to time by the Masters and Scholars and others of or belonging to the said school.' Some of the resolutions are curious. The qualifications of the master are defined as follows :

' Item, one that frequents the Holy Communion.
' Item, one that hath a good government of himself and his passions.
' Item, one of a meek temper and humble behaviour.
' Item, one of a good genius for teaching.
' Item, one who understands the grounds and principles of the Christian religion, and is able to give a good account thereof to the minister of the Parish or Ordinary on Examination.
' Item, one who can write a good hand and who understands the grounds of Arithmetic.
' Item, one who keeps good orders in his family.'

The chief purpose of the school was defined as ' The Education of Poor Children in the knowledge and practice of the Christian religion as professed and taught in the Church of England,' and the master's chief business ' to instruct the children in the principles thereof as they are laid down in the

14—2

Church Catechism.' And though the master was to enforce discipline among the children, not only in school but in the streets and in their homes, yet was he not to whip ' any of the said scholars but in the presence of one or more of the Governors or Trustees for the time being, who shall have power to hear and examine the crime and remit the punishment or to see the correction given as he or they shall judge most proper.'

The children were to go to church twice on Sunday, and as they came out the master was ' to cause them to be ranged or set under the school-room by the vestry and school door, with their caps off, and there to stand until the Congregation be passed by, and to see that they behave themselves decently during the time, and that they be given to understand who are their Benefactors, and instructed that as often as they pass by any of them they pull off their caps and make them a bow.'

These rules are signed by John King, Rector, J. Munden, John Blow, Moses Goodyear, and eleven other governors and trustees.

In 1694 Dr. Chamberlayne settled a rent-charge of £10 per annum on this school. His original idea was to apprentice one lad annually, and to instruct five others. In 1786 a return was obtained of the amount of stock in the public funds standing in the name of the Trustees; it was not complete, but amounted to £455 8s. 4d., made up as follows:

						£	s.	d.
' 1703. Brunswick ...	...	...	...	...	...	20	0	0
' 1766. Charles Larchin	...	...	...	...	...	20	0	0
' 1770. Sloane Elsmere	...	...	...	...	...	115	8	4
' 1771. Henry Huett (or Hewett)	...	...	...	...	50	0	0
' 1772. Stephen Fox	...	...	...	...	...	200	0	0
' 1782. George Beck	...	...	...	...	...	20	0	0
' 1782. William Jousselin	...	...	...	...	...	30	0	0

That these bequests were misapplied long ago is apparent from the following Vestry Minute, March 14, 1811:

' Resolved that it has been always the acknowledged duty of the Rector and Church-wardens of the Parish of St. Luke's, Chelsea, to consider the bequests of a l persons committed to their charge as sacred trusts, not to be perverted even to the most meritorious purposes, but to be carried into execution according to the precise intention of the donors.'

In 1819 one hundred boys and girls were clothed and educated free of expense to their parents. The girls' school was then held in a house in Lordship Place endowed for that purpose by the Rev. Sloane Elsmere.

Faulkner tells us that the funded stock of the Petyt Schools amounted to £1,700 by 1823, but a Vestry Committee, appointed in 1861-2, could only trace the amount recorded in the Gilbert return given above, and was foiled in every attempt to discover what had become of all this money. There can be no doubt, however, that it was spent over the new schools in King Street. When these were built, the original purpose of the Petyt Schools was abandoned. For some years the ground floor or vestry-room was used as a fire engine station, and by 1867 the building was so dilapidated that the Vestry, at the request of the Rev. Mr. Davies, granted £100 for its repair. Mr. Davies obtained a further grant of £300, and the whole building was converted into a school with three rooms. Of late years, however, it has only been used as a Mission Hall and Sunday School, and in 1887 the Surveyor reported that the building was in an unsafe condition, and subsequently it was proposed to rebuild it at a cost of £700. The proposal excited a great deal of contention, and eventually the land was vested in the Charity Commissioners, who, with the consent of the Trustees, have leased it for eighty years to the Rev. R. H. Davies at ten guineas a year. This year (1890) the building was taken down, and has since been rebuilt in *facsimile*. It will henceforward be used as a Church-house and Sunday-school.

Petyt died in 1708, and bequeathed his large collection of MSS. and printed books to the Honourable Society of the Middle Temple, of which he was the Treasurer. A contemporary portrait, which formerly stood in the Vestry-room he built, but has long been neglected, is to be cleaned and hung up in the new building.

Nearly opposite to the school is the White Horse Inn, a modern building. The original, a posting-house, burned down on Monday morning, December 14, 1840, dated from Tudor times, and was a very interesting example of a village inn. Its old, grotesquely-carved panelling and brackets formed of human figures (only one of which was saved from the fire), attracted general attention. The place had a special local interest, for in its large public room the old Parochial Guardian Society met.

A few doors to the north, No. 9, now a draper's shop, lived Dr. King, who had let the rectory, and next to him (now used as a grocer's shop, No. 11) Dr. Edward Chamberlayne. This is ascertained from the 'Land Tax Book' for 1704. Dr. Chamberlayne was a man of very considerable learning, and received the degree of LL.D. from both Universities. His chief work was 'Angliæ Notitiæ,' or 'The Present State of England'; it was first published in 1667, and must have been very popular, for it went through thirty-eight editions. Among the Graham MSS. was a letter from Dr. Chamberlayne to Lord Preston, dated July 11, 1682, in which he refers to this work:

'Both parts of my little treatise of the present state of England (whereof one part is humbly dedicated to your Lordship) being newly finished, I have taken order to have one book neatly bound, and speedily transmitted to your Lordship at Paris, begging your acceptance thereof, wherein are some hundreds of alterations and additions, si..ce the last impression.'

Addison, in one of his Spectators, speaks disparagingly of those 'rural squires whose reading does not rise so high as "The Present State of England."'

Chamberlayne took a long tour through Europe during the Civil War, and was afterwards tutor to the Duke of Grafton, one of the illegitimate sons of Charles II. He also taught English to Queen Anne's consort, Prince George of Denmark.

He was also an active magistrate in the parish for some years : he died at

THE WHITE HORSE, 1829.

his house in Church Street in 1703. His son John Chamberlayne, F.R.S., continued to live in the same house. He was a distinguished linguist and published translations from the French, Spanish, Italian, and Dutch. One of his works was 'The Lord's Prayer in one hundred Languages.' His name, too, is on the later editions of 'Angliæ Notitiæ.'

In Faulkner's time the house was inhabited by a Mr. Eggleton. Frances Elizabeth Eggleton is among the benefactors of the parish ; in 1861 she bequeathed the sum of six pounds to be given annually on Christmas Eve to such twenty poor persons, married and having a family, as shall be recommended by a respectable housekeeper of the parish.

Next door to the Chamberlaynes lived John Martyn, F.R.S., a distinguished botanist of his day, who took an active part in the establishment of the Botanical Society, of which he was the first secretary. In 1723 he married Eulalia, the youngest daughter of Dr. King, by whom he had eight children, all born in the house in Church Street.

Among Martyn's numerous publications are two that concern this parish: 1. 'An Account of an Aurora Australis seen at Chelsea, March 8, 1738-9': the first published account of this phenomenon; 2. 'An account of an Earthquake felt in London, February 8, 1749-50.' The following passage tells us how the earthquake affected Chelsea:

> 'At 40 minutes after noon, all the houses were violently shaken, especially those nearest the river. A maidservant passing from one under office to another, felt the ground, which was six feet below the surface, shake. Of those who were in the street, or on the river, some felt, others not. . . . It seemed to terminate in the west, about two miles beyond Chelsea.'

Near at hand lived John Bowack, writing-master at Westminster School. He was an industrious antiquarian, and projected an extensive history of Middlesex. The first part, in folio, appeared in 1705, with the title, 'The Antiquities of Middlesex; being a collection of the several church monuments in that county; also an Historical account of each church and parish, with the Seats, Villages, and Names of the most eminent inhabitants.' To it all the writers on Chelsea have been indebted for the contemporary account of the parish. It would have been, for its time, a monument of careful collection and research, but only two parts were published, as the author did not meet with sufficient patronage.

Among the inhabitants of Church Street mentioned by Bowack was Admiral Sir John Munden, one of the original trustees of the Petyt School, and an active participator in the affairs of the parish.

The famous and witty Dr. Arbuthnot, whom Swift calls 'the Queen's (Anne's) favourite physician,' and one of a famous group of literary lights, was another resident in Church Street. He was appointed physician to Chelsea Hospital on November 12, 1713. The date of his coming to Chelsea is found in a letter of Erasmus Lewis to Swift, dated August 7, 1714, in which he says: 'Arbuthnot is removed to Chelsea and will settle there.' This intention was soon abandoned, as we find the doctor himself writing to Swift, on October 19 of the same year: 'Shadwell says he will have my place at Chelsea.' This was, of course, Sir John—'hasty Shadwell,' as Rochester styles him—who was also physician to Queen Anne. His father the poet-laureate, the Mac Flecknoe, of Dryden, also lived at Chelsea, and was buried in the church (1692), but his grave is not now known, nor his house, though his widow, a retired actress, was living in Chelsea in 1696.

At the corner of Paultons Street stands the Black Lion, now, like the White Horse, modernized. The old house was very picturesque, and was probably built in the latter part of the seventeenth century. An old pump

THE BLACK LION, 1820.

which stood near, belonging to a house apparently contemporary with the inn, was dated 1691, and had not been removed when ' Old and New London' was first published. The inn itself survived until comparatively recent times, and its appearance has fortunately been preserved in one of Mr. Hedderley's valuable photographs, as well as in several drawings. To compare this quaint old structure with its successor is to see at a glance what we are losing in this vast city of ours by the gradual purposeless destruction of all that is delightful to the eye. The old house had the usual accompaniment of tea-gardens and a bowling-green. The sign is somewhat uncommon, and is traced by Larwood and Hotten to the arms of Queen Philippa of Hainault, wife of Edward III., or to Owen Glendower, who bore 'the black lion of Powyss' on his arms; but it is not to be supposed that the Chelsea tavern has so ancient an origin.

THE RECTORY.

On the opposite side of the road is the Rectory. It stands within an old brick wall, and the front towards Church Street is unpretentious and by no means beautiful, but that towards the east is more picturesque, and the garden of two acres is prettily laid out. The house, which has been much rebuilt, was erected by the Marquis of Winchester, and exchanged in 1566 with Robert Richardson for an older house, which stood on part of the site of Milman Street. Richardson had lived through troubled times; he had been ejected from his living in Mary's reign for being a married priest, but was reinstated in 1558, when Elizabeth sat on the throne.

After John Churchman, Thomas Browne, Richard Warde, and George Hamden, Dr. Samuel Wilkinson was presented (1632), and held the living for thirty-seven years. He was the fourth, and last provost of Chelsea College, and was described by the Parliamentarian commissioners as 'a man of very scandalous report,' by which is meant a Royalist and a High Churchman. The epithet, however, might be taken in a more modern sense, as he was accused of bookstealing on an extensive scale. The library of the College disappeared during his connection with it, and he refused to return a number of valuable books lent to him by the Countess of Nottingham, on the pretence that she had intended them to be handed down to future rectors; none of the books in question were afterwards found in the rectory library. He was collated to the prebend of Neasdon in 1668, and, dying in the following year, was buried at Chelsea, January 7, 1669.

More celebrated was his successor, Dr. Adam Littleton, known in his own day as 'the great dictator of learning.' He was one of the Royal chaplains, and received from Charles II. a grant to succeed the famous Dr. Busby as head-master of Westminster School. Among his many erudite works was a long-celebrated Latin dictionary. He died in 1694, and, like his predecessor, was buried at Chelsea.

Dr. John King is known as 'the antiquarian rector of Chelsea.' His manuscript account of the parish, which has never been printed, and is now

THE RECTORY.

decaying and almost illegible, is preserved in the rectory library, and there are five other manuscripts in the British Museum, including a ' Letter designed for Mr. Hearne respecting Sir Thomas More's house at Chelsey.'

In the first-mentioned MS. he says:

> ' I was inducted into the rectory of Chelsea, having had a presentation from the Rt. Hon. Charles, late Visc. Cheyne. At the same time that I received that presentation, I gave another to the Rev. Mr. Cheyne, of the rectory of Pertenhall in the county of Bedford' (which he had acquired by his marriage with Elizabeth, daughter of Joseph Aris, of Adstone, Northants).

Elsewhere he says:

> ' Upon my coming to Chelsey, I found the parsonage in the following condition : The barns, houses and paling miserably out of repair ; the dilapidations were valued at £150, but nothing was to be recovered, Dr. Littleton dying insolvent, and leaving his widow, who had brought him a large fortune, in mean circumstances, and an object of compassion. So that instead of recovering from her towards the repairs of the houses, barns and fences, I gave Mrs. Littleton freely the current half year, she supplying the cure by some friends and neighbours.'

It was for this reason, perhaps, that Dr. King did not live in the rectory, but took the house in Church Street.

Dr. Sloane Elsmere was presented by his relation Sir Hans Sloane. He founded the ' Girls' Charity School' in Lordship Place, and died at Chelsea in 1776.

The Rev. Reginald Heber, who succeeded Dr. Elsmere, was the father of the celebrated Reginald Heber, Bishop of Calcutta. The latter, however, was not a native of Chelsea, as he was not born until after his father had exchanged his living at Chelsea with the Rev. Thomas Drake for the rectory of Malpas.

The Hon. and Rev. William Bromley Cadogan, M.A., who succeeded the last-named, was intimately connected with the Methodist movement, and much esteemed by the followers of George Whitfield. During his time the pulpit of Chelsea Church was frequently occupied by some of the leaders of this great revival—John Wesley, Cecil, Venn, Romaine, etc. Mr. Cadogan preached a funeral sermon on the last-mentioned. He held the vicarage of St. Giles', Reading, and during the latter part of his career he let the rectory, and left Chelsea in charge of his curate, the Rev. Erasmus Middleton, editor of the *Biographia Evangelica*, and compiler of a dictionary of arts and sciences. The Rev. W. B. Cadogan died in 1797. At Reading there is a monument to his memory, with a bust by Bacon.

Subsequent rectors of Chelsea were the Rev. Charles Sturgess, M.A., the Hon. and Rev. Dr. Wellesley (brother to the first Duke of Wellington), the Rev. Charles Kingsley, M.A., father of two literary sons, and the present holder of the living, the Rev. G. A. Blunt, M.A.

15—2

CHURCH PLACE.

Not far from Danvers House, and nearly on the site of what is now Paultons Terrace, stood another of the old Chelsea houses, variously known as Essex House, Queen Anne's Laundry, and Church Place. Faulkner tells us that the date, 1641, was cut in brick on 'the back front,' and that the structure standing in his time was 'evidently only a portion of the original fabric.' The view

THE CHURCH PLACE, 1829.

he gives of it, which is here reproduced, represents a house jo considerable size, and apparently a complete structure. It is strange that no history of its building or its inhabitants has been preserved.

Faulkner mentions the tradition that the Earl of Essex, the Parliamentarian General, once lived there, but, like many other Chelsea traditions, this cannot be traced to any satisfactory source, and Dr. Martin falls into the curious error of associating with this house Thomas Cromwell, Earl of Essex, the son of the Putney blacksmith, who became Henry VIII.'s vicar-general, and went to the block in 1540, just one hundred years before the house was built.

When Bowack wrote his account of Chelsea (1705), Church Place was in the occupation of ' Mr. Moses Goodyear, a gentleman well known by most of the Ingenious Men in the Kingdom,' who had resided there for some years. The Goodyears appear to have been an old Chelsea family, for among the baptisms in the Chelsea Register we find :

'1596. Avelina Goodyear. 24th October.'

Among the Clarendon Papers is a warrant of Lord Nottingham, dated August 17, 1608, for the apprehension of William Gorringe and William Goodeare, who, we find from a subsequent paper, were keepers of disorderly alehouses in Chelsea.

The burial of another Goodyear is mentioned in the Register :

'1715. Mr. Aaron Goodyear. Jan. 11.'

Nine years previously Ralph Palmer, of Little Chelsea, had written to his nephew, Lord Fermanagh :

' Your old acquaintance, Aaron Goodyear, is in a lamentable condition at Richmond.'

The name of Moses Goodyear occurs frequently in the Parish Papers, and he was one of the original trustees of Petyt's School. Among the MSS. of Sir H. Ingilby, Bart., is a copy of a prayer of the Lord Strafford's at his execution. It is endorsed in the handwriting of Ralph Palmer :

' Given me by Moses Goodyear, Esq., who stood by him at his execution for being in the Popish Plot, in King Charles II.'s reign.'

The Copes of Little Chelsea also seem to have been among his acquaintances, as among the same papers are several witty letters of Anthony Cope, addressed to him from various parts of the Continent.

The record of his burial is found in the Register :

'1728. Moses Goodyear, Esq. March 14th.'

In the same year died ' Elizabeth, daughter of William Goodyear.' Her father, whose name is the last of this family found in the Parish Records, died in 1736.

It is probable that Church Place was then purchased by Sir Hans Sloane, for when Faulkner wrote, in 1829, it was the property of William Sloane Stanley, Esq. He says it was in a very dilapidated condition, and let out in tenements. Here it was that Henry Kingsley placed the Burton family, in his novel of ' The Hilliers and the Burtons,' where he gives many interesting descriptions of Chelsea as it was some forty years ago.

Church Place was taken down in 1840-42, and Paultons Terrace, which stands upon its site, was then built. This terrace bears the date 1843.

UPPER CHURCH STREET.

The northern portion of Church Street has also had a few inhabitants of distinction. Alexander Stephens (1757-1821) a prolific writer on biography, history and belles-lettres, lived at Park Lodge. Hughson says that this house, which is still standing, was designed by a pupil of James Adams, the well-known architect, and gives the following account of it :

> ' It has a field in front and Chelsea Park behind, in the latter of which are a small lawn and kitchen garden, surrounded by a shubbery. Although in the cottage style, the apartments are of considerable dimensions. The windows are of German glass, and the upper apartments of the principal rooms being adorned with stained glass, a very picturesque effect is produced.'

Mr. A. H. Haworth, an industrious entomologist, lived in Upper Church Street for some time previous to 1825, and there accumulated a very fine and well-known collection.

Among the artists who have lived in Church Lane are Anker Smith, A.R.A., an engraver and miniature painter (1792-8) ; W. H. Davis, at No. 8 (1805-1815), and J. F. Sartorius (' Queen's Elm,' 1811), two animal-painters whose works were much patronised by the sporting fraternity ; and Philip Reinagle, R.A. The son of the last-named, Richard Ramsay Reinagle, R.A., also died ' at his house in Chelsea ' in November, 1862.

SIR THOMAS MORE'S HOUSE.

There is ample evidence to prove that there were important houses in Chelsea before the coming of Sir Thomas More in 1520 ; but there can be no doubt that it was his residence that gave Chelsea its fame in Tudor times and attracted the attention of other eminent men. More's life has been written so often, and is so well-known, that it would be waste of space to enter upon it at that length to which one is naturally tempted by the greatness and nobility of the subject.

When More came to Chelsea he had been Under-Sheriff of the City of London for more than ten years ; he had distinguished himself as an orator and champion of Parliamentary liberty, as a pleader at the bar, and as a man of letters, and the historian of his country. He counted the greatest men of this momentous time among his intimate friends, and stood very high in the King's favour, which, however, he well knew how to esteem at its proper value: 'Sonne Roper,' he said, on one occasion, 'I have no cause to be proud thereof. For if my head would win him a castle in France it would not fail to go.'

The house he built stood at a short distance from the river across the site of Beaufort Street. Dr. King took great pains to fix the situation of this

BEAUFORT HOUSE.

house. Two manuscripts of his conclusions are in existence; one is in the British Museum, and the second, apparently an earlier draft, was printed in *Notes and Queries* (Second Series, Vol. ii., p. 324). The argument begins quaintly:

'As there were 7 Cities in Greese which contended for the birthplace of Homer, so there are in the parish 4 houses which lay claim to the place where Sir Thomas More's house stood. To wit:

'1. The Duke of Beaufort's. 2ly. The old house of Mes Butler's, lately Mes Wood-cock's School House. 3. That wch was once Sr Reginald Bray's at the Arch, wch is now built into several Tenements, and 4ly, Sr John Danvers', wch is now pulled down, and upon that part of the Ground a short street is built, called Danvers Street.'

Dr. King decided on Beaufort House for two reasons: Firstly, because More's grandson (Cresacre More) said it was the house which the Earl of Lincoln bought from Sir Robert Cecil, and this was easily proved to be Beaufort House; and secondly, because the More Chapel in the old church went with that house until Sir Arthur Gorges reserved it for himself. Dr. King's conclusions have been generally accepted; but Mr. Walter Rye thinks 'much may be said in favour of the pretensions of Danvers House,' relying mainly on the fact that the Earl of Lincoln's son sold 'the lands called *Moor House*' to Sir John Danvers in 1618. The name, however, can, I think, be more satisfactorily accounted for, and will be dealt with later on in the account of Danvers Ho use. It is curious to note that so industrious a historian as Faulkner fixed the site of More's House at Shewsbury House (the second of those mentioned by King), in his first edition. The Rev. A. L'Estrange tells us that when collecting materials for his 'Village of Palaces,' he was told by some Chelsea residents that the house they then inhabited was that of Sir Thomas More!

No view of More's house and garden is known to exist. We must therefore picture them from the general characteristics of English architecture at that time, and from such scant descriptions as we are able to find. Erasmus tells us: 'It was not mean, nor invidiously grand, but comfortable.' Ellis Heywood calls it 'The beautiful and commodious residence to which, when fatigued with his occupation in the City, he returned for the refreshment and solace of retirement.' English gardening was then in a very elementary stage; the range of cultivated flowers was very limited, and no treatise on the subject had as yet appeared. Judging from Heywood's glowing description, More's garden was a great advance on the ordinary practice of the time:

'The gentleman of whom I have spoken being one day at dinner with Sir Thomas More, afterwards descended about two stones' throws into the garden, walked on a little lawn in the middle, and up a green hillock, where they halted to look round them. It was an enchanting spot, as well from the convenience of the situation—from one side almost all the noble city of London being visible, and from the other the lovely Thames, surrounded with green fields and wooded hills—as for its own beauty, being crowned with an almost perpetual verdure, and covered with lovely flowers and the sprays of fruit trees, so admirably placed and interwoven that, looking at them, they appeared like a veritable piece of living tapestry made by Nature herself, so much more noble than the works of art, as she gives fuller satisfaction than that imitation of beautiful things, which leaves the mind more dissatisfied than content.'

More's family life had previously been sketched by himself in the dedication of Utopia:

'For when I am come home, I must common with my wife, chatte with my children, and talke with my servauntes, all the whiche things I recken and accompte among businesse, forasmoche as they must of necessity be done; and done must they needs be, onelesse a man wyll be a straunger in his owne house. And in any wise, a man muste so fashyon and order hys conditions, and so appoint and dispose himselfe, that he be merie, jocunde, and plesaunte among them, whom eyther Nature hath provided, or chaunce hath made, or he himselfe hathe chosen to be the felowes and companyons of hys life.'

At Chelsea there lived with him, besides his wife and son, three married daughters with their husbands, eleven grandchildren, and a poor relation, Margaret Giggs, whom he had adopted. All lived in peace and harmony. 'There is not a man living so affectionate to his children as he,' Erasmus writes, 'he loveth his old wife as well as if she was a young maid.' All his biographers agree in drawing an unflattering portrait of his 'old wife.' His grandson describes her as ' of good years, of no good favour, nor complexion, nor very rich, her disposition very near and worldly.' Thus there is a special significance in an Epigram composed by More after his second marriage :

> Some men hath good,
> But children hath he none ;
> Some men hath both,
> But he can get none health :
> Some hath all three,
> But up to honour's throne
> Can he not creep by no manner of stealth.
> To some she sendeth children,
> Riches, wealth,
> Honour, worship, and reverence all his life,
> But yet she pincheth him
> With a shrewd wife.
>   Be content
> With such reward as fortune hath you sent.'

While he was careful to unite his family by the ties of affection, he was none the less diligent in maintaining discipline in his household. 'He suffered none of his servants either to be idle or to give themselves to any games ; but some of them he allotted to look to his garden, assigning to every one his sundry plot ; some again he set to sing, some to play on the organ. He suffered none to give themselves to cards or dice. The men abode on one side of the house, the women on the other, seldom conversing together. He used before bedtime to call them together, and say certain prayers with them. He suffered none to be absent from Mass on Sundays, or upon holy days ; and upon great feasts he ordered them to watch the eves until Mattins time. He used to have one to read daily at his table, which being ended, he would ask of some of them how they understood such and such a place, and so then grant a friendly communication, recreating all men that were present with some jest or other.'

He shared the common belief that the practice of music was a great sweetener of the temper, and it is amusing to read that he persuaded his ' old

16

wife' to play the lute and viol. The great reformer, Erasmus, tells us of his daughters and their occupations :

> 'If you should hear them playing skilfully on various instruments of music, or watch them poring over every kind of Latin or Greek author, like little busy bees, here noting something to copy, here culling something to be used as a maxim, here learning by heart some little story to repeat to their friends, you would say that they were muses toying sweetly in the loveliest paths of Aonia, collecting flowerets and sweet marjoram to weave their chaplets.'

To this happy household came many notable visitors. There one might have seen Warham, Archbishop of Canterbury ; Stokesley, Bishop of London ; Fisher, Bishop of Rochester (doomed to die in the same cause as his friend) ; Heywood the poet ; Sir William Sandys (Lord of the Manor, and associated with More at Calais) ; Sir Richard Southwell (who bore witness on his behalf at his trial) ; Sir Thomas Pope (who carried to him the sad tidings of the date fixed for his death) ; the Duke of Norfolk ; John Clement, M.D. (More's physician, who, about 1526, married his patron's adopted daughter, Margaret Giggs) ; and, besides many others, the King himself.

It has been generally assumed that Hans Holbein, the famous painter of Augsburg, was also a visitor, and that he lived at Chelsea for three years preceding an introduction to the King, who at once made him chief Court painter. A new terrace at Sloane Square has been named Holbein Place, in memory of this supposed residence.

The first notice of Holbein's proposed visit to England that I have been able to find occurs in a letter from Sir Thomas More to Erasmus (December 18, 1525), in which he says :

> 'Your painter is a wonderful artist, but I am afraid he will not find England so fertile as he expects, although I will do the best as far as I am concerned, that he may not find it altogether barren.'

From the tone of this letter, we might assume that Holbein was already in England, but there is ample evidence to show that this was not so. On August 29, 1526, Erasmus wrote to Petrus Ægidius, at Antwerp :

> 'He who gives you this letter is the man who painted me. I will not trouble you with his praises, though he is a distinguished artist. . . . Here the arts are torpid ; he seeks England in order to scrape together a few angels.'

It is very probable that, on his arrival in England, Holbein at once introduced himself to Sir Thomas More. Mr. Henry Huth has an important portrait of More, dated MDXXVII., which was esteemed one of the best of Holbein's works when shown at South Kensington in 1866. We may, perhaps, be allowed to suppose that in fulfilment of his promise of assistance, More caused Holbein to paint this portrait as a specimen of his skill, and subsequently introduced him to the several persons whom we shall presently mention. The portrait of More in the National Portrait Gallery is similar in type to that of Mr. Huth.

In May, 1527, the King ordered 'a pastime to do solace to strangers.' A house called Long House, at Greenwich, was furnished 'for the disguising and meskelyng of lords and ladies.' Among the items of expenditure we find money spent by 'Master Hans un the mayn cloothe,' and by 'Master Hans and his Company on the roof [decoration of the ceiling].' Master Nykolas (a Florentine painter) and Master Hans were paid four shillings a day.

In this same year, among the 'Payments of Sr Henry Gwildford, knight, and Sir Thomas Wyat, knight, in building a banquetting house for the king his manor of Greenwich,' we find:

> 'Paid to Master Hans for the painting of the plat of Tirwan, which standeth on the backside of the great arch, in grete [gross], iv *li.* x*s.*'
> 'Black collars [colours?] for Master Hans, iij*s.* iv*d.*'

I have very little doubt that these payments refer to Hans Holbein, and that these were his first engagements in the Royal service. Nor do I hesitate to recognise the 'plat of Tirwan' as 'The Battle of Spurs,' with a landscape in the background inscribed 'Terwaen' (now at Hampton Court, No. 339), traditionally ascribed to Holbein, and a subject in which Guildford would take particular interest, as he had borne the royal standard at Terouenne.

Holbein was certainly known to Guildford in this year, when he painted his portrait (now at Windsor Castle) and that of Lady Guildford (exhibited at Burlington House, 1880). He was also known to Sir Thomas Wyat, and painted the little portrait of him now at the Brussels Museum, which Dr. Martin imagined to represent Sir Thomas More ' " in his habit as he lived " in the later years of his life.'

Another evidence of Holbein's early engagement on royal work is a memorandum (undated, but *circa* 1527) in the accounts of Sir Thomas Cawarden (Losely Papers):

> 'Item, for a paynted boke of Hans Holby's making, vj *li.*'

This gives support to the tradition that the first work of Holbein in England was the illumination of the margins of the 'Moriæ Encomium' of Erasmus.

It is clear that if the quotations given above refer to Holbein he could not have been in Chelsea during a considerable part of 1527, for he was engaged at Greenwich; and in 1528 he was at Basle.

In 1529 Holbein painted the More family, and it is probable that he lodged at Chelsea while preparing his studies, if not during the execution of the picture. More sent the sketch of it (now at Basle) to Erasmus, who acknowledged it in a letter (September 5, 1529):

> 'I should like to see again the dear friends Holbein has exhibited in his picture.'

The finished picture is lost, and now known only by the copy at Nostell Priory (which was once the property of the Ropers at Well Hall), the sketch at Basle, and the studies at Windsor. It is, of course, quite possible that Henry saw this portrait group during one of his visits to More at Chelsea, and there may, therefore, be some foundation for the story that the King saw some works of Holbein at More's house, and exclaimed in astonishment : ' Is there such an artist alive, and can he be had for money ?'—a discovery which was followed by the engagement of Holbein as Court painter.

It will be seen from the above that there is but little evidence in favour of Holbein's supposed residence at Chelsea.

Dean Colet, the founder of St. Paul's School, has been named as a visitor to More at Chelsea, but as he died in 1519 this is improbable. Erasmus, too, was never at Chelsea, though he has left us the most vivid account of More's life and home : his information was obtained from one of More's domestic servants.

But there were other and unwilling visitors to More's ' poore house at Chelchithe.' It was part of the Lord Chancellor's duty to search out heretics, and More performed it with a zeal that ill accords with the broad religious tolerance of his earlier years as expressed in ' Utopia.' Ready for conscience' sake to oppose the King even unto death, he yet hated heresy as a damnable thing, and even in the epitaph which he composed for himself classed heretics with thieves and murderers. Nevertheless, we must weigh the charges preferred against him in Foxe's ' Boke of Martyrs ' with great care ; they were written in a time of extreme bigotry, are opposed to the whole tenor of his life, and were specifically denied by More himself, who says :

> ' There are divers who have said such as were in my house while I was Chancellor, I used to examine with torments, causing them to be bound to a tree, and there piteously beaten. This tale some of these good brethren so caused to be blown about, that a right worshipful friend of mine heard it commonly spoken of. . . . As to heretics, save only their safe keeping, I never caused any such thing to be done to any of them in my life, save two.'

These were a child, one of his own servants, who blasphemed the Holy Sacrament, and received a whipping, and a half-mad fanatic, who disturbed the service in church, and was publicly whipped before the whole town.

> ' Of all that ever came into my hands for heresy, not one of them, so help me God, had any stripe or stroke given them, not so much as a fillip on the forehead.'

The petition of John Field to the Lord Chancellor and Council sets forth that the day after Twelfth day, 21 Henry VIII., Sir Thomas More, being then Lord Chancellor, had the petitioner, with others, brought to his place at

Chelsea, and there kept them for eighteen days, then set them at liberty, taking bonds for their appearance in the Star Chamber eight days after. This is probably a typical case, but the graver charges—the torturing of John Tewkesbury, Master John Baynham, and John Frith—have no earlier authority than the 'Martyrology' of John Foxe.

In Chelsea, More's kindly nature showed itself in his unstinted charity. It is well known that he built or hired a house to be used as a poor-house for the relief of the needy, and that his daughter, Margaret Roper, was appointed to see that his pensioners wanted for nothing. His grandson tells us that 'he seldom used to feast noblemen, but his poor neighbours often, whom he would often visit in their houses, and bestow upon them his large liberality, not groats, but crowns of gold, even more than according to their wants.' Hoddesdon says that when More was a private lawyer he would take no fees from poor folk, widows or pupils. And yet he was not at any time a rich man: his income never exceeded £2,000 a year of our money.

His liberality was equalled by his humility. Almost every Sunday he might have been seen in Chelsea Church, carrying the cross in the procession, singing in the choir, or responding for the clerk. Thus the Duke of Norfolk, coming to Chelsea to dine, found him, and exclaimed afterwards: 'God's Body, my lord Chancellor, what, a parish clerk, a parish clerk! You dishonour the King and his office.' 'Nay,' quoth the gentle Sir Thomas, 'your grace may not think that the King, your master and mine, will be offended with me, for serving God, his Master, or thereby account his office dishonoured.'

Towards the end of his life he became more intensely religious, and, it must be admitted, somewhat fanatical. He built himself an oratory near his house, and spent a portion of every day in devotion there; he wore a hair shirt next his skin, and is said, even, to have flagellated himself daily.

More's steadfastness in searching for and holding by the truth comes out above every other feature in his character. Ellwood's words—applied to George Fox—may well be said of him:

'He was valiant for the truth, bold in asserting it, patient in suffering for it, unswerving in labouring for it, steady in his testimony to it, unmovable as a rock.'

On being summoned to Lambeth to take the Oath of Supremacy, he set out by barge, accompanied by his son-in-law Roper. On the journey he long kept silence, wrestling with a great temptation. At Lambeth was an eager crowd of men jostling one another in their haste to take the oath: but to More death itself was easier, and, at length, he exclaimed: 'I thank the Lord, son Roper, the field is won!' He refused the oath, and four days later was committed to the Tower.   Conscious of his triumph over his weaker nature, he maintained his cheerful temper through all his trials, even to the block.

In the Harleian collection of manuscripts is the unique copy of ' Sir Thomas More, a play,' written probably about 1590, and very little known, as only a limited edition — for the subscribers of the Shakespeare Society— has been printed.   Nothing is known either of its author or of its performance.   A portion, however, was evidently prepared for representation at Court, as the manuscript bears various stage and other directions in the handwriting of E. Tyllney, Master of the Revels.   Many of the incidents are apocryphal, but the author was well acquainted with his subject, and a few extracts cannot fail to be of interest in this place.

The family is represented as filled with alarm while More was absent at Lambeth, and made to discourse of their ominous dreams :

> ' LADY MOORE (*to her Daughters and* MASTER ROPER).
>
> > To-night I had the straungest dreame
> > That ere my sleep was troubled with.
> > > Methought 'twas night,
> > And that the king and queen went on the Thames
> > In bardges to hear musique ; my lord and I
> > Were in a little boat methought,—Lord, Lord,
> > What straunge things live in slumbers !—and, being neere,
> > We grapled to the bardge that bare the king.
> > But after many pleasing voyces spent
> > In that still mooving musique house. methought
> > The violence of the streame did sever vs
> > Quite from the golden fleet, and hurried vs
> > Vnto the bridge, which with vnused horror
> > We entred at full tide : thence some slight shoote
> > Beeing caried by the waves, our boate stood still
> > Iust opposite the Tower, and there it turnde
> > And turnde about, as when a whirlpool sucks
> > The cirkled waters ; methought that we bothe cryed
> > Till that we sunck ; where arm in arm we dyed.'

A little later on Roper calls to his wife :

> > ' Come hether, wife,—
> > I will not fright thy mother, to interprete
> > The nature of a dreame ; but, trust me, sweete,
> > This night I have bin troubled with thy father
> > Beyond all thought.
> > ROPER'S WIFE.   Truely and so have I :
> > Methought I saw him heere in Chelsey Church
> > Standing vppon the roodloft, now defac'de ;
> > And whilste he kneeld and prayde before the ymage,
> > It fell with him into the vpper quier,
> > Where my poor father lay all stainde in blood.
> > ROPER.   Our dreams all meet in one conclusion,
> > Fatall, I feare.

Presently enters 'SIR THOMAS MOORE *merily, seruaunts attending.*'

> DAUGHTER.   See where my father comes, ioyfull and merie.
> MOORE.   As seamen, hauing past a troubled storme
> Daunce on the pleasant shoare ; so I—
>   Oh I could speake
> Now like a poett ! now, afore God, I am passing light !—
> Wife give me kinde welcome : thou wast wont to blame
> My kissing when my beard was in the stubble ;
> But I haue been trimde of late ; I haue had
> A smoothe court shauving, in good faith I haue.

He bids farewell to Chelsea in these words :

> ' Moore now must marche. Chelsey, adiewe, adiewe,
> (Straunge farewell !) thou shalt nere see More true
> For I shall nere see the more.'

After a year's confinement in a miserable closet he was condemned to be half hanged, decapitated, disembowelled and quartered—a barbarous sentence, subsequently commuted to decapitation only.   His last words to his judges are very characteristic of the greatness of his nature : ' I verily trust and right heartily pray that though your lordships have on earth been my judges to condemnation, yet we may hereafter meet in heaven merrily together to our everlasting salvation, and God preserve you all, especially my sovereign lord the King, and grant him faithful counsellors.'

Some relics of this valiant soul, besides those mentioned in the account of the cenotaph at Chelsea, are still preserved with loving care by those into whose hands they have fallen.   His hair shirt is at the Augustinian convent at Abbotsleigh, near Blandford : a piece of it was shown by Father Morris at the Festival of the Chelsea martyrs in 1888.   His clock is, or was until recently, at Walton Hall, near Wakefield, the residence of Charles Waterton, the famous traveller ; and his oaken, silver-mounted pint-cup, belongs to Mr. Eyston, of East Hendred.

The vindictive King did not confine his resentment to his victim, but visited it on the whole family.   There is a story that, on receiving the news of his death, Henry, who was playing draughts with Anne Boleyn, rose suddenly and hurried out, exclaiming, ' Thou art the cause of this man's death,' from which it would seem that some pang of remorse for the evil deed he had wrought had seized him.   If so, it was but short-lived.   As a matter of course, More's estates had been confiscated, though they could have been of little moment to a king sated with the plunder of numberless monasteries ; and Mistress More was so poor that she wrote to Cromwell that in order to find ' bord wages for her poore husband and his servant ' while in prison, she had of very necessity been compelled to sell part of her apparel.   Nevertheless, twenty pounds a year was all that she was allowed to live upon. Some ten years afterwards the King leased to her a certain messuage, parcel of the lands and possessions of Sir Thomas More, for twenty-one years, at a rental of twenty shillings and two-pence. This house, I take it, was that which afterwards went by the name of ' Moorhouse,' and will be referred to again in the account of Danvers House.

There was more than one applicant for the confiscated estate. In the papers at the Record Office is a letter (dated July 24, 1535) from the Duke of Suffolk asking that the King would grant no part of Sir Thomas More's lands lying about Chelsea, as he wished to have the house and lands adjoining, which were not above the yearly value of sixteen pounds, as part recompense for a certain reversion.

The Duke was doomed to disappointment, for on April 20 of the fol-lowing year a warrant was issued giving to Sir William Poulett (Pawlet) custody, during pleasure, ' of a chief messuage, curtilages, etc., lately belonging to Sir Thomas More, deceased.' Pawlet, whose pliability must have been truly phenomenal, contrived to retain position and favour under such oppositely disposed sovereigns as Henry VIII., Edward VI., Mary and Elizabeth. He was made Lord St. John by Henry VIII., and Marquis of Winchester by Edward VI. What a pitiful contrast to the brave spirit who had gone before him ! He and his widow occupied More's house for nearly fifty years, and he is reported to have made several alterations and reconstructions in it. From the ' Particular of Chelsea Manor ' drawn up in 1544, we find he already held by lease :

4 closes in Gospelshott ;
30 acres in Themyshott ;
12 acres near the cross in the same field ;
1 acre called ' wyffes acre ' ;
A meadow called ' Stoneybridge Close ' ;
A close called ' blakelands.'

A portrait of Pawlet, holding the white staff of Lord Treasurer, by an unknown painter, is in the National Portrait Gallery, and came from Holme Lacy, the seat of the Scudamores. His present representative is premier marquis of England.

Among the Additional Charters at the British Museum (No. 16,153) is the following, dated October 23, 1572 (A° 14 Eliz.) :

' Whereas the right honourable William, late Marques of Winchestre, and father unto the said now Marques, was indebted and stood bounden to our said Soveraigne Ladie the Quene's Majestie that now is, by his deed obligatorie bering date the xvij^th daie of June in the tenth yere of her highnes raigne, in the sume of thirty and five thousand poundes, with and upon the condition to content and paie or cause to be contented and paied to her highnes, etc., the sume of thirty four thousand one hundred and fortie pounds xv^s 1^d ob. of good and lawfull money of England, at any such daies and tymes as our said Soveraigne Ladie the Quene, her heires or Successours, should demaunde or require the same ; sithence the making of which bound the said William, late Marques of Winchestre, is departed out of this lif. The said John, now Marques of Winchestre, in consideration and for satisfaction of the sume of foure thousand poundes, parcell of the saied debt of xxxiiij m cxl^{li} xv^s 1^d ob., is contented and agreed to give, graunt, bargaine, sell and assure, and by these patents doth give, etc., unto the said Sir Walter Mildmay, knt., etc., all that his newe buildinges, chiefe mancion, or capitall messuage and mannour house, in Chelsey, in the countie of Midd. with all and singular houses and buildinges, barnes, stables, dove houses, orchardes, gardaines, lands, tenements, rentes, and all and singular other the appurtenances, whatsoever, which lie or at any time were belonging unto the said nowe Marques of Winchestre, sett, lying, and being in Chelsey aforesaid [besides sundry other landed possessions].

'And that the premises in Chelsey aforesaid, in the said countie of Midd. be and for ever hereafter shallbe and continue of the cleare yerely rent and value of nyneteen poundes, fourteene shillinges, and three pence, over and above all charges and reprises.'

It is further covenanted that on the payment by the said John of this £4,000 'before the Feast of the Purification of our Lady, Blessed Mary the Virgyn,' next after date, this mortgage shall be null and void.

There is no record to show how this very large debt had been contracted, but it is possible that Pawlet, like Sir Christopher Hatton and Lord Burleigh, had exceeded his purse in extravagant building. Four years after the date of the above, John, the second Marquis of Winchester, died in this house, which passed to Anne, Lady Dacre (daughter of Winifred, Marchioness of Winchester, by her first husband, Sir Richard Sackville), and her husband, Gregory Fiennes (or Fynes), Lord Dacre of the South. The Dacres are still remembered in Chelsea for the presentations to Emanuel Hospital bequeathed by Lady Dacre on the condition that her tomb should be kept in good repair. There is a curious paper concerning this charity, preserved with the Scudamore Papers (MSS. Add., B.M., 11056, f. 289) :

'Whereas there is a place voyd in ye Lady Daker Almshouses and wch is to be bestowed either by ye free choice of ye Inhabitants of this Parish or else by her successors, that hath ye repayring of her Ile and Monument in ye Parish Church according to the purport of her last will and testament, So it is, that you are to give warning to ye Church-wardens, to the Overseers for the Poor, and to ye rest of ye Parish, that there be a day appointed for ye generall meeting of ye inhabitants at the Parish Church concerning this Election, whereby it may be performed according to ye last Will and Testament of the Foundresse, wch course ought not in any sort to be so anxiously violated as hath bin of late practised by some of the Inhabitants : For ye avoyding of wch odious disorder and indirect practise, you are to give warning to ye whole parish in manner as followeth. And that a day of meeting for ye due performance there to be nominated and publique warning to be given there so at ye church accordingly. As you will aunswere ye neglect of yor duty on y^t behalfe at yor perille.

'Septemb^r 9th 1624.   'A. GORGES.

'To ye Constable and Headborough
  of Chelsey in ye County of Mids.
  and to any other officers of y^e
  same to whome it does or may
  appertayne.'

Lady Dacre died childless a few months after her husband in 1594. In her will, dated December 20, 1594, she bequeathed to Sir William Cecil, the great Lord Burghley, her neighbour at Brompton Hall, 'My house at Chelsey, and all the buildings, courtes, yardes, gardens, ortchards, backsides, grounds enclosed, and all my other lands and tenements in Chelsey, Kinsingtoune and Bromptone, in the said county of Middlesex,' with remainder to his youngest son Robert; but Lysons tells us he had seen, at the Rolls Chapel, a pardon of alienation to Sir Robert Cecil, dated June 21, A° 39 Eliz. (1597), for acquiring these premises of Thomas, Lord Buckhurst.

Cecil altered the old mansion in grand style. In building Wimbledon House he had employed the most celebrated English architect of the time, John Thorpe ('John of Padua'), and it would be interesting if we could find, what is not altogether improbable, that the alterations at Chelsea were his work also. Cecil's initials, 'R. C.,' and those of his wife, 'R^c. E.,' with the date, '1597,' remained on the pipes and other parts of the house in Dr. King's time. I do not think, however, that Cecil rebuilt the house, as some have supposed, or that it was an entirely new erection, as Mr. Rye suggests, for the architecture is of an earlier type than that which prevailed at the latter end of the sixteenth century, and its main features are characteristic of the time of Sir Thomas More.

Cecil appears to have tired of his new house shortly after he had obtained it, and found a purchaser in Henry Clinton, Earl of Lincoln. The date of this transfer is obtained, very nearly, from a letter of John Chamberlain to Dudley Carleton (London, March 15, 1597-98), in which, with various items of current news, he says :

'The Earl of Lincoln has bought Chelsea of Mr. Secretary.'

The year before Cecil had been appointed principal Secretary of State. The house, however, was never called Salisbury House, as Mr. L'Estrange and others have supposed, for Cecil was not created Earl of Salisbury until 1605.

The Earl of Lincoln was a strange, wild-tempered man, who had played some part in the moving events of the time. He had sat on the trial of Mary Queen of Scots, and on that of Elizabeth's whilom favourite, the Earl of Essex. He lived at Chelsea about seventeen years, and his name frequently occurs in the parish records.

Arthur, Lord Gray (died 1593), had for his second wife Jana Sibilla, daughter of Sir Richard Moryson, of Cashiobury, Hertfordshire, and sister of the Countess of Lincoln. This connection, perhaps, accounts for the following entry among the Chelsea baptisms :

'1626. Henry, son of Lord Gray, June 22.'

George, Lord Carew, writing to Sir Thomas Roe, September, 1615, says:

'The Erle of Lincoln is dead, and Sir Arthur Gorges is in possession of his house at Chelsey.'

Sir Arthur already had a house near, and four years later sold the late Earl's house to Lionel Cranfield, afterwards Earl of Middlesex, the Lord Treasurer, for £4,300. It was then described as 'the greatest house in Chelsea,' with 'two fore great courts adjoining, environed with brick walls, also a wharf lying in front, having a high brick tower on the east and west ends, and a high water tower standing upon the west corner of the wharf, and the watercourse belonging thereto. An orchard, a garden, having a peryment standing up in the middle, and a terrace on the north thereof, with a banquetting house at the east end of the terrace having a marble table in it. A great garden, dovecote close, containing five acres; the kitchen garden, brick barn close, containing ten acres' (Rot. Claus., 18 Jac. I., pt. 18, m. 38). Many of these features had disappeared when Kip took his view at the beginning of the eighteenth century.

In the following year (1620) Cranfield bought from William Blake (who, two years previously, had become the owner of Chelsea Ferry), 'All those closes of Pasture now divided into five, ditched, and being known by the name of Sandhills, containing, by estimation, 32 acres, abutting on the King's Highway from Chelsea to London on the South, on the lane leading from Chelsea to Brompton [now Upper Church Street] on the East, on the Highway from Fulham to London on the North, and on the close called Brickbarn Close on the west.'

The Earl of Middlesex held this house for six years only, but during this time much of the State business was transacted in it; a very large number of papers, warrants and grants, issued by him in virtue of his office, and dated from Chelsea, are still extant. For a time he stood high in the King's favour, as appears from various contemporary letters. Thus, on January 4, 1622, Chamberlain writes to Carleton of 'a great christening of the Lord Treasurer's son at Chelsey; the King, who was godfather, gave the child £1,000 in land.' The baptism of the child is recorded in the Chelsea register:

'1621. James, son of Lionel, Lord Cranfield, Dec. 27.'

(He succeeded his father in the title in 1645; he had taken the Parliamentary side on the outbreak of the Civil War.) Again, the same writer, on May 11, 1622, intimates that 'the King supped . . . with the Lord Treasurer on May Day.'

This favour, however, did not last. Cranfield was the chief of the Spanish party who desired to see Prince Charles wedded to the Infanta of

Spain. The project was highly unpopular in the country, and when the negotiations fell through, all who had advocated the scheme came in for a share of the blame. Cranfield was impeached and dismissed from office—chiefly at the instigation of the Duke of Buckingham. He was committed to the Tower, and his fine was at first fixed at £50,000, but afterwards reduced to £20,000. He was released in May, 1624, and proceedings were for a time suspended. In June he wrote to the King, protesting his innocence, and imploring protection; but the 'British Solomon' was almost entirely under the control of his favourite 'Steenie,' *i.e.,* the Duke of Buckingham—Cranfield's bitter enemy—and little or nothing could be expected without first gaining his goodwill. Accordingly, in August, we find Thomas, Lord Cromwell, writing to Middlesex the substance of a private conversation he had had with Buckingham, in which he takes very little pains to hide his opinion that the *Pardon* and *Protection* of the favourite must be purchased, and suggests that the resignation of Chelsea House, as a bribe, might be agreeable.

Meantime James I. died, and his son ascended the throne, amid the enthusiastic and hopeful loyalty of the nation. The change, however, brought no relief to Middlesex; Charles was quite as much under the influence of Buckingham as his father had been. From a letter of another of Cranfield's friends, Dr. John More, written about a month after the new King's accession, it appears that Cranfield, knowing the Duke was hankering after Chelsea House, had offered it to him at a certain price. The offer was rejected, and the same More again writes :

'My Lady [Middlesex] wishes you will not only pay your fine, but also give your house freely to the king, and then you can keep the sugars.'

At length Middlesex surrendered Chelsea House as part payment of his fine. Chamberlain writes (May 21, 1625) :

'The Earl of Middlesex has retired to Copt Hall, having compounded for his fine with £5,000, his farm of sugars, and his house at Chelsey.'

It is in this sense that we must understand the statement in the Cadogan title-deeds that he *sold* the house to the King. Cranfield's opinion of the sale is significantly expressed in some letters to Nicholas Hermon (May, 1626), in which he complains of 'the indecent use of the King's name in the business of the fine' : £5,000 was demanded of him, and Chelsea House was 'forced from him like Naboth's vineyard.'

Charles bestowed Chelsea House on Buckingham 'to be held of the manor of East Greenwich, paying to the King and his heirs twenty shillings yearly' (Pat. 3, Car. I., pt. 35, n. 4). After this there is a touch of grim humour in the letter of Francis White, Dean of Carlisle, written to Middlesex about the same time, in which he says the Duke was 'willing and desirous to be reconciled,' and if Cranfield would meet the Duke at York House or Chelsea, 'he doubted not a loving peace should be renewed between them.' These assertions were perhaps not without weight on Cranfield's mind, for, in the draft of an unfinished letter to the Duchess of Buckingham (Knole MSS.), written apparently in 1631, he says:

'The Duke told the Duchess in bed that he pulled Middlesex down, but never had a good day after, and cursed them that made the misunderstandings between them,'

INIGO JONES'S GATEWAY.

and that Lord Savage said the Duke resolved to make reparation. Perhaps when troubles began to gather round him, Buckingham remembered the words of shrewd but helpless King James when urged to sign the decree for Cranfield's dismissal, 'You are making a rod for your own back.'

The house was now known as Buckingham House. The Duke figures but little in Chelsea history: he was frequently away from England on State service, and had but three years of life after getting his 'Naboth's vineyard.'

Yet he must have spent much of such time as remained to him at Chelsea, whence many of his letters are dated, and where he was visited by the Court and all those parasites to whom the great man's smile or frown meant deep-laid schemes lost or won. A letter to the Rev. Joseph Mead (July 7, 1626) tells us:

> 'Yesterday at Chelsey House the duke feasted the king and queen.'

A letter from Mead (whose correspondence is preserved in the Harleian collection) to Sir Martin Stuteville, written May 11, 1627, just before Buckingham set out on the disastrous expedition to Rochelle, gives us another glimpse of his life at Chelsea:

> 'They say the Duke will have another masque before he goes, which will be chargeable [? to the state]. His friends feast him every day, and on Tuesday he feasted the Queen at Chelsey.'

On August 23, 1628, he was stabbed to death at Portsmouth by John Felton, an act which was hailed with shouts of exultation by the mass of the people. Crowds came forth to cheer the assassin on his journey to London, and the general feeling was well expressed by one old woman, who shouted to him, 'God bless thee, little David!' The national hatred of the slain Duke vented itself in scores of bitter lampoons, but none more bitter than that of a certain John Heape:

> 'I that my country did betray,
> Undid the king that let mee sway
> His sceptre as I pleased ; brought downe
> The glory of the English crowne ;
> The courtier's bane, the countrie's hate,
> An agent for the Spanish state ;
> The Romists' friend, the gospell's foe,
> The Church and Kingdome's overthrowe ;
> Here a damned carcase dwell,
> 'Till my soul returne from hell.
> With Judas then I shall inherit
> Such portion as all traytors meritt.
> If Heaven admit of treason, pride and lust,
> Expect my spotted soule among the just.'

The Duchess continued to live at Chelsea after the death of her husband, and to receive some share of royal favour. To quote from another letter of Mead to Stuteville, October 11, 1628:

> 'On Tuesday and Thursday, the last week, the king and queen were in London, and both days, as they returned to Hampton Court, visited the Duchess at Chelsea.'

Another notice of her connection with Chelsea is to be found in her letter to Secretary Dorchester, July 28, 1631, in which she asks him to move the King to pay Orazio Gentileschi (an Italian painter much patronized by the King and the late Duke) what is owing to him, so that he can leave England,

and she keep York House to herself, 'for want whereof she is constrained to keep a family at Chelsea to look after her laundry.'

The following extract from the destroyed parish books probably refers to this house :

'1632. Given the ringers at his Majestie's coming to the Duchess's House, o 1s. od.'

The Duke, like his master, had been a great collector of works of art, and an inventory of pictures, cabinets of jewels, etc., in Buckingham House, Chelsey (1635), is preserved among the Rawlinson MSS. (A. 341, 30) at the Bodleian Library.

As the Duke's heir was very young, and travelling with his tutor, Buckingham House was occupied for some years by his daughter Mary, who had married James Stuart, Duke of Richmond and Lennox, one of the four faithful adherents of Charles I. who offered their lives to save his. From the 'Perfect Occurrences,' April 10, 1646, we learn that

'The Duchess of Lennox, daughter of the Duke of Buckingham, being then at Oxford, petitioned the Lords for leave to come to London, or to her house at Chelsey, to be under Dr. Mayerne's hands for her health ; a pass was ordered for her, and the concurrence of the Commons desired.'

Both of Buckingham's sons returned to England while Charles was in prison, and took sides with the Royalist party, whereupon Buckingham House was confiscated by Parliament (August 2, 1648). A passage in a letter from Rowland Marston to his brother Edward (September 27, 1642) is evidence that the house had been seized on the outbreak of the Civil War. He requests his brother to use his best endeavours towards the liberation of some of his friends' kindred 'at present detained in Chelsea House, London.' As we have already mentioned, it was used as a barrack in 1649, and was so much injured by this occupation that a considerable sum had to be expended in its repair, 'the walls and wainscot of the house being much pulled down, the windows unglazed, the gardens destroyed, and the whole house much defaced by the soldiery quartered in it.'

In R. H. Whitelocke's 'Memoir of Sir Bulstrode Whitelocke' we read :

'The Attorney General, at the instigation of Lord L'Isle, moved the House to bestow it [Buckingham House] as an official residence on the two first commissioners, with a lease of twenty-one years from Haberdashers' Hall, at the moderate rent of £40 per annum. It was instantly granted, and here our first keeper [*i.e.*, Whitelocke] resided till the Restoration [June-July, 1649].'

John Lisle, one of these Commissioners of the Great Seal, afterwards fell under the ban of the Commonwealth, retired to the Continent, and was shot by an unknown assailant at Lausanne. He was thus the third resident in this famous house who met with a violent death.

While at Chelsea, Whitelocke was sent by Parliament as Ambassador to the Court of Sweden.

He often entertained distinguished visitors at Chelsea. In one of his letters he particularly mentions that the Swedish Ambassador often visited him there, and on the occasion specially referred to 'did much commend the sports in England of hawking and hunting.' This was Christer Carllson Bonde, whose diary is preserved in the Royal Museum at Stockholm, and contains several notices of visits to Whitelocke. On August 11, 1656, for example, he went with Fleetwood to Hampton Court, picking up Whitelocke at Chelsea. He goes on to describe how they hunted a buck, had an interview with the Protector, kissed his lady on the hand and his daughter on the cheek, feasted merrily, and had a merry journey home. Other entries refer to 'notable discourses' and 'prolix discourses' with Whitelocke at Chelsea.

On the return of Charles II., Whitelocke purchased his pardon for a considerable sum, and was allowed to withdraw into the country to 'take care of his wife and sixteen children.' He then retired to Chilton Park, near Hungerford, in Wiltshire, an estate which he had purchased with the dowry of his third wife, there to spend the remainder of his days in study and meditation.

After the Restoration, the second Duke of Buckingham, 'the last and lowest of all the Villierses,' recovered his father's estates, and spent some of his time at Chelsea; but his dissolute and vicious life soon involved him in such difficulties that he was compelled to part with his property, and Buckingham House was sold to John Godden and others in 1664.

In 1674, James Plummer, one of the creditors, sold the Chelsea estate to Strode and others in trust for George Digby, Earl of Bristol, the boon companion of its late owner. This remarkable man, who had played such an extraordinary part in the affairs of the times, is said (by Anthony à Wood) to have died at Chelsea, and to have been buried in the old church; but no record is to be found in the register, nor is his grave known. He demised the house at Chelsea to his countess, who engaged John Evelyn to find a purchaser for it. On January 15, 1679, he wrote in his journal:

'I went with my Lady Sunderland [daughter of the late Earl of Bristol] to Chelsea, and dined with the Countess of Bristol (her mother) in the great house, formerly the Duke of Buckingham's, a spacious and excellent place for the extent of ground and situation in good air. The house is large but ill contrived, though my Lord Bristol, who purchased it after he sold Wimbledon to my Lord Treasurer, expended much money on it. There were divers pictures of Titian and Vandyck, and some of Bassano, very excellent, especially a Venus and Adonis, a Duke of Venice, a butcher in his shambles selling meat to a Swiss, and of Vandyck, my Lord of Bristol's picture with the Earl of Bedford's at length in the same table. There was in the garden a rare collection of orange-trees, of which she was pleased to bestow some upon me.'

These pictures are now at Althorp, the seat of Earl Spencer, and were lent to the South Kensington Museum some years ago.

Several interesting papers relating to Evelyn's efforts to sell Chelsea House are preserved among the Ormonde MSS. He had offered it to the Duke of Ormonde, who refused it, whereupon he wrote to his son, Thomas, Earl of Ossory (February 14, 1679-80) as follows:

'My Lord, I am extreamely sorry for my Lord Duke's sake, but especially for your Lordship's, that you reject the opportunity that is presented to you for the purchasing of that sweete place at Chelsey, vpon such easy termes, because I am certaine that if ever the times should settle into any tollerable composure, it will not lie vpon their hands who have interest in it for a much more considerable summ than is now demanded for it, and that then it may not possibly be in my power to serve your Lordship as now it is. I have formerly acquainted your Lordship with the particulars ; that besides a magnificent house capable of being made (with small expense) perfectly modish ; the offices, gardens, and other accommodations for aire, water, situation, vicinity to London, benefit of the river and mediocrity of price nowhere to be parallel'd I am sure about this towne, or any that I know in England. There are with it to be added, as many orange-trees, and other precious greenes, as are worth 500*l.* The fruits of the gardens are exquisite ; there is a snow-house—in a word, I know of no place more capable of being made the envie of all the noble retreats of the greatest persons neere this court and citty, so that it ever grieves me your Lordship should not be master of it. I almost forgot to tell your Lordship that there is neere one hundred pounds a yeare in good tennements vnder-rented ; so as vpon the matter I do not esteame your Lordship giues about 3,500*l.* for the whole, which realy is not aboue a third part of what it would sell in any other circumstances. Not one argument of all this would I vse to your Lordship after what your Lordship has communicated to me, since you went into Ireland (where my Lord Duke cannot have so perfect a notion of it as your Lordship who is so neere it every day) because methinks I cannot have acquitted myselfe of the many obligations I remaine vnder to your Lordship without making your Lordship this second offer of my service, etc.'

A week later Lord Ossory wrote to his father :

'Having received from Mr. Evelyn the enclosed, which by Sir Stephen Fox, who was once about purchasing of the house mentioned in it, I doe finde it to be a very greate bargain, and the summe demanded not very considerable, besides a morall certainty, if the time be quiet, that at any time it may be parted with at advantage. I thought it not amiss to send you the proposal ; the conviency and indeed the decency of your hauing an abode in England, if your affairs can permitt your laying out so much money hauing inclined me to make this stepp, which, if proceeded in, I doubt not but you will be satisfied of the price and the good repayre that boath house and gardens are in.'

With this was enclosed 'a perticular of Chelsey House':

'There belongs to Chelsey house 16 acres of ground, with several large gardens and courts, all wald in and planted with the choycest fruite that could be collected either from abroad or in England.

'The whole house is in perfect good repaire, the apartements alterd according to the mode, my Lord of Bristoll hauing laid out upon it 2000*l.*

'The outhousing is very good, ample and commodious, and all the offices supplied with excellent water.

'The tenements belonging to it are now let for 100*l.* per annum, and may be very considerably improved as the leases expire.

'The purchase was at first 7,000*l.*

'For this particular, with the addition of all orange-trees, and other greenes, fruite and flowers of all kinds, with seates, rowlers, tables, and all garden vtencills. Allsoe, within

18

the house all fixt necessarys, as greates, chimney pieces, and wainscot, the billiard table, and a pare of marble tables and house clocke there will be p^d 5,000*l.*
'" Thus offerd 26th June, 1679.
' By Sir Step. Fox.'

Evelyn twice refers to the negotiations with Sir Stephen Fox in his journal:

June 17th, 1679. 'To Chelsey to Sir Stephen Fox, and my lady, in order to the purchase of the Countess of Bristol's house there, which she desired me to procure a chapman for.'
Nov. 8th, 1679. 'At Sir Stephen Fox's and was agreeing for the Countess of Bristol's house at Chelsea within 500*l.*'

All these preliminaries, however, resulted in nothing, and on September 3, 1681, Lady Sunderland wrote to Evelyn:

' I must now tell you what is my opinion as to Chelsea—that my mother had better take 6,000*l* for it than live a melancholy life there another winter. I am ever to trouble you with my affaires, but now we come upon you double. My mother and I do earnestly beg that you will be so kind as to negotiate the sale with Monsieu Foubert, who has told Sir Gabriel Sylvius that he will give 4,000*l* for it. Although this offer is so inconsiderable, there is no hearkening to it yet, from its coming voluntarily from him, I conceive he may be brought to give this 4,000*l.* for the house and gardens, and leave my mother mistress of the little houses called tenements. If he will agree to this, we beg you to conclude with him, and do all you can.'

In the following year, 1682, ' the sweete place at Chelsey ' was sold to Henry Somerset, first Duke of Beaufort, in whose family it remained for about thirty years, and henceforth bore their name. Evelyn does not record that he had anything to do with this sale, but on September 3, 1683, he writes:

' I went to see what had been done by the Duke of Beaufort on his late purchased house at Chelsea; which I once had the selling of for the Countess of Bristol ; he made great alterations, but might have built a better house with the materials and the cost he had been at.'

The Duke of Beaufort was a steady supporter of the House of Stuart, and brought about the initial disaster to Monmouth's troops in their ill-fated rebellion. Monmouth marched on Bristol, where he had hopes of finding friends, money, and arms. The Duke of Beaufort, warned of this, declared to the people of Bristol that if they offered any assistance to the rebels he should fire the city. When Monmouth heard of this threat, he exclaimed, 'God forbid that I should bring the two calamities of fire and sword together upon so noble a city!' He then marched to Bath, where he was again foiled.

Henry, Earl of Clarendon, records several visits to Beaufort House in his diary. The following, March 27, 1689, has a particular interest:

' In the afternoon I went to Chelsey to the Duchess of Beaufort, whom we found alone. She told me the whole story how Lady Essex had sent for her and her lord, and all the relations, Lord Bedford, Devonshire, Bishop Burnet and young Mr. Hampden, about the matter relating to Lord Essex's death, now depending before the committee of the Lords ; that she had declared that she believed that he killed himself ; and therefore desired that the business might fall.   She told me Burnet and Hampden both owned the conspiracy against King Charles II.   I should have been there had I been in town.'

The first Duke of Beaufort refused to take the oaths of allegiance to William and Mary, and lived in retirement until his death in 1699.   His son Henry, the second duke, occasionally resided in Chelsea.   Luttrell wrote in his diary, September 1, 1702 :

'The Duke of Beaufort's house at Chelsey is fitting up for his reception against winter.'

Ralph Palmer, again, writing to Lord Fermanagh in 1708, says :

' The Duke and Duchess of Beaufort are come to reside at Chelsey.'

Later evidences of their occupation are to be found in the marriage register of the old church.   On December 24, 1711, the Hon. Mary Somerset, grand-daughter to her grace the Dowager-Duchess of Beaufort, was married to the Hon. Algernon Greville; and on April 10, 1713, the Right Hon. Lady Henrietta Somerset was married to the most noble Charles, Duke of Grafton. The year after, Mary, the widow of the first duke, died at Chelsea at the age of eighty-five years.

Bowack, writing in 1705, said of Beaufort House :

' It is so pleasantly situated, that the late queen Mary had a great desire to purchase it before King William built Kensington, but was prevented by some secret obstacles.'

What authority Bowack had for this statement does not appear, but supposing it to be well founded, it is easy to understand the secret obstacles.

Faulkner printed the following curious extract from the will of Samuel Travers, July 16, 1724 :

' Having long and seriously considered how I might do the most and most lasting good to mankind, with that wherewith it had pleased God to bless me, I bethought myself of introducing a better way of educating young men of quality and condition in the principles of virtue and honour, and in useful learning, in order whereunto I agreed for Beaufort House at Chelsea, as the properest situation for that purpose.   But meeting with some discouragement therein, which made me apprehend the age was not disposed to receive so great a benefit, I leave that benefit to some future and happier season, and have now turned my thoughts another way, wherein I may hope to do some good without encountering so many difficulties.'

Thus the famous old mansion was once more waiting for a tenant, and so stood until 1736, when Sir Hans Sloane bought it for £2,500.   Sir Hans had been in possession of the manor since 1716, and his object seems simply to have been the extension of his landed possessions in Chelsea, which were already considerable.   As the house still continued tenantless, he pulled it down in 1740, and the materials were carted away. Inigo Jones' gateway, built for the Earl of Middlesex, was given to the Earl of Burlington, an amateur architect, who carried it to his gardens at Chiswick, where it was re-erected. On a stone tablet was inscribed:

'Builded by Inigo Jones, at Chelsea, MDCXXI.';

and on another tablet:

'Given by Sir Hans Sloane, baronet, to the Earl of Burlington, MDCCXXXVII.'

Its removal occasioned the well-known lines of Alexander Pope beginning 'O gate, how cam'st thou here?' A letter from Cranfield to the architect (1622) is preserved among the Sackville MSS.

Such is the history in brief of this famous house, which affords material and interest enough for a volume to itself. There are very few houses in the land that can present such an array of distinguished residents. Across its site Beaufort Street (formerly Row), commenced in 1766, now runs; a portion of the cellarage existed in the basement of No. 17. On the opposite side is a house, lately inhabited by Mrs. Jopling, the artist, which has recently been purchased by the Roman Catholic Church in commemoration of Sir Thomas More, for the garden is undoubtedly a portion of those celebrated by Heywood. In it stands a mulberry-tree, which is not improbably a descendant of one dating from More's time. The garden walls at the back of Paultons Square and Danvers Street are undoubtedly those which separated the gardens of Chelsea House from those of Danvers House, and may be contemporary with the original planning of the grounds. If we proceed a few steps westward along the King's Road we come to a public-house, the Globe, by which is a gate leading to the Moravian burial-ground. This, too, is a portion of More's gardens. The massive walls are built of the narrow, bright-red bricks peculiar to his time, and they may be seen also in the chapel or aisle he built in the old church. One of the largest pieces exhibits the remains of a fireplace, the bricks blackened with smoke, a portion of an archway, and remnants of beams, silently reminding us of the home of the great man, after all the changes and accidents of 350 years. The keeper's cottage, over-run with vines, is evidently a structure of the same age, and the schoolhouse was originally the stables of Beaufort House, as shown in Kip's view. In the garden is an old twisted mulberry-tree, from which, according to the usual tradition, Queen Elizabeth had many a plate of fruit.

Beaufort Street is, of course, comparatively modern (it was laid out as Beaufort Row in 1766), but has already had several noteworthy inhabitants. John Varley, of water-colour fame, lived at 10, Beaufort Row, and made many sketches of the neighbourhood during his stay there. A drawing of the church from near Winchester House was shown at the Exhibition of 1862 by Mr. J. H. Chance. Members of his family are still resident in Chelsea. When John Varley left Chelsea, his house was taken by Edmund Dorrell, another water-colourist, and subsequently by James Stark, one of the best pupils of John ('Old') Crome, the founder of the Norwich School. Varley's son-in-law, Wilson Lowry, F.R.S., eminent for his attainments in natural philosophy and metaphysics, also lived near Battersea Bridge. John Galt, the novelist; Ralph Wedgwood, of the famous pottery firm (which had a

THE CLOCK HOUSE.

branch at Chelsea); and 'Chinese' Gordon, the hero of Khartoum, are also among the former residents of Beaufort Row.

When the demolition of Beaufort House was decided upon, the lodge to the stable-yard gate was, with a piece of the ground, given to one Howard, a Quaker, who had been gardener to Sir Hans Sloane. His herb-garden, one of the last of a species that was once common, was well known for many years. Among the MSS. collected by Faulkner was a very interesting note on this garden by the Rev. John Mitford, of Benhall, Suffolk (October 6, 1828),

which was first printed by the Rev. A. G. L'Estrange in his ' Village of Palaces.'
From it I take a few extracts :

> ' The walls are covered with ancient fig-trees and fine old vines of the choicest sort.
> Vines also are grown on treillages (trellises) near the walks.   This is a mode of culture
> now passed away, and bespeaks a reliance on summers warmer and more genial than
> those of the present time.   There are four large standard pomegranates, some of which
> are in full flower at this present time ; these fine and beautiful plants, in modern gardens,
> have always the warmth and protections of a wall ; but were formerly grown like the
> present specimens in the open border.
> ' A remarkable shrub that adorns the venerable garden is a large Camellia Japonica
> growing in the open grounds without even the protection of a wall.   It is of the single
> red species, apparently uninjured by the severity of our winter, and may be considered, at
> least in this part of England, as a remarkable curiosity.   Near the entrance is a most
> beautiful specimen of the Gleditsia Triancanthos of unusual size, at least I have never
> seen it equalled, but by two trees of the same species in the gardens of Lord Tankerville
> at Walton Bridge. . . .
> ' Mr. Howard's garden possesses a fine plant of the Althœa Frutex, the Arbutus, and
> Myrtle ; these exotic shrubs flourish here in perfect health and beauty.   A Calycanthus
> Floridus still in full vigour is known to have been here more than 60 years, but the
> oldest tree in the garden is the mulberry, now decaying fast, and which probably must
> have seen more than two centuries.   The profits attending the culture of this small and
> curious garden are chiefly drawn from the sale of fruit and the distillation of waters,
> which used to be considered as possessing great medicinal virtues. . . .
> ' The venerable old lady who resides at the Clock House . . . remembers the old-
> fashioned families in the country coming with their coaches and four in the autumn of
> every year to lay in their annual stock of spear-mint, penny royal, peppermint, and other
> waters, good for the gravel, stone, and of great efficacy in inward bruises, and even at
> this day an advertisement in the window reminds the public of the great and specific
> virtue of these bottles, whose general fame has long since expired. . . . This was the
> kind of garden old Tradescant cultivated, which Compton loved, and which Evelyn
> described . . .'

Howard's brother was of a mechanical genius, and the wooden clock which
he fixed upon the wall gave the house its name of ' The Clock House.'   A
Vestry minute, September 25, 1760, tells us :

> ' At a vestry, Mr. Edmund Howard, of Chelsea, was ordered to make a new Parish
> clock, for the sum of 50*l*., which was fixed up in May, 1761.'

The quaint old house, of which a sketch is here given, was pulled down
about thirty years ago.

' The Sandhills,' which formed part of Sir Thomas More's estate, were, as
we have seen, purchased by the Earl of Middlesex from William Blake in
1620.   On Hamilton's Survey, as corrected by Dr. King, this land is called
Wharton Park, after Lord Wharton, who lived in Danvers House.   Lord
Wharton gave up his Chelsea property about 1714, and some four years later
Chelsea Park, as the ' Sandhills ' came to be called, was purchased by a company to form a mulberry-garden.

About 1716, Henry Barham, F.R.S., who tells us he had been surgeon-
major in the island of Jamaica, came to England, and settled at Chelsea.

Here he gave up his mind to the rearing of the silkworm, and apparently succeeded in persuading a good many people that this might be made a profitable
industry in England. Among these was one John Appletree, to whom a
patent was granted, under the Great Seal of England, on May 23, 1718. He
issued 'Proposals for an Undertaking to Manage and Produce Raw Silk, of
the growth of England; and to raise a Fund for the carrying on of the
same.'

The total number of shares was to be 10,000, one-half of which was to be
for the benefit of the patentee. These shares were of the value of five pounds,
and when the proposals were issued 500 had already been subscribed for.
The patentee, with Richard Musgrave, Jonathan Jarrett, and Hercules Coyte
were declared directors for life, and seven others were chosen by the share-
holders.

The matter contained in these proposals, together with a disquisition on
the whole subject, is to be found in 'An Essay upon the Silkworm,' written by
Barham, the preface of which is dated Chelsea, March 25, 1719. Speaking of
the culture of the mulberry-tree, he says:

> 'A light dry mould, and exposed to the sun and air is best for them, low ground being
> pernicious to them ; and therefore we have made choice of Chelsea Park as proper ground
> to make a nursery.'

Again, on 'The manner of building proper house,' etc.:

> 'First chuse a place in good air, and near the mulberry-trees. This direction we have
> followed, in making choice of Chelsea Park for our houses and plantations, which is as
> good air as any in England.'

With regard to the scale on which they started he says:

> 'Having mention'd Mr. Evelyn's computing one mulberry-tree feeding as many silk-
> worms with its leaves in one year, as made 7 pounds of silk : according to that estimate
> those 2000 trees already planted in Chelsea Park (which does not take up one-third of it)
> will make 14,000 pound weight of silk : then allowing one pound weight of silk to be
> commonly worth but twenty shillings a pound, those trees must make 14,000 pounds
> sterling per annum (which is but a small number of trees to what the Company intend to
> plant).'

He also tells us that the estimated outlay for the whole would be about
£25,000, a great part of which was already paid in. Appletree, in his proposals, says that all the expenses up to the time of their issue, including the
leasing of Chelsea Park for 122 years, and the planting of the 2,000 trees, had
been borne by himself. The premises of the company are rated in the parish
books at £200 per annum.

Another pamphlet was issued in 1720, entitled 'The Produce of India,
Italy, and France raised in England by the Silk Manufacture.' This is a short

abstract of Appletree's proposals and Barham's essay, together with a copy of Apletree's (*sic*) patent.

When the company got into working order it attracted considerable attention, and the affair became one of the 'lions' of fashionable society. The venture seems to have been attended with some success at first, and Thoresby, writing in his diary in 1723, mentions that he saw 'at Mr. Gates' a sample of satin made at Chelsea of English silkworms for the Princess of Wales, very rich and beautiful.' In this year proceedings were instituted against the Park Company for some offence against the parish, and a Vestry minute orders that John Turner, Surveyor of the Highways, should be indemnified for his costs in the matter.

The novelty of the thing soon wore off. There was no society for the protection of home industries to lend the company a helping hand, and after a few years' struggle the premises were closed. The park and its trees, however, remained, and during the early years of this century mulberry-trees were very plentiful in Chelsea. A few of those originally planted were still surviving, near a pond, when the Elm Park Estate was planned, some ten years ago, and there yet remain two or three in different parts of the gardens.

Christopher Le Blon, an engraver of Flemish birth, came to Chelsea between 1732-34, and set up a factory on the Mulberry Ground, Chelsea, for the purpose of weaving tapestries after Raphael's seven cartoons, which are now hung in the Raphael Room at South Kensington Museum. The looms were set, and some drawings, characterized by Walpole as 'very fine,' were made, but Society did not respond to this endeavour. Le Blon had been concerned in a 'picture company' some years previously, when his conduct did not inspire public confidence. Moreover, the taste for tapestry decoration had died out. The famous Mortlake Works had closed at the beginning of the century; the Fulham, Soho, Exeter, and Stamford factories had all failed, and that at Chelsea does not appear to have made more than a start.

Park Chapel was built within the precincts of Chelsea Park in 1718 by Sir Richard Manningham, M.D., to meet the growing requirements of the parish, which then possessed no Episcopal place of worship but the old church. It is wrongly described as a French chapel on Rocque's map, 1751. Sir Richard died on May 11, 1759, and was buried at Chelsea. The lease was granted to the Rev. William Lacey, of Battersea, in 1730, and the following have been the ministers since his time:

1736.	Rev. Sloane Elsmere, D.D., rector of Chelsea.		
1766.	„	—	Gower, schoolmaster, of Chelsea.
—	„	—	Jacobs, rector of St. Dunstan's in the West.
1785.	„	—	Kelly, D.D., vicar of East Meon, Hampshire.

PARK CHAPEL.

1792.   Rev. James Ward, Fellow of Queen's College, Cambridge.
1797.   „   Thomas Ellis.
1800.   „   James Manning.
1802.   „   J. Gee Smith, M.A., rector of Chellesworth, Suffolk. He made very exten-
             sive alterations in the chapel about 1810, when it was practically rebuilt.
1812.   „   John Owen ; he was previously curate of Fulham under Bishop Porteus,
             who also bestowed on him the rectory of Paglesham, Essex. He took a
             distinguished part in the foundation of the British and Foreign Bible
             Society, served as its honorary secretary for eighteen years, and wrote
             its history. He died at Ramsgate in 1822.
1822.   „   Henry John Owen, son of the preceding. He became the first minister of
             the Catholic Apostolic (Irvingite) Church in College Street, Chelsea, in
             1835. The school attached to the chapel was built during his ministry
             in 1828, chiefly owing to the exertions of Samuel Gower Poole, of Poole's
             (or Green's) Brewery at Stanley Bridge.
1834.   „   John Harding.   1846. Rev. W. Cadman.
1836.   „   Henry Vaughan.   1852.   „   C. J. Goodhart.
1836.   „   Thomas Vores.   1868.   „   J G. Gregory.
1841.   „   John C. Miller.   —   „   W. J. Bennett.
                                     1888.   „   Sydenham L. Dixon.

The chapel is extra - parochial, and is held on lease of Sloane Stanley, Esq.

Piece by piece Chelsea Park was cut away for building purposes. Park Walk (previously called Lover's Walk and Twopenny Walk) was built at the latter end of the eighteenth century, and the Camera Square district about sixty years since. The last remnant of the park was that attached to the mansion built by Mr. William Broomfield, a surgeon, and afterwards occupied by Sir Henry Wright Wilson, Bart., M P. In 1810 the grounds were reduced to that piece which is now the Elm Park Gardens Estate.

The mansion was pulled down in 1876, and the Estate was laid out ; it will probably supply Chelsea of the future with many eminent inhabitants ; it already reckons among its residents the Right Hon. John Morley, M.P., R. H. Scott, Esq., F.R.S., of the Meteorological Office, R. N. Cust, Esq., a distinguished philologist, William Kuhe, the musician, and some eminent artists, as Henry Pilleau and Paul J. Naftel.

GORGES HOUSE.

In Kip's view of Beaufort House we see to the west of it, and almost adjoining, another house of much less size, but of notable appearance, and built in the style characteristic of the latter half of Queen Elizabeth's reign. This was the house of Sir Arthur Gorges, who has already been mentioned as the son-in-law of the Earl of Lincoln.

In 1567 the Marquis of Winchester demised to Nicholas Holborne, of

Chelsey, gent., and to Katherin his wife, the mansion or farm-house nigh unto the south-west side of the Marquis's own mansion, 'one quyll of water coming to the said farm-house,' 130 acres of arable land in Chelsea and Kensington, the messuage 'late called the Parsonage of Chelsey,' and fourteen acres of land obtained by exchange with Richardson, the Rector. The lease was for fifty years at a rental of £13 6s. 8d. Nicholas Holborne, 'paterfamilias et senex,' died in 1592, and was buried at Chelsea on October 4 of that year.

Although we have no documentary evidence, yet it seems fairly clear that when Sir Arthur Gorges married the Earl of Lincoln's daughter Elizabeth, he obtained the mansion house above mentioned, and rebuilt it in the manner shown in our sketch. There is no evidence of the presence of the Gorges

GORGES HOUSE, 1705.

family in Chelsea previous to this time. An undated letter of Lady Elizabeth Gorges (Scudamore Papers, British Museum), stating that her son (probably Timoleon, baptized in the old church October 1, 1600) roused all her family, and also the Earl of Lincoln, on the occasion of an attempted burglary at the Gorges House, proves that these were near neighbours; while another letter from Rowland White to Sir Robert Sidney, November 15, 1599, proves that the house was then newly built:

'As the Queen passed by the faire new House in Chelsey, Sir Arthur Gorge [knighted October 29, 1597] presented her with a faire Jewell.'

Sir Arthur had been the friend of Edmund Spenser, who has some interesting remarks concerning him and his family in the dedication of the 'Daphnaïda: an Elegie upon the Death of the noble and vertuous Dovglas Howard, daughter and heire of Henry, Lord Howard, Viscount Bindon, and wife of Arthur Gorges, Esquier.' It was printed in 1596, and dedicated to the Right Honourable the Ladie Helena, Marquesse of Northampton :

> 'I have the rather presumed humbly to offer vnto your Honour the dedication of this little Poëme, for that the noble and vertuous Gentlewomā of whom it is written, was by match neere alied, and in affection greatly deuoted vnto your Ladiship. The occasion why I wrote the same, was as well the great good fame, which I heard of her deceased, as the particular goodwill which I beare vnto her husband, Master Arthur Gorges, a louer of learning and vertue, whose house, as your Ladiship by mariage hath honoured, so doe I find the name of them by many noble records, to be of greate Antiquity in this Realme ; and such as haue euer borne themselves with honourable reputation to the world, and un-spotted loyaltie to their Prince and countrey ; besides so lineally are they descended from the Howards, as that the Lady Anne Howard, eldest daughter to John, Duke of Norfolke, was wife to Sir Edmund, mother to Sir Edward, and grandmother to Sir William and Sir Thomas Gorges, Knights. And therefore I doe assure myselfe that no due honour done to the White Lyon, but will be most gratefull to your Ladiship, whose husband and children do so neerely participate with the blood of that noble familie,' etc.

The lady thus celebrated, one of the richest heiresses of the day, died in 1590, and left an only daughter, Ambrosia Gorges, who survived her mother ten years, and was buried at Chelsea. A curious note upon her death occurs in a letter from Sir Robert Cecil to Sir George Carew, dated November 8, 1600 :

> 'Sʳ Arthur Gorges' daughter is dead, which works in him shrewd effects, but he hath some relief by a composition made between him and the Viscount, who must pay him 400ˡⁱ a yeare during his lyf, which will keep the staff from the dore.'

The Viscount was her uncle, Thomas Howard, who had succeeded her grandfather as third in the title. She had been made a ward of the Queen on the 10th of May preceding her death, much to the annoyance of her father, who naturally wished to dispose of her himself, and had a husband in view for her, in the person of Thomas Howard, Lord Howard of Walden. She was evidently an heiress of some consequence, for we find that Sir Philip Herbert, afterwards Earl of Pembroke and Montgomery, offered the Queen £5,000 in money and jewels for her hand. Her early death, however, put an end to all intrigue.

Sir Arthur married secondly, as we have seen, Elizabeth, the only daughter of the eccentric Earl of Lincoln. In the Additional MSS. of the British Museum are two papers relating to this lady. One is the complaint to Sir John Danvers of the conduct of his workmen already referred to. She was afterwards engaged in a lawsuit with Danvers ; and among the MSS. of the Duke of Bedford at Woburn is a ' Note of the proceedings in the Star Chamber, Hil., 3 Car. I., Sir John Danvers v. Lady Gorges.' The second paper in the British Museum, which is signed ' E. Gorges,' relates to this ' long and tedious suite;' and is a certificate on behalf of Mr. Day, 'late curate of Chelsey,' who appears to have fallen under Sir John's displeasure for the part he had taken in the dispute.

Sir Arthur Gorges was a prolific writer; most of his verses still remain in MS., but his translations of Lucan's ' Pharsalia ' and Bacon's ' Wisdom of the Ancients' have been published. The former, published in 1614, has a curious dedication, from which the following are extracts :

'To the Right Noble and Vertuous Lady Lucy, Comtess of Bedford, my most Honoured Lady and Mistresse,—

'. . . . This Poeme by chance I did see in my Father's study, amongst many other of his Manuscripts. And because it lay idly there, I desired him to give it me. When asking what I would do with it, I told him that I would present it to my Lady my Mistresse. Which humour of mine he seemed very well to like : but he answered that it was not faire enough written for her reading. Whereunto I replied that if I might haue it, I would amend that fault, and get it prented by the helpe of my Schoole-maister, and in that sort offer it. Whereto my Father said that he liked well my deuotion to so Noble a Mistresse as that hee would freely giue it mee. . . .

'Now if this may but receive your honourable applause, as some pledge of my Deuotion, I will neuer thinke that I need to be ashamed to flutter with my Father's Feathers.

'Your Ladiships most humble and faithfull seruant,

'Carew Gorges.'

Sir Arthur wrote an account of the Earl of Essex's ' Islands,' or ' Azores Voyage ' (1597), which has been printed by Samuel Purchas (1625) in his ' Pilgrims,' x. 9. Sir Arthur commanded the *Wast Spite* in this expedition, and Sir Walter Raleigh, rear-admiral, sailed in his ship.

Sir Arthur Gorges died on September 28, 1625, and was buried at Chelsea on the tenth of the following month. He died possessed of 17 messuages, 120 acres of land, 12 of meadow, and 50 of pasture in Chelsea, Kensington, and Brompton.

The Chelsea estate of his son, Sir Arthur Gorges, was assessed at £60 by the Committee for the Advance of Money on August 24, 1643 ; and on September 15 of the same year it was ordered that the £30 deposited by him should be considered a discharge of his assessment. In 1647, the Committee for Compounding with Delinquents fixed the fine for his whole estate at £806, notwithstanding his assertion that he had never been in arms against the Parliament. Two years later this fine was reduced to £512.

The parish registers record that his son, Sir Arthur, died in October, 1661 ; and Evelyn makes note that he came to Chelsea in the February following to see Sir A. Gorges' house, but does not say for what purpose or with what result. In 1664 Arthur Gorges, son of the second Sir Arthur, sold Gorges House, together with the chapel (reserving to himself the right of burial there) to Thomas Pritchard. The reason for this sale is not recorded ; but Bowack mentions (apparently as a certificate of honour) that he was the intimate friend of the Duke of Buckingham and the Earl of Rochester, so that, if a man may be known by the company he keeps, his character was none of the steadiest. He died in 1668, and was buried beside his ancestors at Chelsea.

The following advertisement appears in the *London Gazette*, November 25, 1680:

> 'Josias Priest, dancing master, who kept a boarding school for gentlewomen in Leicester Fields, is removed to the great house at Chelsey, that was Mr. Portman's. There will continue the same masters and others, to the improvement of the said school.'

Priest here gave the first performance of Purcell's 'Dido and Æneas.' An original copy of the libretto is still extant, and bears the following title:

> 'An opera performed at Mr. Josias Priest's Boarding School, at Chelsey, by young gentlewomen, the words made by Mr. Nat. Tate. The musick composed by Mr. Henry Purcell.'

Among Dr. Urfey's 'New Poems' (1690) is 'An Epilogue to the Opera of "Dido and Æneas," performed at Mr. Priest's Boarding School at Chelsey; spoken by Lady Dorothy Burk.'

When Bowack wrote in 1705, Gorges House was still a 'famous boarding-school for young ladies' kept 'by Mr. Jonas Priest.' Parsonage Close, which went with this house, was, therefore, sometimes called 'Priest's Close.'

Subsequently Gorges House became the property of Sir William Milman (or Millman), who died September 13, 1713, and lies in the old church. The houses at the water-side end of Milman Street are apparently about 300 years old; others, of the genuine Queen Anne style, were, according to a note on a plan in the Moravian Archives, built in 1726. Gorges or Milman House, therefore, must have been demolished shortly before that date.

In 1793 Abraham Pether, a well-known painter of moonlight scenes, gives his address in the Royal Academy Catalogue as '2, Millman Row, Great Chelsea,' and continued to exhibit regularly from this address until 1797. One of his pictures in 1796 was 'An Iron Foundry by Moonlight,' possibly Janeways, which his windows overlooked. An excellent specimen of his work is now in the South Kensington Museum. In 1776 another artist, a Mrs. Wright, landscape painter, exhibiting with the Incorporated Society of Painters, gives her address as 'Mrs. Ralph's, Millman Row, Chelsea.'

Some years ago, when sewage-works were being carried out in this street, the workmen opened a vault of some size, built of red brick, in the rear court of the house then numbered 19. It probably belonged to Gorges House, and in it were found an old jar and some Elizabethan coins.

STANLEY HOUSE.

Elizabeth, daughter of the first Sir Arthur Gorges, by his second wife, married Sir Robert Stanley, the second son of William, the 6th Earl of Derby. This marriage seems to have greatly displeased the Stanley family. A letter in the Harleian Collection, dated March 16, 1626-7, and addressed to the Rev. Joseph Mead, says:

'On the Friday night, or Saturday morning, died the good Countess of Derby, mother to the Lord Strange, and was buried on Sunday, by night, at Westminster. It is said, of grief she took for Sir Robert Stanley her second son's marriage, killed her; yet she saw both him and his lady before her death, prayed God to forgive, and left unto him 400*l*. per annum.'

We catch a glimpse of Sir Robert Stanley in the account of Ben Jonson's masque, 'Love's Triumph through Callipolis,' acted at Court in 1630. 'Fifteen lovers ranged themselves seven and seven on a side with each a Cupid before him with a lighted torch.' The King was in the centre, Lord Strange playing the 'Secure Lover' and Sir Robert Stanley the 'Substantial' (Works, ed. 1816, viii. 93).

Sir Robert evidently lived in Chelsea from the time of his marriage. We find his daughter Mary buried in the old church in June, 1629, a son James baptized there in 1631, and Sir Robert himself buried in January, 1632.

On the death of her husband, Lady Stanley pressed very hard for an annuity from the Stanley family, and was awarded one by the King. Lord Strange took her efforts in very ill grace, and, writing to Sec. Windebanke, March 7, 1634, says that his wife was unfit to travel, 'but it were better if wee both slept in o^r graves than be thus perpetually vext by the misinformation of a most unconscionable woman.'

In 1637, Lady Elizabeth Gorges leased to her daughter a messuage called 'Brickills,' and lands containing five acres, for thirty-one years, at an annual payment of £20, payable to James Stanley, her second son. In Scharf's catalogue of pictures at Knowsley, Stanley House, or 'Brickills,' is said to have been built in 1625, but no authority is given, nor do I know of any.

Lady Gorges bequeathed this house to her daughter:

'I, the Right Honourable Lady Elizabeth Gorges, widow, being weak in body, but in perfect memory, thanks be to God, doe ordeyne this my last Will and Testament in manner and Forme following. Imprimis, I bequeath to my eldest sonnes children all those Tenements and Lands, lyeing and being in Chelsey, to be equally divided amongst them, provided my said eldest sonne suffers my daughter, the Lady Stanley, and her heirs, quietly and peaceably to enjoy one house and land called the Brickills, which she purchased of me, but if my said sonne or his heirs doe make claim or title to the said Brickills, and either of them Interrupt or trouble the possession or Title of my said Daughter, then I will that my eldest sonnes children or any of them shall not have the said Tenements or Lands in Chelsey, but my said Daughter, the Lady Stanley, and her heirs shall have them.'

STANLEY HOUSE (OR GROVE), 1890.

This will is dated July 18, 1643, and Lady Gorges died four days afterwards. Her daughter subsequently married her cousin Theophilus, Earl of Lincoln, and she is probably the Countess of Lincoln buried at Chelsea on May 5, 1675.

On August 24, 1643, the Committee for the Advance of Money assessed the estate of Lady Elizabeth Stanley at £60; but, on April 26 of the following year, ordered the assessment to be discharged, and her goods re-delivered, as she could receive no rents from her remote estates in Lancashire and Oxford.

Sir Charles Stanley ' of Chelsea,' son of Sir Robert, is also buried in the old church. His portrait at Knowsley, probably by Robert Walker, was exhibited at South Kensington in 1866, and said to have a distant view of Stanley House in the background. Mr. George Scharf, however, in his catalogue of the Knowsley pictures, calls this alleged view, 'a castle gateway among trees and distant hills,' seen ' through an open window to the right.'

Stanley House (or Grove) remained in the possession of Sir Robert Stanley's widow and her descendants until 1691, when William Stanley the last male in direct line died. It was then rebuilt (though left unfinished and unoccupied for some years), a few yards to the north of the original site. In 1887 the foundations of the first house were partially exposed. The next occupant we hear of is Henry Arundell in 1724, and a Thomas Arundell, of Stanley House, Chelsea, is mentioned in the report of a trial for violent assault in the *Monthly Chronicle*, May 20, 1729. Admiral Sir Charles Wager, to whom there is a monument by Scheemakers in Westminster Abbey, died there in 1743. Then we find that a Miss Southwell, who married Lord Chief Justice Eyre, sold this place, in 1777, to the Countess of Strathmore, an enthusiastic botanist. The Countess built extensive conservatories and hot-houses, and stored them with a valuable collection of exotics. The miserable story of this lady's sorrows, after her unfortunate marriage with a rascal named Bowes, is related by Jesse Foot, and also at some length by Faulkner.

The Countess sold Stanley House to Mr. Lochee, of the Military Academy at Little Chelsea; and among its subsequent occupants we find Richard Warren, M.D., who died in 1797, Mr. Leonard Morse, of the War Office (died about 1815), and William Hamilton, British Envoy at the Court of Naples, and a famous virtuoso. He built a large hall on the east side, and the casts from the antique mentioned below are still in their place.

In a letter of Miss Burney's, September 24, 1821, we read:

' Luckily the house rented by Mrs. Gregor from William Hamilton, Esq. (who accompanied Lord Elgin into Greece), abounds with interesting specimens in almost every branch of the fine arts. Here are statues, casts from the frieze of the Parthenon, pictures, prints, books, and minerals, four pianofortes of different sizes, and an excellent harp. All this to study Desdemona (that's me) seriously inclines, and the more I study, the more I want to know and see. In short, I am crazy to travel in Greece.'

20

DOORWAY IN STANLEY HOUSE.

Theodore Hook, who lived at Egmont Villa, Fulham, noted, in his journal, his attendance at ' W. Hamilton's party, Stanley Grove,' on July 5, 1826.

About 1828 this house was occupied by the Marquis of Queensberry, and in 1830-1831 by Colonel Grant (at a rental of £1,000 a year). Finally, in 1840, Mr. Hamilton sold the house and grounds to the National Society (for £9,000), who built there, after the designs of Mr. Blore, a training-school for teachers known as St. Mark's College. The first principal was the Rev. Derwent Coleridge, son of Samuel Taylor Coleridge and brother of Hartley Coleridge, a man of high culture, who inherited some share of the family genius. The present principal is the Rev. G. W. Gent, M.A., who succeeded

CREMORNE HOUSE, 1789.

the Rev. Canon Cromwell in 1888. Stanley House, which is in excellent condition, and but little altered, is used as the principal's residence. The view from the upper windows, before the Cremorne and Ashburnham estates were cut up for building, was very pleasing, and admired by the late Matthew Arnold as one of the finest in London.

CREMORNE HOUSE.

Westward of Sir Thomas More's house was a piece of open land called the West Field, separated from the lands on the east by Hob Lane, which led from the World's End to the river-side. This lane, now marked by Seaton Street, is mentioned in an indenture in the Cadogan Records :

20—2

> '20th of January, 1620. Sir Arthur Gorges, Knt., and Lady Elizabeth, his wife, demised to Blanch Kingston, daughter of Sir Richard, late of Chelsea, dec^d, a messuage, with a long shed ; the back of the said messuage abutting upon an orchard belonging to Sir Lionel Cranfield, late in the tenure of the same messuage, and the highway commonly called Hob Lane.'

The lane is mentioned also in the verdict of the Court Leet, 1681 :

> 'We present there is an ancient cart-way to and from the land of Samuel Bishop, poulterer, lying in the West Mead of this Manor, leading by Hob Gate to the north-west corner of the said Land.'

The messuage, which was very small, is not marked on Hamilton's survey, but is shown in a view of Chelsea, 1759. Near to it, about 1740, Theophilus, Earl of Huntingdon, built a villa known as Chelsea Farm. He died in 1746, and his widow (Lady Selina Shirley, daughter of the Earl Ferrers), lived in the house for about two years longer. This lady is well known for the important part she played in the great religious movement originated by John Wesley, and is sometimes called the ' Queen of the Methodists.' During her life she founded more than sixty chapels, and was the principal patron of George Whitfield. Howel Harris brought him to Chelsea in 1748, and on several occasions he preached at Chelsea Farm. On August 21, 1748, Whitfield writes :

> ' I received your Ladyship's letter last night, and write this to inform you that I am quite willing to comply with your invitation. As I am to preach, God willing, at St. Bartholomew's on Wednesday evening, I will wait upon you the next morning, and spend the whole day at Chelsea. Blessed be God that the rich and great begin to have hearing ears.'

He also writes of another reception at Chelsea :

> 'On Tuesday I preached twice at Lady Huntingdon's to several of the nobility. In the morning the Earl of Chesterfield was present ; in the evening the Lord Bolingbroke. All behaved quite well and were in some degree affected. Lord Chesterfield thanked me and said : " Sir, I will not tell you what I shall tell others, how I approve of you," or words to this purpose. Lord Bolingbroke was much moved, and desired I would come and see him the next morning. I did, and his lordship behaved with great candour and frankness. All accepted of my sermons, and seemed surprised, but pleased. Thus the world turns round. " In all time of my wealth, good Lord, deliver me."'

It must be to some later occasion that Bolingbroke refers in writing to his friend, Lord Marchmont, in November, 1748 :

> ' I hope you heard of me by myself, as well as of me by Mr. Whitfield. This apostolic person preached some time ago at Lady Huntingdon's, and I should have been curious to hear him. Nothing kept me from going, but an imagination that there was to be a select auditory. That saint, our friend Chesterfield, was there, and I heard from him an extreme good account of the sermon.'

Walpole wrote to his friend Montagu upon these matters in his usual jeering strain :

'Whitfield preaches constantly at my Lady Huntingdon's at Chelsea; my Lord Chesterfield, my Lord Bath, my Lady Townshend, my Lady Thanet, and others, have been to hear him. What do you lay that next winter he is not run after instead of Garrick?'

At the end of 1748, Lady Huntingdon left Chelsea Farm and took a house in Park Street, in order to give Whitfield better opportunities, and there he preached twice a week.

Chelsea Farm was sold to Richard, Viscount Powerscourt (d. 1751). He

CHELSEA FARM, 1829.

was succeeded by the Countess-Dowager of Exeter, widow of Brownlow, the eighth earl. Then came Sir Richard Lyttleton (d. 1770), the friend of the poet Shenstone, who addressed a poem to him on his marriage with Rachel, the Dowager-Duchess of Bridgwater (d. 1777).

Thomas Dawson, Baron Dartrey (created Viscount Cremorne in 1785) was the next occupant. He enlarged the house, and made many alterations in it, from the designs of James Wyatt, an architect of the pseudo-classic taste. Chelsea Farm, afterwards known as Cremorne House or Villa, had little or no architectural merit. Faulkner's and other views represent a building without any claim to beauty, but the grounds about it were fine and richly wooded. They are mentioned by Hassell in his 'Excursions on the Thames' (1823):

> 'Lord Cremorne's park is seen on the right, protruding considerably into the Thames, with the mansion at the upper end of the grounds ; abundance of noble elms, ash and oaks, enrich its area, and impart classical effect to its scenery.'

Cremorne House may be regarded as one of the last of the great houses that gave dignity to Chelsea, and its park one of the last 'spreads of fine home scenery' that beautified it.

Lady Cremorne is celebrated in the 'Percy Anecdotes' as the best mistress of a household that ever lived, and there are many references to her goodness and gentle nature in Mrs. Carter's memoirs. This lady, the translator of Epictetus, addressed several short poems to her friend and her children. In one of these, written in 1795, she addresses her as

> 'Friend of my soul ! with fond delight each hour,
> From earth to heaven I see thee urge thy race,
> From ev'ry virtue crop the fairest flower,
> And add to Nature ev'ry waning grace.'

Lady Cremorne enjoyed the particular friendship of Queen Charlotte, who often visited her at Chelsea. One of these visits is mentioned by Mrs. Carter in a letter to Mrs. Montague, 1791 :

> 'I perfectly subscribe to all your encomiums of the Queen and the Princesses. I had the honour to be an eye-witness of the truth of them two days before I left town, when I received Her Majesty's command to attend her at Chelsea.'

Bryan says that Lady Cremorne resided at Chelsea the greater part of the year, and kept a large establishment. She was greatly liked in the parish, as she gave her household special orders to patronize the local tradesmen as far as was practicable. Every year, too, she gave an entertainment to all the school-children in the parish, and these entertainments were repeated whenever Queen Charlotte visited Cremorne House.

Viscount Cremorne died in 1813, leaving no surviving issue either by his first or second wife, and his titles of Baron Dartrey and Viscount Cremorne became extinct, but his other title, Baron Cremorne (created 1797) devolved on his great-nephew. His 'Villa of Chelsea Farm' he bequeathed absolutely to his wife.

Philadelphia Hannah, Lady Cremorne, was the great-grand-daughter of William Penn, founder of the State of Pennsylvania, and was born in its splendid capital, after which she was named. When she died in 1825, she bequeathed her estate in Chelsea to her cousin, Granville Penn. He resided there for some years, and put it up for sale in 1826-27 and 28, but it was bought in on each occasion.

A large but not very notable collection of paintings at Cremorne House was sold by auction in 1827. Faulkner gives the complete list, in which we find views of Chelsea Farm and Battersea Bridge by De Cort of Antwerp, with others by the same hand, and important stained-glass window by Jarvis,

THE STADIUM, 1831.

examples by Teniers, and Copley's fine copy of Correggio's masterpiece, ' The Communion of St. Jerome,' bought by the painter's nephew, the celebrated Lord Lyndhurst.

Cremorne House was at length purchased by Charles Random de Bérenger, Baron de Beaufain, who established here a ' National Club' for the cultivation of ' various skilful and manly exercises, being a British arena for such pursuits.' It was named the Stadium.

In the *New Sporting Magazine* for 1831 we read :

' The Club is to be divided into three branches. No. 1. The department for cultivating perfection in shooting generally. No. 2. For aquatic pursuits, sailing, rowing, swimming, fishing, waterfowl shooting and bathing. No. 3. The department for general purposes, and for investigating improvements. Its care, says the prospectus, will be to promote, by a variety of means, all matters connected with the manly, skilful, or useful exercises, not already set forth, such as fencing, archery, riding, driving, skating, coursing, hunting and racing.'

There is an interesting lithographed view of the grounds, with the members engaged in these various exercises, published by the proprietors at the Stadium, May 28, 1831. A portion of it is here reproduced.

In a letter to the Earl of Lichfield, March 3, 1838, the Baron, in asking for Government support, states that the Stadium had 'engrossed alike his attention and his means for the last eight years.' This forerunner of the Hurlingham and Ranelagh Clubs was still flourishing in 1841; in a handbook to Chelsea published in that year we read that 'galas are likewise given here on a most magnificent scale, which are patronized by most of the nobility.' The name of this club has been perpetuated in one of the recently-built streets, Stadium Street.

In 1845 the estate was opened as Cremorne Gardens. These never acquired the aristocratic reputation enjoyed by Ranelagh Gardens in the previous century, but after some years of disreputable existence, became such a nuisance to the neighbourhood that they were closed on October 4, 1877. The grounds are now almost entirely built over, and nothing remains to recall the varied associations of the spot but some grottoes and plaster figures in Messrs. Wimsett's nursery, and the large gates at Mr. Bowden's brewery, near Stanley Bridge. Dartrey Road and Cremorne Road, however, preserve the name of the best-remembered owner of the estate.

ASHBURNHAM HOUSE.

To the west of Chelsea Farm, Dr. Benjamin Hoadley built a house in 1747, consisting, says Faulkner, 'of a centre and two wings, being joined on the west by a noble conservatory, built in the antique style.' Antique marble busts of the Emperors Galba and Domitian flanked the principal entrance on the south side; and statues of Flora and Ceres adorned a fine lawn, shaded by a noble cedar, and studded with evergreens, magnolias, orange-trees and various flowering shrubs.

Dr. Hoadley was the eldest son of the famous bishop, who lived at Winchester House, and must be included in the long list of eminent physicians who have made Chelsea their home. On his death the house was bought by Sir Richard Carr Glynn, who in turn sold it to the Earl of Ashburnham, whence it became known as Ashburnham House.

Dr. Cadogan, another eminent physician, was the next inhabitant. During the three years he occupied it, the garden became interesting to the medical faculty for the large number of medicinal herbs planted by him.

Lady Mary Coke, the youngest daughter of John, Duke of Argyll, succeeded Dr. Cadogan. In 1786, Mrs. Carter wrote:

> ' Lady Mary Coke has purchased Lord Ashburnham's house, next to Lord Cremorne's, at Chelsea. She has had a great deal of vexation and expense at Notting Hill, which, after all she has done, is tumbling down. One may venture to say of her new abode that, in the style of Mr. Christie [the auctioneer], she will have a most agreeable vicinage.'

After the death of her husband, Lord Coke, eldest son of the Earl of Leicester, some amatory passages seem to have taken place between her and the Duke of York, brother of George III. She always protested that he had contracted an undeclared marriage with her. This was an easy object of ridicule for the wits and would-be wits of the day, and Walpole, especially, has many a jest at the expense of poor ' Mary à la Coque,' as he calls her.

She lived at Ashburnham House for about ten years, and was succeeded by a Mr. Joseph Brown, a Mr. Stevens, and lastly by the Hon. Leicester Stanhope, who became Earl of Harrington.

The grounds were about ten acres in extent, well planted with fine trees and shrubs. About 1862 they were opened as a place of public amusement. The Balloon Tavern, at the angle of Lots Road, was named after a captive balloon which made daily ascents from these grounds.

The Ashburnham Nursery, School, and Road preserve the memory of this estate, now entirely built over.

In front of Ashburnham House were the Lots, about four acres in extent, originally a part of the manor, over which the parishioners had Lammas rights. They are mentioned in the ' Perticular Booke of the Chelsey Manor,' 1544 :

> ' De prefato Bernerdo p. redd iiij^{or} pcell prat voc lez lotte p. a. ... ... ij^s.
> De Johe Patynson p. . . . . vij lotte prate jac in occiden campo
> de Chelsey, &c. [with other holdings] ... ... iiij^{li} vj^s viij^d.'

These Lots were afterwards assigned to Sir Arthur Gorges in lieu of his rights in the Common Pasture. They are now occupied by wharves, saw-mills, etc.; but we have the name preserved in Lots Road.

West of Ashburnham House was Ashburnham Cottage, which, with three acres of garden, belonged to Mr. Edward Burnaby Greene, a gentleman ' well known in the regions of Parnassus,' says Faulkner. He was the author of several poetical paraphrases and imitations, as well as some original poems, all of which appeared with the initials E. B. G. He was the brother of Admiral Sir William Burnaby, whence, perhaps, comes the name of Burnaby Street, close at hand, and assumed the name of Greene on inheriting the property of an uncle, a brewer of Westminster. Here afterwards lived Eliza Gulston, an amateur etcher and artist, who executed a number of drawings, coats-of-arms, etc., for Faulkner. She was industrious, too, in the collection of materials for his ' History of Chelsea'; and one of her letters, concerning Shrewsbury House, has already been quoted. In a letter to the Earl of Buchan, May 3, 1814, preserved in Mr. Mayer's interleaved copy of Faulkner's ' Chelsea,' where there are one or two of her etchings, she claims to have been a descendant of Vandyck.

DANVERS HOUSE.

According to Lysons (' Environs,' ii., p. 123), Sir John Danvers, knt., held lands in Chelsea, to the annual value of £60, in the reign of Queen Elizabeth. He refers to the Harleian MS. No. 1711, in which is a paper entitled ' Syllabus Liberorum Tenentium cujuslibet Hundredi in Com. Midd., an. 17 et 18 Eliz.,' with some others relating to the same subject. I have carefully examined this manuscript, but have found no reference to Danvers. The statement is highly improbable, for Danvers (born about 1588) was still a child when Elizabeth died ; and the amount of the assessment implies a much larger estate than he possessed in Chelsea at any time.

In June, 1618, we find Thomas, Earl of Lincoln, writing to Sir Clement Edmonds to request him to procure the delivery to Sir John Danvers of 'the writings relating to the lands called Moorhouse, in Chelsea, which he has sold to him.' This letter raises some difficulties. Henry, Earl of Lincoln, who had purchased from Sir Robert Cecil the estate formerly belonging to Sir Thomas More, had died two years before, and Chelsea House had passed to his son-in-law, Sir Arthur Gorges. The writer of the letter was the son and successor of that earl, who, although disinherited as regards the house, would appear to have inherited at least a portion of the landed property in Chelsea ; for besides the sale alluded to, we find that he sold the Ferry at Chelsea to William Blake in the same year.

The name ' Moorhouse' naturally suggests the idea that Danvers House was the home of Sir Thomas More ; and, as Aubrey clearly shows, Danvers himself thought so. But it seems to me that the most probable explanation of the name is that the ' Moorhouse' was that messuage leased to Alice More in 1543. It is thus described in the lease :

'Unum messuagium in Chelsey cum pertinentis in Comitatu nostro Midd', quondam Mewtes ac nuper in tenura Edwardi Barker at Edmundi Middelton et modo in tenura rectoris ecclesiæ parochialis de Chelsey; Quod quidem messuagium cum pertinentis fuit parcella terrarum et possessionum nuper dicti Thome More militis de altu proditione attincti, ac in manibus nostris ratione ejusdem attincturæ modo existunt.'

The lease was for twenty-one years, and the rent twenty shillings and twopence, being twopence more than the last tenant paid.

The Earl of Lincoln's letter, however, mentions lands only; and the house inhabited by Danvers was evidently leased from Mr. Shuckborough. A paper relating to an exchange of 'pues' in Chelsea Church between Sir John Danvers and the Countess of Nottingham, 1626 (Add. MSS., British Museum, 11,056, f. 290), says:

'The r^t wor^ll Sr John Danvers, b^t was likewise possessed and did use one other pue or seate belonging to Mr. Shuckborough's house, wherein he now lives.'

Again in the list of proprietors of common for 1647, we find:

'Mr. Shugbury, for two houses; one called the dog [now the Rising Sun], the other Sir John Danvers.'

In 1645, the Committee for the Advance of Money assessed Christian, the widow of —— Shugborow, of Chelsea, at £200, and she was ordered to be brought into custody to pay her assessment. In July of the following year, however, she deposed that £35 was the full third (the proportion payable) of her revenue, and that all debts paid, her personality, except desperate debts, was not worth £100. She was accordingly discharged from further liability on the payment of this £35.

Danvers appears to have altered or rebuilt this house on a grand scale, but at what date I have been unable to discover. Among the Additional MSS. at the British Museum is the rough draft or copy of a letter from Lady Gorges, complaining of Sir John's workmen, who had attempted a robbery on her premises. Unfortunately it bears no date; but as it mentions the Earl of Lincoln being disturbed in his sleep, it must be anterior to 1615, the date of his death. Nicholas Stone, the best English sculptor of his time, wrote in his Diary (1622?):

'Unto Sir John Danvers at Chelsey I made the statues of an old man and a woman, and a diall, for which I had 7 li. a piece.' (Walpole, Anec., i. 241.)

The new house was evidently a building of some architectural pretension. It stood in what is now Paulton's Square, which, before being thus laid out, was a nursery ground in the occupation of a Mr. Shepherd. In September, 1822, extensive remains of the house were discovered—the foundation walls, a large bath, fragments of columns, capitals, etc. As they occupied considerable space, Mr. Shepherd considered they were too extensive to be preserved, and caused them to be covered up again. They are therefore still *in situ*.

Aubrey, whose grandmother was a Rachel Danvers, says:

> 'The chimney-piece in Sir John's chamber was the chimney-piece of Sir Thomas More's chamber, as Sir John himself told me. Where the gate is now, adorned with two noble pyramids, there stood anciently a gate-house, which was flatt on the top, leaded, from whence was a most pleasant prospect of the Thames and the fields beyond, and in this place the Lord Chancellor More was wont to recreate himself and contemplate.'

The garden extended from what is now the King's Road nearly to the river bank, and enjoyed considerable celebrity. Sir John is believed to have introduced the Italian taste in gardening into this country, and the gardens of Danvers House were a fine specimen of the style. They are described in a paper among the Ashmolean MSS., which has not yet been printed.

Sir John Danvers was the youngest son of Sir John Danvers, of Dauntsey. Joined to a 'harmonical mind,' he had a goodly person and 'complexion so exceeding beautiful' that Thomas Bond, of Ogborne, his companion in travel, says that people 'would come after him in the street to admire him.' These qualities combined would, as Dr. Donne puts it, 'have promised him acceptance in what family soever or upon what person soever he had directed his affection.' Accordingly, when he was little more than twenty, they secured a wife for him in the person of Magdalen Newport, the widow of Richard Herbert, of Montgomery Castle, and an excellent lady. Her age was more than double his, a fact quaintly commented on by Donne:

> 'As the well tuning an instrument makes higher and lower strings of one sound, so the inequality of their years was thus reduced to an evenness, that she had a cheerfulness agreeable to his youth, and he a sober staidness conformable to her more years. So that I would not consider her so much more than forty, nor him so much less than thirty at that time; but as their persons were made one, and their fortunes made one by marriage, so I would put their years into one number, and finding a sixty between them, think them thirty apiece, for as twins of one hour they lived.'

By her first husband she had seven sons and three daughters, or, to quote Donne again, 'Magdalen Newport, as a flower that doubles and multiplies by transplantation, multiplied on leaving her father's house into ten children.' The most famous of her sons were Lord Herbert of Cherbury and George Herbert of Bemerton.

This lady deserves to be placed among the many noble ladies whose lives have graced the history of Chelsea. Everything that is recorded of her redounds to her honour; her wit, her piety, her hospitality, and her care for the poor. One of the most intimate of her friends was Dr. Donne, Dean of St. Paul's, whose mother was a descendant of Sir Thomas More; another was Bacon, Earl of Verulam, of whom we catch a glimpse in the 'curious garden' at Chelsea. On one occasion he fainted there after a long walk. 'Lady Danvers rubbed his face, temples, etc., and gave him cordial water.

As soon as he came to himself he said, " Madam, I am no good foot-man." '

Lady Danvers died in 1627, the year following the terrible visitation of the plague, during which Chelsea suffered so severely. Her burial is recorded in the register :

> ' 1627. Magdalen Danvers, wife of Sir John Danvers, buried the 8th of June.'

The funeral sermon was preached in the old church by Donne, and is a remarkable example of his style—full of quaint conceits and fancies. Isaac Walton was there, and saw the good Dean weep with the fervour of his discourse and the memory of his lost friend.

In the year following Danvers married Elizabeth, daughter of Ambrose (son of Sir John) Dauntsey, and thus came into possession of the estate of Lavington in Wiltshire. Here he indulged his taste for gardening on a scale even more extensive than he had at Chelsea. His second wife died in 1636. Several children were the fruit of this marriage. Among the baptisms in the Chelsea register we find :

> ' 1629. Elizabeth, daughter of Sir John Danvers and Elizabeth his wife. May 1st.'
> ' 1631. Mary, daughter of Sir John Danvers. Sept. 29.' [The notice of her burial occurs on June 25, 1638.]
> ' 1532[-3]. Charles, the son of Sir John Danvers. Feb. 1.' [He died an infant, and was buried on the 7th of the same month.]

Sir John's third marriage is recorded in the Chelsea register :

> ' 1648. Sir John Danvers and Mrs. Grace Hewit. Jan. 6.'

Sir John Danvers has been generally described as a spendthrift who dissipated his means by extravagant living. There is ample evidence that he was a very bad financier, and constantly struggling with money difficulties; but there are other causes besides his extravagance to account for this. He held at different times several Court appointments, but both James I. and Charles I. were bad paymasters, from whom the Court officers obtained their salaries with difficulty, and frequently after long arrears had accumulated. Thus, in 1620, we find Sir John writing to the Duke of Buckingham, begging his help to obtain payment from the King. Again, in 1623, he wrote to Secretary Conway that he had often petitioned for the payment of his pension, and had received gracious replies from the King, Buckingham, and the Lord Treasurer, but nothing had been done. He asserts that he has neither money nor credit left, and entreats speedy payment for his relief. Probably he only received more 'gracious replies,' for three years after we find him borrowing £30 from the parish, and in 1629 another £10. The parish books recorded that he honourably paid interest for these loans at the rate of 8 per cent. per annum until he repaid in full in 1655. Further difficulties were in store for him. In 1644, the Parliamentary Committee for the Advance of Money, having sequestrated the estate of Angel Gray, of the Temple and Kingston Marwood, found that Danvers had owed Gray the sum of £3,000 since 1641, and called upon him for immediate payment. This he was unable to do, as his Wiltshire estates lay under the King's quarters, and nothing was obtainable thence. However, in the course of time he succeeded in paying off two-thirds of the debt, but as the balance was not forthcoming, the County Commissioners of Middlesex reported that on May 12, 1653, they 'sent in and seized and inventoried all Danvers' goods in his house at Chelsey, and took security for them, but they are claimed by Judge Atkins on a bill of sale at the suit of Wm. Toome for a debt of £2,000.' The judge's claim was set aside, and the Commissioners reported again on November 25 that they had levied and received the £1,000 balance of Danvers' debt.

Much unmerited obloquy has been cast on the memory of Sir John Danvers by previous Chelsea historians, for the share he took in the political events of his time. Early in life he had shown a disposition to resist the arbitrary conduct of the Crown. In 1624 he heard that the Government intended to seize the papers of the Virginia Company, and with the aid of the secretary he caused the whole of them to be copied out and placed under the care of his friend Lord Southampton. In 1636 he took part in the Chelsea protest against the levy of ship-money, and three years later refused to contribute towards the expenses of the King's expedition to put down the rising of the Scots. In 1640 he sat in the Short Parliament as member for Oxford University. When the Civil War broke out in 1642, he took up arms for Parliament, and received a Colonel's commission, but took little or no part in the military operations. The opening incidents of the struggle are described by him in several letters to his friends written from Chelsea in July and August, 1642. His brother Henry, Earl of Danby, who had often been a isitor at Danvers House, died in 1644, and left the whole of his property, valued at £1,500 a year, to his sister, Lady Gargrave. Danvers immediately took steps to dispute the will. He petitioned Parliament to set it aside, on the ground that he was deprived of his inheritance because of ' his affection and adherence to Parliament.' A committee was appointed to inquire into the matter, and, after long and careful consideration, decided in favour of Danvers' petition, and eventually, on October 9, 1649, the House resolved ' That Sir John Danvers, from this time, have the benefit of so much of the proper estate of the Earl of Danby, both real and personal, as is sequestrable, until the same shall be compounded for.'

Meantime Danvers was taking a leading part in the momentous events of the time. He was ordered by Parliament to receive the Dutch Ambassadors at Chelsea in 1644; elected member for Malmesbury in the room of Anthony Hungerford in 1645; in 1648 he sat on the trial of Charles I., and signed the death-warrant; and in February, 1648-9, he was appointed a member of the Council of State. He held this position for one year only, his re-election being negatived in February, 1649-50, by forty votes to thirty-four.

Sir John Danvers died a natural death at his house in Chelsea in April, 1655, and was buried at Dauntsey. Echard says he died a professed Papist, and Bate thinks that Fuller, who often preached before him in Chelsea Church, led him to repent of the part he had played in the Revolution.

Fuller preached the funeral sermon over Danvers' eldest son Henry, who died in 1654. He bequeathed the whole of his estate in his power to Ann, daughter of his sister Elizabeth, who had married Sir Henry Lee, of Ditchley. Her daughter Elinor married the Earl of Abingdon, who thus came into possession of a remnant of the property.

The baronetcy became extinct in 1796.

Danvers House was purchased by the Hon. T. Wharton, who thus had his sister, the Countess of Lindsey, for a near neighbour; but I have not found the date of the transfer. He was in Chelsea, however, at least as early as 1674, when 'Esq. Wharton' appears among the proprietors of common for the house called 'the Goat' in Little Chelsea. In 1683 we find he was amerced two shillings by the Court Leet 'for an encroachment on the highway by a wall next the Goat.'

Wharton was one of the leading Whigs of the day, and of course reaped a full harvest of abuse from the political scribes of the other side. Bolingbroke calls him 'the scavenger of his party.' Swift, who had some personal disappointment to colour his opinion, sums him up as 'a Presbyterian in politics and an atheist in religion.' He was undoubtedly a man of ability. Dr. Percy says he wrote 'Lilliburlero,' the famous political song which Sterne's Uncle Toby was always whistling, and which was said to have 'sung a King out of three kingdoms,' referring of course to the precipitate flight of James II. in 1688. The stirring music (a 'Quickstep,' composed by Purcell in 1687) is still sung by Orangemen in the north of Ireland and by the peasants of Sussex.

Burns used this old song as the foundation of his 'Castle of Kellyburn Braes.'

Wharton seems to have left Chelsea in 1705 (the year of his sister's death), when the great stable in Church Lane was converted into a playhouse. Part

of the ground had been cut off in 1696, as we learn from the name-plate on a
house at the south end of Danvers Street :

'This is Danvers Street, began in yᵉ year 1696 by Benjamin Stallwood.'

This house was originally a fine large building, the Bell Inn, shown in
Preist's view, 1738. One of the old houses at the south end has an early
association with the practice of inoculation for the small-pox on the plan
of Baron Dimsdale. Faulkner quotes the following advertisement (about
1764) :

'Inoculation at Chelsea. Mr. Reid having taken into partnership Mr. Peake, Surgeon

HOUSES AT CORNER OF DANVERS STREET, DEMOLISHED 1889.

and Apothecary, the business of Inoculation will be carried on as usual at the house in
Danvers Street, where Mr. Peake constantly resides.

'The Apartments are pleasant and commodious ; and Patients are inoculated, and
attended with the utmost care and Tenderness, for Ten, Five, or Three Guineas, according to their choice of accommodation.'

Mr. Alexander Reid was assistant surgeon at Chelsea Hospital, and a
friend of Smollett.

J. Dobbin, the water-colour artist, was living at 4, Danvers Street in
1843.

Wharton became Marquis of Wharton in 1714, and entirely gave up the Chelsea property. The Goat, now the Goat in Boots, already belonged to Sir Hans Sloane in 1713 ; and Danvers House was demolished in 1716.

Wharton's sister, Lady Philadelphia Lockhart, widow of Sir George Lockhart, of Carnworth in Scotland, died (July 3) and was buried at Chelsea in 1722 (Mawson's Obits, College of Arms MSS.).

LINDSEY HOUSE.

About 1611 there came to England a famous physician, Theodore Turquet de Mayerne, a native of Geneva, previously Court-physician to Henry IV. and

LINDSEY HOUSE IN 1750.

Louis XIII. of France. He was well versed in chemistry, and imported this knowledge into his prescriptions, a revolution in medical practice which exposed him to the abuse and derision of the faculty of his day. His first residence was in St. Martin's Lane, but he afterwards came to Chelsea and built a house on the site of the present Lindsey Row. The date of his coming is not known ; but it seems that he was in Chelsea at least as early as 1639, when the burial register records the death of one of his servants. His daughter Elizabeth was born in 1633 ; and as no record of her baptism is found in the

22

Chelsea register, we may infer, perhaps, that it was between that year and 1639 that he settled in this parish. This daughter married the Marquis de Cugnac, a French Protestant who immigrated to this country. She died soon after her marriage, at the early age of twenty-three. A tablet to her memory stands in the old church.

Sir Theodore—he was knighted by James I.—only survived his daughter by two years. His portrait prefixed to his works, taken in the last year of his life, represents him as still a fine man, and his death in 1655 is said to have been due to the effects of bad wine. He was buried at St. Martin's-in-the-Fields. During his long life he served four Kings as chief medical adviser— the two French monarchs already named, and James I. and Charles I. of England. His manuscripts are preserved in the Sloane Collection at the British Museum and Ashmolean Library at Oxford. They contain ample material for a history of the medical science of his time, but have not yet been edited.

Four years after his death another daughter married another French Protestant. In the Chelsea marriage register we find this entry :

'1659. The Rt. Hon. Armand de Coumond, Lord Marquis de Montpolion and Mrs. Adriana de Miherne.'

Some time after this the house was sold to the Berties. Montagu Bertie, second Earl of Lindsey, has been named as the purchaser; but I cannot find that he had any connection with Chelsea. He died at Campden House, Kensington, in 1666. His son Robert, third Earl, was already in possession in 1671, when the following notice occurs in the register of baptisms :

'1671. The Lady Elizabeth Bartie, daughter to the Right Hon. Robert, Earl of Lindsey, Lord Great Chamberlain of England. June 23.'

He rebuilt or repaired the house in 1674 or 1675. Sir Christopher Wren has been suggested as the architect ; but no design or drawing for it is to be found in the collection of his drawings preserved at Oxford. The sketch here given (taken from a drawing in the Moravian Archives at Herrnhut) differs somewhat from that in Kip's view of Beaufort House and grounds. In this house the first performance of an Italian opera in this country is said to have taken place.

The Earl of Lindsey died in 1701 ; the family retained possession of the house until 1750, but do not appear to have again lived there, although the name of the Countess of Lindsey, Chelsea, appears among a list of peers, peeresses, etc., summoned to Court in 1716 (Coke MS., Melbourne Hall). Several important persons, however, occupied it in the meantime. After the death of the Earl of Lindsey the house was leased to Ursula, Countess

Dowager of Plymouth, and her son, Lord Windsor. Various entries concerning them occur in the parish registers. Among the marriages we have:

'1703. Thos. Lord Windsor, Visc. Blackwater, in the Kingdom of Ireland, and Charlotte, Lady Dowager Jeffries.'

This Lady Jeffries was the widow of that infamous judge whose bloody career after the battle of Sedgemoor has made his name a synonym for all unjust judges. The register of baptisms gives us:

'1704. Ursula, daughter of Lord Viscount Windsor. Dec. 2.'
'1706. Thomas Philip, son of Lord Viscount Windsor. February 7.'
'1707. Herbert, son of Lord Viscount Windsor. May 1.'

This last succeeded to the title, and was the last to hold it.

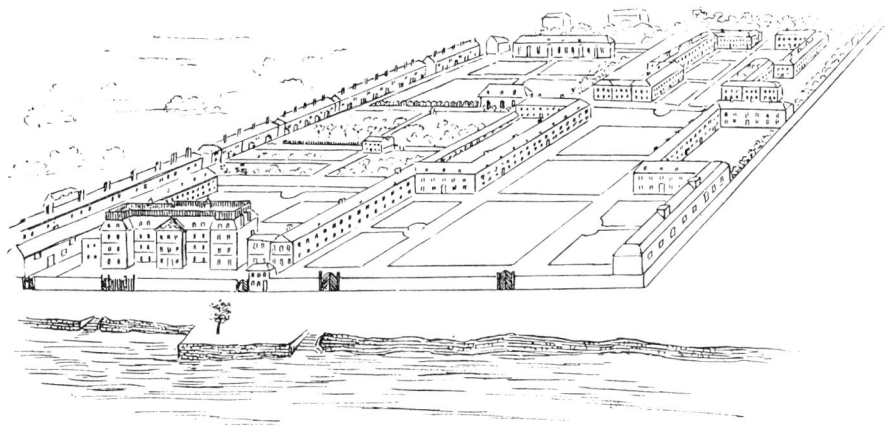

PLAN OF 'SHARON.'

Lindsey House was next in the occupation of Francis Seymour, Lord Conway. His third wife, Charlotte, was the sister of Lady Walpole, and their son Francis, afterwards Marquis of Hertford, was born at Chelsea; in the register we read:

'1718. Francis, son of Francis, Lord Conway, Baron of Ragley, and Charlotte, Lady Conway his wife, born July 5, and baptized August 2 following.'

In 1750 the Duke of Ancaster (the Earl of Lindsey had been so created in 1718) sold Lindsey House to Nicholaus Ludwig, Count von Zinzendorf, 'a colossus of faith in the midst of the cold unbelief of the eighteenth century,' who intended to establish in Chelsea a Moravian settlement under the name of Sharon. Negotiations were opened for the purchase of the site left vacant by the demolition of Beaufort House, but they fell through. The stabling of

22—2

Beaufort House was converted into a chapel; Lindsey House was renovated in excellent taste, and a portion of the grounds of Beaufort House laid out as a cemetery.

John Wesley, writing to Professor Liden, on November 14, 1769, says:

'The Count's house at Chelsey is a palace for a prince. Truly they are wise in their generation.'

The autograph of this letter, which gives many interesting particulars of the condition of the Methodists at that time, is preserved among some 'Observations détachées sur l'Angleterre dans les Années 1788-90' in the Bibliotheca Bruckmanniana.

LINDSEY HOUSE AS RENOVATED BY COUNT ZINZENDORF, 1750.

These good Christian people, as remarkable for their goodness of heart and strict morality as for their extreme simplicity of manners, lived together as one large family. It is, perhaps, only in the natural course of things that they were much assailed and ridiculed in their early years. The Chelsea colony did not prosper, and the house was chiefly used as a pilgrim home for the Herrnhutters, as they were originally called, passing through the country. Count Zinzendorf himself lived there whenever he was in England. His death in 1760 undoubtedly injured the prospects of the society, and ten years later they sold Lindsey House. However, they continued to worship for some years in the chapel now used as a boys' school. The burial-ground was specially excepted from the Burials Act of 1855, because the brethren bury but one person in a grave, and that very deeply. At a recent synod (1888) it was decided to recommence their services in the chapel at Chelsea.

This burial-ground is itself an impressive illustration of the simplicity of the sect ; it is laid out in four square parts, the married males separated from the unmarried, and so with the female members. Each grave is covered with a flat stone, bearing simply the name and age of the deceased. James Gillray, father of the caricaturist, was for forty years the sexton, and was buried among the brethren (1799). His famous son was born, perhaps, in Chelsea, in

MORAVIAN CHAPEL AND BURIAL GROUND, 1890.

1757, when his father was an out-pensioner of Chelsea Hospital. There can be no doubt that his boyhood was spent in Chelsea, and a square opposite the burial-ground, formerly called Strewan Square, has recently been renamed Gillray Square, on the suggestion of Sir Charles Dilke. Among the Moravians buried at Chelsea are Count Henry the 73rd of Reuss ; Petrus Bœhler, 1770, one of their most celebrated missionaries ; William Hammond, 1783, author of ' The Marrow of the Gospel ;' Benjamin La Trobe, 1786, and his son the Rev. C. J. La Trobe ; James Hutton, 1795, whose character is portrayed in Fanny Burney's novel of ' Cecilia,' under the name of Albany ; James Frazer, 1808, who had made no less than fifty-six missionary voyages ; and Christian

Renatus, 1832, the only son of Count Zinzendorf. In the south-west corner of the cemetery, separated from the graves of the chosen, is the memorial-stone, with inscription now illegible, of one of the brethren who committed suicide.*

After the house was sold by the Moravians in 1770, it was considerably altered; the gables were taken down (though the finely proportioned roof was otherwise left intact), and the house itself partitioned into five separate dwellings. It is shown thus divided in a view engraved by Malcolm in 1809. Since then it has been still further altered; the fronts have been plastered over, and the easternmost house has had bays built out through its whole length. The last house and its neighbour have been formed into one for the Hon. Miss E. Egerton.

There are still remains of the original house scattered through the different portions. Number 97 contains what is probably the original staircase, broad and substantial, with a handsome balustrade. In the next house, 96, are some fine oak-carvings dating from the seventeenth century.

Since the division Lindsey Row has had several notable residents. Sir Mark Isambard Brunel, the engineer of the Thames Tunnel, lived for a long time in the centre house, as also his son, another celebrated engineer. In the next house lived Joseph Bramah, the inventor of the famous lock and the hydraulic press. John Martin, K.L., the painter, whose remarkable compositions were at one time regarded as truly sublime, and who counted the Prince Consort as a frequent visitor to his studio, lived near; the remains of a fresco on the garden wall still exist, as a memorial of his occupation. The painter's brother, William Martin, died at Chelsea on February 15, 1851, presumably in this house. This remarkable person, one of the strangest characters of modern times, styled himself 'The Philosophical Conqueror of all Nations,' and claimed to have discovered the secret of perpetual motion. He exhibited his machine in 1821, when it failed as a matter of course. He also published 'A New System of Natural Philosophy, in Refutation of Sir Isaac Newton and other Pretenders to Science.'

Henry Constantine Jennings, a connoisseur, who ruined himself by his passion for collecting, was a neighbour (in the easternmost house of the Row). He was a descendant of 'La Belle Jennings,' Duchess of Marlborough, and suggested the formation of the famous collection known as the Marlborough Gems. He came to Lindsey Row in 1792. James Abbott McNeill Whistler, the

* The views of Lindsey House, the Moravian Chapel, and the plan of the proposed settlement, are taken from 'The Moravians in England,' by E. M. C., and published by special permission.

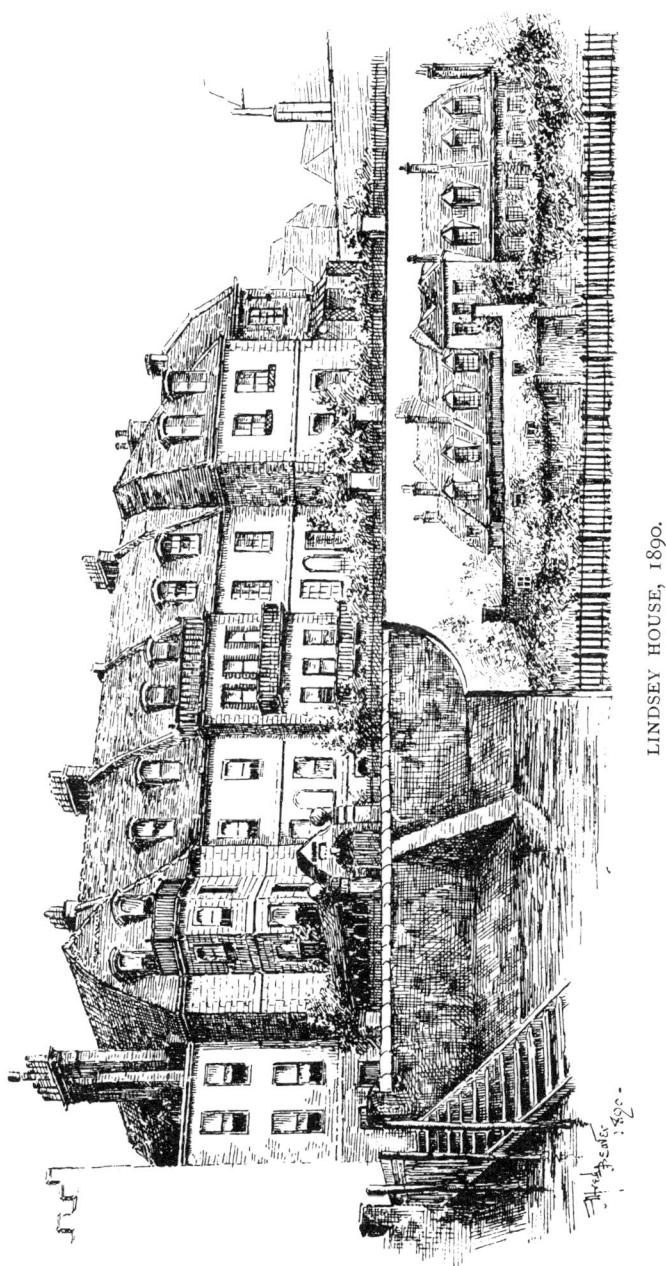

LINDSEY HOUSE, 1890.

famous painter and etcher, whose nocturnes, symphonies, and arrangements have had so great an influence over the younger generation of painters, lived at No. 96. The hall was for some time painted with masts and sails, the work of his hand. The Earl of Buckinghamshire (died 1804) also lived in Lindsey Row.

No one passing over Battersea Bridge can fail to be struck by the fine proportions of this group. Thus we find Mr. Percy Fitzgerald writing:

'Opposite the boat station stands a most remarkable and imposing building, now cut up into many tenements. The fine roof, the stately proportions, the dignified windows, all point to a mansion of the greatest pretension.'

Belle Vue House was the residence of Mr. Charles Hatchett, an industrious student of chemistry and metallurgy, of whom Faulkner gives a somewhat lengthy account. He had here a small collection of good pictures (including a portrait of Mrs. Hatchett by Gainsborough), and an extensive library. Belle Vue House was built by Mr. Hatchett's father in 1771. For many years this house was inhabited by Mr. W. B. Scott, the painter-poet, and friend of Dante Rossetti. During his occupation the house was a museum of almost every species of articles of vertu — a fine collection of Blake's valuable drawings and pictures by the old masters, an extensive collection of rare first editions of the English poets, interesting specimens of Mr. Scott's own work, and that of his brother, David Scott, a gifted and ambitious artist, besides engravings, pottery and china, carvings and old armour. All were sold by auction in December, 1889. The house was then taken by the celebrated anatomist, the late John Marshall, F.R.S., who died in December, 1890.

At Belle Vue Cottage lived Luke Thomas Flood, a respected justice of the peace for Middlesex, and a generous benefactor to the parish. Flood Street has borne his name since 1865, and every year a service in memory of his benefactions is held in St. Luke's Church on 'Flood's Day.' Mr. J. T. Crossley, Q.C., now lives in this house.

The houses beyond Lindsey Row—from Milman Street to World's End Passage—were formerly called Lindsey Place, in the easternmost house of which lived Paul Bedford, the comedian.

This portion of the riverside, though unkempt and neglected and lacking the surroundings of trees and meadows, yet gives us some idea of what old Chelsea was once like. Mr. Seymour Haden and Mr. C. W. Sherborn (of Stonyhurst, King's Road, Chelsea) have both made very interesting etchings from it.

THE NEW MANOR-HOUSE.

As we have already stated, Henry VIII. acquired the Manor of Chelsea by exchange with William, Lord Sandys, the King's Chamberlain. In consideration of the surrender ' of the manor of Chelshith, and of divers lands and tenements in Chelshith and Padyngton, Midd.,' the King granted to Lord Sandys, K.G., and to Margery, his wife, ' the site, etc., of the late priory of Holy Trinity, Motisfount, Hants, and the church, churchyard, messuages, etc., of the said priory, and the mansion of Motisfount-cum-Fride, *alias* Motis-

THE NEW MANOR-HOUSE, OR CHELSEA PLACE.

phount Bentley, etc.' The King's grant is dated July 14, A⁰ 28 Henry VIII. (1536), and Sandys' charter of concession May 28 in the same year. Henry acquired other lands in Chelsea from the Abbey of Westminster (1536), from Thomas Keyle (1539), and Robert White (1542).

Having obtained the manor, Henry soon set about building a new manorhouse, possibly because the old one was neither large enough for his needs, nor luxurious enough for his tastes. We get the exact date of the commencement

23

of the new building from a warrant (January 1, 1536-7, six months after the exchange) to pay Anthony Dennye £2,000 to be employed on buildings at 'the King's manors of Westminster, Chelsey, and Hakeneye.' This accords with a statement that the King found the new place suitable for the residence of his daughter Elizabeth, and sent her here when she was three or four years old, and it is probable that a considerable portion of her girlhood was spent in Chelsea.

The architecture of the earliest portion resembled that of St. James's Palace, built about the same time. From Dr. King's MS. we learn that it adjoined Winchester House, and extended eastward as far as Don Saltero's coffee-house, both subsequent buildings.

In 1540 Sir Francis Bryan was appointed 'Keeper of Chelsey' for life, and we may probably take this appointment as marking the completion of the mansion or palace. Three years later, when Henry married Katherine Parr, Chelsea Place became part of that Queen's jointure, and after the King's death she came to live here. She was a woman of high culture for those times, and corresponded with the new King, Edward VI., in English, French, and Latin; she also wrote pious works—'Prayers and Meditations' and 'Lamentations of a Sinner.' It is, therefore, easy to understand why she was entrusted with the education of the Princess and of Lady Jane Grey.

Very shortly after the death of the King, Katherine began a secret courtship with a former suitor, Thomas Seymour, Lord Admiral. Seymour, who was mercenary and unscrupulous, had no love for the Queen, but hoped to use her as a lever to his ambition.

On the Queen's side, the engagement appears to have been one of affection, of which we find evidence in the following letter:

'My Lord,—I send you moost humble and harty comendations, beyng desyrous to knowe howe ye have done syns I saw you. I pray you be not offended with me in that I send soner to you than I sayd I wold. For my promys was but one in a fourtened. Howbeyt the tyme is well abrevyated, by what means I know not, except the weakes be shorter at Chelsey than in other places. . . .

'I wold not have you to thynke that thys myne onest good wyll towards you to procede of any sodayne motyon of passyon. For as truly as God ys God my mynde was fully bent the other tyme I was at lybertye to marye yew before any man I knewe. Howbeyt God withstode my wyll theryn most vehemently for a tyme, and through his grace and goodness made that possible whyche seemeth to me most impossible, that was, made me to renownce utterly myne owne wyll, and to follow hys wyll most wyllingly. Yt were too long to wryte all the process of thys matter. Yf I lyve I schall declare yt to you myself. . . . By her that ys yours to serve and obey duryng her lyfe,
'Kateryn the Quene. K. P.'

Seymour persuaded her to marry him secretly within two or three months of the King's death; the date is not known, as the marriage was not avowed until some time afterwards, and Seymour kept up a succession of clandestine visits to his wife at Chelsea. It says something for the audacity depicted in his countenance that he should thus have dared the nightly dangers of Chelsea fields and woods. In another letter the Queen gives him directions for his coming:

'When it shall be your pleasure to repair hither, yᵉ must take some pain to come early in the morning, that yᵉ may be gone again by seven o'clock, and so I suppose yᵉ may come without suspect. I pray you lett me have knowledge over-night at what hour yᵉ will come, that my porteress may wait at the gate to the fields for you. By her that is, and shall be, your humble, true, and loving wife during her life,
'Kateryn the Quene.'

Notwithstanding their caution, the secret gradually leaked out, and on May 17, 1548, Seymour wrote to his wife how Lady Herbert, his sister, 'waded further with me touching my lodging with your Highness at Chelsea, which I denied lodging with your Highness, and this point stood with her for a long time, till at last she told me further tokens, which made me change colour, who, like a false wench, took me with the manner.'

When Seymour came to live openly at Chelsea Place, he subjected Princess Elizabeth to a course of persecution which seems to have been deliberate, and designed so to compromise her that she must, perforce, eventually agree to his aims. At length matters came to a crisis. Katherine, suspecting her lord, came suddenly upon him, and found the Princess in his arms. A recriminatory scene followed, and about a month after Whitsuntide, 1548, Elizabeth was removed to Cheshunt. All this was disclosed at the evidence given at Seymour's trial, and is printed in the Burleigh Papers.

The princess, then a girl of fourteen, is portrayed in the poem called 'Throckmorton's Ghost,' supposed to have been written by Nicholas Throckmorton, cupbearer to Katherine:

'Elizabeth there sojourning for a time,
Gave fruitful hope of blossoms bloom in prime.
For as this lady was a princess born,
So she in princely virtues did excel ;
Humble she was, and no degree would scorn
To talk with poorest souls she liked well.
. . . .
If some of us that waited on the Queen
Did aught for her, she passed in thankfulness.
I wondered at her answers, which have been
So fitly placed in perfect readiness.
She was disposed to mirth in company,
Yet still regarding civil modesty.'

Katherine only lived a few months after the rupture, and died at Sudley on September 5, 1548, not without a suspicion of poison. A few months later her husband was charged with treason, and, without any real trial, brought to the block on March 20, 1549. The death-warrant was signed by his own brother, Edward Seymour, Duke of Somerset, and 'Protector of the Realm,' who himself, in January, 1552, less than three years after, was executed for high treason.

The death of the Protector was the climax of a long series of plottings fomented by Queen Katherine's successor in Chelsea Place, John Dudley, created Earl of Warwick, and afterwards Duke of Northumberland. The Manor of Chelsea must have been given to him shortly after the Queen's death, for we find him surrendering it A° 5 Edward VI. (1551). On March 13 of the same year it was granted to his son John, Earl of Warwick. Proofs of the residence of this family in Chelsea are to be found in a letter in the Record Office from the Earls of Wiltshire (Pawlet, afterwards Marquis of Winchester) and Warwick, dated from Chelsea, November 5, 1551; a letter from the Duke of Northumberland, dated Chelsea, November 23, 1552; and another to the King's Commissioners of Sales (Harl. MSS., 284, 76), dated Chelsea, January 17 (no year given), recommending Sir John Ransford to them for the purchase of a piece of land lying by his park pale, which another person was about to buy out of his hands. On March 2, 1553, the Manor of Chelsea was once more granted to the Duke in exchange for the Manor and Castle of Tonbridge with appurtenances.

After the execution of Somerset, the Duke of Northumberland became the chief power in the State. His fourth son, Lord Guildford Dudley, had married Lady Jane Grey, great-grand-daughter, on her mother's side, of Henry VII. This noble-minded and highly-educated lady had passed some time in Chelsea Place under the care of Katherine Parr, and on her death Seymour made great efforts to keep her in his own hands, doubtless hoping to make some use of her in the struggle for power in which he was one of the first to fall. It was now her evil fortune to be made the most unwilling instrument of her unscrupulous father-in-law in his boldest bid for power. The King's health was visibly failing, and Northumberland persuaded him to set aside the claims of his two sisters, Mary and Elizabeth, as well as those of Mary of Scotland, and name the Lady Jane as his successor. Shortly afterwards Edward VI. died, but the attempt to place Lady Jane Grey on the throne met with little response in the nation, and Northumberland, Lady Jane, her husband, and many more paid for the failure with their lives. All Northumberland's property was, of course, confiscated, but the Duchess obtained a re-grant of Chelsea Place, where she died in January, 1555, having survived her husband less than eighteen months. Her will mentions 'the green and gold hangings in the gallery in the Manor House, waterside, Chelsea, with my lord's arms and my own,' with many other luxurious articles of furniture and apparel.

Again the history of this house is somewhat involved. According to the Cadogan title deeds, it was granted in fee on April 11, 1557, to John Caryll, who sold the property to James Basset on June 1 of the same year. There is no known record of Basset's surrender; but in July following we find from the Heralds' account of the funeral of the Lady Anne of Cleves, that she died 'at the King and Quene's Majestie's Palace at Chelsey.' To overcome this difficulty Lysons conjectured that Caryll's grant related to the *old* manor-house, but this is a point on which we have no information. The lady who took her repudiation by Henry VIII. so philosophically was possibly a visitor at the time, as she may have been when the manor was held by her Master of the Horse, the Duke of Northumberland; there is no record of any grant to her. Besides the Heralds' account of the funeral, we have another con-temporary account in the diary of Henry Machyn, which is less known:

'1557. [The xvj day of July, died the Lady Anna of Cleves, at Chelsea, sometime wife and queen to King Henry the] viij[th], but she was never crounyd, butt [remained] in England, and she was seyryd the night following (*i.e*, cered, wrapped in wax cloths). . . .

'The [xxix of July] sam day began the hers at Westminster for my lade Anne of Cleyff, with carpynters worke of vij prensepalles as goodly a hers a . . . .

'The iij day of August my lade Anne of Cleyff, sum time wyff unto kyng Henry the viij[th] cam from Chelsey to be [buried] unto Westmynster, with all the chylderyn at Westmynster and many prests and clarkes, and then the gray ames [amice] of Powlles, and the monkes of Westmynster, and my lord Bishop of London, and my Lord Abbott of Westmynster, rod together next the monkes, and then the two sekturs [executors] ser Edmond Peckham and ser Robert [this should be Richard] Freston, cofferer to the quen of England; and then my lord admerall, my lord Darce of Essex, and many knyghts and gentylmen; and afore her servandes and after her baner of armes; and then her gentyllmen and here hed offesers; and then her charett with vij baners of arms of dyvers armes, and viij baners of emages of whytt taffata, wroght with fyne gold and her armes; and so by Sant James, and so to Charying-crosse, with a c torchys bornyng, her servandes beyryng them, and the xij bedmen of Westmynster had new blake gownes; and they had xij torchys bornyng, and iiij whytt branchys with armes; and then ladies and gentyll-women all in blake, and horsses; and a viij haroldes of armes in blake, and ther horses; and armes sad [set] abowt the herse behynd and befor; and iiij haroldes baryng the iiij whytt baners; and at the chyrche dore all dyd a-lyght and ther dyd reseyvyd the good lade my lord and my lord abbott in ther myteres and copes, sensyng her, and ther men dyd bere her with a canepe of blake welvett, with iiij blake stayffes, and so browthe in-to the herse and tared dirige and so ther all nyght with lyght bornyng.

'The iiij day of August was the masse of requiem for my lade prenses of Cleyff, and dowther to William [this should be John], duke of Cleyff; and ther my lord abbott of Westmynster mad a godly sermon as ever was mad and then . . . . the byshope of London song masse in ys myter, [and after] masse my lord byshope and lord abbott, mytered, dyd [cense] the corsse; and afterward she was caried to her tomb [where] she lays with a herse-cloth of gold, the wyche lyys over her, and ther alle her hed offesers brake ther stayffes [and all] her hussears [ushers] brake there rodes, and all they cast then into her tombe ; the wyche was covered her corps with blake, and all the lords and lades and knyghtes and gentyllmen and gentell-women dyd offer, and after masse a grett [dinner] at my lord [abbott's], and my lade of Wynchester was the cheyff morner, and my lord admerell and my lord Darce whent of eyther syde of my lade of Wynchester, and so they whent in order to dinner.'

' My lady of Winchester ' is, of course, the Marchioness of Winchester, who lived at Sir Thomas More's house to the west of the King's manor-house.

A letter from Margaret, Countess of Bedford, to Sir William Cecil, dated August 9, 1557, probably refers to the Lady Anne's effects. She says she is ' going to Chelsea to see stuff and jewels there to be sold, where she wishes she might see Lady Cecil, who, however, is not likely to bestow much money, nor is she [the writer], yet her mother would have her bestow some for her lord's daughter.'

In 1559 Queen Elizabeth leased the manor for life on a yearly payment of £13 6s. 8d. to Ann, Duchess of Somerset, widow of the Protector. Thus, by the strange working of events, she came to live in the same house as her husband's great rival, Northumberland, whose Duchess had received a large share of the Duchess of Somerset's confiscated robes, etc.

The Duchess of Somerset died in 1588, and on April 15 of the next year the Queen granted Chelsey Place and Manor to John Stanhope, Esquire, for life, rendering the like rent as the Duchess had paid. In the May following he was married at Chelsea, a fact duly recorded in the register :

' 1589. Johannes Stanhope Armiger, et Margaritta Mack Williams, alias Cheecke, traxerunt matrimonium, 6 die Maii, et regni Elizabeth 31.'

The register of baptisms shows that he retained a connection with Chelsea for some years :

' 1593. Elizabeth filia Johis Stanhope armi: and Margaritæ uxoris ejus, 14th August.' [She married Sir Lionel Talmash.]
' Carolus filius Johs Stanhope armi: April 27th.' [He succeeded his father as second Lord Stanhope of Harrington.]

It is questionable, however, whether Stanhope ever lived in the manor-house. In 1592 it was granted (on the same terms) to Katherine, Lady Howard, wife of the Lord Admiral who, in 1588, had gained much glory and the gratitude of the whole nation by dispersing the Spanish Armada. But there is ample proof that Howard was living in Chelsea for some years before the grant of the manor to his wife.

Howard was a man of ' proper person ' ; and to his father's fidelity to her cause, it may be Elizabeth owed even her life. It is not surprising, therefore, that she often visited him in the house where her own girlhood had been spent. Nicholls, in his 'Progresses of Queen Elizabeth,' says that the earliest visits were in 1581 and 1585; but I have not been able to verify this statement. The churchwardens' accounts of two neighbouring parishes, however, prove a royal visit as early as 1587; the Lambeth ringers received eighteenpence 'when the Queen came to dine with my Lord Admiral at Chelsey,' and the bells of St. Margaret's were rung when she returned to Richmond. Another visit is recorded on July 5, 1588. Letters of the Lord Admiral (Harleian MSS.) are addressed from Chelsea in 1589 and 1591. The bells at Fulham celebrated a visit of the Queen in 1592; and there is proof of others in 1594 (Molyneux Papers), 1596, 1597 (Fulham Registers), 1599 (two), and 1600 (Sidney Papers).

In 1597 Lord Howard was created Earl of Nottingham for his share in the capture of Cadiz. Boissise, the French Ambassador (who had gone to plead the cause of the Earl of Essex), mentions a royal visit to Chelsea shortly after this:

PORTRAIT OF EARL OF NOTTINGHAM.

> 'Having been informed that the Queen would return to this city the day before yesterday, I went to meet her at Chelsea, where she had already arrived to dinner. The Admiral had invited me as a guest, and received me with all possible courtesy.'

There is a well-known story of a ring in which the Earl of Nottingham and his Countess are involved. Elizabeth is said to have given the ring in question to the Earl of Essex, telling him that if ever he was in trouble to send it to her, and it should intercede with her on his behalf. When committed to the Tower, the Earl bethought him of his ring, and entrusted it to Lady Scrope to give to the Queen. She gave it to her sister, the Countess of Nottingham, and the Earl forbade her to send it on. Meanwhile, Elizabeth was expecting the return of the ring, and put it down to the Earl's obstinacy when she did not receive it. She therefore allowed him to be executed. Of course the Countess confessed on her deathbed; and the Queen, roughly shaking the dying woman, exclaimed: 'May God forgive you! I never can.' The story is apocryphal, perhaps an amplification of some slight incident. Lady Cork possesses a ring said to be the very one in question; and in the Louvre is a miniature of the Countess painted by Hilliard, in which she wears a ring round her neck, doubtless in reference, says M. de Sauzay, to this 'historical fact.'

In the Sidney Papers we read that on Saturday, January 10, 1600:

> 'Her Majesty dined at Chelsea at my Lord of Nottingham's; Yt is thought that she will stay there till Monday. She took with her but the Lord of Worcester, Sir John Stanhope, and two or three ladies.'

A passage in the Cabala refers to this same visit:

> 'Thither are gone Sir R. Cecil, Lord Cobham and Sir Walter Raleigh. An opinion is held that Councillors and Offices shall be made and bestowed there, but I will not believe it. The Lord Treasurer, the Lord Keeper, Mr. Chancellor, were going to Richmond, but stay till they see what the Queen will do, and to-morrow they will go where the Queen will be.'

On February 25, 1603, the Countess died; her burial is recorded in the parish register:

> 'Catherine, the Countess of Nottingham, died the 25 day of February at Arundell House, London, and was buried at Chelsey, the 28 day of the same, whose funeralls were honorably kept at Chelsey, the 21st of March, 1603.'

The Earl was not long in marrying again. His second wife was the Lady Margaret, daughter of James Stuart, Earl of Murray. On June 12, 1603, the manor and mansion-house of Chelsea were granted to her for life. In the register of baptisms we have two entries of the Earl's issue by her:

> '1617. William, the sonne of Charles Lord Admirall. Dec. 5.'
> '1618. Margaret, the daughter of the Right Hon. Charles, Earl of Nottingham, and the Lady Margaret his wife. December 22.' [In the certificate of the death of the Countess this daughter is called 'the Lady Anne.']

In the latter year the Earl of Nottingham was eighty years old. He died in 1624, and was buried, not at Chelsea, as has been erroneously stated, but in a vault in the parish church of Reigate, where, strange to say, there is no monument to his memory. In the register of burials, however, we find:

> '1624. The 23d day of December, at midnight, was buried the Right Honourable Charles, Earl of Nottingham.'

The following inscription is on the coffin:

> 'Here lyeth the Body of Charles Howard, Earle of Nottingham, Lorde High Admyrall of Englande, Generall of Queene Elizabeth's Navy Royall at Sea against the Spanyards Invinsable Navye in the year of our Lorde 1588, who departed this life at Haling House, the 14th day of December, in the year of our Lorde 1624, etatis suæ 87.'

At length, just three hundred years after the performance of this most memorable act, a grateful country set itself to collect subscriptions, in order that a suitable monument might be erected to his memory in the church where his remains have lain so long unhonoured and unthought of.

The Countess Margaret afterwards married Sir William Mounson, Viscount Mounson of Castlemaine in Ireland. By him she had one son, Steward Mounson, who died in infancy.

The certificate of William Ryley, Bluemantle, sets forth that:

'Lady Margaret, Countess of Nottingham, daughter of James Stuart, Earl of Murray, departed this life at her house in Covent Garden, London, on Sunday the 14th August, 1639. . . . Her funeral was solemnly celebrated at Chelsey Church, where she lies in the chancel near her first husband.'

Of course the statement with regard to the Earl is an error.

In 1609 James I. granted Chelsea Place and Manor to James Howard, son of the Earl of Nottingham by his first wife, for forty years after the decease of the Countess, at a rental of £45 15s. 7d. The Countess, however, outlived him, and he never held possession, but the following baptismal and marriage entries make it probable that he lived in Chelsea:

'1597. Dñus Willmus Howard et Agneta [this should be Anna] St. John, filia et hæres Dⁿˢ St. John de Bletsoe, 7th February.'
'1605. Anna, filia dmᵘˢ de Effingham et Anna uxor. 12 October.'

The next occupant was James, Marquis of Hamilton, and Master of Horse to Charles I. By indenture, March 10, 1628, Sir William Monson and the Countess of Nottingham sold what right might remain to either of them in the property, after the death of the Countess, for £2,000 to Sir John Monson of Burton and Robert Goodwyne of Horne, Surrey. In 1636, the Marquis of Hamilton had a grant of the manor and house from the King, to be held in socage, as of the Manor of East Greenwich, at £10 yearly, and two years after Sir John Monson and Robert Goodwyne assigned their interest to Francis Vernon in trust for the Marquis of Hamilton.

The Marquis was created Duke of Hamilton in 1643. Clarendon, in his 'History of the Rebellion' (book x., sec. 158), says:

'The Duke Hambleton, who had been sent prisoner by the king to the castle of Pendennis, and had been delivered from thence by the army when that place was taken in the end of the war, had enjoyed his liberty and his pleasure at London, and in his own house at Chelsy, as long as he thought fit, that is, as long as the king was with the Scots' army and at Newcastle.'

His steadfast loyalty to the cause of Charles I. brought him to trial and execution in 1649. From the papers of the Committee for the Advance of Money we learn that on September 20, 1648, one Mary Searle informed the Committee that Duke James's own house and divers other of his houses at Chelsea, value £500 a year, were unsequestered, and on October 6 they

24

ordered that on proof being given that he had levied war on Parliament, and had thereby become a delinquent, his house, goods, rents, etc., in Chelsea or elsewhere, were to be seized and secured. From the description of the house rendered to Parliament we learn that it then consisted of:

> 'three cellars in the first floor, three halls, three parlours, three kitchens, two parlours, larders, and nine other rooms, with a large staircase, in the first story; three drawing-rooms, seventeen chambers, and four closets with garrets over part of them; and summer rooms, with a bedroom, and garden and orchard on the north side of the said capital messuage, and a court-yard on the south side thereof; and one stable, and one coach-house, three little gardens, and one parcel of ground enclosed with a brick wall, formerly called the Great Orchard, now ploughed up.'

The grounds contained over five acres.

On June 21, 1651, an information was laid before the Committee for the Advance of Money that the inheritance of Chelsea Manor belonged to William, Duke of Hamilton, brother of the late Marquis [Duke James]. He had mortgaged it to Lord Monson for £2,600, who entered into it for non-payment, and enjoyed about £400 a year. The Duke died on September 12, 1651, of a wound received in the battle of Worcester.

From the Cadogan title-deeds we find that the Parliamentary trustees sold the manor to Robert Austen, Thomas Smithby, and others, who were probably acting as trustees for the heirs of the late Duke of Hamilton; in 1657 they were joined with William, Lord Douglas, and Ann, Duchess of Hamilton, his wife, in conveying the house to Charles Cheyne, to whom in 1660 the same parties sold the manor also. Pardon for this alienation was granted to 'Charles Cheyney of Chelsey, Middlesex,' in February, 1662-3.

Lady Jane Cheyne is one of the several noblewomen whose lives have added such lustre to the record of Chelsea. Her father, the first Duke of Newcastle, had fought valiantly for the Stuart cause, and his great bravery and his victories had brought him his titles, and his daughters, Lady Jane and her sister, also defended one of his houses against the troops of Parliament until overpowered by numbers. When the Royalist outbreak was finally suppressed at the battle of Worcester, the Duke retired to the Continent, and lived in banishment until the Restoration. Lady Jane remained in England, and supplied him with money by the sale of her jewels and plate. There is an inventory of her jewels, drawn up in 1656, preserved with the Cheyne Papers in the Bridgwater Trust Office at Walkden, Lancashire. Among the items are:

> 'A neclase of pearls, wherein is 36 pearls, 725*l.*'
> 'A pare of lockets, wherein is 18 great diamonds and 16 little ones, the prise, 342*l.*'

Notwithstanding her losses and expenses, she brought her husband a great fortune. Dr. Adam Littleton mentions their marriage in his funeral sermon, or rather panegyric:

> 'And then with what Condescending, Prudence and Judicious Moderation did she make her Choice, when having through the Iniquity of the Times observ'd the Desolation made in the Greatest Families, and the little Choice then amongst those Few left of the Higher Nobility (for she resolv'd to match with no Family, which had ill-treated her King and Father, how advantageous so-ever), she suiting her Judgment to her Inclination accepted a Gentleman, yet One (besides his other Accomplishments, and the merit of his most Affectionate Respects) of an Ancient Family and a very Noble Descent, with whose Principles and Fortune she had persuaded herself of Content. And she found that Persuasion did not deceive her, having here in Chelsey lived there 14 years and few Months, as Well to her Own, as to the great Satisfaction and Joy of everybody else that knew her.'

They were living in Chelsea in 1655, two years before the purchase of the Manor-House, and Blacklands House has been named as their probable residence. It may well be supposed that Chelsea had many associations that would attract them to it. The Duke of Newcastle's uncle, the first Earl of Devonshire, had lived at Shrewsbury House (bequeathed to him by the Countess of Shrewsbury), and his aunt, the Countess, died there in 1643.

Three children were born unto Charles Cheyne at Chelsea—Elizabeth in 1656, William in 1657, and Katherine in 1658. The last-named was baptized in Chelsea Church by the famous Jeremy Taylor; two entries in Lady Cheyne's household accounts, 1656-64, refer to him:

> 'Oweing Mr. Cheyne more, what I had for Doctor Taler's chrisninge, 2*l.* 10*s.*
> Owing more, what I gave Doctor Taler at his goeing into Irland, 5*l.*'

Lady Cheyne's character was that of a true Lady Bountiful; her charity and devotion were unbounded. Like one of her predecessors in the Manor-House, Katherine Parr, she wrote volumes of pious meditations, and her only objection to Chelsea was that its nearness to London caused too great an attendance of visitors, and interfered with her devotions. In conjunction with her sister, Elizabeth Brackley, she wrote a play, 'The Concealed Fansyes,' which is preserved among the Rawlinson MSS. at the Bodleian Library. None of her works are published.

In her epitaph her husband touchingly says she never caused him any sorrow but in her death. This occurred in 1669, when she was only forty-eight years of age.

Her virtues were thus estimated by Dr. Littleton:

> 'Her Noble Father stiles her the Best of Daughters; so her Husband praises Her for the Best of Wives; Her Children rise up and call her the Best of Mothers; Her Servants (for whose encouragement and Reward she took care to the Last) own Her as the Best of Mistresses; Her Allies lookt upon Her as the Best of Friends; those that had the Honour to know Her, the Best of Acquaintances; and those that liv'd near her, the Best of Neighbours.'

An elegy on her death, written ' By a Person of Quality and Neighbour in Chelsey,' is bound up with the British Museum copy of the sermon; it contains these lines :

> ' Ye Chelsey Fields no more your pleasures boast,
> Your greatest pride is with your Lady, lost ;
> No more cry up your sweet and healthy Air,
> Now only fit for such as breathe despair ;
> Of your delightful River brag no more,
> Briny its waves, and fatal its shore ;
> Not all its Sands can count the Tears we spilt,
> Not all its streams can wash away this Guilt.'

Richard Flecknoe, the poet whose name was used by Dryden to satirize Shadwell, the poet-laureate, also has an epigram ' On the Death of Lady Jean Cheynee ' :

> ' The softest Temper, and the mildest Breast,
> Most apt to Pardon, needing pardon least,
> Whose Blush was all her Reprehension ;
> And none e'er heard her chide, or saw her Frown ;
> All Sweetness, Gentleness, and Mildness, all
> Without least Anger, Bitterness, or Gaul,
> Who scarce had any Passion of her own,
> But was for others all Compassion.
> A Saint she liv'd, and like a Saint she dy'd,
> And now is gone where only Saints abide.
> What will she be in Heaven now she is there,
> Who led so heavenly a life when she was here ?
> And who so Angelical was, what will she be
> Now she is there in Angel's Company ?
> Make much of her, ye Saints, for God knows when
> Your Quires will ever have her like agen.'

Charles Cheyne was created Viscount Newhaven in 1681 ; he made many improvements on his estate, especially in the gardens. Evelyn records a visit to them on June 20, 1696 :

> ' I made my Lord Cheyney a visit at Chelsey, and saw those ingenious water-works, invented by Mr. Winstanley, wherein were some things very surprising and extraordinary.'

' Mr. Winstanley ' was, of course, the ill-fated architect of the first Eddystone Lighthouse, destroyed with its designer in the great storm of 1703.

Viscount Newhaven married, secondly, his near neighbour, Isabella, the Dowager-Countess of Radnor, who lived in Paradise Row, at the end of what afterwards became Cheyne Row. He died in 1698.

In his will he desired to be laid by his first wife in the chancel of Chelsea Church. His estate was thus disposed of :

> ' I do will and bequeath unto the Lady Isabella, Countess of Radnor, my now present dearly beloved wife, all those arable lands, being in the east field of Chelsey, with all the buildings and tenements thereon, and such houses in the town of Chelsey as were not

settled on my son William by his last deed of marriage, to the said Countess of Radnor, my wife, during her life, and after her decease to my son William and his heirs for ever. And this bequest to the said Countess of Radnor is given only in case the Privy Seal, granted to me by King James, be not granted to her ; with this desire to my son William, that he would permit my dear wife, the Countess of Radnor, to have and enjoy one of my two mansion houses in Chelsey or Bois, with such household stuff as shall be therein at the time of my decease, if she pleases to live in the same, during her life ; being sorry I can do no more for her. Item, I do, by advice and counsel, give and bequeath all my right, title, and claim or interest whatsoever in a legacy given to my dear deceased wife's mother, by her grandmother, Lady Ogle, as by her will in the Prerogative Court may appear, unto my son William ; hoping he may sometime receive the benefit thereof without the expense and trouble of law, though I have received but little, as by some of my papers may appear. I also give and bequeath to my son William all my lands in Chelsey, commonly called Blacklands, with all edifices and buildings, and all my estate, real and personal whatsoever, in goods and chattels, lands or tenements, in England or Ireland, except what is before given, during the life of my present wife, by this will.'

His son and successor, William, had been married at Chelsea during his father's lifetime. The first marriage is thus noticed in the register :

'1675. 'William Cheyne, only son of Charles Cheyne, Esq., Lord of this Manor, and Mrs. Elizabeth Thomas, grand-daughter to the Lady Morgan, and both of this parish, were married by the Right Rev. Father in God, George [Morley], Bp. of Winton. Dec. 16.'

She died in less than two years ; and in 1680, on May 6, William Cheyne married, secondly, Madame Gertrude Pierrepoint. Lady Mary Wortley Montagu spent part of her girlhood at Chelsea with 'her beloved Aunt Cheyne.' Lord Cheyne was appointed Lord-Lieutenant of Buckinghamshire in 1712, and made his chief residence at the old family seat of Drayton Beauchamp. He resided little, if at all, at Chelsea after his accession to the title. Bowack, in 1705, mentions that Chelsea Place was then let as a French boarding-school ; and in 1712 the manor was sold to 'the father of Natural History,' Sir Hans Sloane.

A letter in the Verney MSS. from Ralph Palmer, of Little Chelsea, to Viscount Fermanagh, New Year's Day, 1712-13, says :

'Dr. Sloane is likely to be a purchaser for Lord Cheyney's whole estate and living of Chelsey ; he has been some time upon it, he was at first but about part of it.'

As we have already stated, he also bought Beaufort House, and eventually became the owner of more than half the parish. He was probably attracted to Chelsea by early associations, for in its botanic garden, then under the care of Mr. Watts, he had laid the foundation of his future greatness. After his settlement in Chelsea he bestowed this garden upon the Apothecaries' Company at a nominal rent, and contributed liberally in money to its improvement.

In February, 1742, he began to move his great natural history collection from Bloomsbury to Chelsea Place. The fame of this museum naturally brought many visitors to Chelsea, among them the Prince and Princess of

Wales in 1748. By his will he gave the nation an opportunity of buying it at about one-fourth of its value. He intended it to remain in the Manor-House at Chelsea. By a codicil annexed to his will, and dated July 10, 1749, he says :

> 'I do will and desire, that, . . . my collection in all its branches may be, if possible, kept and preserved together, whole and entire, in my manor house, in the Parish of Chelsea, situate near the Physic Garden, given by me to the Company of Apothecaries for the same purposes. . . . And I do hereby request and desire, that the said trustees, or any seven or more of them, do make their humble application to his Majesty, or to Parliament, at the next session after my decease, as shall be thought most proper, to pay the sum of 20,000*l.* unto my executors, or the survivors of them, within twelve months after my decease, in consideration of the collection, or musæum, it not being, as I apprehend or believe, a fourth of their intrinsic value, and also to obtain such sufficient and effectual means, powers, and authorities, for vesting in the trustees all and every part of my collection or museum before mentioned, in all its branches ; and also my capital manor house, with such gardens and out-houses as shall thereunto belong, and be used by me at the time of my decease, in which it is my desire the same shall be kept and preserved. . . . And that the same may be from time to time visited and seen by all persons desiring of seeing and viewing the same, under such statutes, directions, rules, and orders as shall be made from time to time by the Trustees.'

Walpole mentions the opening incidents of the purchase in a jocular letter to Sir Horace Mann, February 14, 1753 :

> 'Sir Hans Sloane is dead, and has made me one of the trustees to his museum, which is to be offered for 20,000*l.* to the King, the Parliament, the Royal Academies of Petersburgh, Berlin, Paris, and Madrid. He valued it at four score thousand : and so would anybody who loves hippopotamuses, sharks with one ear, and spiders as big as geese ! It is a rent charge to keep the fœtuses in spirits ! You may think that those who think money the most valuable of all curiosities, will not be purchasers. The King has excused himself, saying he does not believe there are twenty thousand pounds in the Treasury. We are a charming set, all philosophers, botanists, antiquarians and mathematicians ; and adjourned our first meeting, because Lord Macclesfield, our chairman, was engaged to a party for finding out the longitude. One of our number is a Moravian, who signs himself Henry XXVIII., Count de Reuss. The Moravians have settled a colony in Sir Hans' neighbourhood, and I believe he intended to buy Count Henry the XXVIIIth's skeleton for his museum !'

A letter from Ames to Mr. T. Martin on March 22 continues the history :

> 'I cannot forbear to give you some relation of Sir Hans Sloane's curiosities. The Parliament has been pleased to accept them on the condition of Sir Hans' codicil ; that is, that they should be kept together in one place in or near London, and should be exhibited freely for public use. The King, or they, by the will were to have the first offer. The 19th inst. being appointed for a committee of the whole House, after several speeches, the Speaker himself moved the whole House into a general regard to have them joined with King's and Cotton libraries, together with those of one Major Edwards, who had left seven thousands to build a library, besides his own books ; and to purchase the Harleian manuscripts, build a house for their reception, etc.'

Sir Hans Sloane's last years are feelingly described by George Edwards, F.R.S., in the preface to his 'Gleanings of Natural History' :

> 'Sir Hans in the decline of his life left London, and retired to his manor house at Chelsea, where he resided about fourteen years before he died. After his retirement to Chelsea, he requested it as a favour to him (though I embraced it as an honour to

myself), that I would visit him every week in order to divert him for an hour or two with the common news of the town, and with everything particular that should happen amongst his acquaintance of the Royal Society and other ingenious gentlemen, many of whom I was weekly conversant with ; and I seldom missed drinking coffee with him on a Saturday, during the whole time of his retirement to Chelsea. He was so infirm as to be wholly confined to the house, except sometimes, though rarely, taking a little air in his garden in a wheeled chair ; and this confinement made him very desirous to see any of his old acquaintance to amuse him. . . . During the latter part of his life he was frequently petitioned for charity by some decayed branches of families of eminent men, late of his acquaintance, who were famous for their learned works, etc., which petitions he always received and considered with attention ; and, provided they were not found fraudulent, they were always answered by his charitable donations. The last time that I saw him was on the 10th of January, 1753 ; and he died on the 11th, at four o'clock in the afternoon.'

Sir Hans Sloane was buried in the graveyard of Chelsea Old Church, where his monument, designed by Joseph Wilton, R.A., still attracts the passer-by. He had named this place of burial in his will (dated October 9, 1739) :

'I will that my body shall be buried in a decent manner in the churchyard at Chelsea, about noon, or at a convenient time of the day.'

After his death the manor was divided into two portions, the one going to Lady Cadogan, his second daughter, and the other to his daughter Sarah, wife of George Stanley, of Paultons in Hampshire. The latter left her share to her son, Hans Stanley, who died in 1780, bequeathing it to his sisters Anne, Lady Mendip, and Sarah, wife of Christopher d'Oyley, with reversion to Lord Cadogan. Thus the greater part of Chelsea is now in the hands of the Cadogan family.

After the demolition of the Manor-House about four acres of its grounds were leased to the Rev. Thomas Clare. This gentleman built a house adjacent to the Bishop of Winchester's. He made horticulture his hobby, and his garden was one of the last of the many fine ones which adorned Chelsea at different periods. They are thus described in 'The Beauties of England and Wales,' published in 1815 :

'They are laid out with an accuracy of taste that cannot too highly be commended. Mr. Clare has taken nature for his guide, and has studied the attainment of variety by means at once simple and elegant. From each devious walk and intervening plot of green sward, the clustering buildings in the neighbourhood, and every mean or ill-assimilating object, are excluded by plantations, which would seem to have been planted without design, and which are trained to assume a natural and irregular form. The straight line and fantastical parterre find no place here. Few grounds in the vicinity of the metropolis evince more decidedly the superiority of the present age in the disposal of garden scenery.
'In one part of the garden is a mulberry-tree, banked round and propped some ages back, which probably yielded fruit and afforded shade, even in the days of the "Virgin Queen."'

The original wall of the palace garden was then standing almost entire. It extended eastwards as far as Durham Mews, broken only by Robinson's Lane, now Flood Street. Remnants of the stone work of the old Tudor mansion may yet be seen in the foundations of the houses which occupy its site; doors studded with heavy nails, which doubtless belonged to the old palace, are to be found in them; and not long since there was still standing (in the garden of Mr. Druce) a bit of crumbling wall with the arch of a gateway, possibly belonging to that very gate through which Seymour passed on his daring nocturnal visits to Katherine Parr.

WINCHESTER HOUSE.

The palace of the Bishops of Winchester at Southwark was confiscated by Act of Parliament, and partly demolished in 1647; and in 1663 another Act was obtained empowering the then Bishop—George Morley—to lease out what remained.

Adjoining the new Manor-House, James, Duke of Hamilton, had built a large brick house. The authors of 'The Beauties of England and Wales' say this had existed since the fifteenth century; but they are clearly in error, for in a Cadogan MS. (mid. 17th century) it is called 'Hamilton House, a *new* brick-built house.' It was purchased for the Bishops of Winchester 'of Charles Cheyne, Esq., for the sum of four thousand two hundred and fifty pounds, and the water agreed to be kept up at the expense of the Lord of the Manor, except the pipes in the house.' By the Act of Parliament it was held to be in the diocese of Winchester. The water was supplied from an ancient conduit built by Henry VIII. at Kensington, of which Faulkner gave a view in the second edition of his work on Chelsea. This stream still runs underground, and was the cause of a subsidence of the embankment at Albert Bridge a few years ago. It is now diverted into the sewer.

Winchester House faced the Thames, and had a raised terrace in front; Oakley Street cuts across its site, and a short crescent, Winchester Terrace, perpetuates its memory. It was a plain red-brick building without a pretence of ornament, quadrangular, and two stories in height, with a tiled roof, an excellent specimen of the old English substantial and comfortable mansion. The entrance-hall was forty feet long and twenty wide. 'The great staircase at the western end of the hall,' says Faulkner, 'led to three grand drawing-rooms, which extended the whole length of the south front, and which, during the residence of the late Bishop, were splendidly furnished. The walls were covered with beautiful paper, having gold borders; the ceilings were richly ornamented in stucco work, and the chimneypieces composed of various coloured marbles, put up at considerable expense by the Bishop [North] after his return from Italy.'

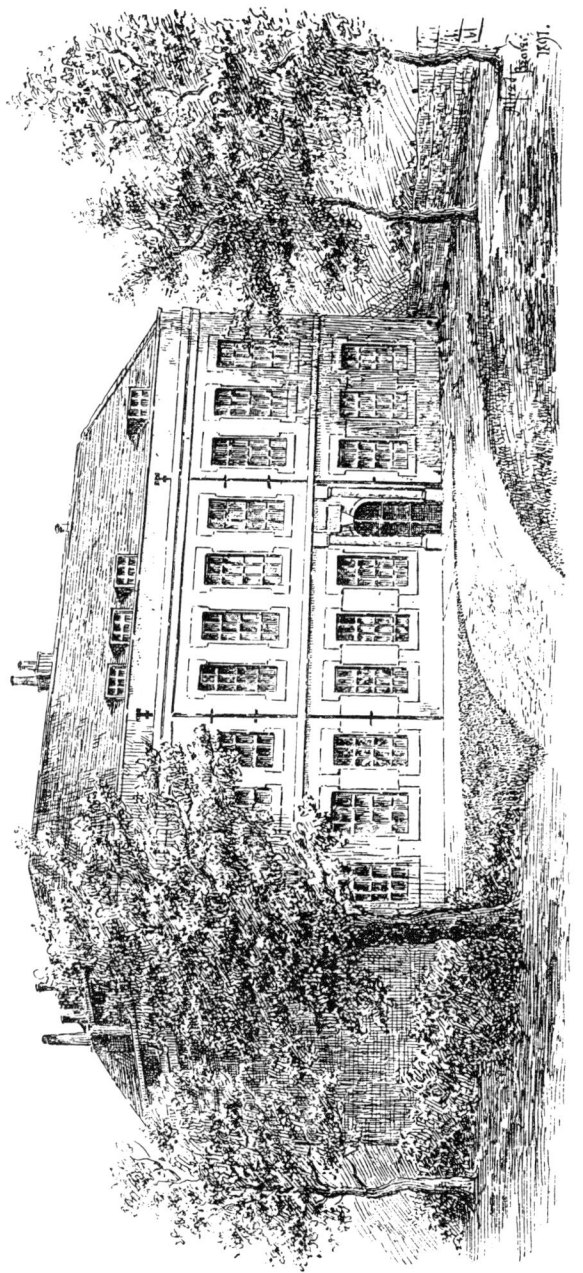

WINCHESTER HOUSE.

25

From the restoration of Charles II. until the demolition of the house eight Bishops of Winchester lived at Chelsea.

The first was George Morley, translated from the See of Worcester in 1662. In 1664 he petitioned the Crown that the fee-farm rent of £10 per annum on the house and grounds he had bought at Chelsea might be discharged; and on January 27 of the following year his petition was recommended to the attention of Lord Treasurer Southampton and the Attorney-General.

In 1678, when the Commission for taking evidence upon the alleged Popish plot of Titus Oates was sitting, the Bishop of Winchester was accused of taking part in the preparations for the supposed rising. Here is the evidence as given in the calendar of the House of Lords' MSS.:

'1678. 5 Dec. Richard Gervais is called in. He says he had heard Geo. Osborne, a bricklayer, say that about a year since, he with another plastered up about 200 or 300 arms in the Bishop of Winchester's House in Chelsea. Captain Daniell and Mr. Richard Young say that they heard Osborne say the same thing yesterday. Ordered, That Osborne attend at 3 Eod. die p.m. George Osborne, bricklayer, who lives in Harts-horne Lane, by Charing Cross, is sworn by Earl Clarendon and the Bishop of London as Justices. Being asked whether he knows anything of arms being sealed up in the house, he says that about a year and a half since, when he wrought at the Bp. of Winchester's house at Chelsea, he was employed by one of the Bp's. servants, whose name he knows not, to seal up some arms in a garret; he supposes there might be 200 muskets. Thos. Arnold, a bricklayer, assisted him. Believes he can go to the same room again. E. Clarendon is desired to write to the Bishop about this business and desire his answer. 10 Dec. Mr. Snow is directed to take Osborne and Arnold, and search the Bp's. house for arms; he is not to search trunks or boxes, but may break down walls, ceilings, or doors, etc.

'14 Dec. Ordered that Osborne and Arnold attend on Monday. 16 Dec. Mr. Snow informs the Committee that he could not find Arnold, but he left the order for his and Osborne's attendance with Osborne's wife yesterday. Ordered, that if Osborne attend not this morning, the House be moved that he be taken into custody.

'17 Dec. Osborne is called in. Sir G. Charnock informs the Committee that he had absented his lodging at Charing Cross, and that he found him at Southwark, and that he was unruly. Osborne denies it. Says that about a year and a half or two years since he and Arnold made up arms in the east end of the Bishop's house in the ceiling; they did it privately, and a gentleman, whose name he knows not, paid him; Arnold spoke to him to do it. He never worked there before nor since, nor can he now find Arnold. He withdraws. Ordered, that the House be acquainted with what Osborne said. Osborne recalled says Arnold used to lodge in St. Giles, but is not there now. Believes if he might have his liberty, he might still find him. 27 Dec. Capt. Daniell is called in. Says he knows nothing concerning arms in the Bishop's house, but that Osborne told him he walled up arms there. He withdraws.'

Here the evidence on this matter ends. There is no further reference, so that in all probability we may conclude that no arms were found at Chelsea, and that the 'evidence' given was too slight and untrustworthy even for the alarmed credulity of the Commissioners.

Morley died in 1684, and was succeeded by Peter Mews, translated from the See of Bath and Wells. Then came Sir Jonathan Trelawney, Bishop of

Exeter, 1707, the friend of Atterbury, and one of the Seven Bishops whose trial in 1688 had caused such an agitation in the nation. Charles Trimnell was promoted from the Bishopric of Norwich in 1721, and Richard Willis, Bishop of Salisbury, two years later. Willis made the Chelsea house his principal residence, and died there suddenly on August 10, 1734. His wife Isabella is buried in the north vault of the chancel of the old church.

Benjamin Hoadley, Bishop of Salisbury, succeeded him. When the house was pulled down a curious relic, supposed to date from his time, was discovered. On the plaster of a small room, at the north-west corner, were found 'nine figures of the size of life, viz., three men and six women drawn with black chalk in a bold and animated style. Of these,' says Faulkner, 'correct copies have been taken by an ingenious artist, who intends to publish them.' Hogarth, who counted Hoadley among his few patrons, and often visited him at Chelsea, was generally credited with these designs; but it must be remembered that several members of Hoadley's family were amateur artists, as is mentioned by Faulkner. It is said that Hogarth once directed a letter 'To the Doctor at Chelsea,' which, strange to say, reached the Bishop, for whom it was intended, and was preserved as a curiosity.

After Hoadley's death in 1761 came John Thomas, Bishop of Salisbury, who died at Chelsea on May 1, 1781.

He was succeeded by the Hon. Brownlow North, Bishop of Worcester, to whom Faulkner dedicated the first edition of his 'History of Chelsea,' and 'by whom,' he says, 'he was ever treated with respect and kindness.' During Bishop North's residence in Italy, he made a considerable collection of antiquities, which were disposed about the Chelsea palace. Faulkner mentions a bust of Bacchus in the great entrance-hall, a Roman sepulchral vase on the staircase, and mosaics and frescoes from Herculaneum in the drawing-room.

Madame d'Arblay, in her Diary, mentions several visits to Winchester House, during his stay. Here is a sketch of Lady North :

> '1783. July 5. My father and I went to dinner at Winchester House, Chelsea. Mrs. North was rather cold at first, and reproached me with my long absence, but soon made up, and almost forced from me a promise to go to Farnham, as the only condition of her forgiveness. She is clever, bright, pleasing, eccentric, and amusingly whimsical ; and she is also beautiful ; but her manner has something in it alarming, that seems always upon the qui vive.'
> '1784. May 7. My father and I dined at the Bishop of Winchester's. . . . The Bishop is charming, and the children are very interesting.'

Bishop North, who had taken an active interest in Chelsea during the thirty-nine years that he held the See of Winchester, died at this place on July 12, 1820. He was succeeded by Dr. George Tomline, Bishop of Lincoln.

Lady Tomline conceived some dislike to Chelsea, and this Bishop obtained the consent of Parliament to sell the premises, which were bought by the lord of the manor. The house was subsequently sold by auction and pulled down.

SHREWSBURY HOUSE.

When Faulkner wrote the first edition of his 'History of Chelsea' in 1810, there was still standing to the west of the site of the Pier Hotel a very old house, the origin of which is unknown. It was then called Alston House. Three years afterwards it was removed, and now there is no trace of it except a few remnants of garden wall, an underground passage, and an old gateway in Dr. Phené's grounds.

The first owner that we hear of is George, Earl of Shrewsbury, a Privy Councillor to Henry VIII., and one of his train at the meeting with Francis I. at Guisnes. When the rebellion known as 'The Pilgrimage of Grace' (1536-7) broke out in the North of England, after the suppression of the lesser monasteries, this Earl of Shrewsbury was named the King's Lieutenant, and, with the Duke of Norfolk, succeeded in quelling it. His sixth son by his first wife was, according to Dugdale, born in this house.

His son Francis, who succeeded to the title in 1538, is mentioned as a freeholder in the court rolls of the manor in the 35th year of Henry VIII. (1544-5). He, too, played a prominent part in the affairs of his time, and was appointed President of the Council of the North shortly after Mary ascended the throne.

One of his entries into Chelsea is mentioned by Machyn, from which we may gather that this nobleman moved about with considerable state :

> '1551. The v day of June cam to Clessay [undoubtedly it is Chelsea that is meant— Machyn's spelling is everywhere most eccentric] the yerle of Shrusbery with vij^{xx} [seven score] hors, and afer hym xl. welwett cotts and chynes [chains], and in hys owne leveray, to his plasse, and the resydew of his servandes.'

He died in 1560, and was succeeded by his son George.

Like his father and grandfather, the sixth Earl of Shrewsbury occupied a very distinguished place among the great men of his time. To his care, in 1568, Mary Queen of Scots was committed ; his lenient treatment of her induced Elizabeth to replace him by a stricter guardian, but so great was his influence, that when he demanded that Mary should again be placed under his charge, the Queen did not care to refuse him. However, he was afterwards glad to relinquish it. His wife, jealous of his attention to the prisoner accused him of an improper intimacy with her—a charge which she had afterwards to retract upon her knees. Elizabeth, to put an end to all this, gave the Earl a command in Lancashire, upon which he thanked her Majesty for relieving him of 'two she-devils.'

His wife, the famous 'Bess of Hardwick,' was at once rich, beautiful, accomplished, and ambitious. Henry Constable (c. 1590) addressed two sonnets to her, in one of which he compares her to the Virgin Mary (Harl. Misc., ix. 507). A co-heiress of her father, John Hardwick, of Hardwick in Derbyshire, she married three rich husbands, became possessed of their fortunes, and then for her fourth married the Earl of Shrewsbury, one of the

SHREWSBURY HOUSE.

richest and most powerful nobles of the day. It is quite apparent that she did not get on very well with her fourth husband, and there are a number of letters among the Duke of Rutland's MSS. referring to their quarrel. Queen Elizabeth herself undertook to reconcile them, and appears to have commanded the Earl not to leave Chelsea pending the settlement. On March 11, 1584-5, he wrote to his brother-in-law, John Manners:

'My wife, with the help of the Master of the Rolls and of her purse, has many friends, and I know not how the matter will turn out. All may be for the best, though I get little I shall be rid of my mortal enemy.'

In this, however, he was to be disappointed. A news-letter (Rutland MSS.) of July 18, 1586, informs us :

> ' It is given out that her Majestie hath reconciled the great Earle and his wief, which was solempnely don in her Highness presence, when the Lord Treasurer used som large speach in comendacion of that most gracious and Christian acte. And so we nowe say, the Erle and she, lovingly together will shortely into the countrey and make it appeare to the world that all unkindenesse arre appeased. Thus may your Lordship see that things desperate arre oftentimes recovered, and no man's hart so strong which a woman cannot make softe. It cannot but be a presage to a generall peace throughout Christendom ; for in common opinion more likely were the warres in the Low Countreys to take end than these civill discords between him and her.'

How lovingly the Earl felt towards his Countess is shown in a letter to her (Salisbury MSS.), August 5, 1586 ; after referring to the various items of reconciliation, he says :

> 'You still pressed her Majestie further that you might come to me to my house at Chelseye, which I granted, and at your coming I told you that you were welcome upon the Quene's commandment ; but that though you were cleared in her Majestie's sight of all offences, yet I had not cleared you, nor could trust you till you did confesse that you had offended me.'

Bess of Hardwick was a great builder, and erected three of the grandest houses in this country—Chatsworth, Oldcotes, and Hardwick, which still preserve their original grandeur, and remain in the possession of her descendant, the Duke of Devonshire.

The Earl of Shrewsbury died in 1590, and was buried at Sheffield. 'An Inquisition, taken at Derby, 3d of April, 33 Elizabeth, on the Death of George, Earl of Shrewsbury,' mentions 'one capital messuage, etc., in Chelsea, county Middlesex,' among his possessions ; but the value is given with his other estates in a gross total of £800 a year.

There is a reference to the Chelsea house and its furniture in the Harleian MS. No. 6,853, Article 88, which is entitled, 'The pticulers of sutch thinges as were taken from me Elinor Breton by [Gilbert] the [seventh] Earle of Shrewsburye and his servauntes,' with the Earl's answers to the charges. The tenth count in the plaint is :

> 'There were taken out of a wardrobe nere Charinge Crosse, certaine hangings, turkey carpetts, ffeather bedds and other stuffe wch my lord [the late Earl] bestowed upon me to furnishe my howse at Coleherbert wth all to the valewe of ...   ... vj li' [£600].

To this the Earl of Shrewsbury answers :

> 'Theis pticulers were my lord my fathers howsehold stuffe appointed cheifelie for his howses at Chellseye & Coleherbert and ptlie used when he attended at the Courte both of good valewe, rytche and honourable, farr unfitt for the Comp^{lts} base qualitie,' etc.

The house at Chelsea appears to have been bequeathed by the sixth Earl to his widow, Bess of Hardwick, who survived him seventeen years, and bequeathed all her estates to her son William by her second husband, Sir William Cavendish.

This son was created Baron Cavendish, and afterwards Earl of Devonshire, by James I. He died at Hardwick in 1625. His widow appears to have constantly resided at Chelsea; the burials of several of her servants are recorded in the register, and among the Duke of Devonshire's MSS. are several 'Household Books for Chelsea.'

Some time after her death the house became the property of the Alstons. Mary Alston died here in 1670-71. Dr. Littleton preached the funeral sermon, and upheld her as an ideal wife:

> 'Shall I tell you of her conjugal affection, and her chast conversation coupled with fear? who, besides the advantage of a great Fortune, brought that to her husband, which was a more valuable Portion, a lowly Mind; paying that constant respect to his Person, and that due submission to his Pleasure, and that sure Friendship to all his Concerns, and demeaning herself so humbly, as if she had brought him nothing but her Vertues?'

Sir Joseph Alston, knt., was buried at Chelsea on May 31, 1688.

Dr. King, in his letter to Hearne, alludes to this mansion as 'The Old House of Mes Butler's, lately Mes Woodcock's School House.' From the burial register we find that 'Robert Woodcock, a native of Upton-on-Severn, and kept a school at Chelsey,' was buried at the old church in 1710.

The house was subsequently in the possession of the Tates, an old family in Chelsea, who at one time owned considerable property in the parish. It was eventually converted into a stained-paper manufactory.

In Lloyd's *Evening Post* and *British Chronicle* for August 21, 1771, we read:

> 'The large mansion house at Chelsea, built by Lord Chancellor More, who was beheaded on Tower Hill as long since as the reign of Harry the eighth, is to be converted into a distillery, and buildings erected in the garden behind the house for the feeding of a large number of swine.'

This passage undoubtedly refers to Shrewsbury House, then generally supposed to have been the home of Sir Thomas More. Beaufort House had been demolished some thirty years before.

A subterranean passage connected with Shrewsbury House has been described by Miss Gulston in a letter to Miss Tate:

> 'I have found an old man now living at Chelsea, who worked at the paper manufactory when a lad, and who has established the facts. I have always been laughed at when I mentioned the story. I have gotten two drawings of the room and passage.
> 'The entrance to this passage was from the room used by the paper stainers as a drying place. It had no fireplace in it; the dimensions were nearly as follows: 25 feet high, 50 long, 36 wide; the ceiling was strung with beams, to sustain the upper floors, but without any plastered ceiling. You descended into it by a wide winding staircase, through a circular top-door, strongly fortified with rivets and four large hinges; this door was so contrived that it opened far enough back to hide the approach to the hole, and

could there be fastened so as to have the appearance of belonging to the large room, and the circular steps leading to it caused the more deception.

'The side walls are all brick. This man never could proceed with a light more than a distance of thirty yards, when the light invariably went out. The passage is free from any incumbrance of earth, or from any part of the side walls having given way ; as far as could be ascertained, its direction was towards the river.

'It is regularly paved with two flag stones, having a border of six inches of earth ; width 3 feet, length 5½ feet.

'This passage was discovered owing to the proprietor having been robbed of a quantity of paper for years. The man now alive volunteered to detect the thief; the paper was found in the staircase descending to the passage.'

This passage still exists. An entrance to it has been discovered in the grounds of Cheyne House. It has been partially explored by Dr. Phené, F.S.A., and found to agree very closely with Miss Gulston's description.

Shrewsbury House was an irregular brick building, forming three sides of a quadrangle, and having one story above the ground-floor. It had one great room, 120 feet long, which had been wainscotted with carved oak. Another room, apparently designed for an oratory, was painted in imitation of marble, probably a late 'improvement.' Some badly-used portraits on panel were found and destroyed. As they not improbably represented the former owners of the mansion, and so possessed historical if not artistic interest, their destruction is much to be regretted.

The garden-walls were embattled, and a portion still exists in Dr. Phené's grounds. This remnant contains the old gateway mentioned by Faulkner and Bryan, and has been very carefully restored by Dr. Phené. Carlyle has an interesting note upon another portion in his ' Shooting Niagara : and after ?' written in 1867 :

'Nothing I know of is more lasting than a well-made brick—we have them here, at the head of this garden (wall once of a manor park), which are in their third or fourth century (Henry Eighth's time, I was told), and still perfect in every particular.'

CHEYNE WALK AND NEIGHBOURHOOD.

The Manor-House, Winchester House, and Shrewsbury House, those gray homes of our fathers, have long since yielded to the 'eternal law of metamorphosis'; and now the three old-fashioned terraces which rose about their sites—Cheyne Walk, Cheyne Row, and Upper Cheyne Row—with their air of quiet and homely, unpretentious comfort, are gradually falling before the modern spirit of indifference to the picturesque and the rights of posterity. Even after Don Saltero's famous coffee-house had passed away, after the Yorkshire Grey had succumbed to the fate that befel the watermen who frequented it, and the new embankment had swept away the old river-wall and the path under the screen of weather-beaten trees, Cheyne Walk still recalled to Mr. Percy Fitzgerald the effect of a bit of Dutch canal, to Mr. Hare, 'more than anything else outside Hampton Court . . . . the time of William and Mary,' while to Dr. Martin it was 'the most old-fashioned, dignified, and impressive spot in all London.' Since they wrote there have been further losses, and unless the modernizing spirit is checked or dies out, there is a prospect of losing this old row, with its rich store of memories. Nearly

CHEYNE WALK, 1750.

a dozen houses between Flood Street and Manor Street, including the quaintly designed Gothic house, have been pulled down; and, farther westward, two old taverns have been lost, the Magpie and Stump by fire, and the Cricketers by expiration of lease. A huge ugly block of chambers now occupies the site of the last and its neighbours. Several old houses at the corner of Lawrence Street have also gone to make way for the new Cheyne Hospital for Incurable Children; but in this case we may at least congratulate ourselves upon getting a building in excellent taste and harmony with its

26

surroundings to replace them.   The old houses in Cheyne Walk had, it must be admitted, little or no architectural pretensions, but they possessed that species of picturesque beauty that only comes of age, for which the buildings of to day are only too often a very poor substitute.

The loss of the old weed-grown river-wall, overhung by the fringe of grand old trees, growing at the very water's edge, was too great not to be regretted by all lovers of the picturesque.   It had attracted the pencils of Peter de Wint and John Varley.   Turner, in his old age, had dwelt on it with loving eyes; and when it was finally condemned a score of artists hastened to preserve it for posterity, while Cecil Lawson well expressed the feelings of those who regretted their loss in the earnest picture, 'Chelsea Embankment—A Lament.' But amid all this regret there was one, from whom very different feelings might have been expected, that hailed the new order of things with pleasure.   Thomas Carlyle, who had known the old row for more than forty years before the change came, and had almost nightly smoked his midnight pipe over the river-wall, thought the new embankment the greatest improvement that had taken place in London within his memory.

This 'improvement' had long been proposed.   Faulkner tells us that in his time Mr. Handford, surveyor to the lord of the manor, drew up a plan for extending the embankment from Bishop's Walk to the Engine House, by removing the houses on the south side of Lombard Street and Duke Street. The Bill had even passed the House of Commons, but was thrown out in the Lords, on account of inaccurate wording.   It is something to be thankful for, that another scheme (by Mr. Burnell) for building a great pseudo-classic pile, which would have obliterated everything from this famous spot, was also still-born.

The Magpie and Stump, anciently the Magpye, or simply the Pye, was not a thing of beauty; but it was ancient, a remnant of the old Chelsea that was almost dead a hundred years ago; and visitors, after a long absence, would naturally look for it as one of the landmarks of the old village.   For years the Court Leet and Court Baron held its sittings in it, and there the good men and true of Chelsea drew up their presentments, amercing, impartially or otherwise, all those trespassers who overstepped their boundaries, neglected their piece of river-wall, or let the swine and cattle run at large upon the highway.   I find the tavern first mentioned in the burial register:

'1596. Mr. Coxe his man, of Kynston, was buried fro Jones of the Pie.'

Perhaps the Pie, though we are loth to think so, was one of those 'disorderly alehouses' whose keepers were brought before the Earl of Nottingham in 1608.

When James Leverett (a retired gardener after whom Leverett Street is named) died in 1663, he charged his estate with £10 to be distributed quarterly amongst the poor, and also £4 to provide a quarterly dinner for the parish

DON SALTERO'S, CHEYNE WALK, 1840.

officers. As Mr. Churchwarden Wheeler has wittily remarked in a lecture on the Chelsea charities :

'If any are disposed to save money for the poor, never forget to provide a dinner for the distributors ; it is a wonderful cement to keep things together.'

The bequest was faithfully administered, and the dinner celebrated at the old Magpye for more than two hundred and twenty years, until the tavern was burned down in 1886. The old sign still stands opposite the gaping ruin the

26—2

fire has made, and near is the topstone of the water-stairs, formerly belonging to Shrewsbury House, and worn by the feet of the many great and famous men and women who have played their parts in that old mansion.

The Cricketers in former years possessed one of the somewhat numerous signboards painted by or attributed to George Morland, the unfortunate sot who drank himself to an early and dishonourable death. This sign was in existence in 1824. 'At the above date,' says Larwood, 'this painting by Morland had been removed inside the house, and a copy of it hung up for the sign. Unfortunately, however, the landlord used to travel about with the original, and put it up before his booth at Staines and Egham races, cricket matches, and similar occasions, all of which removals, it may be presumed, did no great good to it.'

More famous, but also gone for ever, was Don Saltero's, 'six doors above Manor Street,' now a private house, No. 18, Cheyne Walk. According to the green and gold signboard which swung in front, it was opened in 1695 by one James Salter, who had been travelling valet to Sir Hans Sloane. He was living in Chelsea, and presumably in the same place, in 1685, when he was amerced by the Court Leet in £6 (as was Dr. Atterbury) 'for suffering the [river] wall opposite to his dwelling to be ruinous.' Coffee had not long been introduced, and coffee-houses were springing up all over London, when Salter opened his establishment at Chelsea. The earliest notice of it that I have been able to find is in an anonymous letter (apparently by Anthony Cope) to Moses Goodyear, of Church Place, Chelsea, 1697, which says:

'Forget me not at Salter's in the next bowle.'

Cope seems to allude to their convivialities also in another letter addressed to the same at 'Chelsey super Punch.' Steele refers to Salter's celebrity in punch-making:

'There are other things which I cannot tolerate among his rarities, as the China figure of a lady in the glass case, the Italian engine for the imprisonment of those who go abroad with it; both of which I hereby order to be taken down, or else he may expect to have his letters patent for making punch superseded.'

Sir John Cope and his son appear among 'the first generous benefactors to the Museum' which his position with Sir Hans Sloane had enabled Salter to form, and was the great attraction of his coffee-house. Steele has celebrated the Don in the *Tatler*, No. 34:

'When my first astonishment was over, comes to me a Sage of thin and meagre countenance, which aspect made me doubt whether reading or fretting had made it so philosophic; but I very soon perceived him to be of that sect which the ancients called Gingivistæ—in our language, tooth-drawers. I immediately had a respect for the man; for these practical philosophers go upon a very rational hypothesis not to cure, but to take away the part affected. My love of mankind made me very benevolent to Mr.

Salter ; for such is the name of this eminent barber and antiquary. Men are usually but unjustly distinguished rather by their fortunes than by their talents, otherwise their patronage would make a great figure in that class of men which I distinguish under the title of Odd Fellows ; but it is the misfortune of persons of great genius to have their faculties dissipated by attention to too many things at once. Mr. Salter is an instance of this ; if he would wholly give himself up to the string, instead of playing twenty beginnings to tunes, he might, before he dies, play Roger de Caubly quite out. I heard him go through his whole round ; and, indeed, I think he does play the Merry Christ Church Bells pretty justly ; but he confessed to me, he did that rather to show that he was orthodox, than that he valued himself upon the music itself. Or if he did proceed in his Anatomy, why might he not hope in time to cut off legs, as well as draw teeth ?'

This coffee-house—'where the literati sit in council'—soon became an object of curiosity, one of the features of Chelsea, which no visitor would omit seeing. Here no doubt came St. Evremond from Paradise Row, Smollett from Monmouth House, Atterbury and Swift from Church Lane, Addison from Sandford Manor-House, Steele from his house near at hand, Bolingbroke from Battersea, old Richard Cromwell 'with a most placid countenance,' Vice-Admiral Munden (who turned plain James Salter into 'Don Saltero'), fresh from the Spanish main, and many others. Benjamin Franklin mentions coming to Chelsea ' to see the college and Don Saltero's curiosities.' Franklin had a purse of asbestos, which excited much wonder at the time ; it was bought by Sir Hans Sloane, and added to Salter's museum. But the curiosities were of little value—the scourings, as it were, of his master's collection. Among them was ' a lignified hog '—otherwise a tree-root grown somewhat into that shape— given by an ancestor of Pennant the topographer. The Don himself gives the following doggerel account of his museum in an advertisement in the *Weekly Journal,* June 23, 1723 :

> ' Monsters of all sorts here are seen,
>   Strange things in nature as they grew so,
> Some relicks of the Sheba Queen,
>   And fragments of the fam'd Bob Crusoe.
> Knick-knacks, too, dangle round the wall,
>   Some in glass cases, some on shelf ;
> But what's the rarest sight of all,
>   Your humble servant shows himself.
> On this my chiefest hope depends,
>   Now if you will the cause espouse,
> In journals pray direct your friends
>   To my Museum Coffee House.'

The date of Salter's death is unrecorded, but the business was carried on by his daughter, Mrs. Hall, until about the time of George III.'s accession. It changed hands in January, 1799, and the collection was sold by auction ; the highest bid was but thirty-six shillings, for a model of the Holy Sepulchre, that stood No. 1 in the catalogue. The whole collection realized little more than £50. Some years later the ornaments of the Don's smoking-room were

CHEYNE WALK, 1810.

offered to Charles Lamb by a fellow-clerk in the East India House. After the sale the house was converted into a tavern, ' most respectably conducted,' we are assured. Mr. Bryan, who lived in Chelsea all his days, tells us :

> ' There was a subscription room, where the gentlemen met and conversed, and which was frequently visited by men of literature and science, many of whom are still living, but of late years it had lost the celebrity of former years.'

Don Saltero's was closed and rebuilt in 1867.

Apart from its three great mansions and its old taverns, the associations of this riverside terrace, which seems to us so representative of Old Chelsea, are

CHEYNE WALK, 1840.

comparatively modern. That portion now lying between Manor Street and Flood Street is marked on Hamilton's Survey (1664, corrected to 1717) ' The Great Garden, 5 ac. o r. 26 po.' Here, it has been said, was laid out one of the several mulberry-gardens which were planted in the neighbourhood of London by the direction of James I. I find no support for this statement, which has probably arisen from confusing this early attempt to acclimatize the silkworm, either with a later attempt, which will be related in its place, or with the royal mulberry-garden at Buckingham House. The houses in this part of the Walk were built at various dates. That now bearing the number four is apparently old enough to appear (but it does not) on Hamilton's corrected survey. The next block, with the exception of Queen's House, was built after the destruction of the Manor-House, subsequent to the death of Sir Hans Sloane. Westward, towards the church, most of the houses are older. Here the Walk formerly ended, but Lombard Street, Duke Street, Lindsey Row and Terrace, are all now included under the name Cheyne Walk.

The houses in Cheyne Walk are mostly unpretentious in style, but the homes of many famous men and women have endowed them with a wealth of associations, and given them a world-wide fame.

In Faulkner's time, a medical gentleman named Powell lived at No. 1. His father had been assistant to the once-notorious Bartholomew de Dominiceti, whose Chelsea establishment will be described presently.

Mr. Powell possessed a panel-portrait of Henry VIII., said to have been originally in More's house, and the work of Holbein. It was sold with Mr. Powell's effects about 1850. The house has quite recently been rebuilt 'in the Old Chelsea style.'

Sir John Goss, the famous organist and composer, lived at No. 3 for many years, not very far from his master, Thomas Attwood. Goss was an unsuccessful competitor for the post of organist to the old church in 1819, but was appointed to the new church in Robert Street when it was opened in 1824. So superior was his performance even in these younger days that it was the invariable custom of the great part of the congregation to remain to hear the concluding voluntary. The description of the organ in Faulkner was 'obligingly communicated by Mr. Goss, the organist to Chelsea New Church.' He retained this post until his appointment to St. Paul's in 1838.

No. 4 is a good example of what our great-grandfathers understood by a comfortable dwelling-house. The interior presents a wide well-staircase with handsome balustrade and frescoed walls and ceiling, in the style of Sir James Thornhill. From the top to the basement of this house there is an extraordinary and inexplicable shoot. Mr. Vaux, who resided here a few years since, had noticed similar shoots in houses occupied by Jonathan Wild and his kind. This house is distinguished as the residence of several notable persons. I can find none earlier than James Neild, a jeweller, of St. James's Street, who retired to Chelsea in 1792 with an ample fortune, to spend the remainder of his life in acts of benevolence. In 1773 he was largely instrumental in founding a Society for the Relief and Discharge of Persons im-

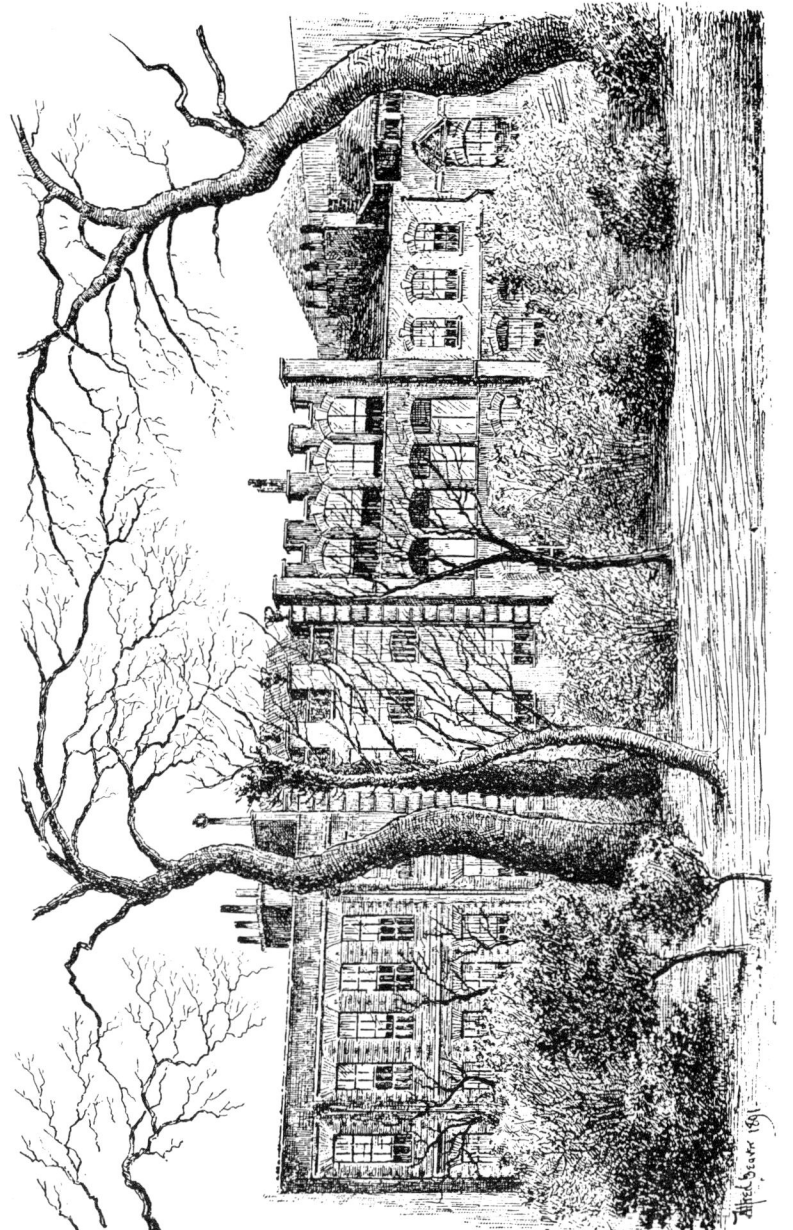

EAST END OF CHEYNE WALK, SHOWING THE HOUSE IN WHICH GEORGE ELIOT DIED

prisoned for Small Debts. The condition of prisoners was a subject that engaged him during his whole life, and in 1812 he published a quarto volume on 'The State of Prisons.' He died in 1814, and was buried in Battersea Church, where there is a monument to the memory of his wife and her father. His son, James Camden Neild, lived a useless, eccentric, and miserly life in this house for some years, and when he died, in 1852, left the whole of his property, worth half a million sterling, to the Queen, who has erected a reredos in Caen stone with stained window above to his memory in the chapel of North Marston Church, where he spent the latter part of his life.

William Dyce, R.A., lived in the same house in 1846-47, during which time he produced several of his best works. His style, though hard and ascetic, is earnest and well suited to the medium in which he worked. The frescoes in the Queen's Robing-room at St. Stephen's undoubtedly form the finest monument to his talents, and there is a very powerful cartoon for stained glass in the South Kensington Museum.

The house was afterwards the residence of Daniel Maclise, R.A., who came here to live about 1861, and remained until his death in 1870. His biographer, Mr. W. Justin O'Driscoll, tells us that in the latter portion of his life, when his health was very delicate, and he was compelled to keep his room, his favourite habit was to sit with his pencil and sketch-book at a window overlooking the river. From this window he could see the ancient free wharf or draw-dock, which disappeared with the construction of the embankment. He gives a plaintive but overdrawn account of the annoyance the wharf caused him, in a letter to the *Times*, entitled 'A Voice from Cheyne Walk':

'I write on behalf of many of my neighbours who are devoted to quiet pursuits in Cheyne Walk, Chelsea. We like the place, and foreigners like it, for I see them meandering in a mal-du-pays sort of way opposite to my gateway, and thinking with sighs how badly it represents the Cours de la Reine and the Lung d'Arno. Yet they come here as the best reminder of what they have left, and they find elm-trees bordering the river, and a really grand expanse over Chelsea Reach to Battersea Park, crowned by the heights of Clapham, and the Crystal Palace gleaming on the nearest Surrey hill.

'Yet what drawbacks are there to our otherwise pleasant situation ! There is a free wharf opposite to us, and for ever come sailing and oaring in, even in the dead of night, with peculiar cries, as they hoist or lower their masts, or do the same with their anchors, certain barges called Billy-boys, laden with every kind of material, from a brick to a balk of pine 40 feet long. Masses of granite arrive here, from monoliths from Mull to what appear to me to be paving-stones of the same material. Three, four or five horses are necessary to pull these importations up an inclined plane from the river, and the horses are immersed before my eyes, above their hocks, on the coldest of winter days in the river waiting for their burdens, and they are daily maimed in their goaded endeavours to bring up their load. I have witnessed since I visited here four horses drowned, to be borne away by means of an apparatus apparently designed for this particular purpose, as if it were a recognised necessity.

'. . . . Its outer form appears only in the shape of a man leaning on a rail all day, and for ever smoking a short pipe. . . .'

He goes on to complain of the out-door worshippers on Sunday evening, the cock-crowing which so disturbed Carlyle, and the clothes-airing.

Fame has been somewhat unkind to the memory of Maclise. Criticism dwells almost entirely on his shortcomings, which, it must be admitted, were not few; but, after all deductions, his two great frescoes in the Houses of Parliament are works such as only an artist of high power could produce.

Some ten years after the death of Maclise, George Eliot and her husband, Mr. Cross, came to this house, intending to make it their home. We gather from several of her letters that the picturesque outlook and the interesting associations of the neighbourhood had much to do with its choice by them. They came to it on December 3, 1880, and proposed to winter there. On the following day she wrote to Mrs. Congreve:

> 'I find myself in a new climate here—the London air and this particular house being so warm compared with Witley.'

Her health was then much broken, and a chill caught at a concert at St. James's Hall hastened the end. Her husband thus writes of her last few days:

> 'The air in the hall was over-heated, and George Eliot allowed a fur cloak that she wore to slip from her shoulders. I was conscious of a draught, and was afraid of it for her, as she was very sensitive to cold. I begged her to resume the cloak, but, smiling, she whispered that the room was really too hot. In the evening she played through several of the pieces that we had heard at the concert, with all her accustomed enjoyment of the piano, and with a touch as true and delicate as ever. On Sunday there was a very slight trouble in the throat, but not sufficient to prevent her from coming downstairs as usual. In the afternoon she was well enough to receive visits from Mr. Herbert Spencer and one or two other friends. . . .
>
> 'Little more remains to be told. On Monday the doctor treated the case as one of laryngeal sore-throat; and when Dr. (now Sir) Andrew Clark came for consultation on Wednesday evening, the pericardium was found to be seriously affected. Whilst the doctors were at her bedside, she had just time to whisper to me, 'Tell them I have great pain in the left side,' before she became unconscious. Her long illness in the autumn left her no power to rally. She passed away, about ten o'clock at night, on the 22nd December, 1880.'

We have another excellent specimen of the domestic architecture of the last century in No. 6. In 1765 this house, truly described as large, pleasant, and convenient, with four spacious and lofty parlours, two dining-rooms, and thirteen bedchambers, was fitted up as a sanatorium by Dr. Dominiceti, a Venetian of an ancient and noble family. A certificate of his nobility, signed by Ralph Bigland, Garter King of Arms, was communicated by Mr. John Eyre to the *Gentleman's Magazine*, January, 1829. His speciality was fumigatory baths, of which a full description is given in 'A plan for extending the use of artificial water-baths, pumps, etc., by Dr. Bartholomew de Dominiceti. Dedicated to Sir John Fielding, knt., Chelsea, November 1, 1771.' The following is an extract from it :

> 'The entrance of the building which contains this apparatus is in Robinson's Lane [now Flood Street], very contiguous to China [Cheyne] Walk, Thames-side, and to the King's Road ; it is situated in my garden, 220 feet in length, 30 in breadth, and two stories high ; it contains 36 Sweating and Fumigatory bedchambers.'

There were also separate departments for infectious disorders, a room for amusement, etc. He professed to have spent more than £37,000 upon this establishment, and his pretensions created no small stir in society and among the faculty. Among his patients were the Duke of York and Sir John Fielding, a magistrate, and son of the novelist. The latter considered himself so much benefited by the treatment that he wrote a 'Vindication of Dr. Dominiceti's practice,' in which he says :

> 'Dr. Dominiceti has most happily situated himself at Chelsea, as the Thames and the gardeners' grounds are his great Apothecary's shop, the one furnishing with water and the other with herbs.'

By the 'gardeners' grounds' were meant the Pharmaceutical Gardens, which no doubt attracted him to Chelsea. But Sir John Fielding cannot be considered an altogether unprejudiced witness, for the pamphlet just quoted says that the doctor gave 'a shilling out of each guinea to Sir John Fielding for his scheme of apprenticing deserted boys,' a give-and-take arrangement that is open to suspicion. Dr. Johnson was among the sceptics, and advised one of the defenders to go there and get his head fumigated, 'for that was the peccant part.'

After some seventeen years Dominiceti fled, hopelessly in debt, and Chelsea knew him no more.

The Rev. Weeden Butler afterwards kept a well-known school in this house for more than thirty years. He had acted as amanuensis to Dr. William Dodd, until the latter's execution in 1777 for forgery, and had a share in the compilation of 'The Commentary on the Bible,' and the editing of the *Christian's Magazine.* His elder son, the Rev. George Butler, D.D., became Head-master of Harrow School. His younger son, Weeden, materially assisted Faulkner in the preparation of his 'History of Chelsea'—translated the Latin inscriptions on the church monuments, etc., and interspersed the narrative with various philosophical and moral reflections. He published a small volume of poems entitled 'Bagatelles,' in which there are several references to Chelsea.

All the houses onwards to Manor Street have been rebuilt in the past year (1888). Those destroyed include No. 13, in which lived a family named Fraine, to whose eccentricities and suicidal tendencies Faulkner devotes several pages; and No. 10, Gothic House, where dwelt Count d'Orsay, 'the mirror of fashion.' Carlyle humorously describes a visit of this 'exquisite' to him soon after his settling in Cheyne Row:

'Chelsea, April 16th, 1839 : I must tell you of the strangest compliment of all which occurred since I last wrote—the advent of Count d'Orsay. About a fortnight ago, this Phœbus Apollo of dandyism, escorted by poor little Chorley, came whirling hither in a chariot, that struck all Chelsea into mute amazement with splendour. Chorley's jaw went like the hopper or under-riddle of a pair of fanners, such was his terror on bringing such a splendour into actual contact with such grimness. Nevertheless, we did amazingly well, the Count and I. He is a tall fellow of 6 feet 3, built like a tower, with floods of dark auburn hair, with adornment unsurpassable on this planet, withal a rather substantial fellow at bottom, by no means without insight, without fun, and a sort of rough sarcasm rather striking out of such a porcelain figure. . . . He admired the fine epic, etc., etc., hoped I would call soon, and see Lady Blessington withal.

'Finally he went his way, and Chorley with re-assumed jaw. Jane laughed for two days at the contrast of my plaid dressing-gown, bilious, iron countenance and this Paphian apparition.'

The south end of Manor Street, until recently, consisted of old-fashioned houses built towards the middle of the eighteenth century. Amongst their inhabitants we notice Montagu Bacon, a scholar and critic, and descendant of the Lord Keeper, who lodged and died here in 1749; William Bromley, painter and engraver, 1793-95 ; and Robert Farrier, the artist, 1842-57. The street was not connected with the King's Road until 1824; previously a large garden stretched across the north end. The new buildings have been named Cheyne Gardens, and are houses of some pretension. Mrs. Trollope, widow of the novelist, Mr. Justin McCarthy, M.P., and his son, Justin H. McCarthy, are among the residents.

A well-known artistic family, the Lawsons, moved into Carlton House in 1869. Three of the sons distinguished themselves—Malcolm Lawson, as a musical composer ; F. W. Lawson, as the painter of an earnest and pathetic series of pictures, 'The Children of the Great City'; and Cecil G. Lawson, as the most promising genius in landscape art since the days of John Constable. The hard formal line of the embankment was not then in existence, and the young genius fell in love with his home, its surroundings and associations, and gave expression to his feelings in a series of fine pictures. In 1870 he sent to the Academy 'Cheyne Walk, 1870,' the first of a series of illustrations of this spot. It was very bold in conception and original in treatment, and drew much attention to the painter. Among the figures was a rear view of Carlyle in the cloak and broad-brimmed hat so familiar to all who knew him. In the following year he exhibited 'A Summer Evening in Cheyne Walk,' bathed in a golden haze, and 'The River in Rain'—the Thames as he saw it from his window one cold raw night, with the rain pelting down and bleak clouds scudding across the gray sky. It was this picture that prompted Theo Marzial's queer little poem, ' Plop !'

Then in 1872, when the workmen were driving the great piles in the shore before his window, he painted his ' Lament.' Millais came to see it, and dashed in a few red sparks above the funnel of a river steamer to relieve the gray. This picture was followed by ' The Bell Inn, Cheyne Walk,' a highly-finished work, rejected by the Academy (1874) ; ' Rus in Urbe : a pastoral in Trafalgar Square, Chelsea ' (1876) ; ' View from Don Saltero's in Cheyne

END OF CHEYNE WALK, 1873.
(*From an etching by Mr. C. W. Sherborn.*)

Walk, 1770 ' (1877). Other pictures of this neighbourhood were ' A Chelsea Garden,' ' Moonlight Memories,' another scene from his window ; ' The Swan and the Iris,' an arch of old Battersea Bridge, which Whistler etched for Gosse's memoir of the painter ; ' Old Battersea,' ' A Wet Moon, Old Battersea,' and ' In Memoriam,' the garden of the sculptor, J. B. Philip, R.A. (whose daughter he married), at Merton Villa, Trafalgar Square.

In the spring of 1880 he opened negotiations for the purchase of a plot of land in Swan Walk, where he intended to build a house overlooking the Physic Garden ; but this was a project he was never to complete. His health broke down with the zeal of his labour, and the keen March winds finished what overwork had begun. He died on June 10, 1882, and was buried at Haslemere.

The next house, Queen's House, No. 16, has also had famous occupants. Catherine of Braganza, the neglected Queen of Charles II., is supposed to have lived here; but I can find nothing in support of this belief, except that it was formerly called Queen's House, that the initials in the gateway agree with it, and that they were formerly surmounted by a crown or coronet. The suggestion presupposes that this house was built before 1692, when she retired to Portugal. Undoubtedly it is a house of some pretension, and good enough to be the work of a pupil of Wren, if not of the master himself. The bay in front is a late addition, and disfigures the simplicity and fine proportions of the original design.

In October, 1862, four men, Dante Gabriel Rossetti, William Rossetti, George Meredith, and Algernon Swinburne, who were exercising a considerable influence in the world of art and letters, came to live here. The aggressive natures of these men doubtless militated against their long association, and brought about an early separation. Meredith stayed but a very short time, Swinburne went next, and finally the poet-painter had the house to himself. With its air of dignity, its noble gates, wrought in a time when blacksmiths were artists, and fine old garden (now partially destroyed by the building of Cheyne Gardens), it would be to a man constituted as D. G. Rossetti an almost ideal residence. He crowded it with objects of beauty, old pictures, carved oak furniture, blue china, etc.; in the garden he kept quite a small menagerie, including a zebu, of which some ludicrous tales are told. A sycamore in this garden appears in many of the pictures he painted in Chelsea. Many brilliant gatherings of the leaders of art and æsthetics were held in this house, especially towards 1871; but his hypochondria, the result of indulgence in chloral hydrate, rendered his last years desolate, and drove from him many friends. He died in 1882 at Birchington-on-Sea, where his friend, J. P. Seddon, the architect, had a villa. Mr. G. P. Boyce, of West House, Glebe Place, has a number of sketches and finished designs for his pictures, and there were others, with a cast of his head taken after death, at Belle Vue House, the residence of Mr. W. B. Scott.

In the Embankment Garden opposite to the house a monument has been erected to the memory of this singular genius. It consists of a gray granite fountain, designed by J. P. Seddon, with a bronze alto-relievo bust, modelled by Mr. F. Madox-Brown, in the baldacchino. It was unveiled by Mr. Holman Hunt on July 14, 1887.

The Rev. H. R. Haweis now occupies Rossetti's house, and has restored the old name of Queen's House.

QUEEN'S HOUSE, CHEYNE WALK.

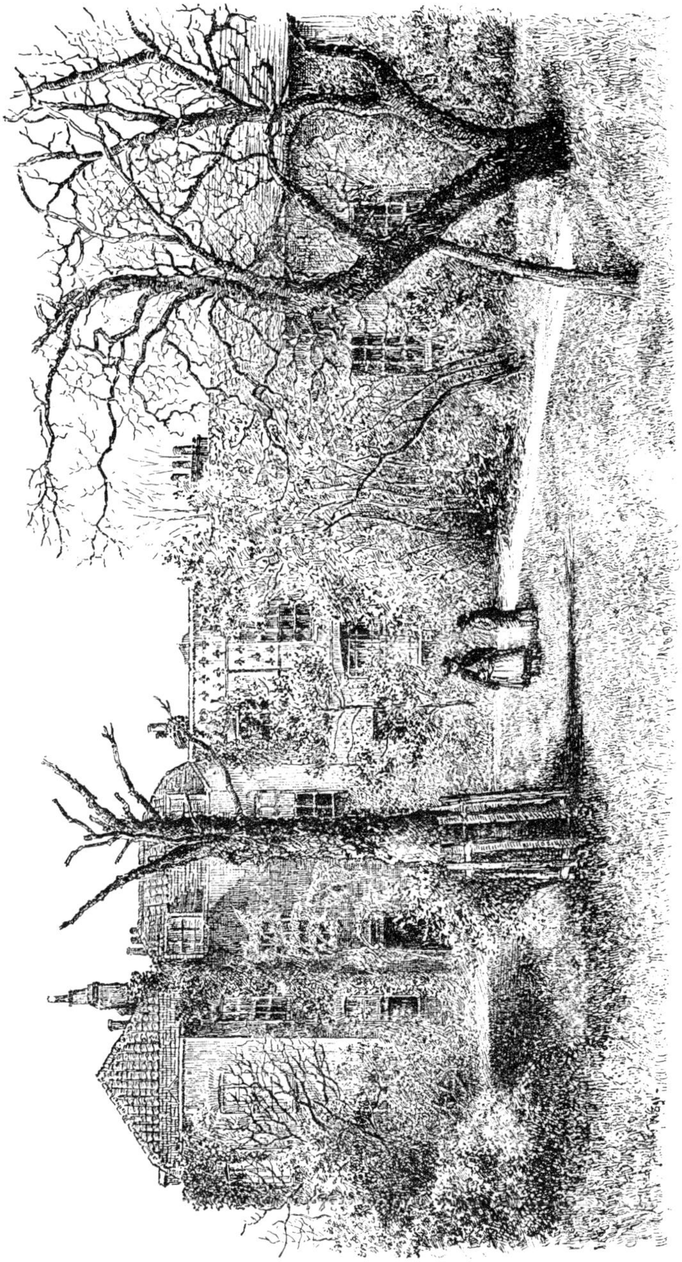

CHEYNE HOUSE AND GARDEN, 1880.

Thomas Attwood, the composer, pupil of Mozart, died at No. 17 on March 24, 1838; Henry Redhead Yorke, a political writer under the name of 'Galgacus,' who had been an officer in the French army, a member of the National Convention, and friend of Condorcet, lived at No. 19; and Mrs. Augusta Webster, the poetess and educationist, at No. 24.

Oakley Street was laid out after the destruction of Winchester House; a piece of the old garden wall may still be seen by the entrance to the Ladies' Dwellings.

William Artaud, a good miniature-painter, lived, in 1791-92, at No. 42, Cheyne Walk, then further westward than at present.

At the corner of Cheyne Row stood an old inn, The Feathers, with gardens extending to Cook's Ground, adjoining Glebe Place. In 1666 the landlord of this inn issued a token, inscribed 'Thomas Munden, his halfe-penny,' specimens of which are still extant.

Upon the gardens Great Cheyne Row was built in 1708. John Hall, who in his youth had worked in the 'nursery' at the china works, and who became historical engraver to George III., lived here from 1769-74. At No. 9 lived John Denyer, a collector of Bibles and missals, whose name is preserved in one of the Chelsea streets. His daughter had some reputation as an illuminator; at her death in 1824 she left a sum of money, the interest of which was to be paid to 'poor spinsters, parishioners, not under 60, of good character, constant at a place of worship, and who have not been beggars.'

But Cheyne Row is famous all the world over as the residence of Thomas Carlyle. Probably the 'sage of Chelsea' first saw the place when he visited Leigh Hunt in 1832, and was so pleased with it that he determined to make it his own dwelling-place. Accordingly he took the house, No. 5 (now 24), Cheyne Row, and has himself described his coming:

> 'We proceeded all through Belgrave Square hither, with our servant, our loose luggage, ourselves and a little canary bird (Chico, which she had brought with her from Craigen-puttock), one hackney coach rumbling on with us all. Chico in Belgrave Square burst into singing, which we took as a good omen. We were all of us striving to be cheerful (she needed no effort of striving), but we had "burnt our ships," and at bottom the case was grave. I do not remember our arriving at this door, but I do the cheerful gipsy life we had here among the litter and carpenters for three incipient days. Leigh Hunt was in the next street, sending kind unpractical messages; in the evenings, I think, personally coming in.'

They had not been long in the house before his wife, Jane Welsh, made it 'a little Eden around her (so neat and graceful in its simplicity and thrifty poverty).' In Froude's 'Reminiscences' we have many interesting glimpses of the friends who came to see Carlyle in Chelsea: of Leigh Hunt (who liked the Scotch porridge and Mrs. Carlyle's Scotch tunes), 'with the airiest kindly style of sparkling talk'; of John Stuart Mill, who for several years walked with Carlyle every Sunday; Mrs. Taylor, 'a very Will-o'-the-wispish

" iridescence " of a creature '; of Edward Irving's first and only visit; of Mazzini (who lived in Chelsea), 'a most valiant, faithful, considerably-gifted, and noble soul'; of Godefroi Cavaignac, 'a fine Bayard soul (with figure to correspond)'; of Allan Cunningham, Harriet Martineau, Tyndall, Emerson, Jeffrey, Tennyson, Ruskin, and scores of others famous in art and learning.

During his residence of nearly fifty years in this house, Carlyle wrote most of his best works, and gradually earned the reputation of being the deepest and most original thinker of the age. But with all his success and greatness, he never lost his simplicity of manners, quaintness of dress, and Scotch accent. During the last ten years of his life he was accustomed to take a daily walk upon the Embankment, and, until his health became impaired, a nightly walk also. Chelsea naturally teems with anecdotes of the great man— of his flashes of wit, outspoken denunciations, and of his kindly sympathy, notwithstanding his rugged exterior and seeming harsh words.

After his death the house remained empty for some six or seven years, and presented a very forlorn appearance. It has since been re-let, and Woolner's alto-relievo bust in marble placed upon the wall. In the garden on the Embankment is a bronze statue by the late Sir Edgar Boehm, R.A., the very presentment of the man and his person; it was erected by the subscriptions of those who honoured and esteemed him during life, and was unveiled on October 26, 1882.

At the north end of Cheyne Row is Upper Cheyne Row, of which Leigh Hunt came to live at No. 4 in 1833, and remained there for seven years.

> 'From the noise and dust of the New Road,' he says in his Autobiography, 'my family removed to a corner in Chelsea, where the air from the neighbouring river was so refreshing, and the quiet of the "no thoroughfare" so full of repose, that, although our fortunes were at their worst, I felt for some weeks as if I could sit still for ever, embalmed in the silence.
>
> 'I know not whether the corner I speak of remains as quiet as it was. I am afraid not ; for steamboats have carried vicissitude into Chelsea, and Belgravia threatens it with her mighty advent. But to complete my sense of repose and distance, the house was of that old-fashioned sort I have always loved best, familiar to the eyes of my parents and associated with my childhood. It had seats in the windows, a small third room on the first floor, of which I made a sanctum, into which no perturbation was to enter, except to calm itself with religious and cheerful thoughts (a room thus appropriated in a house appears to me an excellent thing). And there are a few lime-trees in front, which in their due season diffused a fragrance.'

Here Leigh Hunt wrote his poem of 'Captain Sword and Captain Pen,' several plays, of which 'The Legend of Florence' was performed in 1840, and 'The Lovers' Amazement' in 1858; and the essays written for the *London Journal*, and afterwards collected and published under the title of 'The Seer.' In 1840 he left Chelsea, and went to live in Kensington. The house in Cheyne Row is now numbered 10. Mr. E. A. Ward, the portrait-painter, well known

28—2

as 'Spy' of the *Vanity Fair* cartoons, lived here for some years previous to 1891, when his lease expired.

At the old No. 1, Upper Cheyne Row, lived for some time John Fuge, a water-colour artist, now best remembered for his excellent lithographs of the Physick Gardens, showing the fine old cedars.

At the north-east end of the Row stands a fine old English house, called Cheyne House. The great age of some of the brickwork, and indications of lanceolated openings point to Tudor times, but the chief portions are in the Wrenean style, and were added by the Huguenot ancestors of Dr. Phené, F.S.A., who is the present owner. One of the eastern walls is plastered and ornamented with *fleurs-de-lys*. The grounds, formerly about six acres in extent, were, in part, once occupied by a Mr. Shailer, a lavender-grower, who here raised the first moss-rose. The site is now almost entirely built over, but the portion still attached to Cheyne House is the most interesting private garden in Chelsea. Some of the trees are of considerable age; there is a mulberry supposed to date from Tudor times, the stump of a cedar, which flourished years ago, a beautiful catalpa, still vigorous, planted when this tree was very rare in England, and some old hollies. The walls of the garden, also very old, have already been mentioned, as has the subterranean passage to Shrewsbury House. Worked in the foundations of the wall of the pleasaunce, Dr. Phené has found a large number of Roman bricks, and in other parts of the garden, a Roman skull, an old British stone mortar, and many worked stones. Interesting as these things make this garden, they are surpassed in interest by the valuable collection of architectural relics, gathered during some forty years by Dr. Phené. Here we may see stone vases from Alston and Beaufort Houses, portions of Old Whitehall, Queen Elizabeth's Palace at Mile End, Northumberland House, Ormond House, Wanstead House, Plashet House, pre-historic stones, and much else. Dr. Phené now lives at Carlton Terrace, Oakley Street, a considerable portion of which he built. The trees there were planted by him, and Oakley Street thus enjoys the distinction of being the first London street planted with trees. Prince Albert examined them with interest in 1851, and the planting of the road in front of the South Kensington Museum followed in 1852.

The Rev. Dr. Felix established a high-class Huguenot school in Cheyne House, which was well known in the early portion of the present century.

Mr. C. J. Lewis, the artist, now of River House, Cheyne Walk, lived at Cheyne House from 1858 to 1883.

About 1769 Thomas Bentley came to live in Little (now Upper) Cheyne Row, in order to supervise the Chelsea branch of the firm of Wedgwood and Bentley. This branch was established for the encaustic decoration of vases after the Etruscan manner. A site near London was chosen for the convenience of engaging suitable artists. The work appears to have been carried on in London as late as 1795, though Bentley left Chelsea in 1774.

In this last-mentioned year a German named Ruhl, or Ruelle (who was succeeded by his son-in-law, C. F. Hempel), established a pottery in Little Cheyne Row, which produced the best-reputed crucibles in this country. In the south-east corner of his grounds, Dr. Phené has discovered, at a depth of 25 feet, many fragments of crucibles which show signs of use; the discovery indicates the site of Ruelle's pottery, and Dr. Phené thinks it probable that some of the Chelsea china-glazing was carried on here. On the expiration of the lease, prior to 1790, Hempel's widow, Johanna, removed the works to King's Road.

Some of the homes of famous residents in Cheyne Walk (which formerly ended at the church) or its immediate neighbourhood cannot now be exactly determined. Sir Richard Steele had a house at the waterside, which was rated at £14 per annum. On February 14, 1716, he wrote to his wife:

'Mr. Fuller and I came hither to dine in the air, but the maid has been so slow, that we are benighted, and chuse to lie here than go this road in the dark. I lie at our own house, and my friend at a relation's in the town.'

In the previous year, ' Margaret, daughter of Edward Sent,' was 'buried from Sir Richard Steele's, Nov. 12.'

James Northcote, R.A., pupil of Sir Joshua Reynolds, dates a letter from ' Cheyney Walk, Chelsea,' in 1781 (Colonel Macaulay's MSS.). Henry Sampson Woodfall, the printer of the letters of ' Junius,' those mild polemics (according to modern ideas) which created such a sensation in their day, lived in retirement near the old church, and died there in 1805. Arthur Rawson Ashwell, a well-known theologian and principal of the Theological College at Chichester, was born in Cheyne Walk in 1824.

Mudie, father of the founder of Mudie's circulating library, kept a bookseller's shop in Cheyne Walk, where his son was born.

The five houses to the east of the church (of which only two now remain) were formerly called Prospect Place. From 1850 to 1854 Mr. William Holman Hunt, the famous painter, of the Pre-Raphaelite Brotherhood, lived at No. 5, now pulled down for the Children's Hospital. His name appears in the Royal Academy Catalogue for 1850 as A. H. Hunt, and in the following year as V. H. Hunt. In a room on the first floor of this house in Cheyne Walk, overlooking the river, he painted 'The Light of the World,' now at Keble College, Oxford, and the greater part of 'The Christian Missionaries,' ' The Two Gentlemen of Verona,' ' Claudio and Isabella,' ' The Hireling Shepherd,' ' The Strayed Sheep,' and ' The Awakening Conscience.'

In an adjacent house, No. 2, the brothers G. and E. A. Holmes, both members of the Society of British Artists, have lived for many years.

LOMBARD STREET FROM THE RIVER.

LOMBARD STREET.

The piece of Cheyne Walk from the church to Danvers Street was formerly called Lombard Street, possibly after the first owner or builder. It passed by an archway through a large old house, which has already been mentioned. An old stone name-plate is still in position on the house nearest the church, and the name is preserved in what was once Waterman's Court, but is now called Lombard Buildings. The tavern adjoining, the Rising Sun, where may be seen a small collection of old Chelsea views, was formerly called ' The Dog,' and enjoyed the right of common. Five doors from it lived Smollett's companion, Mr. W. Lewis, who has already been mentioned. Near at hand is a small fish-shop, which is perhaps the oldest house now standing in Chelsea. It appears to be a portion of a larger house, the history of which has not been preserved, but if Dr. King's assertion that Sir William Powell's house ' at the arch,' was originally Sir Reginald Bray's, be correct, it may have formed a portion of the old manor-house. Hereabouts, too, probably stood the house mentioned in the Close Roll, No. 7, Richard II., at which date John de Shordich demised to John Bacon a mansion formerly the property of William 'atte water at Chelchithe, ovec les gardins et toutes les maisons dedeinz le pale et ovec meism les pale—reserves au dit Johan de Shordich le soler oue le chemyne de la novile chambre illocque la chambre de bas dessouz le dit soler.' An old inn stood at the Danvers Street corner, and is shown in Priest's view; its sign of the Bell stretched in the old-fashioned way across the road.

CHELSEA FERRY.

Nearly opposite Danvers Street was the ferry, celebrated by Dibdin in Tom Tug's song. My earliest note upon it occurs in the expenses of John of Brabant, and Thomas and Henry of Leicester, Anno 21 Edward I. (1292-3), when alms were given to a servant for the passage of the Thames at Cenlee, on the journey from Merton (Surrey) to London. Mr. Joseph Burtt (of the Record Office) thinks this refers to Chelsea. In 1592 Norden includes it among the ' horse ferryes and passages over the Thamise—at Lambeth, at Greenwich, and at Battersey or Chelsey.' This is quoted from the author's manuscript, Harleian Collection, n. 570. This ferry was presumably royal property, for in 1618 we find James I. granted to his ' dear relations, Thomas, Earl of Lincoln, and John Eldred and Thomas Henley, Esquires, all that Ferry across the river Thames called Chelcheyhith Ferry or Chelsey Ferry.'

The old spelling is evidently quoted from some early document (about the first half of the fourteenth century), and is indicative of the antiquity of the ferry. The grant carried with it the possession of the adjacent land, which, on the Battersea side, was known as Ferry Mead. The Earl of Lincoln sold his share in it to 'our very illustrious subject, William Blake,' who was then the owner of Chelsea Park.

In August, 1659, when rumours of a Stuart restoration filled the air, the

CHELSEA FERRY, 1709.

Council of State was awake to the necessity of a strict vigilance over incoming strangers; and on the 19th, in their day's proceedings, we find this order:

'All the ferrymen of the ferries between London and Staines Bridge, viz., Lambeth, Chelsey, Putney, etc., not to ferry over, after sunset or before sunrise, any person, horse or coach, without special order from Council, or they are to answer their contempt at their peril.'

In 1695 Chelsea Ferry belonged to one Bartholomew Nutt, and in 1710 we find it rated at £8 per annum. Later on it became the property of Sir Walter St. John, of Battersea; and in 1762 it passed, with the rest of the Bolingbroke estate, to the Earl Spencer, who held it in 1766, when the Act was obtained for building the wooden bridge, beloved by artists, but abhorred by bargees and river captains.

DUKE STREET.

The road from Danvers Street to the bridge was known as Duke Street, and appears to have been built, or at least named, in the days when George Villiers, the first Duke of Buckingham, lived in More's house. The south side, pulled down to make way for the embankment, was very quaint, especially the old inn, the Adam and Eve, which Mr. Napier Hemy has introduced into his picture 'Good-bye.' It had galleries overhanging the river, and some of the rooms had the walls half-covered with fowling-pieces, relics, doubtless, of the days when Chelsea was a favourite shooting-ground. The whole of the buildings on the north side were demolished in 1889, including the tobacco-shop patronised by Carlyle. Mr. Walter Greaves, of Chelsea, has painted Duke Street in its original condition, and quite recently it was sketched by Mr. Ascroft, and painted by Mr. Charles J. Watson.

In 1766 an Act of Parliament was passed empowering the Earl Spencer to build a bridge from Chelsea to Battersea, in place of the old ferry. The tolls were to be one halfpenny for foot-passengers, and fourpence for a one-horse cart. Powers were given to the promoters to sue any waterman or other person who injured the bridge with a boat or vessel, which seems to imply that no very substantial structure was contemplated. The Act also stipulated that if the bridge was rendered dangerous or impracticable by tempest or otherwise, a suitable ferry was to be provided during the reconstruction, and that no more than the bridge tolls should be charged. The bridge was not commenced until 1771, when Earl Spencer formed a company with seventeen other gentlemen, and a contract was entered into with Messrs. Phillips and Holland, who agreed to build it for £10,500. At the end of the year it was opened for foot-passengers, and for carriage traffic in the following year. By 1773 the money expended amounted to £15,662.

It was a timber structure of nineteen spans, varying from 15 feet 6 inches to 32 feet. It was 726 feet in length, and 24 feet wide, with a slight curvature to the west. For many years it yielded little or no return to the proprietors, and in 1795 was so much damaged during the severe frost that no dividend was declared for the next three years. Battersea Bridge enjoyed the distinction of being the first wooden bridge across the Thames to be lighted at night-time; oil-lamps were fixed along one side in 1799, and these were replaced by gas from Chelsea in 1824. The neighbouring roads were much improved by the building of this bridge, as the proprietors at various times expended considerable sums upon them. It remained in the possession of the descendants of the original proprietors until 1873, when the Albert Bridge Company purchased it, and proceeded to carry out certain alterations under the direction of their engineer, Mr. R. M. Ordish. The foundations of the piers were

THE ADAM AND EVE.

strengthened with concrete, and one pier was removed, the two spans being thrown into one for the greater facility of traffic. But notwithstanding these alterations, the bridge became so insecure by 1883, that vehicular traffic was stopped altogether; and in 1887 the old timber bridge, which had lasted for over a hundred years, was entirely removed, and a new one of stone and iron commenced.

The old bridge was utterly detested by 'practical' people, being to them nothing but an eyesore and an encumbrance; but its removal was a sad loss to the picturesqueness of Chelsea. The old weather-worn structure seemed to have adapted itself to the character of the place, and was especially in keeping with the old houses that lined the shore before the embankment swept them away. Many artists have found a subject in it. Girtin, Turner, De Wint, and Varley sketched it; Mr. Whistler brought its weird timbers into many a nocturne; Mr. East and Mr. C. J. Lewis have painted well-known views of it.

CHEYNE WALK (*Continued*).

Beyond Lindsey Row is a humble little house almost covered with ivy, next but one to a small tavern called the Aquatic Stores, the present goal of Doggett's Coat and Badge Race. The road has

BATTERSEA BRIDGE, 1882.

WEST END OF CHEYNE WALK, SHOWING TURNER'S LAST RESIDENCE.

(After an Etching by Mr. C. W. Sherborn.)

been raised considerably in recent years, so that this cottage and its neighbour have a quaint sunken appearance. Here came Turner, the great landscape painter, in the weariness of his old age, to escape the importunities of over-zealous admirers. Everyone knows the story of his coming, of his offer of a roll of bank-notes for reference, of his adoption of the landlady's name, and of the irreverence of little Chelsea Philistines, who shouted ' Puggy Booth' and ' Admiral Booth' after him as he trod the Chelsea streets. It is all pointedly told by Thornberry. Above the house may be seen a small iron balustrade, put there for or by Turner, who often went on the roof to sketch. Nearly opposite, in Battersea Parish Church, with its green copper spire, is the window which Turner also used as a point of vantage. In those days the scene was nothing so grimy and sordid as it now is. Pleasant fields with wooded background, groups of cattle, quiet villas, here and there a barge unloading—such were the scenes on either bank. Towards evening ' the lovely English half-haze' steeped every-thing in a mystic, elusive beauty, enchanting enough to tempt even a Turner. The change to belching chimneys, hideous warehouses, and dirty wharves is sad enough, but even yet at eventide one can imagine the blotted beauty. Thus Mr. C. J. Lewis painted from his window at River View a beautiful picture of this now defiled spot, throwing over the whole one of those lovely golden after-glows which were so common some eight years ago. These wonderfully beautiful sunsets, which have been ascribed to the diffusion of fine volcanic dust in the higher regions of the atmosphere, after the great eruption of Krakatoa in August, 1883, have been skilfully and faithfully registered in a large series of sky sketches taken mainly from the Chelsea Embankment by Mr. William Ascroft, of Queen's Road West. The whole series has been ex-hibited at South Kensington ; a selection has been reproduced by the Royal Society, and others have been purchased by the Austrian Government.

PARADISE ROW.

The portion of old Paradise Row that still remains, between Tite Street and Smith Street, is one of the most picturesque remnants of Old Chelsea. Time has dealt hardly with this part of Chelsea. Most of the old houses which in bygone days sheltered many famous people are now pulled down or disfigured beyond recognition. Facing the Infirmary built by Sir John Soane, however, is the short terrace we have alluded to, in a genuine, unimproved condition, just sufficient to set us thinking how delightful a place Old Chelsea must have been before the greedy city clutched it in its destroying grasp, before land was counted out by the square yard, and before men began blotting out the loveliness of the sky and shutting out the freshness of the air with great towering buildings, when men rarely built beyond two or three stories high, when ample gardens back and front ensured that the breath of life should freely find access, and when even ugly buildings were redeemed by the surrounding beauties of plant life.

Paradise Row, now called Queen's Road West, began at what was then Robinson's Lane (afterwards Queen's Street, and now Flood Street), and ended at Burton's Court, which was not then separated from the Hospital, as at present.

One of the earliest inhabitants of this part of Chelsea was Richard Fletcher, Bishop of Bristol (1589), of Worcester (1592), and of London (1594). The record of his life is scarcely honourable, and seems to have been little more than a continual striving for preferment by means of flattery and sycophancy. He had a house of his own at Chelsea, which he made his chief

PARADISE ROW, 1891.

residence, for he spent more time at Court looking after his worldly interests than attending to the spiritual cares of his see.

Among the baptisms at Chelsea we find :

'1592. Maria, filia Rici Fletcher, Bristol Episc.   14th October.'

Two months later his wife died, and was buried at Chelsea, as recorded in the register :

'1592. Eliz. ux Rici Fletcher, Bristol Epi sepult. in cancello subter, mensa December.'

'William Blocksuche, w^t Dr. Fletcher, Bishop of Bristol,' was buried previously on August 23.   The plague raged in London and its surroundings this year, and possibly both were amongst its victims.

In 1594 he applied for the vacant Bishopric of London, alleging as his reasons that he 'delighted in' London, where he was educated, had many friends to whom he would be useful there, and, above all, he would be near the Court, 'where his presence had become habitual and looked for.' After his appointment he took part with Whitgift in drawing up the Lambeth Articles. This was the beginning of his rapid downfall, for their severe Calvinism was promptly condemned by Queen Elizabeth, and their authors censured. Soon after he offended her still more by his second marriage. The Queen objected to the marriage of Bishops in any case, but this one was peculiarly distasteful. Fletcher's new wife was the widow of Sir Richard Baker of Sissinghurst in Kent, handsome, and possibly wealthy, but with a tarnished reputation, which gave a coarse ballad-monger of the time the opportunity to write that the Bishop 'of a Laïs doth a Lucrece make.' The Bishop was forbidden the Court, and suspended from his episcopal functions, scarcely a month after his confirmation as Bishop of London. He penned many grovelling appeals to Burghley for restoration to favour.

> 'My greatest comfort seculor' [he writes] 'for twenty years past has been to live in her Highness's gratious aspect and favour. Now it is a year all but a week or two since I have seen her.'

At length he was partially restored to the Queen's favour, who is believed to have visited him at Chelsea. Sir John Harrington in his 'Brief View of the Church' (pp. 27, 28) says that the Bishop made 'a stayre and a dore in a bay window' for the reception of the Queen on this occasion. But he never recovered from the loss of royal favour, and died suddenly (while smoking a pipe of tobacco) on June 15, 1596. His whole estate consisted of the house at Chelsea, £400 worth of plate, and other property worth £500 more, while there were heavy debts, and a young family unprovided for. An appeal was made to the generosity of the Queen, who was one of the chief creditors. In vol. cclix., n. 47, of the Domestic State Papers of the reign of Elizabeth is a

> 'Statement of the reason why Her Majesty is to be moved for compassion towards the orphans of the Bishop of London. He served her as chaplain and almoner for 18 years ; his one offence may be satisfied with the service and duties of so many years, and with his untimely death, which followed as an effect of his unhappy marriage. If the rest of the debt be exacted, it must be raised by extent of his house at Chelsey, which is the only means left to relieve his eight children, some of whom are infants. It would be a great discredit to the church of England for a Bishop's children to go begging, which must needs follow if her Majesty does not remit that which remains of her debt, their uncle [Giles Fletcher the elder], who may not forsake them, though it be to his undoing, having nine children, and his estate hardly sufficient to meet his own charge. The Bishop got into debt solely by Her Majesty's favours in his preferments, whereby he was kept in continual payment of his first fruits and tenths, having paid £3,000 in three years. He also made gratifications out of the London bishopric to divers of the court, by her appointment, to the extent of £2,000.'

The application was successful, as on April 27, 1597, the Queen released Giles Fletcher, D.C.L., from payment of the £600 referred to (State Papers, Domestic, Addenda, vol. xxxiii., n. 79), a result which was brought about by the interposition of Anthony Bacon and the Earl of Essex.

The register records the burial of a son of Giles Fletcher, the Bishop's executor:

'1596. Nehemias filius Egidii Fletcher, Legum Doctor, sepult. 12th June.'

Bishop Fletcher was the father of John Fletcher, the dramatist (who was not more than seventeen years old when his father died, and must, therefore, have spent his youth at Chelsea), and uncle of Giles and Phineas Fletcher (sons of Giles the elder), two religious poets of high reputation.

At the western corner of Paradise Row stood the mansion of the Right Hon. John, Lord Robartes of Truro, the son of the Lord Truro who is said to have paid Buckingham £10,000 for his title. Lord Robartes was one of those wary people who managed so to steer his course through the Commonwealth times as to avoid giving offence to Parliament, and yet to be received with open arms by the restored Stuart. His sister, it may be noticed, was married to Edward Montagu, who commanded the Parliamentary army at Marston Moor. Lord Robartes himself was then 'a staunch Presbyterian, sour and cynical,' and commanded a regiment of horse under Lord Essex at Edgehill. In memory of his commander a daughter and grand-daughter were named Essex Robartes.

On September 4, 1660, a few months after the Restoration, the King, we learn from the *Mercurius Politicus*, 'was nobly entertained by Lord Robartes with a supper at his house at Chelsey.'

Lord Robartes, who was undoubtedly a man of some power and learning, made rapid progress under the 'Merry Monarch.' He was made Lord President of the Privy Council, Lord-Lieutenant of Ireland, promoted first to be Viscount Bodmin, and afterwards Earl of Radnor.

In 1661, when Pepys took the coach to Chelsea 'to arrange certain business with him'—then Privy Seal—he 'saw by daylight two very fine pictures in the gallery that a little while ago I saw by night, and did also go over the house, and found it to be the prettiest-contrived house that ever I saw in my life.' He was there again in 1665, and examined the pictures in the waiting-room, where he had the opportunity of indulging his pet weakness by gazing on one of the pictures, that of 'my Lord's son's lady, a most beautiful woman.' 'My Lord's son's lady' was probably the Countess of Radnor who died in 1720.

It was at this house, where the King was visiting, that the Duke of Monmouth, in July, 1673, gave 'a very sumptuous treat' to 'Madam Carwell' (Louisa de Kerhoüel), just created Duchess of Portsmouth, the 'baby faced' beauty sent over to bind Charles II. to the French policy. Several contemporary letter-writers mention the gaieties of this entertainment—the fireworks and the gardens all hung with lamps and great tapers. Thus Henry Ball writes to Sir Joseph Williamson on July 31, 1673:

'On Tuesday last his grace the Duke of Monmouth invited his Majesty to a very noble entertainment at my Lord Roberts at Chelsey, where all the gallants were pleased to be present. The entertainment was intended to be in the Bowling Green, which was enlightened by lamps in an extraordinary manner, but it being too cold for the Ladyes, His Majesty supt within the House, so that all that preparation was to little purpose. On Tuesday next the French Ambassador makes the like feast, but intends to exceed it as much as his master's armes does ours (as his servants pretend) in this warr.'

Another correspondent (Robert Yard to the same) makes it clear that the Ambassador's feast was also given in the house of Lord Robartes.

The Earl of Radnor died at Chelsea in 1685, aged seventy-nine, and his memory is preserved in the name of Radnor Street, not far off. He was buried at Lan Hideck, near Bodmin in Cornwall; but no less than eleven members of his family lie in the old church at Chelsea.

His first wife was Lucie, daughter of Robert, Earl of Warwick, by whom he had three sons—John, baptized at Chelsea, October 14, 1662, and buried

PARADISE ROW, 1740.

there, November 17, 1663; Robert; and Hinder; and two daughters—Mary, baptized at Chelsea, January 18, 1661; and Essex, April 7, 1669, and buried there, January 16, 1694.

His second wife was Isabella, daughter of Sir John Smith (son of Customer Smith). She survived her husband, married Lord Cheyne, and was buried in the middle vault at Chelsea. By her he had three sons—Francis, a President of the Royal Society, buried at Chelsea in 1718, as was his daughter, Elizabeth, in 1696; Henry; and Warwick; and three daughters—Isabella, who married Lord Moore, eldest son of the Earl of Drogheda, and secondly, Wycherly the dramatist, after making his acquaintance casually at the Pantiles, Tunbridge Wells; Aramintha; and Olympia, buried at Chelsea, February 24, 1733.

The following members of the family are also mentioned in the register of burials: Richard Robarts, July 18, 1683; Right Hon. Lady Catherine, September 22, 1700; Hon. Frances Roberts, February 7, 1718; Hon. Russell Robarts, February 1, 1719 (in the middle vault); Right Hon. Countess Dowager of Radnor, September 20, 172c; Hon. John Roberts, September 22, 1746.

The remains of the mansion in Chelsea, for years occupied by Mr. Webb, a wholesale stationer, were pulled down in 1888, and the site is not yet built upon.

Another celebrity of old Paradise Row was Hortense Mancini, Duchesse de Mazarine. As Evelyn wrote in 1678, 'all the world knows her story.' She was the daughter of a sister of the astute Cardinal Mazarine, and made the acquaintance of the future Charles II. when he was 'on his travels,' as his exile was euphemistically termed. It goes without saying that the 'traveller' fell in love with her, and it was proposed that the pair should be married. The uncle, however, disdained the match, as the would-be bridegroom's future was so very problematic, and she was mated in 1661 to Armand, Duc de la Meilleraie, who, to quote Evelyn again, was said to be 'the richest subject in Europe.' He is also described as 'a true son of the Church,' while his lady was a true woman of fashion, as well as one of the most famous beauties of the time. She was so 'impatient of matrimonial restraint,' that the pious Duke found it necessary to confine her in a convent. This effort to reform her was unsuccessful, and eventually, in 1668, she fled from her unloved spouse. In 1675 she came to England, probably because her first cousin was Duchess of York and sister-in-law of the King. She joined his troop of mistresses, and received an allowance of £4,000 per annum. Quarterly payments of £1,000 appear regularly in the list of Secret Service Moneys. This, of course, did not suffice for so extravagant a lady. She was a wild gambler, and constantly in debt and difficulties.

The immediate result of her coming to England was to displace the imperious Duchess of Portsmouth, who had been so nobly entertained at the adjacent Radnor House, in the King's 'affections.' This is what Lady Cowper reports in her diary, March 10, 1716:

'The Duchess of Monmouth entertained us with stories of King Charles's court and death, as follows. . . . The Dutchess of Portsmouth . . . was so blind that for a long time she did not perceive the king's intrigue with Madame Mazarine, long after it was public to everybody else. As soon as she perceived it, she went to everybody to complain that the king forsook her for a woman that had neither Beauty nor Meritt (according to her Opinion). The Dutchess of Monmouth told us that the king had long been weary of the Dutchess of Portsmouth.'

The date of her coming to Chelsea is not recorded, and it was perhaps not until her extravagance had compelled her to give up her house in St. James's.

Here she seems to have spent the summer months, and the little house at the end of Paradise Row became famous for its entertainments. Hither came the Dukes of Devonshire and St. Albans, Ladies Sunderland, Montagu, and Mulgrave, with many others, who amused themselves, we may suppose, with my lady's cats, dogs, monkeys, parrots, and the other items of her zoological collection. The conversation, strange to relate, was literary and Scriptural, the light-hearted Duchess, so we are told, shining greatly in both these subjects.

But literature and theology were not the only entertainments afforded. Music and the drama appealed to the less serious portion of the assemblies, and here the Italian opera is supposed to have been introduced to the English. For her St. Evremonde wrote ' Le Concert de Chelsey,' as well as several other pieces, and much poetry full of adulation. This witty epicurean—Charles de Saint Denis Marquetel, Sieur de St. Evremonde—came of a noble Norman family, had played his part in several battles and sieges, had been confined in the Bastille for satirizing my lady's uncle, the Cardinal, had escaped to England, was made keeper of Duck Island in St. James's Park—a sinecure with a salary of £300 a year—and lived at Chelsea, half lover, half retainer of the ' errant lady ' who was making the place famous. Everyone who knows our National Portrait Gallery will remember the sneering but not disagreeable face, with a large wen between the eyebrows, as represented in Parmentier's portrait. He only survived his hostess by four years, and was buried at Westminster.

The numerous guests of the fascinating Duchess are said by Lysons to have been in the habit of leaving payment for their entertainment under their plates, and this presumably was a considerable source of income. But, however this may be, it is certain that she was always in a more or less impecunious condition, and died at Chelsea in her fifty-second year, 1699, ' a defaulter to the parish rates.' Her funeral oration was composed by St. Evremonde. This is Narcissus Luttrell's comment on the event :

> ' The Duchesse of Mazarine (who for many years kept a gaming table) is dead, by which the government saves £3,000 per annum pention, settled upon her for life by King Charles II.'

On August 5 he tells us :

> ' The Corps of the Dutchesse of Mazarine is shipt off for France, in order to be interred with her Ancestors.'

Time brings about such curious contrasts that it is not surprising to find this scene of so much frivolity and fashionable vice put to as opposite a use as can well be imagined. Here until 1890 was the School of Discipline founded in 1825 by the famous philanthropist Mrs. Elizabeth Fry ; where the refractory

Duchess once disported herself, forty-two refractory girls were reformed for five shillings a week, and trained to earn an honest living as domestic servants. The school is now removed to Fulham. The girls still retain the ugly dress adopted by the foundress, with hair plaistered down on their heads, ugly shoes, and quaint aprons.

Almost as great a contrast was exhibited in Paradise Row in the Duchess's own day, for a few doors off lived Mary Astell, who was the woman's rights advocate of the time, and was freely satirized by contemporary wits, as well as by Addison, Steele, Swift, Smollett, and Congreve. There was really little that was ridiculous, either in her character or her ideas ; her misfortune was, chiefly, that she was born before her time. Had she lived in these latter days, she would have found a great work ready to her hand.

She attempted to persuade her sex to form a community pledged to celibacy, and this college of hers would probably have been established but for the remonstrances of Bishop Burnet, who regarded it as a nunnery.

Her ideas are set forth in a little tract entitled ' A Serious Proposal to the Ladies, for the advancement of their true and greatest interest. By a lover of her sex. London, 1694.' A British Museum copy has the autograph of the writer on the fly-leaf:

'For the Honourable M^d Mountague from her Ladiships Most Humble Servat,
M. A.'

She was, undoubtedly, what our forefathers derided as a blue-stocking. Mathematics, philosophy, and logic ; the works of Plato, Xenophon, Epictetus, Cicero, and Seneca—of all these she was a profound student, and earned the respect of such men as Evelyn, Atterbury, Walker, and Dodwell. Atterbury's opinion of her is sufficiently expressed in the following letter to Dr. George Smalridge, 1706 :

'I happened about a fortnight ago to dine with Mrs. Astell. She spoke to me of my sermon [On the Election of the Lord Mayor, 1706], and desired me to print it ; and after I had given her the proper answers, hinted to me that she would be glad of perusing it. I complied with her [request], and sent her the sermon next day. Yesternight she returned it with this sheet of remarks, which I cannot forbear communicating to you, because I take them to be of an extraordinary nature, considering they come from the pen of a woman. Indeed, one would not imagine a woman had written them. There is not an expression that carries the least air of her sex from the beginning to the end of it. She attacks me very home, you see, and artfully enough, and under pretence of taking my part against other divines, who are in Hoadley's measures. Had she as much good breeding as good sense, she would be perfect ; but she has not the most decent manner of insinuating what she means, but is now and then a little offensive and shocking in her expressions—which I wonder at, because a civil turn of words, even where the matter is not pleasing, is what her sex is always mistress of. She, I think, is wanting in it, but her sensible and natural way of writing makes amends for that defect, if, indeed, anything can make amends for it. I dread to engage her : so I may write a general civil answer to her, and leave the rest to an oral conference. Her way of solving the difficulty about swearing to the queen is somewhat singular.'

Atterbury was generally believed to have aided Mrs. Astell in some of her writings. This opinion is very plainly expressed in a letter from Lord Stanhope to Atterbury, December 17, 1706 :

'I must now quarrel with you, Mr. Dean of Carlisle, because I am informed this day that you have put out in print a mighty ingenious pamphlet, but that you have been pleased to father it upon Mrs. Astell, a female friend and witty companion of your wife.'

The great aim of her life was to raise the social condition and improve the education of her sex. The third edition of her ' Essay in Defence of the Female Sex,' London, 1697, contained some laudatory lines by James Drake—an able physician, who spent a somewhat stormy life as a daring and outspoken political writer—from which I take the following :

'With pure Waves henceforth shall Satyr flow,
And we the Change to your Chast Labours owe ;
Satyr before from a polluted Source
Brought Native Filth, augmented in its course.
No longer muddy shall those streams appear,
Which you have purg'd, and made so sweet and clear.
. . . .
To your correction freely we submit,
Who taught us Modesty as well as Wit.
Our sex with Blushes must your Conquest own,
While yours prepare the Garlands you have won.
Your fame secure long as your sex shall last,
Nor time, nor Envy shall your Laurels blast.'

Chelsea long retained a monument of her philanthropic efforts, for the Asylum for Soldiers' Daughters is the outcome of the school for daughters of pensioners which she induced Lady Elizabeth Hastings and other ladies to establish in 1729.

She died in 1731, aged sixty-one, and was buried at Chelsea. Her last years were embittered by the agonies of cancer, for which she had undergone an unsuccessful operation.

The very large number of notable residents in Paradise Row during the eighteenth century, and especially in the early part of it, prove that it was then one of the most important districts in the parish.

Archbishop Sharp, who preached Queen Anne's coronation sermon, is mentioned by Faulkner as living here in 1691. Among the baptisms we find this record :

' 1691. Anne, daughter of the Right Rev. Father in God, Dr. John Sharp, Archbishop of York, Nov. 25.'

Dr. Dering, Dean of Ripon, mentions the Archbishop's residence in Chelsea in his autobiography :

' 1691. This summer, Dr. Sharp, Dean of Canterbury, was promoted to the see of York, vacant by the death of Archbishop Lamplugh. He made me his secretary. I attended him at his consecration, July 5, but lived not in his family, which was at Chelsey, till he went down the next year to Bishopsthorpe.'

Charles, son of Nell Gwynne, is reputed to have lived in Paradise Row in 1692. When six years old he was created Earl of Burlington, and eight years afterwards Duke of St. Albans. He appears among the visitors of the Duchesse de Mazarine, and has a further connection with Chelsea by his appointment as captain of the band of pensioners at the Hospital. He saw some foreign service, and bore the character of an intrepid soldier. In 1694 he married Lady Diana Vere, the only child of the twentieth and last Earl of Oxford, who brought him a great fortune.

Sir Francis Wyndham, who concealed Prince Charles for several days in his house at Trent after the disaster at Worcester, lived here about 1700, and his wife, Lady Hester, was buried in the old church in 1708.

Fitton Gerrard, the last Earl of Macclesfield of that family, died at a house in Chelsea, presumably in Paradise Row, in 1702. The succession to his property involved the family in a serious dispute, which resulted in a duel between the Duke of Hamilton and Lord Mohun, when both disputants were fatally wounded. The Duchess of Hamilton lived in Paradise Row until 1714.

A strange, wild career, shrouded in doubt and mystery, was that of Alexander Blackwell, apparently a resident in Paradise Row between the years 1736 and 1739. He was the son of Thomas Blackwell of Aberdeen, and brother of Dr. Thomas Blackwell, both well-known Scotch divines. Though he pretended to have studied medicine at Leyden under Boerhaave, we find him in 1730 engaged as a corrector for the press by a printer named Wilkins. He then married an excellent woman, Elizabeth, daughter of a well-to-do merchant, who brought him a handsome portion, by means of which he set up as a printer. Prosperity seemed assured, when he was utterly ruined by a combination of London printers, who regarded him as an intruder, and thrown into a debtors' prison. From this he was rescued by the exertions of his wife. Aided by Rand of the Botanic Garden, and encouraged by Sir Hans Sloane and Dr. Mead, she set to work on the publication of 'A Curious Herbal, containing five hundred cuts of the most useful plants which are now used in the practice of physic.' For this work she made the drawings from the plants in the garden opposite her lodging, engraved them on copper, and coloured the prints with her own hands; her husband having supplied the names of the plants, with descriptions abridged from Miller's 'Botanicum Officinale.' The work appeared in two folio volumes in 1737, and its value was shown by its republication, with one hundred additions, by Trew of Nuremberg, 1757-73. Nothing is heard of this worthy woman after the publication of her 'Herbal.'

The register of Chelsea records the burials of two of their children :

' 1736. William, son of Alex. Blackwell. May 3.'
' 1739. Blanch Christian Blackwell. May 11.'

After the publication of the ' Herbal,' Alexander Blackwell obtained the post of director of the improvements at Cannons, the Duke of Chandos's estate, but was dismissed with discredit. He next appeared in Sweden, where he represented himself as a physician, successfully prescribed for the King, and was appointed one of his physicians in ordinary.

Sweden was then under the weak rule of King Frederick, and divided between two factions, known as the Hats and Caps. Blackwell plunged into the intrigues of the time, was arrested, tortured into a confession, and beheaded on August 9, 1747. The exact nature of his crime is still a mystery. It is asserted that he sought to bribe the King to alter the succession to the exclusion of the Crown Prince, but it is suspected that he was ensnared into a bogus plot by the minister, Count Tessin, partly out of jealousy of Blackwell's influence over the King, and partly to injure the rival faction. The proceedings of the tribunal which condemned Blackwell were sealed up by order of Tessin, and remained unexamined for thirty-three years, when Gustavus III. deposited them in the public archives. Their contents were first made public in 1846 in an essay by N. Arfvidsen. Blackwell suffered with remarkable fortitude, and died with a jest on his lips. All the incidents in his life tend to show that he was a man of intelligence, but utterly wanting in principle.

Among other residents who must be rapidly enumerated were William Aglionby, 1704-6, envoy from Queen Anne to the Swiss Cantons ; Sir Thomas Pelham, 1705, politician ; George Stepney (died here, 1707), friend of Addison, and British Envoy at Berlin—a large number of his valuable despatches are in the British Museum ; John Pennant (cousin of the topographer's father), died 1709; Edward Fowler, Bishop of Gloucester, 1714, a good harmless man, who believed in witches ; Richard Mead, M.D., 1714 ; Henry, Duke of Kent, 1715 ; Rev. James Miller (died 1743), author of the ' History of the Bible'; Rev. Thomas Stackhouse, 1750 ; Richard Suett, the comedian, died 1805.

Some early English artists had their home in Paradise Row. William Hamilton was born in Chelsea in 1750, and lived here for some years. His father was an architect, and one of the assistants of the celebrated Robert Adam. William Hamilton was a historical and fancy subject painter, but did not reach any great eminence. He exhibited with the Incorporated Society of Artists in 1771, and also with the Royal Academy in 1774 and 1775, when he gave his address as Paradise Row, Chelsea. Faulkner says that John Collet died here in 1780, after a long residence. Redgrave says that he lived and died in Cheyne Row, but there is no doubt that Faulkner is correct. We find John Collet exhibiting from Chelsea as early as 1770, and continuously for some years, at the Free Society of Artists. He is best described as a plagiarist of Hogarth; his copy of Hogarth's 'Affiliation' is among the Dyce pictures in the South Kensington Museum. Another artist, known as Collet, Senr., but no relation to this painter, died at Chelsea in 1771. John Giles Eccardt, a portrait painter, to whom Walpole addressed his poetical epistle of 'The Beauties,' also died in Paradise Row, after a residence of some years, in 1779, as did Samuel Cotes, a miniaturist and draughtsman in crayons, brother of the more famous Francis Cotes, in 1818.

In 1730 Mary, Duchess of Ormond, daughter of the Duke of Beaufort, was living in a large house at the east end of Paradise Row, near Burton's Court. She was the wife of James Butler, second Duke of Ormond, who died in exile at Madrid in 1745. Possibly she came to Chelsea on his impeachment and hasty flight in 1715.

The first Duchess of Ormond appears to have been resident in Chelsea in 1664, when her name appears as a customer for the salmon caught by the Chelsea fishermen.

Ormond House was subsequently occupied as a naval school. The date of this conversion is obtained from a pamphlet, copies of which are still extant, entitled, 'Reasons for opening the Maritime School proposed in 1777, and now established on the Banks of the Thames at Chelsea, Lond., 1779.'

A later pamphlet (October, 1781) thus describes the situation:

'It is truly on the banks of the Thames, being in Paradise Row, Chelsea, on the water side, in a fair healthy, detached spot. It is an old house, properly cleansed and fitted up, to contain 26 scholars, with the several officers and servants, who are necessary to reside in the house.'

Among the officers were the following:

Superintendent ...	...	Lieutenant Edward Howorth.
Secretary	...	Mr. John Pugh.
Mathematical and Navigation Teacher	}	Mr. John Bettesworth (a well-known name in Chelsea).
Drawing Master ...	...	Mr. J. T. Serres (a good painter of marine subjects, son of Dominic Serres. There is an example of his work at the South Kensington Museum).
Treasurer	...	Mr. Jonas Hanway (a very benevolent gentleman, now best remembered, perhaps, in connection with the introduction of the umbrella, 1786).

The rules were framed in a pleasing, quaint spirit. Religion was the basis of the whole; no lad was admitted until he had had the small-pox, either by inoculation or in the course of nature ; no pocket-money was allowed beyond sixpence a week; the captain of the school wore a medal inscribed, 'Maritime School, Chelsea. The Captain. We hope for glory,' and the lieutenant wore a similar medal; all were in uniform.

When a new scholar was admitted (aged eleven), the captain addressed him in the following words :

'My worthy schoolfellow,—

'By our laws it is my province to address you on this serious but pleasing occasion of initiating you into our society. As it hath pleased Divine Providence to place you under the care of the generous governors of this school, it would be gross folly, as well as ingratitude, if you were not thankful for it, and in all respects obedient to the salutary laws which are here established.
. . . .
'You declare in your Petition that you have read the rules of the School with care ; you must read them again, at least once in six months, and consider how time rolls, and what you are about. . . . .
'May the Almighty guide us in his paths, and bring our learning, religion and good manners to a glorious issue.'

Each boy on leaving (aged fourteen) received a form of caution, enjoining religion, peaceableness, good-humour, purity of speech, and discipline.

In the grounds was a ship of considerable size, which worked on swivels, so that the various evolutions, etc., could be studied as conveniently as could be expected on dry land. Faulkner quotes the following from a contemporary newspaper, August 16, 1782 :

'The ship lately erected in the playground of the Naval Academy, Ormond House, for the instruction of their pupils in ship manœuvres, was, in solemn form, named the Cumberland, by way of compliment to his Royal Highness the Duke of that name, president of the Maritime School. The ceremony was as follows,—The ship being completely rigged, her sails bent, and the young gentlemen drawn up in file, the senior student upon a signal given, advanced and flung a bottle of wine at her head, pronouncing her name. The ship was then put about thrice, the scholars and company repeating "The Cumberland," after which they all returned into the house to dine. Several royal and constitutional toasts were given and an excellent song written purposely for the occasion was sung to the tune of "Rule Britannia." The evening was concluded with great mirth and good humour. All present expressed the highest approbation of the order, regularity and commodiousness of the house, with the warmest wishes for the success of so useful and so national an establishment.'

In advertising some vacancies (November 26, 1782) the governors say :

'It is ever the first object of the institution to assist the families of those brave officers who have sacrificed their lives in the service of their country, or of those who shall live to pursue the same glorious cause, but the fathers of numerous children ; it is hoped the recommendation of the governors will be enforced.'

ORMOND HOUSE.

The site of Ormond House (the name of which is perpetuated in a short squalid street, Ormond Row) is now occupied by a few small shops. At the corner is a public-house, called the Chelsea Pensioners, on the site of which

31

Thomas Faulkner, the historian of Chelsea, kept a bookseller's and printer's shop, and laboured year after year in the collection of material for his local histories.

Faulkner was born in 1777, and commenced his literary career at the age of twenty, by some contributions to the *Gentleman's Magazine*, for which he occasionally wrote during a period of fifty years. In 1805 his ' Short Account of

THOMAS FAULKNER.

Chelsea Hospital ' appeared, and five years later his ' History of Chelsea,' undoubtedly the best work of his life. On its completion the Rev. Weeden Butler, jun., addressed the following lines to him:

> ' To cull correctly from the withering page
> Of ancient lore, sweet Chelsea's site and age ;
> To mark her bounds, inhabitants, and soils,
> Her manufacturing arts and rural toils ;

And paint the beauteous prospects that endear
Our favourite spot through each revolving year ;
This task of taste and judgment might demand
Full many a careful head and patient hand.
Faulkner ! thine unassisted labour proves
How well the heart can trace the scene it loves ;
To thee our warmest gratitude is due ;
A masterpiece of skill thou hold'st to view,
Oh ! may hard-earnèd wreath of fame be thine,
Whose finis'd work exceeds the bright design.'

Mr. Luke Thomas Flood, of Belle Vue Cottage, also addressed some lines to ' T. Faulkner, the immortal author of the " History of Chelsea " ' :

'Oh, Faulkner ! thy work sublime
Is worth a waggon load of rhyme,
And all who live in coming ages
Shall lean in rapture o'er thy pages ;
Tho' dead as Chelsea, a proverb be,
Sweet Chelsea shall ever live in thee.'

His other works were the 'History of Fulham and Hammersmith,' 1813 ; 'History of Kensington,' 1820 ; new edition of Chelsea, in two volumes, 1829 ; 'History of Hammersmith,' 1839 ; and 'History of Brentford, Chiswick, and Ealing,' 1845. His manuscript catalogue of the pictures in Burlington House, Chiswick, is in the British Museum (MSS. Addit., 12,207). Faulkner was versed in the French, Italian, and Spanish languages, and translated 'The Picture of England,' by the Duke de Levis.

He died at 27, Smith Street, May, 1855, at the age of seventy-eight, and was buried in Brompton Cemetery, near the Fulham Road entrance, against the south wall. The epitaph begins with a curious error, 'Ulcior (for Lector) si monumentum requiris, libros ejus diligenter evolve.'

There is a lithographed portrait of Faulkner prefixed to his 'History of Kensington' (1820). There is another and later portrait, a small mezzotint, very unlike the former ; Faulkner sent a copy to Mr. Joseph Mayer, accompanied with the following lines :

'ON MY PORTRAIT, ENGRAVED BY A PUPIL OF QUINTIN MATSYS !

'This seems a Blacksmith, as you plainly see,
But recollect this smith is meant for me ;
Yet never mind though dark his face appears,
His course through life has met with many cheers,
His hard-earn'd merits far extend his name,
And lead him on to Friendship and to Fame.
'Tho. Faulkner.
' Chelsea, March 16th, 1847.'

Faulkner deserves great credit for his conscientious and unremitting industry in the collection of materials for his local histories. His work is, however, by no means without faults. His ' History of Chelsea ' (2nd edition) is very discursive, and swollen to two volumes by the introduction of much extraneous matter and details of the narrowest local interest. Some astonishing errors also appear in his works ; scarcely a single epitaph in the old church at Chelsea is copied correctly ; and in other places he betrays a painful lack of the power of discrimination. Above all, he committed the grave fault, common to many topographical writers of his day, of taking everything upon trust. But still, after all reservations, his books are of high value, and necessarily have formed the basis of all subsequent works on the same subjects. It is hardly too much to say that none of the stories of Old Chelsea, that have appeared in recent years, would have been written had not ' kind old Tom Faulkner,' as Kingsley calls him, worked, year after year, on those dry details of which he never wearied. Much of the historical material which now lies ready to the hand of any who care to seek it, was, in Faulkner's time, quite inaccessible and indeed unsuspected, and the wonder is that he did so well.

GOUGH HOUSE.

Towards the end of the seventeenth century, or at the beginning of the next, John Vaughan, third Earl of Carberry, built what has since been known as Gough House. As Lord Vaughan, Charles II. had bestowed on him, in recognition of the steady loyalty of his family, the governorship of Jamaica, and with the money he amassed there, probably, he bought a piece of land in Chelsea, to the west of the Royal Hospital, and built the house now to be described. The following note relating to the approach to the house was found by Faulkner among the Cadogan Papers (May 30, 1707) :

> ' Be it remembered, that William, Lord Cheyne, pursuant to the intention of the within-written indenture, for the consideration therein mentioned, doth hereby for him and his heirs, grant unto the within-mentioned John, Earl of Carberry, and his heirs, that way or passage, of nine feet broad, beginning at the road which leads through Chelsea [now Queen's Road West], and from thence down and in the Swan next the Thames, and turning and leading from thence eastward, and a new gate passage entering into the garden ground, part of the premises within-mentioned, to be conveyed to the Earl of Carberry,' etc.

He is one of the five presidents of the Royal Society who have been connected with Chelsea. He was of an eccentric nature, and many whimsical anecdotes are related of him. He died in his coach, when on his way to Chelsea, on January 16, 1713. Ralph Palmer, writing to Viscount Fermanagh on January 27, 1713, alludes to his death and character :

> ' Lord Carberry lies in state at his house, and is to be deposited in the Abbey on Wednesday night. His daughter (the Lady Ann Vaughan), who enjoys all he has, except some few legacies, has bought in 6 horses already, her father never keeping above a pair. He had been with his banker, and returning home, sickened and died presently. He had redeemed his estate and amassed wealth by the government of Jamaica, where he carried many *shauntlemen* of Wales with him, and sold 'em there for slaves, as he did his chap-

GOUGH HOUSE.

lain, to a blacksmith ; and tho' he has left 4,000*l*. per annum, besides a great personal estate, was contented rather to keep all he had gotten to himself than to dispose of her well in marriage with any part of it, or the settlement of his estate on or after his death, tho' 84 years old, so that you will not wonder at his servant's answer upon an " How do you " sent him, that his master, he believed, was by that time got half way to hell, whom thro' excessive penury he almost starved living.'

The daughter to whom the property passed, married, a few months after her father's death, the Duke of Bolton. She was not the lady of his choice ; he is said to have been forced into the marriage, and he left her at the church door, and never lived with her. She survived his neglect, however, until 1751, and then her ungallant spouse married Lavinia Fenton, the famous Polly Peachum, whose charming portrait by Hogarth is now in the National Gallery.

The date at which the Earl of Carberry's daughter parted with her Chelsea estate is not known, though it could not have been very long after the death of the Earl, for the purchaser, Sir Richard Gough, a wealthy merchant, died on February 9, 1728, at which date he was member for Bramber, in Sussex (*Monthly Chronicle*). Before his death he sold part of the property to his neighbour, Sir Robert Walpole. Henry, his successor, was made a baronet in 1728, and his first wife, Catherine, died at Gough House in 1731. Through his second wife, Barbara, he acquired the property of Sir Henry Calthorpe, whose name he adopted. This accounts for the name given to Calthorpe Terrace, now merged into the King's Road. He became Baron Calthorpe in 1796, and removed to Edgbaston, near Birmingham.

The Goughs were succeeded by the Pembertons. The elder Mr. Pemberton had gained some reputation in the East India Company's service, and his son, who died in 1816, was apparently a scholar of some position ; he was a tutor of Emanuel College, Cambridge, and Registrar of the University. On the death of her husband, Mrs. Pemberton opened a ladies' school in the house, which was continued by her daughter. Subsequently it was used as a boys' school by Dr. Wilson.

Gough House luckily escaped destruction when the Board of Works acquired the land previous to the construction of the Embankment. It was purchased by a committee of gentlemen, who opened it as the Victoria Hospital for Children. Since then another block of buildings has been placed to the south of the house, and although the old house yet survives, in a measure, it is hardly recognisable from its altered surroundings.

From the views given in Faulkner, we should judge that Gough House originally had very pleasant surroundings. The Dutch taste prevailed when the Earl of Carberry built the house, and its gardens took the trimmest and severest form. Afterwards, as we see from the second view, they assumed a more natural and picturesque character. They sloped to the Thames, whose bank was then a succession of pleasant gardens with riverside summer-houses, as we may see in Vivares' print after Maurer.

TURRET HOUSE.

Turret House was a handsome square brick structure, built in the reign of Queen Anne. Here lived the Rev. William Rothery, a schoolmaster. One of his prospectuses is headed by a small perspective view of the house (Thorogood, sculp.), on which the sketch here given has been founded. The prospectus

TURRET HOUSE.

begins, ' At the Rev. Mr. Rothery's School, the Turret House, Paradise Row, Chelsea, Young Men are Boarded and Qualified for the University or Business.'

Mr. Rothery was elected Lecturer of Chelsea in 1735, in opposition to the Rev. William King, son of Dr. King, the late Rector. Professor Martyn, writing to Faulkner, gives him the following character:

' Mr. Rothery carried the Lectureship against my uncle, Mr. King. He was a very good scholar, and an excellent schoolmaster; but his sermons were composed in haste, and not delivered with any peculiar grace. At the end of his life he became insolvent and lost in drink. I preached for him in Church, and at Ebury Chapel, when he could no longer do it himself.'

In 1761, Mrs. Banks, mother of the famous scientist, Sir Joseph Banks, came to live in the house, and resided in it for many years. In his early Chelsea days Sir Joseph was an ardent angler, and spent many a day and night on the river, frequently in the company of Lord Sandwich, First Lord of the Admiralty; this early connection secured for him a life-long patron.

Turret House was pulled down in 1816.

DURHAM HOUSE.

Durham House, in Smith Street, facing Burton's Court, was a fine old house, with little or no history. It may have been the residence of Sir Edmund Burton in the middle of the sixteenth century, and thus have given the name to the enclosure which stands before it ; but this is merely conjecture. It was standing in 1694, and on Hamilton's Survey is named 'The Ship House.' Tradition says it was a tavern, and was frequented by the workmen engaged in building the Royal Hospital. This may be well founded, but other traditions, which name it as the residence of Katherine of Aragon, Lady Jane Grey, and Nell Gwynne, are certainly baseless. The house is said to have been rebuilt at the beginning of the eighteenth century, and was occupied as a French school successively under MM. Ouiseau, Clement, and Dr. B. Granet. L'Estrange, writing before the last rebuilding, says :

> 'The age of this house is shown by the infirmity of its walls, which, though massive, have bulged inwardly, and would have fallen had they not been strengthened. It was evidently a place of importance, and stands back behind a broad gravel road and green sward. There are eleven large windows in front on the first floor, and a fine massive oaken door, the jambs of which are adorned with carving. The entrance hall is nearly square, and the grand staircase is above seven feet wide, with twisted balusters and low steps. All the rooms are panelled, large, and lofty.'

When Bryan wrote, in 1869, Durham House was occupied by the Rev. Dr. Wilson, of Holy Trinity, Knightsbridge.

It is now the town residence of Sir Bruce and Lady Seton, and though it has been rebuilt with a red-brick front, in not very good taste, the interior retains the characteristics and proportions of an old English manor-house. The walls are oak-panelled, coloured above in a rich Pompeian red ; the ceiling of the hall is crossed with oak beams ; the marble mantelpieces are beautiful works of art ; and the house is crowded with pictures and drawings, old furniture, tapestry, and curiosities. Sir Bruce comes of ancient lineage, counting Mary Seton, one of the Queen's 'Four Maries,' and the celebrated beauty, Elizabeth Gunning (who married the Duke of Hamilton at midnight with a curtain ring) among his ancestors. Here, in Durham House, we may see a piece of lace worn by Mary, Queen of Scots, the night before her execution, and a portrait of the beautiful Duchess. Among other noteworthy objects, a chair which belonged to Alexander Pope; a pen-and-ink drawing by the present Queen, and portraits of Charles I. and Cromwell may be noticed.

SMITH STREET.

Faulkner lived in Smith Street, built between 1794 and 1807 (and named after the builder, Mr. Thomas Smith, of Manor Terrace), after he left Paradise Row. About 1847 he issued the following prospectus :

'Cadogan Library, No. 27, Smith Street, Chelsea.

'Mr. Faulkner has the honour to announce to the Inhabitants of Chelsea and its Environs, that this Library (removed from Paradise Row) has been established upwards of 40 years, and now contains an extensive and valuable collection of Works in History, Divinity, Topography, and Antiquities, Voyages and Travels, Lives and Memoirs, Poetry and the Drama, including the works of Sir Walter Scott and the most eminent periodical writers of the day.

'Literary persons who may be engaged in Historical, Topographical or Antiquarian Researches, will find here ample resources in furtherance of their labours, surpassed only by the great London libraries.'

Smith Street was for a time the residence of Mr. Hubert Herkomer, A.R.A., the remarkable artist whose many-sided talent, in painting, engraving, carving, iron-work, music, and the drama, recalls the great masters of old. Mr. Herkomer's first great picture was a Chelsea subject, 'The Last Muster.'

Durham Place was built in 1794. To the north of it was Manor House, an old-looking house, without any pretensions to beauty, but standing in pleasant grounds. It faced Green's Row, now called St. Leonard's Terrace (built 1765, and named after the owner of the property).

THE SWAN.

Adjacent to the Pharmaceutical Gardens, on the east side, was an old tavern known as 'The Swan.' It stood on the very edge of the water, with projecting wooden balconies, and entrances from road and river. In Pepys' time it was a favourite resort for the townsfolk—a pleasant jaunt by land or water, pleasant gardens to idle in, and, doubtless, good entertainment for man and beast. On April 9, 1666, he, with Mrs. Pearce, and 'that jade Knipp,' whose husband's humour did not always fall in with the easy code of morals that governed the times, went abroad, 'thinking to be merry at Chelsey; but being come almost to the house by coach, near the water, a house alone—I think "The Swan"—a gentleman walking by called to us to tell us that the house was shut up of the sickness [London's annual scourge, the plague]. So we, with great affright, turned back, being holden to the gentleman, and went away, I, for my part, in great disorder, for Kensington.' However, he was there again on another occasion : 'After the play we went into the house, and spoke with Knipp, who went abroad with us by coach to Chelsey, and there in a box in a tree, we sat and sang, and talked and ate ; my wife out of humour, as she always is when this woman is by.' Doubtless the good easy man thought she was as unreasonable as Knipp's husband !

The Swan was the goal of Doggett's Coat and Badge race. Thomas Doggett, an esteemed comedian of the days of Wilks, Booth, and Cibber, was, as Steele put it, 'a Whig up to head and ears'; and so, when George I. came to the throne in 1715, he instituted this race in memory, the coat being of the Whig colour—orange—and the badge bearing the white horse of Hanover. The race is for watermen's apprentices who have just completed their time, and is rowed against the tide every first of August, and Chelsea is still the goal, but the competitors have now to struggle on for an additional quarter mile to a tavern above Battersea Bridge. It has always been very popular among the rivermen. Bryan prints the following chorus, said to have been written by a waterman :

> 'Let your oars, like lightning flog it,
> Up the Thames as swiftly jog it,
> An you'd win the prize of Doggett,
>   The glory of the river !
> Bendin', bowin', strainin', rowin',
> Perhaps the wind in fury blowin',
> And the tide agin you flowin',
>   The coat and badge for ever !'

Doubtless the popularity of the contest is largely due to the fact that each of the many pockets of the coat contains a guinea.

Dibdin came to the old Swan on one occasion to see the finish of the race, and the result was his nautical opera, ' The Waterman.' The gem of the piece is Tom Tug's song :

> ' Then farewell, my trim-built wherry,
> Oars and coat and badge, farewell,
> Never more at Chelsea ferry
> Shall your Thomas take a spell.'

The Swan was the subject of some litigation in 1728. Among the depositions taken by Commission (Exchequer Series) is one giving the value of the plaintiff's (Anthony Bromwich Abbott) lands, situate in or near Chelsea, or elsewhere in the county of Middlesex, particularly the tavern at Chelsea called the Swan.

THE SWAN, FROM THE RIVER.

32—2

Smollett mentions ' Messrs. Wilton and Russell, and all our brotherhood at the Swan,' in one of his letters. The old tavern, which figures in Marryat's novel, ' Jacob Faithful,' was converted into a brewhouse about 1780, and in the records of the Pharmaceutical Garden we find that one Lyall, the owner, was permitted to make a window overlooking the gardens, on an annual payment of five shillings, he agreeing, also, to close it, if required, at three months' notice. The brewery was discontinued about fifty years ago; the grounds extended from where Wentworth House now stands to Monkswell House, and the name is still preserved in Swan Walk.

THE PHYSICK GARDEN FROM THE RIVER, 1882.

The name of the Swan tavern was continued in a house which stood on the west side of the Physic Garden. It had a floating pier for steamboat passengers, and most of the old Chelsea residents can remember its arbours and the gardens sloping to the river. It disappeared with the construction of the new Embankment, and Mr. Wickham Flower's house—Old Swan House— stands almost on its site.

CHELSEA EMBANKMENT.

To the south of old Paradise Row, along the new Embankment, there now stands a terrace of houses of considerable architectural pretensions, interrupted by the Pharmaceutical Garden. Clock House and Old Swan House are from the designs of Mr. Norman Shaw, R.A., who has had so much to do with the revival of old-fashioned English domestic architecture. Monkswell House was built for the first Lord Monkswell, better known to fame as Sir Robert Collier. His well-known artistic skill is inherited by his second son, the Hon. John Collier, whose picture of ' The Last Voyage of Henry Hudson,' in the Chantrey Collection, gives him a high position among contemporary artists. For some years he had a studio in the rear of Monkswell House.

Tite street, leading into Tedworth Square, is named after Mr. W. Tite, M.P. It has a reputation as an artistic and æsthetic colony. White House was built for Mr. Whistler, and later on was occupied by Mr. Harry Quilter, the well-known art critic. Mr. Oscar Wilde lives at No. 16, and the late Mr. F. W. Chesson, of the *Daily News*, and secretary of the Aborigines' Protection Society, lived at No. 3. Among the artists whose names are, or have been, associated with this street, are Mr. Frank Dicey, Mrs. A. Lea Merritt (The Cottage), Mr. J. S. Sargent, Mr. R. Caton Woodville, the late Frank Miles, Mr. A. Stuart-Wortley, and Mrs. Arthur Murch.

THE PHYSIC GARDEN.

On the south side of Paradise Row (now called Queen's Road West) stands a piece of ground belonging to the Apothecaries' Company, and used by them as a Botanical Garden for the growth and study of plants useful in pharmacy. This land is first mentioned in 1647, when

> ' Sir Arthur Gorges, knt., Elizabeth his wife, and Arthur Gorges their son, by deed enrolled in Chancery, 25 October ejusdem, in consideration of 80*l.* grant to Edward Cheyne, Merchant Taylor of London, in fee, All those three several parcels of arable land, lying in the east field, abutting on the south of the Thames, and Cox's close on the north, containing by estimate four acres, more or less, now or late in the possession of J. Burchard, or his assigns.'

It is not clear that this Edward Cheyne was any relation of the subsequent Lord of the Manor. By his will, dated April 4, 1662, he bequeathed a yearly rent-charge of six shillings ' to be paid out of that corner house and ground in the possession of John Casey, situated in Cox's close, at the rent of twenty pounds per annum.' This sum, to be spent in bread, was given in commemoration of his deliverance from fire fourteen years previously.

In 1673 the Apothecaries' Company were seeking a suitable piece of land on which to build a barge-house for the convenience of their state-barge, and could find none more convenient than this piece at Chelsea. Accordingly, on August 23, 1673, Charles Cheyne, Esq., being then Lord of the Manor,

'did demise and grant unto the Master, Wardens, and Society of the Art and Mystery of Apothecaries of the City of London, their successors and assigns, the piece and parcel of ground and premises therein mentioned, to hold from Michaelmas then next ensuing, unto the full end and term of sixty-one years, at the yearly rent of five pounds.'

In the following year the land was walled round, and a piece of it planted with herbs. Thus Chelsea has the interest of possessing the oldest existing botanical garden in England. It had, however, several predecessors. John Gerarde established one in his own garden late in the sixteenth century, and published catalogues of his plants in 1596 and 1599; in 1622 Henry, Earl of Danby, brother of Sir John Danvers, conveyed to the University of Oxford five acres of land, opposite Magdalen College, for the encouragement of the study of physic and botany; the original gateway, designed by Inigo Jones, is still standing. John Tradescant, gardener to Charles I., established a garden for the cultivation of exotic plants about 1630. John Evelyn records another garden at Westminster. On June 10, 1658, he writes:

'I went to see the Medical Garden at Westminster, well stored with plants, under Morgan, a skilful botanist.'

The plants contained in this last garden were removed to Chelsea in 1676; in June of that year the Court of Assistants 'agreed to take Mrs. Gape's lease of the garden at Westminster off her hands for the remaining two years for the sum of £16, the rent being £2 per annum, with the liberty of removing the plants to Chelsea Garden.'

The first gardener appointed appears to have been one Piggott; but nothing more is known of him beyond that he was discharged after about a year's service. In 1680 Mr. John Watts, a learned botanist for his time, who had interested himself in the garden from the first, was appointed curator and manager at a salary of £50 per annum. Under his care the garden rapidly became famous. Dr. Herman, professor of botany at Leyden, visited it in 1682, and brought about an exchange of plants. Three years later the ever-observant John Evelyn came hither, and has recorded his impressions:

'1685, August 7th, I went to see Mr. Watts, Keeper of the Apothecaries' Garden of simples at Chelsea, where there is a collection of innumerable varieties of that sort; par-ticularly, besides many rare annuals, the tree bearing jesuit's bark, which had done such wonders in quartan agues. What was very ingenious was the subterraneous heat, con-veyed by a stove under the conservatory, all vaulted with brick, so as he has the doores and windowes open in the hardest frosts, secluding only the snow.'

This experiment is especially interesting, as it was one of the very earliest attempts in artificial heating made in this country.

THE GAME OF FOUR CORNERS AT THE OLD SWAN, CHELSEA.

Six years later the gardens are mentioned in a MS. description of London gardens, printed in Vol. XII. of the *Archæologia* :

'Chelsay physick garden has great variety of plants both in and out of greenhouses ; their perennial green hedges, and rows of different coloured herbs are very pretty ; and so are the banks set with shades of herbs in the Irish stitch-way ; but many plants in the garden were not in so good order as might be expected, and as would have been answerable to other things in it. After I had been there, I learned that Mr. Watts, the keeper of it, was blamed for his neglect, and that he would be removed.'

Mr. Watts was not 'removed,' but on the expiration of his seven years' lease another man of contemporary eminence, Mr. Samuel Doody, highly spoken of by Ray and Jussieu, was appointed.

Henry, Earl of Clarendon, records in his 'Diary' many visits to this garden, sometimes with his wife, sometimes with Dr. Tenison, and sometimes alone, for meditation. Thus, on May 17, 1689, he writes:

'Being my usual fast-day, I was for above three hours in the Apothecaries' Garden at Chelsea, where I was not disturbed by any company.'

Bishop Cartwright and several other diarists of this period record visits to this garden, which would thus appear to have been generally recognised as a place of interest.

James Petiver, more celebrated as a botanist than either Watts or Doody, was 'Demonstrator of Plants' as early as 1709. His Natural History collection was so important that Sir Hans Sloane offered him £4,000 for it. He purchased it after Petiver's death in 1718, and it is now in the British Museum.

Up to the year 1722 the garden had been for the most part leased to certain members of the company, who for a certain salary agreed to take entire control, provide all expenses, etc. This was almost certain to lead to unsatisfactory results, and the company was unlikely to spend lavishly on a piece of ground that might not improbably go out of their possession in a few years' time. In 1722, however, Sir Hans Sloane, who had purchased the manor from the second Lord Cheyne, by a deed of conveyance :

'grants, releases and confirms unto the said Master, Wardens and Society, and their successors, all that piece or parcel of arable and pasture ground, situate in Chelsea in the County of Middlesex, at that time in their possession, containing three acres, one rood, and thirty-five perches, with the greenhouse, stoves, barge-houses, and other erections thereon, to have and to hold the same for ever, paying to Sir Hans Sloane, his heirs and assigns, the yearly rent of five pounds.'

Two conditions were to be observed : the land was to be put to no other purpose than that for which it was already occupied, and fifty specimens of distinct plants, well dried and preserved, grown in their garden, were to be presented yearly to the Royal Society of London until the number of 2,000 was reached. The first delivery of plants took place in August, 1722, and the last in July, 1774, by which time 2,550 had been presented.

This act of Sir Hans was one of peculiar generosity. He had in former years been much abused by various members of the Apothecaries' Company for his activity in promoting a scheme of the College of Physicians for the establishment of free dispensaries for the poor—a scheme which the apothecaries regarded as opposed to their interests. When Sloane became possessed of the land the apothecaries held on lease, he did a generous act in a double sense in conferring it upon them, and his former opponents did not fail to see it in that light. In 1733 they determined to erect a marble statue to his

STATUE OF SIR HANS SLOANE.

memory in front of the greenhouse. Michael Rysbrach was the sculptor ; he finished his work in 1737, at a cost of £280. Eleven years later it was moved to the centre of the garden, and there it still stands, worn and chipped by the assaults of a hundred and fifty winters.

Linnæus visited this garden in 1736, and made the following entry in his diary :

'Miller of Chelsea permitted me to collect many plants in the garden, and gave me several dried specimens collected in South America.'

33

In many other places Linnæus mentions Philip Miller and his coadjutors, Rand and Hudson, in very high terms.

Philip Miller, called the ' Prince of Gardeners,' was appointed in 1722. Sir Joseph Banks began his botanical studies under him in this garden. It was during Miller's time, too, that Elizabeth Blackwell worked here under the advice of Rand when preparing her ' Herbal' for publication. His ' Gardener's Dictionary,' first published in 1724, passed through many editions, and was translated into Dutch, German, and French. During the fifty years he held the position at Chelsea the garden obtained a European celebrity. He died in 1771, and was buried in Chelsea Churchyard, where, nearly fifty years

THE GREEN HOUSE OF THE PHYSIC GARDEN.

after, the Fellows of the Linnean and Horticultural Societies erected an obelisk to his memory.

One of his assistants at Chelsea was William Aiton, who afterwards, in 1795, became manager of Kew Gardens, and laid the foundation of their present excellence. One of his sons, Charles, educated at Chelsea, became the first curator of the Botanical Gardens at Cambridge.

Miller was succeeded in 1771 by another gardener well known to fame, William Forsyth, who held the position for thirteen years. He was the inventor of a composition for diseased trees, consisting of clay, slaked lime, and fresh cow-dung in about equal parts, which was well known in his own time, and went by the name of ' Forsyth's Plaister.' It does not seem to have been of much use, although Parliament granted him a sum of money for it in 1790-1, and published the recipe.

Among other celebrated botanists and horticulturists who have been connected with the Chelsea Garden may be mentioned William Curtis, demonstrator, 1773; Thomas Wheeler, demonstrator, 1784, who brought up a family of six sons to the same profession; Dr. Lindley, F.R.S., professor of botany; and William Anderson, F.L.S., curator.

The construction of the Thames Embankment increased the size of the Physic Garden by about half an acre, but the growth of the neighbourhood and consequent tainting of the atmosphere renders the rearing of plants in any degree of perfection very difficult. This complaint was first raised in 1837 by Dr. Lindley.

Among the various curious and rare plants which have graced this interesting garden, four cedars, the first ever brought to the country, planted in 1683, have attracted most attention. When planted they were but three feet in height. In 1750 they averaged eleven feet in girth; but twenty-one years afterwards two of them had to be cut down on account of their decayed state. In 1793 the two that were left were more than twelve feet in girth at a point three feet from the ground. Of these one died in 1878 and was removed, and the other will soon follow. A fine oriental plane-tree, one of the finest in the neighbourhood of London, was killed when its water-supply was cut off by the construction of the Embankment. Among the plants mentioned by Faulkner are two specimens of the cork-tree, the paper mulberry, a superb magnolia grandiflora, an old pomegranate, a styrax officinale (still on the wall skirting Swan Walk in 1878), a noble pistachia terebinthus, a maidenhair-tree (still alive), and a Cape tree.

Charles Hatton writes to Christopher, first Viscount Hatton, on April 15, 1690:

> 'I have been to-day at Chelsey Garden, and have made choice of 2 potts of ye passion flower, and am very confident of y^r Lo^ppe need not fear but they will thrive very well, they are soe lusty and stronge,' etc.

Horace Walpole mentions the garden in a letter to Horace Mann, 1742:

> 'I forgot to tell you that I left a particular commission with my brother Ned, who is at Chelsea, to get some tea seed from the Physic Garden.'

A very minute account of the history of this garden is given in R. H. Semple's revised and extended edition (1878) of Henry Field's memoir.

Their long support of this garden is highly creditable to the Apothecaries' Company. Only in the earliest period was it maintained with the idea of making profit out of its produce. Throughout almost the whole period the company has supported it at great expense for the benefit of botanical, and especially, of course, pharmaceutical students. In recent years the question of its discontinuance has more than once been under discussion, but it is to be hoped that this will not be necessary, and that the old Physic Garden of Chelsea, with all its associations with the development of botanical science, will continue to flourish as a green oasis in the wilderness of houses that have grown up about it.

THE THEOLOGICAL COLLEGE.

Early in the reign of James I., Matthew Sutcliffe, Dean of Exeter, projected a theological College, having for its special object the defence of the reformed religion against the attacks of Romish writers. The proposal was heartily taken up by Bancroft, Archbishop of Canterbury, and by him brought under the King's notice. With this King Bancroft would have an easy task; anything in the way of religious controversy was to his liking, and for this particular enterprise he made many well-sounding promises. He endowed the proposed college with the reversion of certain lands in Chelsea, called Thame Shott, then leased to the Earl of Nottingham; he granted the provost and fellows the right of bringing water from the river Lea to London, with power to pass through any man's ground (paying him for damages); he promised them all the timber they should require from Windsor Forest; and he declared his intention of reviving the ancient tribute of 'King's silver'—a poll-tax payable on taking the oath of allegiance and supremacy—'to be yearly enforced as a safeguard against popery,' and the proceeds to go to the building expenses of Chelsea College. But his support proved to be of a very half-hearted character, and of little value to the college. The Earl of Nottingham's lease had thirty-seven years to run, and he charged the fellows £7 10s. per annum for the use of it; the water monopoly, which, it had been expected, would have yielded an ample revenue, became valueless on the completion of Sir Hugh Middleton's New River Scheme; and the poll-tax was not carried out.

The King, however, gave the undertaking the moral support of his presence by laying the foundation-stone on May 8, and lending it the lustre of his name. The Royal Charter, dated May 8, 1618, orders that it should be known as 'King James's College at Chelsey.' On the day following it is mentioned in a letter—Mr. Beaulieu to Mr. Turnbull:

> 'Heretofore I did write unto you of a certain project which was here in hand, for the erecting a colledge at Chelsey, for the studying and handling Controversies on Religion.

VIEW OF JAMES THE FIRST'S COLLEGE.

Which work doth now begin to go forward, the king having passed his grant of the place and the lands about it, which he doth give them for the building and accommodating the same ; especially at the solicitation of the Dean of Exeter, who doth give £1,000 out of his purse, and £300 a year towards the building and making the same. The number of those that are to be entertained there is (as I hear) 20 Doctors, amongst which there will be two for history, besides other students, whereof a good number shall be entertained and instructed there for that function.   This work is the more commendable for that it is most necessary.'

The project is also believed to have had the earnest support of the King's eldest son, Prince Henry, of whom the King and people had such great hopes. Fuller doubted this, as he could find no reference to him in the papers of the college.   But the interest taken by the Prince in the college is mentioned in a circular-letter of the Archbishop of Canterbury, and we find him visiting Chelsea (probably to inspect the works) in 1611.   Among the Ashmolean MSS. (857, n. 159) is a ' Narrative of the Procession of the Mayor and Citizens of London, by water, to meet Prince Henry, and conduct him from Chelsey to Whitehall, upon Thursday the last day of May, 1611.'

The promoters intended to build a large double quadrangle, flanked with towers and side-wings ; the main buildings were to be two stories high, with a piazza along the inner sides of the smaller court.   English architecture was then in a low condition, but this building would have been at least imposing in its dimensions.   The scheme, however, did not obtain the support that its projectors had anticipated, and after Sutcliffe had expended about £3,000 of his own money, scarcely one-eighth of the original design had been realized. Thus the project languished until 1616, when the King again lent his name to an effort to obtain funds.   Royal letters were sent to the Archbishop of Canterbury and to the Lord Mayor.   In the former, Abbot, the Archbishop, was requested to stir up the clergy in his province to make collections for this purpose ; and in the latter, the Lord Mayor was asked to deal with the aldermen, who in turn were to use their influence with the inhabitants of their wards.   Some efforts were made, but with little or no result, as the money collected seems to have been mainly swallowed up in expenses.   After this failure, practically nothing was done in the interest of Controversy College, as Laud nicknamed it, though it dragged on a lingering existence for some forty years.

In the Commonwealth Survey, 1652, it is described as :

'A brick building, 130 feet in length, from east to west, and 33 in breadth, consisting of a kitchen, two butteries, two larders, an hall, and two larger parlours below stairs ; on the second story, four fair chambers, two with drawing-rooms, and four closets ; the same in the third story ; and in the fourth a very large gallery, having at each end a little room, with turrets covered with slate.'

There was a row of elms on the south side of the college.   The building was valued at £30 per annum, and the whole premises, twenty-eight acres, at £69 10s.

The following is a list of the fellows on the foundation :

Matthew Sutcliffe, Dean of Exeter, Provost. He was a born controversialist, and greatly distinguished himself in a famous conflict with a Jesuit named Parsons. His difficulties in connection with the Chelsea College had doubtless much to do with the peevishness and moroseness of the latter portion of his life. Notwithstanding the lack of support, Sutcliffe still clung to his idea, and struggled with great determination to maintain the college. He even willed his property away from his own family for its support. This property con-sisted of four farms in Devonshire, worth about £300 a year ; an 'extent' of £4,000 against the estate of Sir Lewis Stukeley ; a share in the *Great Neptune*, a ship of Whitby ; and all his 'books, household stuff, and such things as he has in Chelsey Colledge.' Misfortune, however, still dogged the progress, if so it might be called, of the college. The profits of the *Great Neptune* were consumed in the repair of the ship ; there proved to be a prior charge on Stukeley's lands ; and in after-years, when the college had ceased to have any function, and had almost died out of memory, the farm-lands were restored to Sutcliffe's descendants. In his will we find this reference to the college :

> 'The college of Chelsey, procured, founded, and built almost all at my charge, prin-cipally for the maintenance of the true catholic, apostolic, and christian faith ; and next for the practice, setting forth, and encrease of true and sound learning, against the pedantry, sophistries, and novelties of the jesuits and others, the pope's factors and followers ; and thirdly, against the treachery of pelagians and arminians, and others that draw towards popery and Babylonian slavery, endeavouring to make a rent in God's church, and a peace between heresy and God's true faith—between Christ and Anti-christ,' etc.

Sutcliffe's eccentricities made him a frequent butt for the wits of the time. Thus Francis Beaumont writes :

> ''Tis liquor that will find out Sutcliffe's wit,
> Lie where he will, and make him write worse yet.'

And Cartwright, in his ' Ordinary,' 1651 :

> ' Old Sutcliffe's wit
> Did never hit
> But after his bag pudding.'

John Overall, Dean of St. Paul's, Bishop of Norwich ; d. 1618. He was one of the translators of the Scriptures, the books from Joshua to Chronicles being entrusted to him. Camden says he was 'a prodigious learned man.'

Thomas Morton, Dean of Winchester, Bishop of Durham ; d. 1659. He was a descendant of Cardinal Morton.

Richard Field, Dean of Gloucester; d. 1616. James I. said of him, after hearing one of his sermons, ' This is indeed a Field for God to dwell in.'

Robert Abbott, Bishop of Salisbury; d. 1617.

John Spencer; d. 1614.

Miles Smith, Bishop of Gloucester; d. 1624. Wrote the preface to the translation of the Bible. Anthony à Wood calls him ' A walking library.'

William Covitt (or *Covill*).

John Howson, Bishop of Durham; d. 1631.

John Layfield; d. 1617. One of the translators of the Bible.

Benjamin Chariott (or *Chasyer*).

Martin Fotherby, Bishop of Salisbury; d. 1619.

John Boys; d. 1643. Translator of the Bible, and one of the revisers. He is said to have been able to read in Hebrew at the age of five.

Richard Brett; d. 1637. Translator of the Bible.

Peter Lilly; d. 1614.

Francis Birley.

William Hellier, Archdeacon of Barnstaple; d. 1645.

John White, Fellow of Manchester College.

William Camden, Clarencieux, and *Sir John Hayward, LL.D.,* were the historiographers.

Among those appointed in after-years were Isaac Barrow ; Mark Antony de Dominy, famous as the Bishop of Spalatro, and for his several changes of faith ; Isaac Bargrave, Dean of Durham ; John Young, Dean of Winchester ; John Prideaux, D.D. ; William Slater, D.D. ; Alexander Strange ; Richard Fitzherbert ; John Saltells ; William Watts ; Alexander Ely ; Theodore Heape ; Samuel Purchas ; John Burley ; and Richard Dean, a young merchant admitted contrary to the design of the institution.

Dr. Featley, known as ' acutissimus ' in controversy, was Sutcliffe's successor. Although somewhat Calvinistic in his opinions, he yet so incurred the hatred of the Puritans, that his church was broken into and damaged, and he himself thrown into prison. There he remained for some months, until, in March 1644, he was permitted to return to Chelsea College for six weeks, where, strange to say, he died on the day that his term expired. He was succeeded by a Dr. Slater, who only held office for one year. The fourth and last provost was Dr. Samuel Wilkinson, Rector of Chelsea.

In Wilkinson's time, Chelsea College became the subject of dispute and litigation. Lord Monson took formal possession of it, on the ground that his wife, the Countess of Nottingham, had a lease of it from the Crown. Dr. Wilkinson demanded £30 a year as the condition of his resigning it ; but this claim was not allowed. In 1651 the Commonwealth Government were seeking suitable places for the safe keeping of their prisoners, and a committee was appointed to inquire ' whether Chelsea College belonged to the State, or to particular persons; if to the State, to make use of it; but if to particular persons, to treat with them that it might be made use of for accommodating some of the Scotch prisoners.' They reported that they had ' conferred with Lord Mounson and Dr. Wilkinson, both pretending an interest therein, and find that there is a suit in Chancery depending between them touching it; but as Dr. Wilkinson, who is in present possession, has a house and parsonage at Chelsey, and it will be no prejudice to the title of either party, if the college, being very convenient, be appointed for keeping some of the Scotch prisoners, they think it should be appointed for the Marshall-General to keep some of his prisoners in, until further order, Lord Mounson consenting thereto; that the said house, after putting to the use, be re-delivered to Dr. Wilkinson, unless law meantime order to the contrary; and that the Surveyor-General survey and make it fit for securing the prisoners, according to the direction of the Marshall-General.'

Thus, in the words of the Rev. J. Darley, Chelsea College became 'a cage for unclean birds.' Among the State papers of this period are many documents relating to the prisoners—their petitions to Parliament, orders for their release on parole and otherwise, and warrants for the payment of their maintenance. Among those whose names have been thus preserved are Major Andrew Cave, Major James Mercer, Major Thomas Henderson, Major William Erskine, General James Wemys, Captain Roger Alsop, James White (Marshall of the Scotch Army at Worcester), Colonel James Graham, and Colonel David Law.

In 1653 seven boatloads of Dutch prisoners were sent to Chelsea, but so crowded was the place at the time that huts were erected for the Dutchmen under the walls.

Meantime there were some who remembered the original purpose of the building, and wished to see it restored to that use. Chief among these was Samuel Hartlib, who published, in 1652, a quarto pamphlet dealing with the subject, entitled, ' The Reformed Spiritual Husbandmen.' In it he proposed that

'The patent for the Foundation of Chelsey Colledge should be reviewed and enfirmed by the authority of Parliament and an addition made unto it of means to maintain more Fellowes, not onely to oppose Popery (for which it was at first founded) but also to maintain an Evangelicall Intelligence and Brotherly Correspondency with Foreign Divines, that by a mutuall concurrence between them and us, the means and helps to propagate true Godlinesse and sound learning everywhere may be set on foot and advanced.'

He develops his ideas at some length, but his scheme was not taken up and the college continued in use as a prison.

On December 12, 1655, three years after the pamphlet appeared, we find Hartlib writing on the same subject to Dr. Worthington, who would be interested in Chelsea matters, as he knew Dr. Wilkinson, and had preached in Chelsea Church in 1651:

> 'I am in hopes that the foundation of Chelsea College will be minded. I am informed by one that well understood the secrets of that society, that their present rents do amount unto £200 per annum, besides moneys bequeathed to them yet in private hands; and that after the expiration of a lease, not a very long one, some hundred more by the year will come to them. I have learned where £2,000 was entrusted in one man's hands, whose friends having divided his estate since his death, must doubtless answer that money as executors of their own wrong. The £200 per annum hath been received of late years by one who is better able than willing to accompt for what he will hardly acknowledge to have received. There are those who endeavour to bag the revenue, or buy it as concealed lands,' etc.

If these assertions be true, it is evident that the provost had been enjoying a very snug sinecure for some years in Chelsea College. The truth seems to be that no one but the founder had cared very much about the college—James I. not enough to support it, Charles I. not at all. The Commonwealth was engaged in sterner work, and ignored it; and when Charles II. was restored, notwithstanding Darley's appeal in 'The Glory of Chelsey Colledge Restored,' no one seriously thought of refounding it.

There was one, however, who thought the building could be put to some philanthropic use. On October 15, 1660, Hartlib wrote to Dr. Worthington:

> 'The honest Earl of Newport hath begged the foundation of Chelsey Coll. to be turned into a Hospital, and hath obtained the grant.'

The last statement was premature, as we find Hartlib again writing, June 4, 1661, in answer to an inquiry:

> 'Chelsey Coll. is not yet set apart for a workhouse for the poor, according to the design and endeavours of the Earl of Newport.'

Nothing more is heard of the Earl of Newport's design, and the college was now a sort of useless derelict cared for by nobody.

On December 4, 1663, John Sutcliffe, a spendthrift nephew of the founder, petitioned the King for a pension, or a grant of the buildings. He states that he had been plundered during the troubles (*i.e.*, the Revolution), and had taken refuge in the college, 'whence he and his wife carried letters to Charles I. through the lines of communication.' He thought he had a right to the buildings, which, indeed, had already been promised to him, and only wrote the petition because he had heard that the King had thoughts of disposing of it otherwise. This rumour proved to be correct, for although his petition was granted, with full power to pull the college down and convert it to his own uses, this grant was subsequently revoked. On June 10, 1664, the president, council, and fellows of the recently-established Royal Society petitioned the King for a grant of Chelsea College and lands, 'that they might be able to prosecute the design for which they were constituted a corporation.' Their application was supported by the Archbishop of Canterbury, the Lord Chancellor, and others. The college was then held on lease by a Mr. Cole, with whom the society proposed to compound for his interest.

Though powerfully supported, the Society's request was not immediately granted, as the Government had another use for it. In January, 1664-5, a warrant was issued to pay Sir George Carteret (Treasurer of the Navy) £5,000, in addition to a previous sum, for the relief of the sick and wounded at sea, the maintenance of Dutch prisoners, and the repair of Chelsea College, to be again used as a prison.

The learned and refined John Evelyn had charge of Chelsea College at this time. He had been appointed one of the four commissioners deputed to look after the sick, wounded, and prisoners; his province included all the ports from Dover to Portsmouth. On February 8 he entered in his journal:

'I visited our prisoners at Chelsey College, and to examine how the Martial and Suttlers behaved. These were prisoners taken in war; they only complained that their bread was too fine.'

Things, however, became very serious as time went on, and Evelyn would probably never have accepted the post had he foreseen how burdensome and repulsive it would become. On October 3 he wrote to Pepys of the increasing numbers he had to provide for, and of the difficulty of finding room for them. He had agreed to hire Leeds Castle (in Kent) from Lord Colepeper, if only money could be found to repair and fit it up. He had deputies and surgeons at Chelsea, two hospitals in London, nine in large towns, and others in villages. In another letter he gives a despairing account of the horrors he had to cope with; the wounded were 'dying like dogs in the street,' and the prisoners 'begged them to knock them on the head,' for there was no food for the wretched creatures. Money it was almost impossible to obtain, the plague had broken out with exceptional virulence among the prisoners, crowded together under what must have been the most unsanitary conditions. Doubtless Chelsea saw many of these dreadful sights; and some years after, in digging up the western court of the Royal Hospital, a great quantity of human bones was discovered in a spot that had probably been used as the prison burial-ground.

Amid such horrors it is not surprising to learn that the prisoners were constantly in a state of mutiny, or that some of them were ready to forget their national feelings and take service with their captors. Among the State Papers is a note by Mr. Tooker, May, 1665, to the effect that the masters who complained of want of hands on account of the severity of the impressments, wished to employ the Dutch prisoners from Chelsey College to load their ships; and in July the Ambassador Van Gogh, living at Chelsea, said in his report to the States-General, that he 'feared that as the plague increased, the Dutch prisoners at Chelsea College and elsewhere would take service under the English, as those who had done so brought home money in their pockets and accounts of their good entertainment.'

Sutcliffe again appealed for royal relief in 1665, saying that when the college building was granted to him, he sold it to one Colebancke for £400; but subsequently the grant was stayed, as the King had decided to present the building to the Royal Society. Thereupon Colebancke threatened to arrest him for breach of contract, and he therefore begged the King to bestow £400 or a pension upon him; the Royal Society, in charity, had promised to give him £100. It appears that some sort of compensation was eventually given him.

The warrant for the grant of the Royal Society is dated November 8, 1666. It was 'to be holden of the manor of East Greenwich by fealty only.' The Society did not immediately obtain possession of the building, as it was still required for the prisoners of war. As an example of the hardships suffered by them, we may turn to 'The supplication of the French prisoners taken in the *Ruby*, and kept at Chelsey College.' They complain of their 'poverty and misery and of the cruelty of their officers.' Then follows a relation which it is to be hoped is overdrawn:

> 'One of their number having attempted to escape, was beaten, all his goods taken away, he put in irons, and shut up in prison 24 hours without food, on which his friends took out some bricks and released him; but he was retaken, and sent back to his prison, and Nicholas Blondel, suspected of aiding him, was sought for. He hid in the pavilion of the prison, resisted orders to come down, threw bricks against two of the officers, but at length came down on their oath not to injure him; in spite of which they murdered him cruelly with many blows, and put his corpse in the same prison with the other offender, though it endangers infection. The gaoler tried in vain to persuade the officers to leave Blondel to him, but in their rage they treated him like the worst offender.'

At length, when the college was no longer required for this purpose, Evelyn notes in his 'Diary':

> 'September 24th, 1667.—I had orders to deliver yᵉ possession of Chelsey Colledge (used as my prison during yᵉ war with Holland, for such as were sent from the Fleete to London), to our Society as a gift of his Majesty our founder.'

The gift was not a very valuable one. It was in such a ruinous condition that it would have cost a large sum to make it serviceable. The Society, moreover, discovered that their legal title was so dubious, that they decided not to risk any money on it at all. We may judge of its dilapidated condition when we read that in 1678 the tiles and timber were stored away under cover to prevent their further decay.

The Society retained possession of this roofless ruin for about eighteen years, during which time several proposals were made concerning it, but all proved abortive. Evelyn suggested that they should let it for £100 a year; another proposed to convert the lands into a nursery garden for choice vegetables, and to repair the buildings at his own expense, if he were appointed perpetual steward; and in 1674 Sir Jonas Moore offered to take a lease of it, and build an astronomical observatory at his own charge, to the care of which he proposed to appoint Flamsteed, the first Astronomer Royal, then a young man. When the King took up the proposal of founding an observatory, Flamsteed favoured the choice of Chelsea College, but eventually Wren decided on Greenwich Hill, a more suitable position in every way.

Meanwhile Prince Rupert, whose attainments in the arts of peace almost equalled his achievements in war, had established a laboratory for glass-making in the neighbourhood of the college. According to the representations of the Society, these works were very detrimental to the college, and had stood in the way of an advantageous sale. The council therefore requested the Prince to take possession of the whole, and recompense them for their loss. Pepys and Sir Richard Southwell joined in these representations, but the Prince did not agree to their request. However, the useless building was not to remain on the hands of the Society much longer.

THE ROYAL MILITARY HOSPITAL.

The constant wars in which England had been engaged had crowded the country with disabled men, for whom there was little or no provision. From the reign of Elizabeth, the State Papers record numerous instances of grants of lodgings, etc., to worn-out veterans, but the number that wandered about the country, living precariously on casual charity, must have been very large indeed. The Parish Books of Chelsea contained several references to such cases. Thus, in 1695:

'Oct. 19. To two poor Souldiers of Coll. Eade's regiment travelling
from Flanders ... ... o o 6d.
To James Cowen, a Souldier in Coll. Graham's regiment,
now come from Flanders ... ... o o 6d.

The problem had for some years engaged the attention of more than one thoughtful mind. As early as 1666 Evelyn, who had witnessed so much of the misery during the time he was a Commissioner, proposed the establishment of an infirmary for disabled soldiers at Chatham. He communicated the details of his plan to Pepys, and, on the whole, they bear a close resemblance to those afterwards adopted at Chelsea. Some fifteen years later, when Sir Stephen Fox, the first Paymaster-General of the Army, was arranging a plan on similar lines, it was natural that he should seek the counsel of Evelyn. The latter records in his 'Diary,' 1681, that he 'dined with Sir Stephen Fox, who proposed to him the purchasing of Chelsey College, which his Majesty . . . would purchase again to build an hospital or infirmary for soldiers there, in which he desired his (Evelyn's) assistance as one of the Council of the Royal Society.'

From this it would appear that Fox had already discussed the matter with the King, who had agreed to the plan, and the recent establishment of the Hôtel des Invalides at Paris may have helped to bring this about. There is no historical support for the more romantic story which credits Nell Gwynne with the original suggestion, and it has no better foundation than an anonymous life of 'honest Nell,' which appeared in 1752. Mr. Peter Cunningham, who made very extensive researches for his biography of her, could find no evidence in favour of the story. Of course it is possible that Fox may have moved her to introduce the matter to the King, and Mr. Hare, in his 'Walks in London,' suggests that the figure of the Orange-girl in Verrio and Cooke's picture in the Hospital refers to her part in the scheme; but this is mere conjecture, and we shall probably be correct if we decide that Nell Gwynne had nothing whatever to do with the establishment of Chelsea Hospital.

On January 27, 1682, Evelyn again records:

'This evening Sir Stephen Fox acquainted me with His Majesty's resolution of proceeding in the erection of a Royal Hospital for emerited soldiers on the spot of ground which the Royal Society has sold to His Majesty for £1,300, and that he would settle £5,000 per annum on it, and build to the value of £20,000 for the relief and reception of four companies, namely, four hundred men to be as in a college or monastery. I was therefore desired by Sir Stephen (who had not only the whole managing of this, but was, as I perceived, himself to be a great benefactor, as well it became him who had gotten so vast an estate by the soldiers) to assist him, and consult what method to cast it in as to government. So in his study we arranged the governor, chaplain, steward, house-keeper, chirurgeon, cook, butler, gardener, porter, and other officers, with their several salaries, and entertainments. I would needs have a library, and mentioned several books, since some soldiers might possibly be studious, when they were at leisure to recollect. Thus we made the first calculations, and set down our thoughts to be considered and digested better, to show His Majesty and the Archbishop. He also engaged me to consider of what laws and orders were fit for the government, which was to be in every respect as strict as any religious convent.'

Sir Stephen Fox, it should be explained, had made a considerable fortune out of his office by a discount transaction, which, from a certain point of view, was not strictly honourable. The troops were then very irregularly

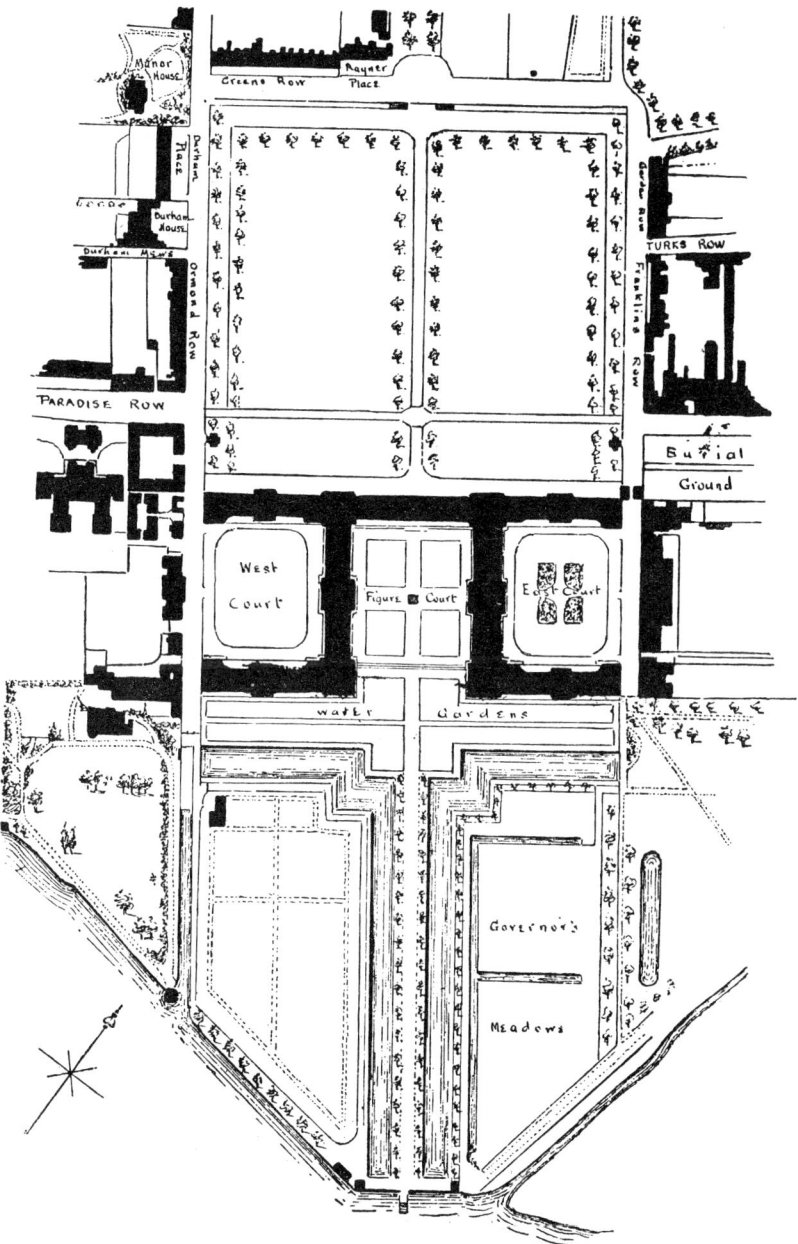

PLAN OF CHELSEA HOSPITAL AND NEIGHBOURHOOD, 1836.

paid, and rarely received their money oftener than twice or thrice a year. Constant murmurings and discontent were the natural consequence, and Sir Stephen conceived the idea of paying them regularly out of his own pocket, charging them one shilling in the pound for the convenience. The payments on which he received this five per cent. amounted to about £130,000 annually, and it is to this arrangement that Evelyn refers when he remarks on the especial fitness of Sir Stephen's benefactions to the hospital.

By the last date the ground must have been cleared of the ruinous college buildings. No trace of these now remain, except some foundation-walls, which

PORTRAIT OF SIR STEPHEN FOX.

may be seen in the cellarage of the chaplain's quarters. During the progress of some sewage works in the western court of the present buildings in August, 1838, some more foundation-walls were discovered at a depth of 15 feet. In parts these were from 15 to 20 feet thick, of brickwork, and so solid and compact, says Faulkner in a letter to the *Gentleman's Magazine,* as to be almost impenetrable to the pickaxe. Other portions were found in Sir Willoughby Gordon's garden.

The following survey of the lands allotted for the hospital (incorrectly printed by Faulkner) was made by Mr. James Hamilton some time after 1687:

	ac.	r.	p.
' 1. The great court, half a parcel of 28 o 4 comes to	14	o	2
2. Thames Shot, arable	19	o	13
3. Medow next Stone Bridge	2	1	30
4. A medow lower at the elbow of the rivulet	1	3	9
5. A parcell of medow to the stairs next the Thames	12	3	28
6. Another parcell belonging to Arnold	2	o	8
7. A parcell of medow where is the kitchen garden	7	1	34
8. Old college site	6	3	32
9. Next the old college where the stable-yard is	2	2	30
10. Taken out of the next ground belonging to my Lord Orford's garden to the quantity of	o	3	18
	71	1	4

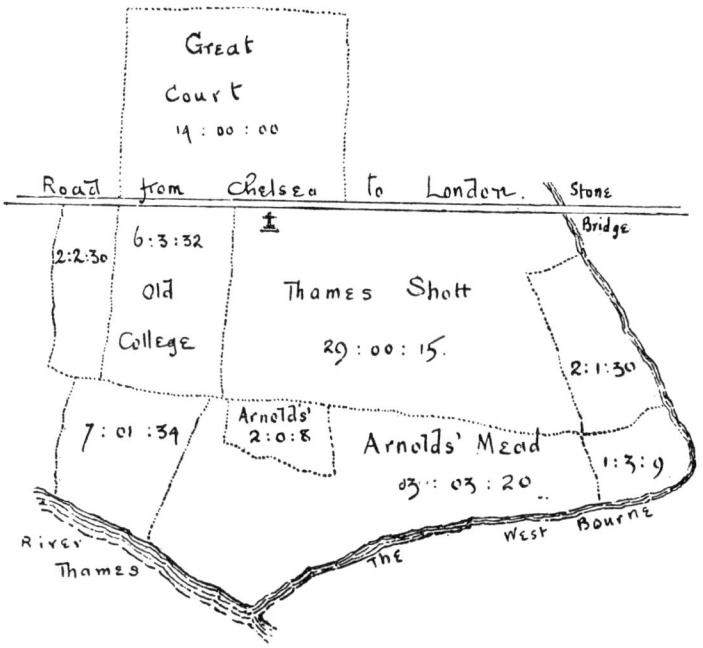

PLAN OF LAND, ABOUT 1680.

There is another survey by the same, which makes the lands slightly larger. Land was purchased from Lord Cheyne, and 3 acres 2 rods from Sir Thomas Grosvenor. The lands purchased from Lord Cheyne were:

1686. Swede Court, on the west.

1687. Burton's Court, 14 ac. o r. 2 p. from Lord Cheyne, since reduced by cutting a roadway through it, in continuation eastward of Old Paradise Row. The origin of this name is unknown. The land is called the Great

Court in the above Survey, but in the Building Accounts we find payment 'to Robert Streeter, serjeant painter, for the two lodges at Burton's.' There was a Sir Edmund Burton living in Chelsea in the reign of Edward VI., and this court possibly indicates the site of his residence. Burton's Court was formerly the Governor's hayfield; latterly it was open to the public as a recreation ground, but is now confined to the military as a cricket-field.

In 1690 the grounds were reduced by the lease of 4½ acres on the west to William Jephson, secretary to the Treasury; and in 1698 by the grant to Lord Ranelagh of the 23 acres previously held by him on lease. The former was redeemed from Lord Yarborough in 1809, and most of the latter has been re-purchased by the authorities.

In 1742, 4 acres were bought for £461 5s., curiously enough out of a legacy by Lord Ranelagh. In 1826 another portion of the Ranelagh estate, 6 a. 3 r. 8 p., was purchased for £9,000 out of a legacy of Col. Drouly.

In 1843, 4 a. 13 p. for £11,970, from the Grand Junction Waterworks Company.

In 1857, 3 a. 13½ p. from Mr. Brett, for £13,886 1s. 7d. (unclaimed prize-money).

The last addition to the hospital lands was made in 1858, when a portion of lands reclaimed from the river was bought from the Crown for £16,500.

When the hospital was completed, the following survey was made (1702):

	ac.	r.	ft.
1. Great Court, north of the building	13	8	124
2. East and west courts	3	29	152
3. Grass-plots and walks between the quadrangle courts and canals...	2	160	180
4. Garden on the east side of the hospital, now called the Governor's	1	156	138
5. Kitchen-garden towards the river	3	80	0
6. Sixty-foot walk between the two canals	1	16	0
7. Walk outside the right-hand canal	0	44	0
8. Walk from the porter's lodge to the king's highway	0	139	0
9. Burial-ground on the eastern side of the hospital	1	80	0
10. Apothecaries' garden	0	50	0
11. Bleaching yards	0	55	0
12. Two forty-five feet footways, one from the east, the other from the west, together	1	14	0

When the building had been finally decided on, very little time seems to have been lost in commencing. In the *Monthly Recorder* we read that on February 17, 1682,

'His Majesty went to Chelsey Colledge to lay the first stone, with several of the Nobility, which is a place designed to be built and endowed by his Majesty for the reliefe of Indigent Officers, and Incouragement to serve his Majesty.'

On May 25, Evelyn again refers to the hospital:

'I was desired by Sir Stephen Fox and Sir Christopher Wren to accompany them to Lambeth, with the plot and design of the college to be built at Chelsey, to have the Archbishop's approbation. It was a quadrangle of 200 feet square, after the dimensions of the large quadrangle at Christ Church, Oxford, for the accommodation of 440 persons with governor and officers. This was agreed on.'

On August 4 Evelyn went with Sir Christopher Wren to survey the foundations. When the building was well on its way the usual lack of money was felt, and as in the case of its predecessor, an attempt was made to collect funds by the aid of the clergy, and apparently with as little success.

The King's letter to Archbishop Sancroft is preserved in several copies. The following is taken from the Tanner MSS., Bodleian Library, 290, f. 223; there is a duplicate in the Cholmondeley MSS. at Candover Hall, Shropshire:

'October, 1684 (probably).—Having oftentimes wth great grief observ'd y^t many of o^r loial subjects, who formerly took up arms for us, and o$_r$ roial father of blessed memory, to resist that torrent of prosperous rebellion, wch at last overturn'd this monarchy, and Church, or who afterwards followed us into forain countries w^n we were driven hence are now by old age, or wounds or other accidents befalling them in y^t service, and disabling them for all other, reduc'd to so extreme poverty, y^t some of them have been forced to beg bread. And farther foreseeing, y^t in our guards, and standing garrisons, and other of o^r forces, necessary to be kept on foot for the safety of o$_r$ roial p'son, and goverm^t there will be many from time to time, who by reason of age, or sickness, or other disabilities will become unfitt to be continued in o^r service and pay and so unavoidably fall under y^e same miserable circumstances with y^e former; We, therefore, out of a tender and deep compassion of ye sad and deplorable condition of so many loial and brave men and being desirous (as much as in us lies) to remove this also among other discouragem'ts which else hinder even men of courage from entring into this kind of service to ye Crown; have upon mature consideration of ye best means, and methods of obtaining so good an end, resolv'd to found and erect at Chelsey (in a place very proper for such a design) a perpetuall hospital, in which more than 400 aged or otherwise disabled soldiers may at present (and so successively y^e same number for ever) be lodged and supplied wth y^e necessary supports of life suitable to their respective conditions. In y$_e$ beginnings and carrying of wch so pious, and charitable a work we have of o$_r$ own roial bounty already expended great sums of money, as by y^e goodly fabrick and to y^r purpose in great part erected is visible to all beholders. But now being sensible, y^t y$_e$ complete finishing of so chargeable an erection and much more y^e perpetual endowm^t thereof for y^e constant maintenance of so many aged and infirm persons will require a greater expence than o^r particular bounty (as o^r affairs now stand) can well extend to; we have thought fitt to call in y^e aid, and assistance of all o^r charitable and well-disposed subjects of estate and quality, and particularly of those of ye clergy who are such, and do therefore hereby will and require you, y^t you forthwith send y^r circular letters to all ye B^{ps} of yor province; earnestly inciting them both by their own example (if they be men of plentifull estate) and however by such topics, and arguments of perswasion wherwth so great and good a cause will abundantly furnish them to deal effectually wth such clergymen wthin their respective dioceses, who beg ye bounty of their patrons, or otherwise are masters of considerable estates, exhorting them to contribute liberally to this good design so manifestly tending to ye glory of God and service of y^r kg. and country. And we do assure both you and them all, that whatsoever hath to be done shall be done in compliance wth this o^r command and sure so just expectations shall be by us most graciously accepted as a p'tic. evidence of yor good affection toward us and of y^r zeal for o^r service.'

That some, at least, of the clergy did not greatly relish their task is apparent from the following letter of the Archbishop of York to Sancroft (Tanner MSS., 32, f. 176):

'Nov. 19 [1684].
'May it please y[r] Grace. I have bin long designing to give yo[r] Grace account of my Visitation of y[e] D. and Chapter, etc.
'My businesse is this. I haue received a second letter from y[e] King about Chelsey Colledge, wherein a change is made of some words particular to y[e] clergy for some other y[t] may comprehend the laity and fetch them in to y[e] same contribution. This I fear will be, not only very troublesome to all ye Bps, but (at least) of no use to ye King. We can neither follow L[ds] gentlemen to their houses, nor summon them to meet us. If we light on them we shall talk with small authority and they will heare wth as little regard. Hatred and contempt we may get, but no money. This I write a la rotée. I beseech yor Grace to consider the thing itself, not my reflexions on it, and speak with whom you think proper, if you do think fit to speak with any or to take notice of the matter.'

Chelsea Hospital was left unfinished on the death of Charles II., and also on the precipitate flight of James II. It was completed in 1691, under William and Mary, having cost altogether about £150,000. By 1872 no less than £289,580 had been expended in buildings and lands.

The following legacies have been left to Chelsea Hospital :

Lord Ranelagh's daughter Catherine greatly offended him by her marriage with Lord Coningsby, and the portion of the estate which would have been hers was set aside for the benefit of the hospital. In 1720 it was invested in South Sea stock, whereby a considerable loss was suffered. It is now in the 3 per cents., and yields about £180 a year.

John de la Fontaine, in 1706, bequeathed £2,000 for the benefit of lame and disabled soldiers. This bequest was transferred to the hospital in 1718, and amalgamated with the Ranelagh legacy in 1725.

In 1818 Col. John Drouly bequeathed property to the hospital which, when realized, amounted to £25,069 13s. 4d. It was invested in the 3 per cents., and after £20,970 had been expended in the purchase of land, as shown above, there yet remained a sum of £7,460 18s. 7d.

In 1845 John Stuart, of Prescot, Lancashire, bequeathed the residue of his estate to the hospital. It was invested, and by 1872 amounted to £3,061 14s. 2d.

When the building was nearing completion it was visited by many who took a keen interest in its object, among others by the King and Queen. Luttrell notes in his Diary :

'March 14th, 1690-1.—The Queen did the Lord Ranelagh the honour to dine with him at Chelsey Colledge, and afterwards viewed that stately fabrick, which will be finish'd this summer, and contain above 400 old and decripit soldiers.'

Again, on April 29 :

'The King dined at the Lord Ranelagh's at Chelsey Colledge, and took a view of the same.'

The building consists of a quadrangle, with two wings and detached offices, and bears a general resemblance in design to the Ospedale dei Mendicanti at Venice, and the Hôtel des Invalides at Paris—both earlier buildings than Chelsea Hospital. In 1693 Wren received £1,000 'for his great care and pains in directing, etc., the building of yᵉ hospitall and settling workmen's bills for ten years past, as per Treãry warrant, dated 9 June, 1693.' In 1687 'Hawsemore' (Hawksmore, Wren's best pupil) had been paid £10 'for drawing designes for yᵉ hospitall' (doubtless from the master's materials; but no designs for Chelsea Hospital are found in the Wren Collection at the Bodleian Library, Oxford).

The merits of Chelsea Hospital as a piece of architecture are undeniable. With very simple materials, Wren has contrived to give us a building perfect in proportion and dignified in effect—one on which the eye dwells with pleasure. Its regularity suggests no monotony; its simplicity no poverty of design; it bears the stamp of genius. Its red bricks have darkened with time, and the Portland dressings are streaked with the grime and dirt of the great city, but still harmonize finely with the delicate greens of the slate roof. The severely formal Dutch water-gardens, as we may see them in the views of Inglis and Kip, were more in keeping

ROYAL MILITARY HOSPITAL, RIVER FRONT, 1805.

with the architecture, and more suggestive of the time of its building, than the richer and more ambitious efforts of our own day; but while the building itself remains unaltered, the spot can never entirely lose that old-world air, picturesqueness, and sense of fitness that has attracted the pencils of Canaletti, Turner, Prout, De Wint, Malton, Pether, and many others, and awakened the enthusiasm of Samuel Rogers.

The large central quadrangle is open towards the river, and cloistered on its inner sides. The north front, looking towards Burton's Court, contains the hall and the chapel.

The chapel, consecrated by Dr. Compton, Bishop of London, on August 30, 1691, is 110 feet long and 30 feet wide. It is paved with black and white

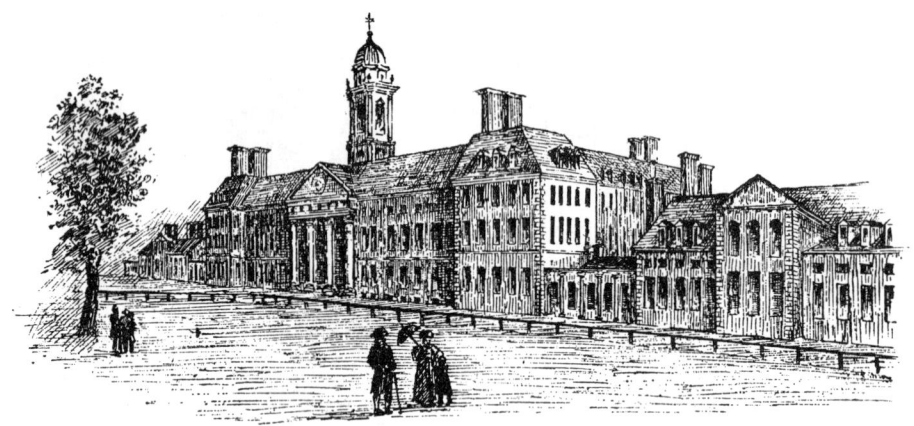

ROYAL MILITARY HOSPITAL, NORTH FRONT, 1841.

marble, and wainscoted with Dutch oak. On each side of the altar are wood-carvings by Grinling Gibbons; and above the communion-table is a fresco by Sebastian Ricci, representing the Resurrection—the Roman soldiers standing lost in fear at the apparition of the risen Christ. Ricci, the rival of Sir James Thornhill in the huge mural decorations so much admired in the seventeenth and eighteenth centuries, is little esteemed now. His works are cleanly painted and dexterously finished, but otherwise have little merit. There are some good specimens of his style at Hampton Court. The service of silver plate, valued at £500, is said to have been given by James II., but in the accounts, 1687-92, we find that there was paid to

> 'Mr. John Rogers, goldsmith, for a great guilt Bason, a salver, three flagons, four chalices with cover, ij great altar candlesticks, for ye use of ye chappell, and other plate by him delivered for ye use of ye hospitall, as by his bills and acq'ues appeares v^{c}xlij (542) li. viijs.'

Around the chapel hang nearly 100 flags, captured in bygone wars, mementoes of the prowess of the worshippers and their predecessors during the last two centuries. They were removed from St. Paul's, Whitehall, in 1835. Among them are thirteen French eagles, including that captured by Sergeant Ewart of the Scots Greys. This incident is represented in one of the best pictures of Richard Ansdell, R.A., which was sold at Christie's some years ago for 700 guineas. It is a pity no generous-minded person thought of buying it for Chelsea Hospital—no more suitable place could be found for it. Besides the eagles there are American, Dutch, Russian, Indian, Afghan, and Hessian colours, eighty-four in all; but, unfortunately, all the captures of Marlborough's campaigns are lost. The assembly of the veterans in this chapel is one of the most impressive sights in all London, and when Herkomer took it for the subject of his great picture, 'The Last Muster,' he touched a chord to which all patriotic hearts responded.

The first organ was the gift of Major Ingram. Dr. Burney is doubtless the best-known musician who presided at it. He was in his time a famous man, wrote a history of music, composed various pieces well-esteemed in their day, and found a place in Barry's ambitious series of pictures illustrating 'Human Progress,' in the Great Room of the Society of Arts. He was the father of Mme. D'Arblay (Fanny Burney), author of the once famous novels 'Evelina,' 'Camilla,' and 'Cecilia.' She was often at Chelsea, and mentions the place several times in her Journal, where we find the following note on her father's appointment to the hospital:

> 'Dec. 16th, 1783.—You have heard the whole story of Mr. [Edmund] Burke, the Chelsea Hospital, and his most charming letter? To-day he called, and as my father was out, enquired for me. He made a thousand apologies for breaking in upon me, but said the business was finally settled at the Treasury. Nothing could be more delicate, more elegant, than his manner of doing this kindness. I don't know whether he was most polite or most friendly in his whole behaviour towards me. I could almost have cried when he said, "This is my last act in office;" he said it with so manly a cheerfulness, in the midst of his undisguised regret.'

Dr. Burney himself acknowledged his indebtedness to Burke for his appointment, and his generosity in not demanding his political assistance in a matter in which they differed. The appointment was very agreeable to Dr. Burney in every way, as the following extract from Mme. D'Arblay's memoir of her father (1832) shows:

> '1791. Dr. Burney at this time resided entirely at Chelsea College; and he found his sojourn so perfectly to his taste, that, though obliged, some years afterwards, to remove from the ground-floor to nearly the highest range of rooms in that lofty edifice, he never wished to exchange the place of his abode.
> 'The distance from town was just sufficient to avoid its bustle, its smoke, its dust, and its noise; yet not enough to impede any evening engagement, as it was not above an hour's walk, and consequently half an hour's drive to Piccadilly. Operas, concerts, con-

versaziones, were all within reach of his time, when without obstruction from his health. And Chelsea air is even proverbially salubrious, Doctors Arbuthnot, Sloane, Mede, Cadogan, Farquar, etc., having given it a medical celebrity by making it their chosen residence.

'He had also the pleasure in the college itself of some very agreeable, hospitable and respectable neighbours, to all of whom he was an acquisition equally valuable and valued. And to which the tastes and pursuits of a man of letters was still more important, he found here safe, lofty, and well fitted-up chambers, that were spacious and ready for the accommodation of his books. Here, therefore, and completely to his satisfaction, he placed his learned, classical, scientific, and miscellaneous library.'

William Mason, the poet, author of 'The English Garden,' was one of his visitors; and in 1791 Haydn came to see him. Mdme. D'Arblay writes, on May 22:

'I had the pleasure one evening at Chelsea, of meeting our ever-valued Mr. Twining, and seeing the justly-renowned Haydn. There was some sweet music of his performed; but Esther, his best exhibitor, was not well, and we missed her in all ways.'

Dr. Burney died April 12, 1814, aged 85, and was buried in the hospital burial-ground. Faulkner, says Mdme. D'Arblay, was also organist at the hospital for some years; but this is a mistake.

Ingram's organ became worn out, and in 1817 was replaced by one by Gray, set up in the original case at a cost of 400 guineas.

The following is a list of the chaplains:

Rev. Augustus Frazer, 1689. Mary, his wife, d. 1710, is buried in the hospital burial-ground; he himself was buried there, September 29, 1722.

Rev. Charles Ashton, 1699.

Rev. Francis Hare, 1703.

Rev. Henry Bland, 1715.

Rev. Emanuel Langford, D.D., d. 1724, buried in the hospital burial-ground.

Rev. William Barnard, 1727-8.

Rev. William Ashburnham, 1741-2.

Rev. Philip Francis, D.D., 1764.

Rev. W. Haggitt, M.A.

Rev. Richard Yates, D.D.

Rev. G. R. Gleig, M.A., 1834. He was the author of several novels dealing with the history and traditions of the hospital.

Rev. G. Matthias, M.A.

Among the marriages solemnized in this chapel, the following are noteworthy:

1701. June 15.—Edward Hamey, M.D., and Ann Bull, of Oxford.

1703. April 15.—Charles Hickman, LL.D., Bishop of Londonderry, and Anne Burgoyne, of the county of Warwick.

1713. August 4.—Hon. James Brydges and the Hon. Cassandra Willoughby.

1717. February 21.—John Berkeley, Esq., of Stoke, co. Gloucester, and the Right Hon. Elizabeth, Viscountess Dowager of Hereford.

1737. September 12.—John Chamberlayne, of the Middle Temple, and Anne Latton.

1747. April 7.—Sir Thomas Parkyns, Bart., of Bunny, co. Nottingham, a minor, and Jane Parkyns.

1748. May 26.—Hon. John Grey (brother of the Earl of Stamford), and Lucy, daughter of the Hon. Sir John Danvers, Bart., of Swithland, co. Leicester.

The great hall is of the same size as the chapel. It was designed for the college refectory, but the practice of dining together was found to be very inconvenient on account of the infirmity of many of the inmates, and has long since been discontinued. The men now dine in their own wards. In the hall is a large equestrian portrait of Charles II., painted by Antonio Verrio, the Neapolitan artist, who was so much favoured by that monarch, and whose 'sprawling' allegories disfigure so large a portion of the walls and ceilings of Windsor Castle and Hampton Court. The portrait in question is painted in an allegorical vein, contains figures of Hercules, Peace, Minerva, and Father Thames, and has a view of the hospital in the background. It was finished by an Englishman, Henry Cooke, pupil of Salvator Rosa. The inscription on the picture credits Lord Ranelagh with presenting it to the hospital:

'Carolo Secundo Regi Optimo Hujus Hospitii Fundatori Dominoque suo clementissimo, Ricardus Jones, Comes de Ranelagh, Hanc Tabulam Posuit.'

The following extract from the accounts (January, 1687, etc.), however, shows that he has no such claim:

'Seign^r Anthonio Verrio, on acco^t of painting in ye Hall at ye said Hospitall, as by his acq'es.   ...   . ccv^{li}. xv^s.'

Another large picture hangs over the gallery of this hall. This is an allegory of Wellington victorious; he stands in a triumphal car crowned by Victory and riding over War, Anarchy, and Rebellion. This picture is the work of William Ward, R.A., a great animal and landscape painter; in the latter department his works had much of the manner and feeling of Rubens, but he had no capacity for allegorical art, and the present work brought him no small share of derision. It was presented to the Hospital by the

British Institution, an association of gentlemen formed to promote British art, which did much service in that direction.

There are, however, very few military pictures in the hospital, and it is somewhat surprising that no such collection has been formed similar to that at Greenwich Hospital, which illustrates (though very imperfectly) the great achievements of the British sailor.

Among the events which have taken place in this hall we may notice the concerts in honour of the Coronation of Queen Anne, given by Mr. Abel (whose fine portrait by Gainsborough hangs at Hampton Court); the entertainment of the Turkish Ambassador, Yussuf Adijah Effendi, on June 29, 1795; the trial

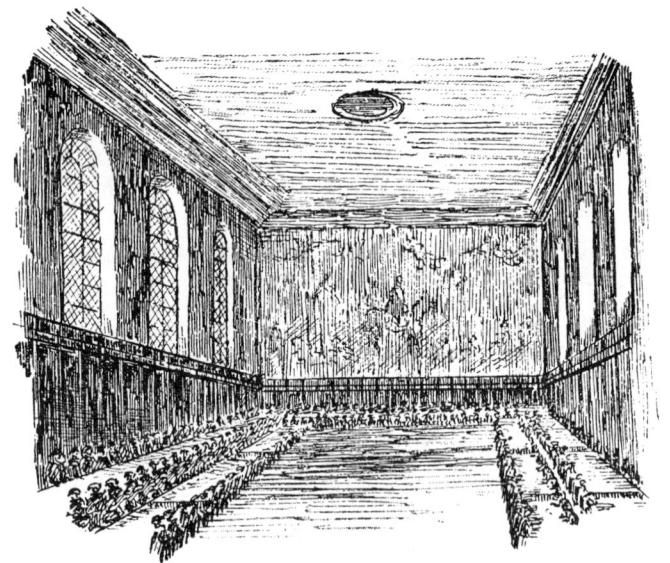

HALL OF CHELSEA HOSPITAL.

of General Whitelock for disobedience, bad generalship and cowardice, which began on January 30, 1808; and the lying in state of the Duke of Wellington, 1852.

The east and west sides of the quadrangle, 365 feet in length and 40 in width, are chiefly occupied with the pensioners' wards, sixteen in number, each containing twenty-six beds.

On the frieze of the colonnade before the chapel and hall is the following inscription:

'In subsidium et levamen, emeritoram senio, balloque fractorum, condidit Carolus Secundus, auxit Jacobus Secundus, perfecere Gulielmus et Maria Rex et Regina. M.DC.XC.'

Within the cloisters are several monuments—to Colonel Arthur Wellesley Torrens, mortally wounded at Inkermann in 1854; to Colonel Seton, who, with his 357 companions met an heroic death in the *Birkenhead*, off the Cape of Good Hope in 1852, as is feelingly told in Doyle's verses; and to Colonel Willoughby More and the men of the Enniskillen Dragoons, lost in the burning of the *Europa* in 1854. The tablets to these two last were erected at the command of Queen Victoria.

In the centre of the quadrangle is a brass statue of Charles II., by Grinling Gibbons, the gift of Tobias Rustat, Page of the Back Staircase, whom Evelyn describes as 'a very simple, ignorant, but honest and loyal creature.' The statue, which cost over £500, is draped in the usual Roman habit, which the artists of former days thought so essential to dignity, but which to us looks so ridiculous. Every year, on May 29—'Royal Oak Day'—the pensioners decorate this statue and themselves with oak-leaves and oak-apples, while at dinner they enjoy a somewhat more luxurious fare than usual. In the court, also, are four French guns, captured at Waterloo (placed here in 1848), and two Sikh guns, captured at Chillianwallah.

At the extreme end of the eastern wing is the Governor's house. The council chamber, or the State apartment, is 37 feet long, 27 feet wide, and 27 feet high. The ceiling, divided into oval compartments, is ornamented with the Royal arms, military trophies, and the initials of Charles II., James II., and William and Mary. There are the following pictures in this room:

Van Dyck (?)	Charles I. and his family. This is mentioned in the accounts, 1699-1702: 'Ireton for the picture of King Charles the 1st, and his children sett up in the Councill Chamber, and for a frame for the same ... ...xlvij. li. vs.'
Lely	Charles II.
„	Catherine of Braganza.
„	James, Duke of York, afterwards James II.
Kneller	James II.
„	William III.
„	George I.
E. Seaman	George II., after Kneller.
„	Caroline of Brandenburg-Anspach.
(The last four were bequeathed by Major-General William Evans in 1739.)	
A. Ramsay	George III.
„	Queen Charlotte.
D. Maas (?)	View of the Royal Hospital, Chelsea, presented by General Charles Churchill in 1722.
P. Tillemans ...	Another view of the same, presented by General Evans in 1729.

In the hall of the secretary's office is another gift of the British Institution —a large picture of the Battle of Waterloo, 15 feet by 11 feet, painted by George Jones, R.A.

GOVERNORS OF CHELSEA HOSPITAL.

Colonel Sir Thomas Ogle	November 1, 1686.

(He died November 23, 1702, and is buried in the hospital burial-ground.)

Colonel John Shales	November 17, 1702.
Brigadier Thomas Stanwix, M.P.	January 13, 1714-15.
Colonel Charles Churchill, M.P.	June 6, 1720.
Lieutenant-General William Evans	October, 1722.
Field-Marshal Sir Robert Rich	May 6, 1740.
„ Sir George Howard	February 3, 1768.
„ the Marquis of Townshend	July 16, 1795.
General Sir William Fawcett	July 18, 1796.

(He died in 1804, and is buried in the hospital burial-ground, where there is a monument to his memory.)

General the Right Hon. Sir David Dundas	April 9, 1804.

(Buried in the hospital burial-ground, March 2, 1820.)

Field Marshal the Right Hon. Sir Samuel Hulse ...	February 19, 1820.
General the Hon. Sir Edward Paget	January 10, 1837.
„ Sir George Anson	May 18, 1849.
„ Sir Colin Halket	November 26, 1849.
Field-Marshal Sir Edward Blakeney	September 25, 1856.
„ Sir Alexander Woodford	August 3, 1868.
General Sir John L. Pennefather	August 27, 1870.
Lieutenant-General Sir Sydney J. Cotton	May 10, 1872.
General (now Field-Marshal) Sir Patrick Grant... ...	February 20, 1874.

LIEUTENANT GOVERNORS.

David Crawford	January 1, 1694-95.

(Buried in the hospital burial-ground).

Colonel Thomas Chudleigh...	January 14, 1714-15.
Colonel William Wyndham, M.P.	April 15, 1726.
„ Thomas Norton, M.P.	April 22, 1730.
„ John Cossley	July 23, 1748.

(Buried in the hospital burial-ground, 1765.)

Nathaniel Smith	November 6, 1765.

(Buried in the hospital burial-ground, 1773.)

Colonel John Campbell	February 11, 1773.

(Buried in the hospital burial-ground, 1773.)

„ Bernard Hale	May 1, 1773.
General William Dalrymple	May 22, 1798.
„ Sir Thomas Trigge	April 2, 1804.
„ William Dalrymple	October 12, 1804.

(Buried in the hospital burial-ground, 1807.)

„ Samuel Hulse	February 25, 1807.
„ Sir Harry Calvert	February 19, 1820.
„ the Hon. Sir Alexander Hope	September 6, 1826.
„ Sir George T. Walker	May 24, 1837.
„ Sir William H. Clinton	November 17, 1842.
„ Sir George Anson...	February 23, 1846.
„ Sir Colin Halket	May 18, 1849.
Lieutenant-General Sir Andrew F. Barnard	November 26, 1849.
General Sir Edward Blakeney	February 6, 1855.
„ Sir Alexander Woodford...	September 25, 1856.
Field-Marshal Sir Henry D. Ross	August 3, 1868.
General the Hon. Sir Charles Gore	December 11, 1868.

[On the death of this last, September 4, 1869, the office of Lieutenant-Governor was abolished, and the duties assigned to the Major.]

Colonel Thomas Chudleigh was the father of the once notorious Duchess of Kingston, who spent her childhood in the hospital. She married the Hon. Augustus Hervey, and one of her children was baptized in the old church at Chelsea, as appears by the register :

> 1747. 'Augustus Henry, son of the Hon. Augustus Hervey, baptized by the Hon. and Rev. H. Aston. Nov. 2nd.'

The story of the scandal may be shortly told in Walpole's words (letter to Sir H. Mann, February 28, 1769) :

> 'Well, to come to goddesses : after a marriage of twenty years, Augustus Hervey, having fallen in love with a physician's daughter at Bath, he attacked his spouse, the Maid of Honour, the fair Chudleigh, and sought a divorce for adultery. Unfortunately, he had waited till all the witnesses of their marriage, and of her two deliveries, are dead, as well as the two children. The provident virgin has not been so negligent. Last year she forced herself into the house of the parson who had married them, and who was at the point of death. By bullying, and to get rid of her, she forced the poor man to give up the certificate. Since that she has appeared in Doctors' Commons, and sworn by the Virgin Mary and Diana, that she never was married to Mr. Hervey. The Ecclesiastical Court has admitted her corporal oath, and enjoined silence to Mr. Hervey. Next week this fair injured innocence, who is but fifty, is to be married to the Duke of Kingston, who has kept her openly for almost half that time, and who by this means will recover half his fortune which he had lavished on her. As a proof of her purity and poverty, her wedding-gown is white satin, trimmed with Brussels lace and pearls. Every word of this history is exactly true. The physician, who is a little more in his senses than the other actors, and a little honester, will not give his daughter, nay, has offered her five thousand pounds not to marry Mr. Hervey, but Miss Rhubarb is as much above worldly decorum as the rest, and persists, though there is no more doubt of the marriage of Mr. Hervey and Miss Chudleigh than that of your father and mother.'

The second marriage of Mr. Hervey did not take place, but on March 8, 1769, 'the Chudleigh' was publicly married to Evelyn Pierrepoint, Duke of Kingston, for which she was impeached before the House of Peers. The marriage was declared illegal, and she retired to the Continent, where she died in 1788. Colonel Chudleigh was buried in the hospital burial-ground 1726.

MAJORS.

Major Henry Skipwith	... ...	About October 19, 1691.
„ Matthew Ingram	... ...	About February 28, 1692.
„ Richard Bettesworth	... ...	December 12, 1694.
(Buried in the hospital burial-ground, 1745.)		
„ Launcelot Storry	... ...	January 7, 1745-46.
„ Nathaniel Smith	... ...	January 27, 1761.
„ William Spath	... ...	November 6, 1765.
Lieutenant-Colonel John Wrightson	... ...	April 3, 1775.
Captain William Bulkeley ...	... ...	October 21, 1779.
(Buried in the hospital burial-ground, 1801.)		
Lieutenant-Colonel Robert Matthews	... ...	October 6, 1801.

Lieutenant-Colonel William Osborne Hamilton			...	July 21, 1814.
„	Henry Le Blanc	...	...	...	September 22, 1814.
Colonel Sir John M. Wilson	...	...	...	...	July 14, 1855.
„	Charles L. B. Maitland ...	...	...	...	January 7, 1871.

The gardens were originally laid out in the trim Dutch taste, with broad walks, formal avenues, and long canal-like slips of water leading to the river at right angles to the building. The kitchen-garden lay along the Thames on the south-western corner of the grounds. These lands lay low, and were subject to inundation. Payments made to the gardener for repairing the damages caused by floods are recorded in March, 1774, and February, 1775.

In 1784, Vincent Lunardi, the aeronaut, who came to this country as secretary to Prince Caramanico, the Neapolitan Ambassador, obtained permission from the King and the Governor to make an ascent from the hospital gardens. In the meantime, a Frenchman, named De Maret, determined to be beforehand, announced that he would attempt an ascent from another garden in Chelsea, near at hand. He endeavoured to inflate his balloon with rarefied air, in Montgolfier's method, but the balloon accidentally sank on the fire, and was destroyed. The assembled multitude regarded the whole thing as a fraud, and expressed their indignation by demolishing everything within reach. The authorities at the hospital, fearing a repetition of these scenes, wisely cancelled their permission to Lunardi.

Ballooning was the great sensation of the day. Walpole, writing to Sir Horace Mann, on December 22, 1784, says:

'Lunardi, the Neapolitan secretary, is said to have bought three or four thousand pounds in the stocks, by exhibiting his person, his balloon, and his cat and dog at the Pantheon, for a shilling each visitor. Blanchard, a Frenchman, is his rival, and I expect they will have an air-fight in the clouds, like a stork and a kite.'

In 1812 Captain M'Guir, chief engineer to the Shah of Persia, assisted by Captain Minn, carried out some demonstrations of an improved method of blowing up fortifications, ships, etc. The captain blew up part of a tower-wall, and the experiments were considered highly successful.

The grounds were altered to their present form when the Embankment was built, in 1872-3. Near the river is a tall obelisk, inscribed with the names of the officers and men who fell at the battle of Chillianwallah, where the British forces were so nearly defeated by the brave Sikh warriors. The precipitate flight of the 14th Dragoons on a supposed order from their commander, was a main cause of the heavy British loss, and the charge of cowardice brought against Colonel King so preyed on his mind that he committed suicide at Lahore. An extraordinary story has recently appeared in an Indian paper, which, if true, removes the stain from the memory of the commander and the fame of his regiment. It is said that there was in the ranks of the dragoons a soldier who bore a grudge against the Colonel. This man was a ventriloquist, and at a critical moment, assuming the Colonel's voice, and throwing it near him, gave the order 'Threes about!' Then followed the wild retreat of the dragoons with all its terrible consequence, of which this monument is the mournful record. One hopes for the honour of the regiment that this strange story is a true one, as it accounts for the fact that while Colonel King positively denied giving the order, the men as positively declared they heard it given.

The old men's gardens, formerly the governor's garden, form one of the

OBELISK.

most interesting features of these grounds. Mrs. Allingham has painted a very pleasing picture of this subject.

WALPOLE HOUSE AND THE INFIRMARY.

The land on which the infirmary stands was a piece of four and a half acres, parcel of Great Sweed Court, leased in 1687 to William Jephson, Secretary to the Treasury, for sixty-one years at £9 per annum. His widow, with her second husband, Sir John Awbrey, Bart., assigned the lease to Charles Hopson, from whom it passed to Edward Harley, Earl of Orford (the victor in the fight off Cape La Hogue), on July 10, 1696. The Earl of Orford dwelt here until 1707, and from 1714 to 1719 the rent was paid by Sir Richard Gough. On January 28, 1730, the lease was granted to Thomas Ripley for twenty-nine and a half years, commencing from June 16, 1751, and a fortnight later Ripley assigned his lease to Sir Robert Walpole.

The infirmary of Chelsea Hospital has an interesting history. Elmes, in his 'Topographical Dictionary of London' (1831) says that Nell Gwynne had lived in the house built on its site, but this is entirely erroneous, and it is very doubtful whether she ever lived in Chelsea at all. Her son, the Duke of St. Albans, who held the appointment of Captain of the Guard of Pensioners, does appear to have lived in this neighbourhood, but there is no evidence as to the site of his residence.

It has been said that Walpole lived in Chelsea before he took this house, and Walpole Street has been named as the site of his previous residence, which has been thought identical with that in which the Earl of Sandwich came 'to take the ayre'; but these are points on which I find no evidence.

Walpole made the house (which we may suppose was built by Jephson) his summer residence from 1723 to 1746, and there can be no doubt that much of the State policy and business, during his long reign of power, was settled here, and that most of the famous men of that peaceful period have sat and conversed in these rooms and lounged in the gardens.

Walpole enlarged his garden by a purchase from the Gough family, and built in them a summer-house and green-house, from the design of Vanbrugh. The following letter probably refers to their building:

'*To the Rt. Hon. Robert Walpole, Esq., at Chelsea.*

'*October 27th,* 1725.

'The enclosed is the second part of what I troubled you with the other day, which I hope you will think a most reasonable application. I have made an estimate of your fabrick, which comes to £270, but I have allowed for doing some things in it in a better manner than perhaps you will think necessary; so that I believe it may be done to your mind for £200. But for your further satisfaction, I desire you will send your Clerk of the Works to me, and I will explain it so to him that he may likewise make his calculation without showing him mine, or telling him what I make the expense amount to in the total. And when this is done we will give each particular article to the respective workmen, and they shall make their estimation, too. So that you shall know the bottom of it at last, or the devil shall be in it.

'Your most humble obedient architect,

'J. VANBRUGH.'

Walpole frequently entertained Queen Caroline and other members of the Royal Family in this house, standing behind her Majesty's chair while she dined. On August 27, 1729, he gave them a grand entertainment in the greenhouse, which excited much comment at the time. The following contemporary account is taken from the *Monthly Chronicle* :

> 'This Day Her Majesty, the Prince of Wales, the Dukes, and all the Princesses were splendidly entertained by the Right Hon. Sir Robert Walpole at his House at Chelsea. The Dinner was in Sir Robert's Green House. A kitchen was built on purpose in the stable-yards, near as big as that erected for the Dinner of the Knights of the Bath, with above 20 places for Fires, etc. The Fruit for the Dessert was collected for a week preceding from all Quarters of the Town. After Dinner, Her Majesty and the Royal Family retir'd to the Banquetting House on the River, to drink Tea ; where were several Barges of fine Musick playing all the Time. After which they returned to the Green House, where the illustrious company were entertained with a Ball, and afterwards supp'd in the same place.'

It was on this occasion that Sir Paul Methuen uttered a well-known bonmot. He was remarkable for a love of romances, and the Queen, thinking to joke him on his fancy, asked him what he had been reading of that sort lately. 'Nothing, Madam,' he replied ; 'I have now commenced, instead of romances, a very foolish study, " The History of the Kings and Queens of England." '

In Horace Walpole's copy of Grammont's ' Memoirs,' there is a curious MS. note on the Duchess of Marlborough — 'La Belle Jennings' of the ' Memoirs ':

> ' I remember her coming when a boy, to my mother at Chelsea, to solicit a pension ; and her eyes being dim, and she full of flattery, she commended the beauty of the prospect ; but unluckily the room in which they sat looked only against the garden wall!'

He also mentions the place in a regretful tone in a letter to Montagu, on August 5, 1746 :

> ' I went t'other night to look at my poor favourite Chelsea, for the little Newcastle is gone to be dipped in the sea. In one of the rooms is a bed for her Duke, and a press-bed for his footman, for he never dares lie alone, and till he was married, had always a servant to sit up with him.'

Lady Walpole indulged in the fashionable whim of the hour, and had a grotto built at Chelsea ; this was not so celebrated as Pope's at Twickenham, which is still preserved, but was well known, and is the subject of some satirical verses in the *Gentleman's Magazine*, December, 1734 :

> ' On presents of shells (mentioned in the *News*) from the islands of Guernsey, Jersey, Sark, and Alderney, for Lady W.LP.E's grotto at Chelsea :
>
>> ' Whilst patriots murmur at the weight
>> Of taxes that support the state,
>> See how the isles obedience pay
>> To W.LP . . E's most auspicious sway,' etc.

Here, too, was that famous collection of pictures, afterwards removed to

Houghton Hall, and described in the ' Ædes Walpoliana,' which now form the staple of the magnificent Imperial Gallery at St. Petersburg.

Of Sir Robert Walpole in private there is a pleasing picture by Pope, who was a frequent visitor to the Chelsea house:

> ' Seen him I have in his happier hour
> Of social pleasure, ill-exchanged for power ;
> Seen him uncumbeied by the venal tribe,
> Smile without art, and win without a bribe.'

The eccentric Messenger Monsey, physician to the hospital, and a very notable man, who concealed his ability under a cloak of oddity, was one of Walpole's most welcome guests. Walpole is said to have asked him on one occasion how it was that no one else dared to contradict him or beat him at whist; to which the doctor bluntly replied, ' Because they come for places, but I for a dinner only !' A small volume might be filled with the whimsical anecdotes related of him. He held his post at the hospital so long that the reversion of it was granted to several successive applicants. He died at the hospital on December 26, 1798, and left his body for dissection. There is a long letter, apparently dictated, relating to this matter, preserved in Mr. Joseph Mayer's copy of Faulkner in the Chelsea Free Library. The apartments he occupied were supposed to have been part of the old Theological College; they have since been removed.

Walpole was attended in his last illness by the principal surgeon of the hospital, John Ranby, who published an account of the case. Ranby died in 1773.

There are two portraits of Walpole in the National Portrait Gallery, one in the robes of the Chancellor of the Exchequer, with the ribbon of the garter, and one by Francis Hayman, represented in the studio of that painter.

On October 13, 1749, Walpole House was leased to John, Earl of Dunmore, for fifty years; ten years later it was assigned to Mr. George Aufrere, who possessed a valuable collection of pictures by Old Masters, and also Bernini's statue of Neptune, which was placed in the octagon summer-house. Mr. Aufrere obtained two extensions of the lease, which would terminate in 1825. Lord Yarborough (son-in-law of Mr. Aufrere) lived here until 1808, when he surrendered the remainder of the lease to the Crown for a compensation of £4,775 15s.

THE INFIRMARY.

The building was bought by the Crown for an infirmary for the hospital, and some additional buildings were erected by Sir John Soane, R.A., architect of the Bank of England, and testator of the valuable museum in Lincoln's Inn Fields, which is so little known to the public. Soane's fame did not outlast his own day, and his works at Chelsea have no architectural merit. Walpole House remains very little altered; the dining-room, with its moulded ceiling and marble mantel is No. 7 Ward, and was to Dr. Martin 'one of the most impressive relics in London.'

The portion of the land not required for the new infirmary was leased to Lieutenant-Colonel (afterwards General) Gordon for eighty years from January 5, 1810, at a rent of £52 14s. It included Walpole's octagonal summer-house; but the greenhouse in which Queen Caroline had been entertained had disappeared by 1815. In the house built by General Gordon he entertained the Emperor of Russia, the Duke of York, the Duchess of Oldenburg and others, on the occasion of their visit in 1814. Gordon House and its grounds, as they appear at the present day, will be familiar to the many thousands who have visited the Military and Naval Exhibitions.

PHYSICIANS TO THE ROYAL HOSPITAL.

Dr. Charles Frazier	1687
Sir Theodore Colludon	1693
(Buried in the hospital burial-ground, 1712.)	
Dr. John Arbuthnot	1712
„ John Smart	1715
„ George Lavis Tessier	1740
„ Messenger Monsey	1742
„ Benjamin Mosely	1788
(Buried in the hospital burial-ground September 30, 1819, æt. 73.)	
Dr. William Somerville, physician and surgeon	1819
„ Daniel McLachlan	1840
„ William Lucas	1863
„ John Alexander McMann	1868

SURGEONS.

John Noades	1690
Alexander Inglis	1706-7
(Buried in the hospital burial-ground, 1736.)	
William Cheselden	1736-7
John Ranby	1752
(Buried in the hospital burial-ground, 1773.)	
Robert Adair	1773
Thomas Keate	1790
(Died July 6, 1821, æt. 76 years; buried in the hospital burial-ground.)	
Sir Everard Home, Bart.	1821

Cheselden, the most famous surgeon of his day, is buried in the hospital burial-ground. Pope, writing to Swift, says:

'I wondered a little at your quære, who Cheselden was. It shows that the truest merit does not travel so far any way as on the wings of poetry. He is the most noted and most deserving man in the whole profession of chirurgery, and has saved the lives of thousands by his manner of cutting for the stone.'

Again, in a letter to the Duchess of Marlborough, 1743, he says:

'Your grace might almost think I told you the thing that was not, and which the very horses in Gulliver's travels disdain to do. But the truth is, the day after I sent to your Grace, when Lord Marchmont was with you, I was taken so ill with my asthma that I went to Chelsea, to let blood by my friend Cheselden, by which I had found more good than by any other practice in four months.'

Faulkner credited Cheselden with the design of Old Fulham Bridge (more commonly known as Putney Bridge). In his 'History of Fulham' (p. 16), he says:

'The plan of this bridge was drawn by Mr. Cheselden, surgeon of Chelsea Hospital, who, in his profession, acquired the greatest reputation, and by the skill displayed in this useful piece of architecture, has shown the affinity that exists among the sciences.'

The following minute of a meeting of the proprietors of old Fulham Bridge (July 2, 1730), built from a design by Sir Jacob Ackworth, proves that though Faulkner was not strictly correct in attributing the design to Cheselden, yet the eminent surgeon deserves some of the credit:

PORTRAIT OF CHESELDEN.

'Resolved, as the bridge is built entirely according to a scheme and principles laid down by Mr. Cheselden, and as he has been very serviceable in directing the execution of the same, that the thanks of the proprietors be given to him for the advantages which they have received from his advice and assistance, they being of opinion that no timber bridge can be built in a more substantial and commodious manner than that which is now erected.'

THE BURIAL-GROUND.

This ground, 542 feet by 105 feet, lies along Queen's Road East (formerly called Jews' Row), between the hospital and Chelsea Barracks. It was consecrated on the same day as the chapel, and closed on January 1, 1855.

The earliest tomb is that of Simon Box, 1692. Among the reputed centenarians buried here we may notice William Hiseland, who, 'when an hundred years old took unto him a wife,' died 1732, æt. 112. There is a portrait of this veteran, at the age of 110 years, painted by George Alsop, a little-known painter, who lived at Wandsworth. When Faulkner wrote, it was in the possession of Mr. Thomas Panister, of Cross Keys Inn, Gracechurch Street, and was recently sold at Christie's, and it is a pity that it did not find its way to Chelsea Hospital. Joshua Cueman, died 1794, æt. 123; Robert Cumming, died 1767, æt. 116; Thomas Ashbey, died 1737, æt. 112; Peter Burnet, died 1773, and John Wolf, 1821, æt. 107; Abraham Moss, 1805, æt. 106; Richard

Swifield, 1805, æt. 105; John Salter, 1827, æt. 104; John Rogers, 1764, æt. 103; Peter Dowling, 1768, æt. 102.

Here are buried two amazons who fought in the British army—Christiana Davis served for several years in the Enniskillen Dragoons, until being wounded her sex was discovered. She died at Chelsea in 1739. Hannah Snell served in Guise's Regiment of Foot, and afterwards in the marines, and was severely wounded. Both were buried here by their own desire.

Among the burials in the ground, in addition to the above, and those given in the lists of the officers of the hospital, are—Colonel Theophilus Cecill, died 1695; Sir Thomas Renton, physician to George I., appointed to attend the pensioners on account of his special skill in the treatment of ruptures, died 1740; Colonel Richard Harward, died 1758; Colonel Arthur Owen, Governor of Pendennis Castle, 1774; John Wilson, deputy-treasurer of the hospital, and Lieutenant-Colonel of the Queen's Royal (Chelsea) Volunteers, died October 17, 1812, æt. 56; William Henry Moseley, M.D., physician to the forces, and son of Dr. Benjamin Moseley, died April 13, 1827, æt. 47; Rev. William Young, lexicographer, the supposed original of Parson Adams in Fielding's novel, died 1757; Lord Lindores, Major-General, died 1765; Rt. Hon. James O'Hara, Baron of Tyrawley and Kilmain, died 1773, æt. 91; Alexander Reid (born in Cheyne Row, 1719), pupil and assistant of Cheselden, died 1789; Samuel Wyatt, architect, died 1807, æt. 70.

RANELAGH HOUSE AND GARDEN.

Richard Jones, 3rd Viscount and 1st Earl of Ranelagh, like Sir John Danvers in the previous reigns, was a man of considerable taste in architecture and gardening. Swift, whose epithets, however, must not always be taken quite literally, says he was 'the vainest old fool he ever saw.' Others tell us he was able but very dissolute. Whether so or not, he was certainly a great favourite with Charles II. In the diary of Henry Sidney, the original of which is in the possession of the Earl of Chichester, we find the following under date March 9, 1680:

> 'The King hath a new mistress, Lord Rane——'s daughter: she hath brought the Duke of Monmouth to the King.'

The name is undoubtedly intended for Ranelagh, and although the reference may be merely an item of scandal, yet it receives some support, or at least identification, from a letter of John to Sir Ralph Verney, June 5, 1679, which mentions 'much talk of a new Miss at Windsor, daughter to my Lord Ranelagh.' If Sidney's statement be well founded, it in some measure accounts

RANELAGH HOUSE AND ROTUNDA.

for Lord Ranelagh's favour and promotion at Court, for history shows only too clearly that such a connection was the best passport to the notice of Charles II.

Lord Ranelagh succeeded Sir Stephen Fox as Paymaster-General to the Forces, and appears to have taken a hint in finance from him, for in 1685-6 we find a Royal Order issued for the deduction of twelve pence in the pound from the pay of the forces. One-third of this was to be applied to the exchequer fees and to the paymaster, and two-thirds were to remain in his hands, either for the service of the hospital, or 'the payment of the establishment of the forces.' So vague an order would easily allow of peculation, and if the rest of Ranelagh's administration was based on the same lines, it is not surprising to find that his expenditure was ere long called in question. The following is extracted from a series of anonymous news letters in the possession of the Earl of Denbigh :

'"Decembre, 1691.—Les Commissaires etablis par la Chambre basse pour examiner la depense des revenus publies depuis l'année 1688 ont presenté un etat du revenu pendant ces trois années qu'on dit monter a dix huit millions de livres sterlins. On a leu cet etat et on dit que my lord Renala et quelques autres n'ont par bien satisfait les commissaires touchant leurs comptes. On les examine à present dans la Chambre et on continuera dans trois jours.'

Some ten years later he was again in trouble, and Luttrell records in his ' Diary ':

' Jan. 1st, 1701-2.—It's discoursed the Earl of Ranelagh, paymaster to the Army, and Mr. Blathwayt, secretary for War, will be discharged.'

But the same writer tell us, on June 18 :

'The Earl of Ranelagh has his commission renewed for continuing paymaster to the Army.'

Public opinion, however, became too strong for him, and though he resigned his office some six months later, he was not allowed to escape without some punishment. Turning once more to Luttrell, we read that on February 1, 1702-3 :

' The Lords . . . debated the Lord Ranelagh's case, and resolved, That he be expelled the house for a high crime and misdemeanour, in misapplying several sums of the public money, when paymaster of the Army.'

Charges of misappropriating the Irish revenue (of which he was Vice-Treasurer) were also brought against him, and in the end he was expelled from his office, and his accounts were not passed until a quarter of a century after his death.

When Chelsea Hospital was nearing its completion, the Earl of Ranelagh obtained several grants of the land belonging to the institution, and lying on the east of it. In 1690, seven acres were leased to him for sixty-one years at £15 7s. 6d. per annum. On this he built a handsome house, and in 1697 had the grounds enlarged by an additional sixteen acres, with an extension of the lease. But this did not satisfy him. Among the ' Treasury Papers ' (vol. xliv., n. 80) is his petition, dated 1697, ' showing that he was a great sufferer by the late war in Ireland, having lost nearly £12,000 in rent, and his castles of Roscommon and Athlone being utterly ruined; his mansion in Dublin being pulled down for timber to build a mass-house there; and praying for a grant of £500 per annum out of the forfeitures of the counties of East and West Meath, and in the province of Connaught; also the inheritance of his house at Chelsea, with the 23 acres thereto belonging, already granted to him for 99 years, in order that he might make a settlement in his family.'

This is minuted :

> ' 4 May, 1697.—Sent to yᵉ Board and the Earl of Sunderland and read. Respited till his Maᵗˢ return.'

In the following year he received a grant in fee of both leaseholds in consideration of paying an annual rent of £5 to the hospital !

The house, as described by Bowack in 1705, was built of brick, and cornered with stone, ' not large, but very convenient, and may well be called a cabinet. It stands a good distance from the Thames. In finishing the whole, his Lordship has spared neither labour nor cost. The very greenhouses and stables, adorned with festoons and urns, have an air of grandeur not seen in many princes' palaces.' The gardens are shortly described in an ' Account of several gardens near London, with remarks on some particulars wherein they excel, or are deficient, upon a view of them in Dec., 1691 ' :

> ' My Lord Ranelagh's garden being but lately made, the plants are but small, and elegantly designed, having the advantage of opening into Chelsea College walks. The kitchen-garden there lies very fine, with walks and seats, one of which being large and covered, was then under the hands of a curious painter [Noble, perhaps, who painted the staircase of Ranelagh House. He died in 1701]. The house there is very fine within, all the rooms being wainscoted with Norway oak, and all the chimneys adorned with carvings, as in the Council Chamber of Chelsea College.'

When Lord Ranelagh died, in 1712, he was possessed of another house at Cranbourne, and ' the little house at St. James's Place,' though Swift says ' he was very poor and needy, and could hardly support himself for want of a pension which used to be paid him, and which his friends solicited as a thing of perfect charity.' He was the first and last holder of the Earldom; the elder title of Viscount passed to a cousin, and only recently became extinct. His widow, the Dowager Lady Stawell, whom he had married in January, 1695-6, survived him for sixteen years.

The Chelsea property passed to his unmarried daughter, Lady Catherine Jones. In 1714 the *Weekly Post* printed a rumour that the house was to be bought and fitted up for the Duke and Duchess of Marlborough, but this intention, if it ever existed, was abandoned. Here, on the evening of August 22, 1715, Lady Catherine entertained King George I., the Duchess of Newcastle, Lady Godolphin, Madame Kilmansegg, and the Earl of Orkney. The royal party had come in open barges, accompanied by hundreds of illuminated boats. Handel, in one of the City barges, conducted his beautiful water music, played by an orchestra of fifty performers, so much to the King's satisfaction that he thrice demanded its repetition. The King landed at Chelsea at eleven, and was conducted to Ranelagh House, where the party was entertained with a concert and supper until two in the morning. Handel's water music was again performed in Chelsea on the anniversary of its first performance for the benefit of the funds of the new Cheyne Hospital for Incurable Children in 1889.

Ranelagh House was destined to be the scene of many brilliant assemblies. In 1730 an Act was obtained vesting the estate in the hands of trustees; and three years later the whole was sold in lots. The house and grounds adjoining were then purchased by Lacy (the lessee of Drury Lane Theatre), and one Rietti, for the purpose of establishing a place of public entertainment on a grander scale than had been previously attempted. The design, however, proved too costly for the original promoters, and as the Royal Hospital authorities not unnaturally opposed it, the gardens were not opened until 1742 (nine years after the purchase), when the property was divided into thirty-six shares of one thousand pounds each. A considerable number of these shares were held by Sir Thomas Robinson. This gentleman, whom Mrs. Carter calls 'the knight of the woful countenance,' built himself a residence called Prospect Place, adjoining the gardens. Its site was afterwards occupied, or very nearly so, by General Wilford's house.

The chief feature of Ranelagh was a large building in imitation of the Pantheon at Rome, called the Rotunda. It was designed by Mr. William Jones, architect to the East India Company, and although not beautiful externally, was considered a triumph of architectural ingenuity. Its external diameter was 185 feet, and internal, 150 feet. As the place was so extensive, and use of stone would have involved an enormous expense, it was built of wood. There were four principal entrances, designed as triumphal arches, the pillars of which formed the chief supports of the great roof. Capon, the most eminent scene-painter of the day, directed the decorations, which, however, do not appear to have been very sumptuous or artistic. This great amphitheatre was lavishly illuminated, and doubtless presented a very brilliant

38

spectacle in its palmy days.   In the *Ambulator*, 1787, we have a description of it which forms the basis of most subsequent accounts:

> 'When all the lamps are lighted, as they emit their rays equally through the whole fabric, it will naturally be imagined that the sight must be very glorious ; no words can express its grandeur ; all parts shine with a re-plendency, as if formed of the very substance of light : then doth the masterly disposition of the architect, the proportion of the parts, and the harmonious disposition of the several pieces, appear to the greatest advantage, the most minute part by this effulgence being open to inspection.   Everyone at first entering the Rotunda at this time feels the same sensation as hearing suddenly a fine concert ; architecture having the same effect upon the eye as music upon the ear,

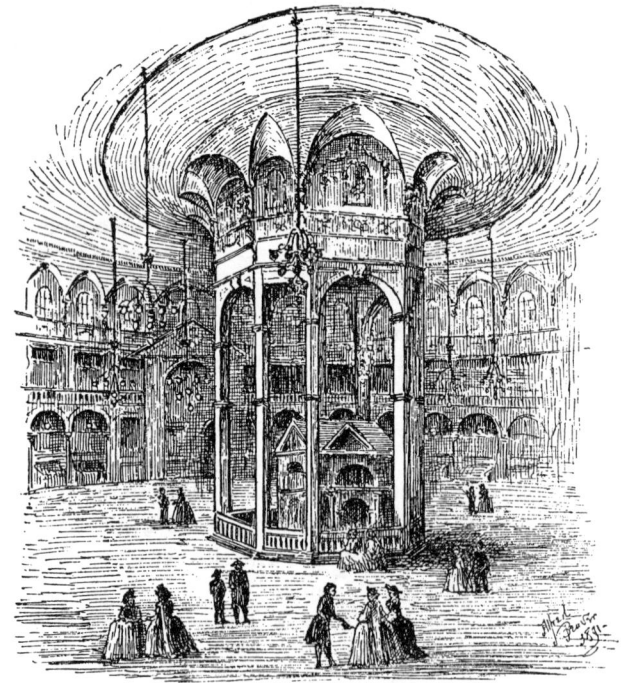

THE FIREPLACE, ROTUNDA, RANELAGH GARDEN.

> the mind is absorbed in an extacy.   The propriety and artful management of the several objects are expressive of the intention of this edifice ; and this, indeed, may be said of Ranelagh, that it is one of those places of pleasure and entertainment, that for beauty, elegance, and grandeur, are not equalled in Europe.'

It is to the contemporary letter-writers of the period, notably Walpole, that we must turn for a vivid description of the social aspects of the place.   It was always essentially a fashionable promenade, and though frivolous and harmful enough, yet it never acquired the disreputable character afterwards borne by

Cremorne, and when the tide of fashion turned from it, it did not descend to catering for a lower stratum of society, but died respectably.

The Rotunda was opened on April 5, 1742, with a public breakfast. This was before the formal opening of the gardens. Walpole was there, of course, and recorded his impressions for the benefit of his friend Mann :

> ' I have been breakfasting this morning at Ranelagh Garden ; they have built an immense amphitheatre, with balconies full of little ale-houses. It is in rivalry to Vauxhall, and costs about £12,000. The building is not yet finished, but they get great sums by people going to see it, and breakfasting in the house ; there was yesterday no less than 380 persons at eighteen-pence apiece.'

These breakfasts were afterwards forbidden by Government as detrimental to public morals.

Mrs. Carter sends an account of the Rotunda to one of her friends on June 1, 1742 :

> ' To untravelled eyes, like mine, 'tis, to be sure, an amazing fine thing, and quite worthy of your coming to town to see it next year, by which time they may possibly have found all that it wants to make it complete, and some use for it answerable to the fineness and stateliness of the structure, for, to be sure, it is quite vexatious at present to see all the pomp and splendour of a Roman amphitheatre devoted to no better use than a twelvepenny entertainment of cold ham and chickens.'

The Gardens were opened on May 24, 1742, and this is Walpole's account of them :

> ' Two nights ago Ranelagh Gardens was opened at Chelsea ; the Prince, Princess, Duke, and much nobility, and much mob besides, were there. . . . The building and disposition of the gardens cost £16,000. Twice a week there are to be ridottos at guinea tickets, for which you are to have a supper and music. I was there last night, but did not find the joy of it. Vauxhall is a little better, for the garden is pleasanter, and one goes by water.'

Many people, however, went to Ranelagh by water. The *Ambulator*, already quoted, tells us :

> ' The landing here is rendered convenient by a flight of steps which lead to an agreeable gravel walk, shaded with trees and hedges, where on one hand is a prospect of the river and the fields on the opposite shore, and on the other a view of the south front of Chelsea Hospital and its gardens. At the end of this walk, which in the evening is lighted with lamps, you enter the gardens.'

This avenue is still flourishing.

A foreigner describing Ranelagh soon after the opening compared the Rotunda to a ' giant's lanthorn ;' the decorations were ' gay as the Asiatic,' and the lights so brilliant that in five minutes his eyes grew dazzled, and all night he ' dreamt of Vanity Fair.'

Ranelagh, patronized as it was by the Royal Family, rapidly gained the public favour. Thus Walpole writes on July 7, 1742 :

> ' I am going to a masquerade at the Ranelagh Amphitheatre ; the King is fond of it, and has pressed people to go ; but I don't find it will be full.'

38—2

Two years afterwards he writes to Conway :

'Every night constantly I go to Ranelagh, which has totally beat Vauxhall. Nobody goes anywhere else ; everybody goes there. My Lord Chesterfield is so fond of it that he says he has ordered all his letters to be directed thither.'

In 1744 Richard Lyttleton, writing to his father, Sir Thomas, says that he went to Ranelagh and had a long talk with the Prince and Princess (Lyttleton MSS. at Hagley).

Its popularity continued undiminished for years, and Walpole has many references to it in his Letters of 1746. For example, on June 5 :

'The Prince of Hesse is come. . . . Monday he went to Ranelagh, and supped in the house. . . . To-night there is a masquerade at Ranelagh for him.'

Some there were, however, who did not find the entertainment very pleasurable. Thus Lord Strafford, in a letter dated May 8, 1746 (MS. of Earl Cathcart), writes :

'Vauxhall and Ranelagh are the present diversions, which one may easily be tired of, I think, for they are always the same, and one's pleasure depends on the party.'

The masquerade is, in its nature, a somewhat disreputable form of entertainment, and could hardly fail to injure the character of the place. Accordingly Fielding laid the scene of the attempted ruin of Amelia in Ranelagh Gardens. The frivolous or worse character they obtained is summed up in George Selwyn's mot on hearing that one of the waiters had been sent to prison : 'What a horrid idea he'll give of us to those fellows in Newgate !' Satirists, naturally, found plenty of material in the masquerades. 'Ranelagh House, a satire in prose in the manner of Monsieur Le Sage,' appeared in 1747, and contains a very harsh character of Heidegger :

'You must know, then, that H-d-g-r, the manager of masquerades, is a Devil disguised in a human shape. I wonder he did not change his face as well as the rest of his body ; that still retains its primitive Diabolicalness. He is called Belial in Hell, and is one of the shrewdest of Pluto's subjects. It is reckon'd he has been more successful in corrupting mankind, than any Devil that ever appeared on earth.'

That even the sober portion of the fashionable world frequented these very questionable entertainments is evident from another letter of Mrs. Carter, June 14, 1748 :

'In the evening my Lord W. carried us to Ranelagh. I do not know how I might have liked the place in a more giddy humour, but it did not strike me with any agreeable impressions ; but, indeed, for the most part, these tumultury torchlight entertainments are very apt to put me in mind of the revel routs of Comus.'

Nor did the Royal Family withdraw its patronage, as we find Walpole writing in the same year of

'Disagreeable Ranelagh, which is so crowded, that going there t'other night in a string of coaches, we had a stop of six and thirty minutes. . . . Princess Emily, finding no marriage articles settled for her at the congress, has at last determined to be old and out of danger, and has accordingly ventured to Ranelagh to the great improvement of the pleasures of the place.'

In 1749 England was celebrating the peace of Aix-la-Chapelle, signed in the previous year, and there were, of course, feasts, ridottos, masquerades, fireworks, and similar rejoicings necessary to such an occasion. Ranelagh, of course, took part in it, and Walpole, equally of course, sends his friends an account of it:

'The next day was what was called "a jubilee masquerade in the Venetian manner." It had nothing Venetian in it, but it was by far the best understood and prettiest spectacle I ever saw: nothing in a fairy tale ever surpassed it. One of the proprietors, who is a German, and belongs to the court, had got my Lady Yarmouth to persuade the king to order it. It began about three o'clock, and about five, people of fashion began to go. When you entered you found the whole garden filled with masks and spread with tents, which remained all night *very commodely*. In one quarter was a maypole dressed with garlands, and people dancing round it to a tabor and pipe and rustic music, all masked, as were all the various bands of music that were dispersed in different parts of the garden; some like huntsmen with French horns, some like peasants, and a troop of harlequins and scaramouches in the little open temple on the mount. On the canal was a sort of gondola, adorned with flags and streamers, and filled with music, moving about. All round the outside of the amphitheatre were shops, filled with Dresden China, Japan, etc., and all the shopkeepers in masks. The amphitheatre was illuminated; and in the middle was a circular bower composed of all kinds of firs in tubs, from twenty to thirty feet high; under them orange-trees with a small lamp in each orange, and below them all sorts of the finest auriculas in pots; and festoons of natural flowers hanging from tree to tree. Between the arches, too, were firs, and smaller ones in the balconies above. There were booths for tea and wine, gaming-tables and dancing, and about a thousand persons. In short, it pleased me more than anything I ever saw. It is to be once more, and probably finer as to dresses, as there has since been a subscription masquerade, and people will go in their rich habits.'

At length the masquerades were suppressed, as we learn from a letter from Thos. Bowlby to Philip Gell, in the MSS. of Mr. H. C. Pole-Gell:

'The foolish Justices of Middlesex so far carried their point that the managers of Ranelagh were obliged to consent that they would make no more masques, and this rural carnival was devised to supply the loss of that entertainment of the town, which was celebrated on Thursday last, Prince George's birthday. The Prince of Wales and his court were present, and much good, but more bad company. The ticket was a guinea, the room and gardens ornamented as at the Jubilee, music and dancing. The company were dressed or undressed as they thought proper.'

The occasion of the king's birthday gave an annual opportunity for an extra display. On June 15, 1761, we find Walpole writing to the Countess of Ailesbury:

'At Ranelagh all is fireworks and sky-rockets. The birthday exceeded the splendour of Haroun Alraschid, and the "Arabian Nights," when people had nothing to do but to scour a lantern, and send a genie for a hamper of diamonds and rubies.'

Ranelagh fireworks were often on a very magnificent scale, as will appear from the following advertisement, Friday, July 17, 1789:

A MAGNIFICENT FIREWORK,

By Mr. Callot,

In the same part of the Garden as that given by his Excellency the Spanish Ambassador,
On the restoration of his Majesty's health;
With the fire music, by a band in the Gardens (during firing),
Composed by Mr. Handel.

On April 17, 1792, the following notice appeared in the newspapers:

> 'A view of Mount Ætna is nearly finished in Ranelagh Gardens, painted by Signor Marinari, which, we hear, is intended to conclude a firework, to be given at the evening masquerade the beginning of May. It is spoke of as a perfect representation, and likely to be the grandest exhibition ever seen in the kingdom.'

'Mount Ætna' is marked on Howard's map (1794).

Music formed an important part of the enjoyment of Ranelagh. There was a good band, and the best singers of the day were to be heard there. Smollett, a resident in Chelsea, has naturally several references to it in his novels. In 'Humphrey Clinker,' we read:

> 'At Ranelagh I heard the famous Tenducci, a thing from Italy: it looks for all the world like a man, but they say it is not. The voice, to be sure, is neither man's nor woman's, but is more melodious than either; and it warbled so divinely, that, while I listened, I really thought myself in Paradise.'

Here is an advertisement of one of his benefit concerts at Ranelagh, June, 1764:

MR. TENDUCCI'S NIGHT.

On Monday the 18th instant, the usual music will be divided into 4 Acts, with the addition of a good choir of singers dispersed over the Orchestra, with some extraordinary bands.

The favourite songs as usual.

At the end of the second Act will be performed the famous Chorus of Mr. Handel in Acis and Galatea. Oh! the pleasures of the plain.

At the end of the 3rd Act will be a grand chorus of Mr. Handel in the Messiah. For the Lord God omnipotent reigneth.

At the end of the 4th Act will be the Coronation Anthem of Mr. Handel. Between the Acts the French Horn and Clarinets will play some favourite pieces in the Chinese Temple in the Gardens.

The whole to conclude with a Ball.

This Tenducci, who was styled Count Palatine and Knight of St. John, married a lady in Dublin, and was subsequently involved in a trial of a very scandalous nature. He obtained great celebrity, especially for his rendering of Handel's airs. Gainsborough painted him in the act of taking a high note, and the portrait is now in the possession of Mr. Gray Hill. Walpole, who became terribly *blasé* after his first few years of society, had, apparently, no very high opinion of him, for he calls him a moderate tenor merely.

In the *Gentleman's Magazine,* we read that on May 12, 1767, 'were performed the much admired catches and glees, selected from the curious collection of the Catch Club, being the finest of the kind publicly exhibited in this or any other kingdom. The entertainment consisted of the favourite catches and glees composed by the most eminent masters of the last and present age, by a considerable number of the best vocal and instrumental performers. The choral and instrumental parts were added, to give the catches and glees their proper effect in so large an amphitheatre, being composed for the purpose by Dr. Arne.'

Sophia Baddely (1745-1786), whose husband instituted the celebrated cake banquet at Drury Lane, was a favourite vocalist at Ranelagh, as were also Charlotte Brant (afterwards Mrs. Pinto), Mrs. Thompson, Dibdin, Bannister, etc.

Dr. Burney, who afterwards received an appointment in Chelsea Hospital, often composed for Ranelagh. Among his works thus produced was the setting of a burlesque ode on St. Cecilia's Day, by Bonnel Thornton, which met with much success.

Entertainments of another character were occasionally given. The following advertisement, April 30, 1784 (in an interleaved copy of 'A Sunday Ramble' in the British Museum), gives us an example:

'RANELAGH.

'A grand Ærostatic Pyramid will be launched into the Atmosphere, from the Gardens, if the weather permits. To-morrow the 1st of May, at two o'clock.

'This pyramidal air-balloon is near thirty feet high, the model of the one erecting in France to the memory of M. Charles, who was the first aërial traveller, on the spot where he made his surprising ascent.

'The caricatures, hieroglyphics and inscriptions, the proprietor flatters himself will be the most entertaining exhibition in this kingdom.

'The above ornaments are descriptive of every remarkable occurrence in the history of air-balloons.

'The Nobility, Gentry, and Public, will most certainly be struck with the Novelty of this figure, which demonstrates how near Ærostatics arrives to Utility, and as an Eminent artist observes, from the situation of the Rotunda and Gardens, will be as fine a *coup d'œil* as any in Europe.'

On July 28, 1802, when the career of the Gardens was nearing its close, M. Garnerin made his first ascent from Ranelagh, accompanied by a Captain Sowden of the Royal Artillery.

Notwithstanding the excitements of the masquerades, carnivals, ridottos, *bals paré*, courts of Comus, concerts and fireworks, the promenade was the great attraction of the place. 'All was so orderly,' says Rogers, 'that you could hear the whishing sound of the ladies' trains, as the immense assembly walked round and round the room.' This must, on the whole, have been rather dull. Bloomfield, the peasant poet, evidently found it so, and gave vent to his feelings in an unwonted piece of sarcasm:

'To Ranelagh, once in my life,
By good natur'd force I was driven;
The nations had ceas'd their long strife
And peace beam'd her radiance from heaven.
What wonders were here to be found
That a clown might enjoy or disdain?
First we trac'd the gay circle all round;
Ay—and then we went round it again.

> ' A thousand feet rustled on mats —
> 　　A carpet that once had been green ;
> 　Men bowed with their outlandish hats,
> 　　With corners so fearfully keen.
> 　Fair maids, who, at home, in their haste
> 　　Had left all clothing else but a train
> 　Swept the floor clean, as solemnly they pac'd
> 　　Then—walked round and swept it again.'

The first twenty or thirty years of the existence of Ranelagh Gardens was a career of uninterrupted prosperity.　To maintain its exclusive character, it was only opened at such periods as society decreed to be ' the season.'　And to prevent ' the offensive admittance of servants, either by mistake or favour,' a special part of the amphitheatre was fitted up for their reception only. Ranelagh took a new lease of life, as it were, when the beautiful Duchess of Devonshire made it again fashionable by her presence, but, by 1788, it was evidently on the decline.　The newspapers of the day were no longer given up to laudation, but contained such paragraphs as the following :

> ' This once agreeable rendezvous of beauty and fashion, has, like all other things, had its day, and now remains a solitary pile, comparative to its former splendour.'
> ' This round-about promenade had very few admirers yesterday evening, the dull insipidity of the bread and butter manufactory—-as poor Sam Foote used to call it—was only rendered endurable by the excellence of the band, rolls, tea and butter.'
> ' The shares of Ranelagh, which sold some time ago for above 1,000*l.*, are now offered at 900*l.*'

Thus passed the glory of this ' Paphian Temple,' which not only appealed to the fashionable loungers of a whole generation, but delighted even such men as Johnson, Goldsmith, Fielding and Addison.　It lingered on, however, for some years, and Rogers in his ' Table Talk ' has an amusing note on the advertising tactics of the proprietor of this garden, and its rival :

> ' The proprietors of Ranelagh and Vauxhall used to send decoy ducks among the ladies and gentlemen, who were walking in the Mall, that is, persons attired in the height of fashion, who every now and then would exclaim in a very audible tone : " What charming weather for Ranelagh " or " for Vauxhall !" '

The last gathering of any importance held at Ranelagh, was an installation ball of the knights of Bath in 1802.

The gardens were finally closed in 1804, and in the following year the buildings were taken down ; some remnants of the ruins, however, remained on the site for some years.　Fifteen years after the demolition, Sir Richard Philips makes the following remark in his journey from London to Kew :

> ' On entering Chelsea, I was naturally led to inquire for the scite of the once gay Ranelagh !　I passed up the avenue of trees which I remember often to have seen blocked with carriages.　At its extremity I looked for the Rotunda, and its surrounding buildings ; but as I could not see them, I concluded that I had acquired but an imperfect idea of the place in my nocturnal visits !　I went forward in an open place, but still could discern no Ranelagh !　At length in a spot covered with nettles, thistles,

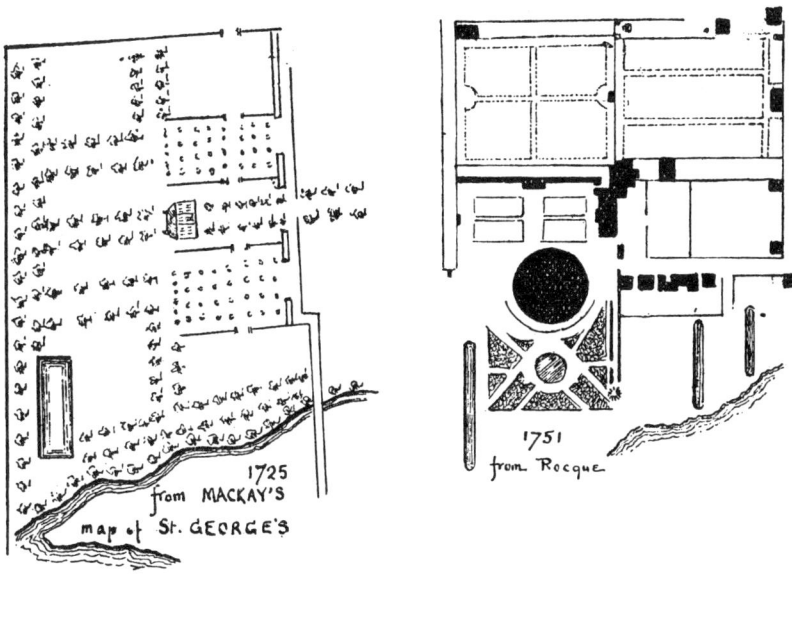

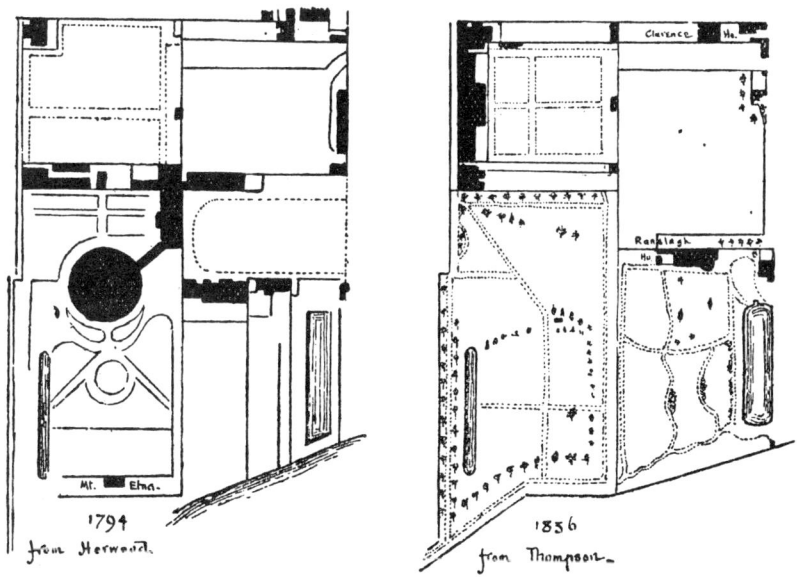

PLANS OF RANELAGH GARDENS.

39

and other rank weeds, I met a working man, who, in answer to my inquiries, told me, that he saw I was a stranger, or I should have known that Ranelagh had been pulled down, and that I was standing on the scite of the Rotunda.'

There are about three pages more of tearful reminiscence, and the following footnote:

' I afterwards learnt in Chelsea, that, latterly, Ranelagh did not pay the proprietors five per cent. for their capital, and therefore they sold the materials to the best bidder.'

Part of the grounds have been bought for the hospital, and formed into a beautiful garden under the old name; but nothing remains to recall the gaiety and dissipation of the past, but a solitary hook, fastened to an old tree, and once used for the lamps that illuminated the nightly revels.

The organ, built by Byfield, which had shared in many notable concerts, was purchased for Tetbury Church in Gloucestershire.

RANELAGH CHAPEL.

A portion of Ranelagh House was certainly standing in 1813, for in that year the Rev. R. H. Shepherd fitted up a room therein, commonly known as ' King William's Drawing (or Dining) Room,' for use as a chapel. It overlooked a lawn, and was therefore sometimes called ' The Chapel on Ranelagh Green.' In 1818 a commodious chapel was built in George Street (opposite the present Sloane Square Station) through the exertions of Mr. Shepherd and his friends, and to it the congregation removed. The service was similar to that used in the Countess of Huntingdon's connection, though the chapel was not connected with it. Mr. Shepherd was greatly respected and highly popular, and continued his arduous labours until 1843, when the chapel became the property of the English Presbyterian Church under the ministration of the Rev. T. Alexander. In 1866 the congregation removed to Halkin Street, Belgrave Square, where it still continues.

The building, that for nearly fifty years had served to supply the spiritual wants of a rapidly increasing population, was soon afterwards converted into the Court Theatre, and thus remained until 1888, when it was demolished. During the course of demolition, a brass plate was discovered recording the fact that Mr. Shepherd himself laid the foundation stone, together with the names of the original trustees, all now deceased.

The Court Theatre now occupies a site on the east side of Sloane Square.

In the latter part of the eighteenth century the neighbourhood of Ranelagh Gardens was somewhat popular as a residence of artists. John Dixon, a well-known engraver in mezzotint, who engraved the ' Ugolino ' and other pictures of Sir Joshua Reynolds', gives his address as ' Kemp's Row, opposite Ranelagh

Walk, Chelsea,' in 1791, and for several years afterwards. Redgrave says that he married a lady of considerable fortune, 'retired to Ranelagh, kept his carriage, and entertained his friends.' Malton the younger was living in Kemp's Row in 1770, and two years afterwards exhibited with the Incorporated Society a 'view of the Royal Hospital at Chelsea, from the entrance at the hither end,' in water-colours. W. Watts, a careful and able landscape engraver, published his 'Seats of the Nobility and Gentry' between January 1, 1779, and May, 1786; the plates are lettered 'published by W. Watts, Kemp's Row, Chelsea,' with dates. Francis Swaine, a painter of marine subjects

INTERIOR OF RANELAGH CHAPEL (AFTERWARDS THE COURT THEATRE).

(by whom there is a small picture at South Kensington Museum, and several others at Hampton Court), lived at 'No. 3, the last house from the Orange Coffee house, Back Road of Ranelagh Walk, Chelsea,' in 1778. The Orange Tavern and Tea-gardens stood where the St. Barnabas Schools are now built, just beyond the Chelsea boundary. In 1780 his address was 'No. 2, next Avery Farm Row, near the Flask, Chelsea.' Swaine died at Chelsea in 1782. Other artists in the same neighbourhood were, Atkinson, a drawing-master, 1774; Allwood, marine painter, and Servandoni, architectural draughtsman, 1776; a Mr. Metz and his two daughters, water-colour artists, in 1788.

'Kemp's Row,' mentioned above, took its name from Nicholas Kempe, one of the proprietors of Ranelagh Gardens. He died in June, 1774. 'Kemp's Acre,' a part of the Common Field, appears on Richardson's 'Survey of the Manor,' 1769.

Another Ranelagh was started in 1772 at Paris, by a gardener of the Bois de Boulogne, and was not finally closed until 1860.

THE CHELSEA ARMED ASSOCIATION.

Before the Rotunda was demolished, the Royal Volunteers of Chelsea held a review there, and this is, perhaps, the best place for a short account of this body.

When

'Napoleon's banners at Boulogne
Armed in our island every freeman,'

the Chelsea freemen were not wanting in martial ardour.

The earliest reference to them that I have found is a sermon in the British Museum with this title-page:

'Philanthropy, Religion, and Loyalty, the best characteristics of a Christian soldier.
'A Sermon addressed to the Armed Association of the Parish of Saint Luke, Chelsea, and to the Inhabitants at Large, on Sunday, 8th July, 1798.
'By the Rev. Weeden Butler, morning preacher of Charlotte-Street-Chapel, and chaplain to the Right Hon. Dowager Lady Onslow. Printed by Request. MDCCXCVIII.'

There is also a

'Sermon preached in the Royal Hospital Chapel before the Chelsea Armed Association on Receiving their Colours from Miss North, daughter of the Lord Bishop of Winchester, May 31st, 1799.
'By the Rev. Weeden Butler, chaplain to His Royal Highness the Duke of Kent.
'Chelsea. Printed by D. Jacques, sold by Davenport and Faulkner, Piccadilly Row, and by Dillon, Lombard Street.'

The preface contains the following resolution:

'The Officers and other members of the Committee beg leave to express their sincere acknowledgments to the Rev. Weeden Butler, for his great attention to the Corps, and for his sermon delivered on the day of presenting the Colours. The Commandant is requested to transmit to Mr. Butler this mark of esteem on the part of the Chelsea Volunteers, and to signify it as their wish, that he will order the discourse to be printed forthwith, together with the detail which has been drawn up of the arrangement of the day.

'Signed, MATTHEW YATMAN, Commandant,
'J. DENYER, Chairman.'

The following account of the ceremony, which acquired dignity and impressiveness from the military associations of the place, is derived from the official detail referred to.

As the Chelsea volunteers marched to the hospital gates, the ground was kept for them by the Kensington Association under the command of Major Torriano. At the gates they were received by Sir William Fawcett, the Governor, Major Bulkeley and the other officers of the hospital in full uniform, and marched through files of the veteran pensioners to the chapel. Dr. Burney presided at the organ, and the chaplains with the Rev. Weeden Butler conducted a service, during which a standard, richly embroidered by the ladies of Chelsea, with the emblems of 'the Union, the Crown and St. Luke,' was brought forward and laid on the Communion Table.

After service, the company adjourned to the quadrangle, where the statue of Charles II. stands. When they were drawn up in line, Miss North, conducted by George Anstey, Esq., Commissary General of his Majesty's Forces, and Mr. Pemberton of Gough House, advanced and presented the colours. Then, after speeches, the volunteers went through their manœuvres, advancing and retiring in line, firing by subdivisions and volleys. On their return they marched to the Lord Bishop of Winchester's, and presented arms to the lady who had done them the honour of presenting the colours; and finished by marching to the commandant's, where, after presenting arms, they lodged the colours, and fired three volleys.

On July 27, 1800, the Chelsea Vestry passed the following resolution:

'At the present most important crisis, when an ambitious and implacable foe has presumed openly to avow his determination to reduce this free and happy country to the miserable and degraded state of a French province, it becomes the indispensable duty of all Britons to stand forward in defence of their native country; the support of the mild and paternal government of the sovereign, and the protection of their rights, their families, and their dearest interests. Resolved, that a subscription be immediately set on foot for defraying the general expense of carrying these resolutions into effect, and that books be opened for the signatures of those persons who wish to become members of the Chelsea Association.'

By 1804, the Chelsea Association, then under the captaincy of Lord Hobart, had advanced to the dignity of the Royal Volunteers, and they received new colours in the Rotunda at the hands of the Countess of Harrington, who, in presenting them, said:

'GENTLEMEN,—Her Majesty having been graciously pleased to confer upon me the honour of presenting to you these colours, I am anxious to express how highly I am flattered by this distinguished mark of the Queen's favour. At a time of all others the most awful, when our country is threatened with the unprovoked attack of a most implacable enemy, and when you have evinced your readiness to stand forward in the defence of everything that is most dear to us all, what can be more gratifying to you than being so particularly distinguished by her Majesty, and receiving your colours from her? Animated as your hearts must be in gratitude to the Queen, in addition to every other noble sentiinent that has guided you, from the moment of the first offer of your services, it would not only be superfluous, but presumptuous, in me, to add anything more upon the occasion, than the expression of my fervent wish for your success, in the event of the enemy carrying his threats into execution ; confident that no power, however strenuously exerted, will ever wrest these colours from you, while there is yet left a man in your corps to defend them.'

Lord Hobart replied suitably, and the colours were presented. This was on January 3, 1804.

The report of the second battalion of the Queen's Royal Volunteers issued on August 31, 1805, and signed by John Wilson, Lieutenant-Colonel, and Richard Downham, Adjutant, says :

'The battalion has supported its effective Force, and the Patriotic members of it have been uniformly advancing in that Discipline and Military Knowledge which are most essentially requisite to qualify them in assisting to repel and subdue an active and hardy Foe, trained to the duties of war, and stimulated to exertion by the Hope of Plunder. This the Committee are warranted to assert from the Observations of Major-General Lord Banbury, who at the last inspection declared himself highly satisfied with the Equipment and Discipline of the Corps ; and that, in making a Report very honourable to the Exertions both of its Officers and Privates, he should state them fully prepared for active service.'

The Chelsea volunteers were five hundred strong, but the successful campaign of the Duke of Wellington robbed them of the opportunity of dying to the last man in defence of their flag. Their triumphs were of a more peaceful if less glorious order, reviews, marches, and such like, and there was living not long since an old inhabitant who remembered with what grand display they marched to Cremorne Villa to be feasted on the occasion of George III.'s Jubilee ! Their colours are preserved in the old church : there they hang thickly on the walls, mournful memorials of a sad period in our history. One of them is a particular object of veneration. It was designed and executed by the Queen and Princesses, and was, says Faulkner and echoes Bryan, 'a superb piece of needlework, the ground being a rich purple silk, having in the centre her Majesty's arms, embroidered and surrounded with sprigs of variegated tints and figures. At the lower corner were the letters C. R., and under the armorial bearings the words, " Queen's Royal Volunteers."' In the porch of the church is a board bearing the following inscription :

'These banners, presented by her Majesty Queen Charlotte to her Royal Regiment on the third day of January, 1804, at a time when the country was threatened with invasion by an inveterate enemy, were deposited in the church in the year 1814. A memorial of Her Majesty's most gracious favour to the Inhabitants of this Parish for their zeal, loyalty and patriotism.'

Bryan, writing in 1869, says :

'There are still living some few old people in the parish who remember, when boys, marching by the side of these colours with all the heroic consequence of supposed military triumph.'

THE KING'S ROAD.

Until Stuart times inland Chelsea was unbuilt on, and almost entirely open. This open land was partly wooded, partly heath and common, and partly cultivated. The estate known as the Blacklands derived its name, it has been supposed, from the heath with which it was once probably covered, as the soil is suitable. This belt of open land remained uncrossed by any road until the reign of Charles II. Previously there was only a field-path following inland the bendings of the river, marking probably an ancient track which, in remote times, may have been the limit of its overflow waters. This path led from a small plank bridge across the rivulet called the Westbourne. This bridge is sometimes called Blandel Bridge; but the name of Bloody Bridge is probably as old as the reign of Queen Elizabeth. From the Parish Books, 1590, Lord Cheyne copied this note:

'John Dakes was this year enjoyned to make a Causie at bloodie Gate.'

On a plan of the Manor of Chelsea, drawn by T. Richardson, 1769 (British Museum), we find a neighbouring meadow (part of the East Mead) called 'Great Bloody Field.' The natural inference to be drawn from this threefold use of the hideously-suggestive adjective is that the spot was in former times the scene of some crime or skirmish.

It was a dangerous spot in comparatively recent times. Thus in August, 1748, 'four gentlemen coming from Chelsea, the King's Road, in a coach, were attacked near Bloody Bridge by two highwaymen, but they all getting out of the coach and drawing their swords, the highwaymen made off without their booty.'—Newspaper notice quoted in *Notes and Queries*, 1868.

The path across the fields extended eastward from Bloody Bridge as far as the town gate in Church Lane, where began the King's highway, which followed the present line of King's Road to the parish boundary at Stanley Bridge. We have no evidence as to the date of the construction of this piece of road, but it is mentioned as early as 1620. There is some evidence that the route through Chelsea to Hampton Court was used in the royal journeys early in the seventeenth century. In 1626 we find an order for Thomas Hebbs, surveyor of the King's Highways, 'to take special care for the repair of the way leading from Chelsea to Fulham.' On September 7 of the same year, Sir John Danvers wrote to Christopher Collam, Richard Stiles, and the Surveyors of the Highways of St. Martins-in-the-Fields, stating that he was commanded by the Earl of Dorset to express 'his just dislike that nothing is done towards the repair of the highway between the

KING'S ROAD, EIGHTEENTH CENTURY.

west gate of St. James's Park and the Stone Bridge at the edge of Chelsey Fields. If a satisfactory account be not given before eight o'clock the next morning, the Earl will conceive it a continual contempt, which he will proceed to censure, and punish, as in his wisdom shall seem meet.' From the Stone Bridge, near the site of the tavern called the Nell Gwynne in Pimlico Road, the highway lay along the present Queen's Road to the waterside, until it reached the present Cheyne Walk. Hence along Church Lane to the highway above-mentioned. In the reign of Charles II. the route was shortened by converting the field-path from Bloody Bridge to the Town Gate into a carriage road ; a new bridge was built at Bloody Bridge (a substantial structure of stone, about 15 feet wide), and the road was continued to St. James's Park, across the Five Fields, where Eaton Square now lies. The date of this improvement does not seem to be known, nor was it in 1719, when a petition to the Lords of the Treasury regarding the right-of-way was drawn up. This petition states :

> 'That before the restoration of King Charles the Second, and some time after, the fields of Chelsea were open fields ; and that the bridge, called Bloody Bridge, was only a foot-bridge, with a plank or board ; and the way leading thence to the lane facing Blacklands House, was then only a foot-path of about five feet wide, and the lands on each side were plowed and sowed close up to the same ; and that from the said lane to the town-gate was only a baulk, or head-land, of about ten or twelve feet broad, or thereabouts ; and the lands on each side of the said head-land were also plowed up to the edges thereof ; and that the said head-land was used by the owners and occupiers of the said lands, for a way, egress, and regress, to their lands, with ploughs and other utensils of husbandry, and to carry off their crops from their lands, time out of mind. That some time after the Restoration, King Charles II. built Bloody Bridge, as it now stands ; and, as we are informed, agreed with the then Lord of the Manor, and others concerned, for the said head-land, for his Majesty's private road, allowing the freeholders their ancient way through the same. Whereupon the King made the road with gravel, and the landowners ditched out their lands on each side of the same ; and the King took upon him the repair of the gate at the town end (which before was maintained by the parishioners), and as soon as the fields were sown, was hung up and shut, and, after harvest, was always open until seed-time returned again, as many yet alive well remember.'

This petition was occasioned by an attempt in 1719 to close the King's Road to all but the Royal family and household. It was in the handwriting of Dr. King, and signed by Sir Hans Sloane. It goes on to say that :

> 'Ever since [its formation] the householders of the said parish have been in possession of a free-way and passage to their lands through the said road (some persons having no other way), and were never denied it through the reigns of King Charles II., King James, King William, and Queen Anne, as we can make appear by sufficient evidence. Now, whereas upon his present Majesty's repairing the said road, the present Surveyor General has given orders to shut the gates against the landholders of Chelsea, to their great detriment, and, as we conceive, to the debarring them of their right.'

The evidence of several freeholders was appended ; an evasive reply was received, upon which the petitioners sent another statement on May 6, 1719, and received the following answer on the same day :

> 'My Lords direct Mr. Watkins to permit the tenants of the lands adjoining to the King's Road, through Chelsea, to have free passage through the same, with their carts and horses, in the manner they have been accustomed to ; and that the ditches which belong to the land, and were lately filled up, be opened again.'

Among the Treasury Papers is a memorial from Joseph Carpenter to the Lords of the Treasury (September, 1721), asking for 'an advance of money for repair of H.M. private road leading to Fulham.' It is minuted :

> '6th Sept., 1721.—600^{li} to be issued to the paym^t upon acco^t of these works now in hand' (Vol. ccxxxviij., n. 69).

There is also the 'Petition of the six poor Gatekeepers in his Majesty's private road leading to Fulham to the Lords of the Treasury' for payment for three years' work on the road, the Surveyor of his Majesty's Private Roads (William Watkins, Esq.) having promised to obtain for each of them £5 per annum. It is minuted :

> '22d Feb., 1722-3.—The allow^{ce} of 5^{li} p ann. each to be established in the Office of Works, and to be p^d from the time they were employed in this service.'

Two letters relating to the claims accompany the petition ; in the second is the following statement :

> 'The Gates on the Fulham Roads are 6, viz., the first at the entrance at the back side of Buckingham House, the 2^d over against Chelsea College, the 3^d at Chelsea Lane End, for which I pay ten shill. p. an., the 4th at the World's End, for which I pay 3 pounds p. an., there being about half an acre of garden ground belonging to it, the 5th at Sandy End, the sixth and last at Fulham, 20 shill. rent ; in all 4*l* 10s. ground rent. The Gatekeepers have worked on the road thro' 3 years past, wch is ever since the houses were built, in hopes and upon my promise that I would use my endeavours to obtain some small allowance for them' (Vol. ccxliij., n. 24).

The road was closed to public traffic for more than a century after this ; the few who were allowed access to it received metal tickets, stamped with the words 'The King's Private Road,' on the one side, and the crown, date, and the letters G. R. on the other. Some of these, with the date 1731, are still extant. The gates and bars mentioned above remained until the present century, as some may even yet remember. It became a public road in 1830. Pope's friend, D'Artiquenave, of ham-pie fame, was at one time surveyor of the King's Road.

For many years the King's Road had a most unenviable notoriety. Crimes were frequent, carriages were stopped, houses broken into, and the law-breakers were sometimes too powerful for the patrol from the Hospital, so that, at length, the inhabitants formed themselves into the self-protecting committee, already mentioned in the introduction. As late as 1812 this was still necessary, as is shown by the following :

'At a meeting of the Committee held this day, Jan. 2nd, 1812,
'It was resolved,
'That the following address to the Inhabitants of Chelsea should be printed and circulated throughout the Parish :
'The Committee appointed at the special Vestry meeting, on Tuesday last, for the purpose of forming a plan for the better protection of the Inhabitants, beg leave to state to them the outlines of the plan which they intend to adopt.
'To establish patroles in every street or Division of the Parish as soon as a Subscription is raised sufficient for the purpose, who shall perambulate every part of the parish continually during the night, shall have the means of communicating with each other and the regular Watchmen, for the mutual support and safety, and shall have authority to apprehend all persons behaving disorderly, or lurking about at unseasonable hours, and detain them in custody, until they can be detained before a Magistrate for Examination. And all those persons who enter their names in the Association will be required to meet occasionally and alternately in such numbers, and at such places and times, as the Committee shall appoint for the purpose of perambulating the parish, etc.
'JOHN GREGORY, Chairman.'

When this notice was issued King's Road had long been famous for its nurseries. In 1784 we find 'a young gentleman, of good estate and honourable position,' advertising for a wife, and offering as a special inducement—over and above that of having so desirable a husband—that ' her home would be in Chelsea, 'midst the floral beauties of the King's Road.' Many years afterwards Miss Landon (L. E. L.) writes :

'How often, at the end of a morning with the fashionable world, afternoon with the more quiet part of the community, and evening with the very respectable indeed, a young cavalier may be seen curbing a horse, impatient of the rein, at the nursery grounds in the King's Road till a bouquet of the most fragrant exotics is brought out.'

And even now, though the old order of things has gone for ever, and Chelsea is no longer rural, the King's Road is still famous in the horticultural world.

Near the bridge built by Charles II. were a few cottages, and an inn, called the Coach and Horses. About 1771 Sloane Square was built, enclosing a small village green, bordered with posts and chains, where the lads of Chelsea enjoyed their village games. Here, too, the Chelsea Volunteers used to drill. Until a few years ago the Square retained something of its original aspect, but recent rebuilding, and the destruction of the trees and gardens, have entirely changed its appearance.

Eastwards is the Royal Military Asylum, on the site of which stood Chelsea House, a ' capital mansion,' which was for many years the residence of the Cadogan family. It has already been shown that the Manor of Chelsea came into the possession of this family by the marriage of Charles, second

Baron Cadogan, with Elizabeth, daughter and co-heir of Sir Hans Sloane. His elder brother William was a trusted subordinate of the Duke of Marlborough, and chiefly associated with the brilliant prowess of 'Cadogan's Horse,' the Inniskilling Dragoons, now known as the Fifth Royal Irish Dragoons. His many services in war and diplomacy gained for him the titles of Baron Cadogan of Oakley, Viscount Caversham, and Earl Cadogan. But he rendered himself particularly obnoxious to the Jacobites, and was accused by them of fraud and embezzlement. The indictment in the House of Commons was supported by Walpole and Pulteney, and only defeated by a majority of ten. Atterbury, stung by Cadogan's remark that he (the bishop) deserved to be thrown to the lions, summed up his character as 'a big, bad, bold, blustering, bloody, blundering booby !' His ability, however, is proved by the high esteem in which he was held by the Duke of Marlborough and Prince Eugene, and when the former died in 1722 Cadogan was chosen to succeed him in the posts of Commander-in-Chief of the Army and Master-General of the Ordnance. He was also appointed a commissioner of Chelsea Hospital. He died at Kensington Gravel Pits in 1726 without male issue, when his titles of viscount and earl became extinct ; but the barony of Oakley passed to his brother Charles above-mentioned, who had also served in Marlborough's campaigns, and in Scotland as a cavalry officer. He died in 1776, and was succeeded by his son, Charles Sloane Cadogan, who became Viscount Chelsea and Earl Cadogan in 1800, and died April 3, 1807.

Colonel Henry Cadogan, son of the last-named by his second wife, a granddaughter of the Earl of Orford, was another brave officer, highly praised by Wellington in his despatches. He served with distinguished bravery at the passage of the Douro, Talavera, Fuentes d'Onore, and at Vittoria, where he was killed at the head of his troops when storming the heights above the village of Puebla (June 21, 1813).

Charles Henry Sloane, second Earl Cadogan, died in 1832, and was succeeded by his brother George, who had been created Baron Oakley of Caversham in the preceding year.

The present earl, George Henry, has earned considerable distinction as a politician on the Conservative side. He was Under-Secretary for War, 1875-8, for the Colonies, 1878-80, and has been Lord Privy Seal since 1886.

Chelsea House, at the corner of Cadogan Place, a stone house built from the designs of Mr. W. Young in 1874, just within the Chelsea boundary, is the present town residence of the Codogan family.

In the latter part of the eighteenth century Chelsea, or Cadogan House, was occupied by Sir Walter Farquhar, a physician who enjoyed a great practice, and was held in high repute, though he does not appear to have made any additions to medical science or literature.

In 1801, the house and grounds were purchased by Government, and to them was added Frazer's meadow at the rear. On the site thus obtained, the Royal Military Asylum was built after the design of Mr. Sanders. The Duke of York (the founder) laid the first stone on June 19, 1801. It is a plain but imposing building with a Doric portico. Beneath the royal arms is the following inscription :

'The Royal Military Asylum for the children of the soldiers of the Regular Army.'

Formerly this school was occupied by boys and girls ; but in 1823, the girls were removed to Southampton, and the boys in that institution brought to Chelsea, where one thousand boys are now accommodated.

About 1810 the grounds were enlarged by the purchase of a piece of glebe land, and in 1848 the sum of £30,000 out of the army prize fund was voted to the service of the asylum. This was followed by £10,000 in 1842.

At the corner of Cheltenham Terrace is the chapel, consecrated by Dr. Howley, Bishop of London, in 1824. It contains a simple but pleasing monument by Westmacott, to the memory of Lieutenant-Colonel George Williamson, the first commandant, erected by the order of the Duke of York.

ROYAL MILITARY ASYLUM (KING'S ROAD), 1830.

The spectacle of the boys leaving chapel, headed by their band, gave Mr. P. R. Morris, A.R.A., the subject of one of his best pictures—'The Sons of the Brave.' The site of this chapel was previously occupied by a cottage, built in 1797, by Mrs. Crouch, a well-known actress and vocalist. She died at Brighton in 1806.

The Royal Asylum was visited by the King and Queen, with the Princesses and Royal Dukes on June 20, 1805 ; by the King and Queen of the Sandwich Isles in 1824 ; and by Prince George of Cumberland in 1828.

On the opposite side of the road were two of the most famous of the Chelsea nurseries, Davey's and Colville's, separated by what used to be called Butterfly Alley, now a portion of Keppel Street. A tavern called the Colville perpetuates the memory of the latter, and both are celebrated by Samuel

MRS. CROUCH'S COTTAGE, KING'S ROAD (ABOUT 1790).

Jackson Pratt, author of 'Sympathy,' in a poem called 'Flowers and Fashion,' which he sent to his friend Faulkner. It begins:

> 'Where smiling Chelsea spreads the cultur'd lands,
> Sacred to Flora a pavilion stands,
> And yet a second temple neighb'ring near
> Nurses the fragrance of the various year.
> Of Davy this, of Colvill that, the care,
> While both the favour of the goddess share.'

After telling us how 'Fashion's suppliants' throng 'to these gay Edens,' he concludes:

> 'Thus, strange to tell! near London you behold
> The age of Fashion, Beauty, and of Gold!'

I take the following lines from another local poet, Samuel Shepherd, F.S.A., 'On the Death of Mr. Thomas Davey, the Florist of Chelsea, who died, April 25, 1833, Aged 77':

> 'Your bloom he did with pleasure view,
> Which Spring did constantly renew,
> And ev'ry plant in order knew,
>   That deck'd each bed.
> 'But from his garden death has borne,
> No more he'll greet the rising morn;
> Be filled with tears, ye flowers forlorn;
>   Your friend is dead.'

Part of Davey's nursery garden, where Glover's gas-meter factory now stands, was afterwards occupied by Downing's floor-cloth manufactory, removed from the opposite side of the road. In the older building the meetings of the Chelsea Auxiliary Bible Society were held; its site is now occupied by Wellington Square, named in compliment to the 'Iron Duke,' whose brother was rector of Chelsea.

Adjoining the chapel of the Royal Military Asylum is an old house, which has, for many years, been connected with education. It appears to have been a school in 1772, when the Rev. John Jenkins, A.M., lectured on 'Female Education and Christian Fortitude under Affliction.' Later on a boarding-school was kept in this house by the Misses Babington, and in 1842 it was purchased by the National Society for the training of school-mistresses, and is known as Whiteland's Training College. This institution has done much good work in its own sphere, but is perhaps most interesting for its annual May Day festival, established in 1881 by John Ruskin. A Queen of the May —elected by popular vote—receives a present from the great man himself; and she chooses a certain number from among the students to receive a gift of one of his books. Need it be said that the students of this college are profound Ruskin students also? This interesting ceremony takes place on a tree-shaded lawn, at the back of the college, and is generally attended by some of Mr. Ruskin's friends and relations. Since 1885, too, the children of the practising schools have had an annual Rose Festival, when the favourite of the school is crowned 'Queen of the Flowers,' and a concert and prize-giving follows.

West of Davey's garden was another nursery, Moore's, on the ground now occupied by Messrs. Weeks and Co.'s horticultural works.

At the corner of Markham Street an old house, still standing, bears the following name-plate :

```
                H

           I         A

           BOX  FARM

              1686
```

The rear of this house is older than the front, and rather quaint. The farm lands stretched across the site of Markham Square ; in 1769 they belonged to Edward Green, Esq., and were afterwards occupied, in part at least, by Moore's nursury. The house has long been in the possession of the Evans family, by whom it is still occupied. The Congregationalist Chapel in Markham Square, built of Kentish rag with Bath stone dressings in 1860 after the design of Mr. John Tarring, is a creditable example of the Decorated style.

Jubilee Place, built in 1809, recalls the fiftieth year of George III., and the celebrations which accompanied that event ; 'Little's Nursery,' the last of the old King's Road nurseries, has but recently been closed, and is not yet built upon; Blenheim Place was named in honour of the Duke of Marlborough, who is believed to have occupied Whiteland's House, until lately part of Messrs. Scott, Cuthbertson and Co.'s wall-paper works ; Flood Street preserves the memory of a worthy Chelsea man, whose benefactions to the parish are celebrated every year at St. Luke's Church on 'Flood's Day,' January 13. Flood Street was formerly known as Queen Street, previously as Robinson's Lane, and earlier still as Pound Lane, the latter name derived from the site of the Parish Pound, which stood at the south end (see Rocque's Map, 1751).

Near Flood Street was Pilton's manufactory of invisible wire fences, with its collection of birds, 'Jimmy's Menagerie,' described in the *Gentleman's Magazine,* April, 1809. Upper Manor Street was first called Wellesley Street in honour of the rector, but the name was foolishly changed some years ago, on account of the murder which took place in one of its houses. Robert Farrier and his sister Charlotte Farrier, two pleasing artists, lived in this street for some years.

Beyond Manor Street is the Town Hall and vestry offices, built in 1859, after the design of Mr. W. W. Pocock. Externally the building is not remarkable, but the hall has been recently rebuilt from the designs of Mr. J. M. Brydon, F.R.I.B.A., and is a very handsome structure. It was near to this spot that the Earl of Peterborough, whose house was at Parson's Green, had a narrow escape from highwaymen. The office of the Board of Guardians on

MANOR COTTAGE, KING'S ROAD.

the opposite side of the road is a handsome red-brick structure designed by Messrs. Harston in 1883.

The burial-ground adjoining, which makes a pleasant green break in the line of dingy shops and houses, was given to the parish by Sir Hans Sloane, and consecrated by Dr. Edmund Gibson, Bishop of London in 1736. Lord Cadogan enlarged it in 1790. Although small, it contains several graves of interest. A tall pillar monument marks the grave of Andrew Millar (d. 1768), the famous bookseller and publisher. Cipriani, a foundation member of the Royal Academy, who died in 1785, lies near ; Bartolozzi, the famous engraver, erected a stone to his memory. On the north side is the grave of John

41

Martyn, F.R.S., professor of Botany at Cambridge University, who lived for many years in Church Street. Dr. Sloane Elsmere (1766), the Rev. Weeden Butler, Mr. Fraser the nurseryman (1811), Dr. Philip Withers (1790), editor of the 'Table of Cebes'; William Powell, the 'Highgate Prophet'; Captain Thomas Baillie, R.N. (1802); John Hamilton (1808), artist, and others of local fame also found here a 'haven of rest.' Its use was discontinued when the new burial-ground in Sydney Street was opened. Behind it is the Workhouse. The building of this institution was first proposed in 1727; in 1733, Sir Hans Sloane gave three-quarters of an acre of land for its erection, situated 'opposite the little houses near the Conduit in the King's Road.' Building was commenced in 1737, and various additions have been made in 1788, 1792, 1797, 1807, 1822, 1827. Since this last date the building has been largely rebuilt, under the direction of Mr. Handford, with subsequent additions by Messrs. Harston. Across the road is the Six Bells, an old-time tavern, which still retains its gardens, bowling-green and sham rockwork. From this point to Glebe Place was Rolle's nursery gardens. An ancient conduit, which supplied the Manor House with water, stood in one corner of the garden. Oakley Street now cuts through the site of this nursery. The four old houses standing between Oakley Street and Glebe Place form what is almost the only 'unimproved' bit of the King's Road left us. Argyll House is said, but with little probability, to have belonged to the Argyll family, and to have been used as a hunting or shooting box. Mr. Mascall, a gentleman who took an active part in local affairs, lived here for many years; afterwards Mr. Boyd, Palmerston's 'man with the white hat'; and until recently, Mme. Venturie, the friend of Mazzini. The house at the corner of Glebe Place is associated with two eminent sculptors, G. B. Fontana and J. Dalou.

Glebe Place itself was originally a back way to Shrewsbury House. The old gateways leading to the gardens of this house are still preserved in Dr. Phené's garden, where several Chelsea and old London relics are preserved. Glebe Place is referred to in a Vestry Minute, September 18, 1755:

> 'Whereas the road leading from the north end of Great Cheyne Row over the Glebe land to the King's Private Road, is the proper right of Mr. John Narbonne, of this parish, and whereas the inhabitants of this parish do frequently pass and repass that way, not only with corpses, to the new Burial Ground, but to the workhouse contiguous, as well as to other places; and as the privilege is only upon sufferance, by consent, and during the pleasure of Mr. Narbonne, therefore we unanimously agree to pay him and his heirs, as long as this privilege shall continue, upon the 1st day of May in every year, being from the day the burying-ground was consecrated, the sum of one shilling, which we order shall be paid by the churchwardens for the time being.'

Towards the south end of this road was one of the earliest houses on the Glebe, 'a capital mansion,' erected in Dr. King's time, and sometimes called

' The Old Rectory House,' though it never seems to have been used as the rectory. When Faulkner wrote (1829) it was inhabited by Mr. W. Cresswell. There was standing in the middle of Glebe Place until recently a small, unpretentious old chapel, built for the Huguenots who settled in Chelsea after the Revocation of the Edict of Nantes. It was afterwards used by the Independents, and among the ministers named by Faulkner, are the Rev. Mr. Trail, the Rev. Benjamin Fielder (who died in the pulpit in 1803), and the Rev. James Bunce.

Between Bramerton Street and Church Street stood Manor Cottage, with a large and secluded garden. This was kept as a private lunatic asylum for ladies, early in the present century, by Mr. and Mrs. Mullins. A portion of it, much altered, is still standing, and occupied by three small shops.

The northern side of the King's Road, from Arthur Street to Carlyle Square was formerly called King's Parade. It was the first portion of King's Road to have a paved footpath. Up to the present it has escaped alteration. Manresa Road leads us into Trafalgar Square, the scene of Cecil Lawson's ' Rus in Urbe.' Here was Merton Villa, where Edward Wright, the comedian of the Adelphi Theatre, lived from 1848 to 1854, and afterwards J. B. Philip, R.A., the sculptor of part of the podium of the Albert Memorial. Cecil Lawson, who married the latter's daughter, Miss Beatrice Philip, made an elaborate pen drawing of the garden, exhibited at the Grosvenor Gallery in 1883. The site of Merton Villa and its garden is now occupied by the Chelsea Public Library, a building of admirable design by Mr. J. M. Brydon. Here are preserved the plaster models of two of Mr. Philip's works—a statue of Sir Joshua Reynolds, given by Mrs. Philip, the sculptor's widow, and an altarpiece, given by Mr. H. Young, of Nelson House, Trafalgar Square. Mr. Young is well known as an art-founder, especially in connection with Steven's Wellington Memorial in St. Paul's Cathedral. In the Library also are plasters by Mr. Fontana, presented by the sculptor; a most valuable collection of Keats' relics, deposited by Sir Charles Dilke; and a large and rapidly-growing Chelsea topographical collection.

Merton Villa Studio is now occupied by Mr. Stirling Lee, the sculptor.

Manresa Road has been famous in the art world for some years as a colony of the ' advanced' school of artists. Holman Hunt had a studio here in 1878, and in it he painted his famous picture, ' The Triumphs of the Innocents'; and among others Messrs. H. H. Lathangue, F. M. Skipworth, Tuke, Llewellyn, Jacomb-Hood, etc.

Carlyle Square, renamed in honour of ' the Sage of Chelsea,' was first called Oakley Square. In the eighteenth century this was a market-garden in the occupation of a Mr. Hutchings. His house was the scene of a murder and robbery in 1771, for which four Jews were sent to the gallows. For years afterwards the Jews in England were jeered with the words 'Chelsea' and ' Hutchings.' There are some very curious illustrations of this crime in the *European Magazine.* Mrs. Kelly, the novelist, lived in a house on the west side of the square, where she kept a school.

The tavern at the corner of Upper Church Street, now called the Cadogan Arms, was originally the Rose and Crown. An old water-colour drawing, preserved in the modern house, represents it as a place of considerable age. It is mentioned in the petitions already referred to.

THE ROSE AND CROWN, KING'S ROAD (ABOUT 1830).

Opposite Paulton's Square is the Vale, a quiet retired nook, now disfigured by the stained paper factory built along its western side. Mrs. Mellon, a favourite actress of the Adelphi Theatre, widow of Alfred Mellon the musician, lived here for many years. Mr. Whistler lived in the Vale for some time, and a curious little sketch of it has been painted by his pupil, Mr. Sickert. North of the Vale was Tebbutt's Nursery, which was closed and the stock sold off in October, 1884.

Near together are the Man in the Moon, the Globe, and the World's End. These three quaintly-named taverns all belong to the old time. The latter appears to have been in existence in the days of Charles II., and it may be that it is this tavern which is mentioned in Congreve's ' Love for Love,' but there was another World's End at Knightsbridge, where Pepys came to disport himself. Faulkner's view of the World's End at Chelsea shows us a wooden structure of considerable age.

The district between Milman Street and World's End Passage was formerly the property of the Norris family, and was sold in lots for building purposes in

THE WORLD'S END, KING'S ROAD, 1790.

1824. The following occurs in the Note-book of Mr. George Skipp, of the Upper Hall, Ledbury, Herts :

'June 17th, 1669.—I married Elizabeth, the daughter of Hugh and Susanna Norris, then living with her sister Prettyman, of Battersey. I had with her in portion betwixt 3,000*l.* or 4,000*l.* ; we were married by Dr. Dixon, in S. Clement's Church in the Strand. We went to Battersey, and continued there about a fortnight, and soe went to live in Chelsey, where we continued one year and a quarter, and thence removed to London for our quarters, and soe to my father's at the Upper Hall.'

William Norris, M.P., wrote to Thomas Norris, High Sheriff of Lancashire, on October 6, 1696 :

'I removed from Chelsea last week, after which came my mother and sister.'

Foundry Place marks the site of Janeway's Foundry, where the bells of the old church were recast, and heavy siege guns were made. Riley Street was built about 1794. The three houses east of Riley Street were formerly called

York Buildings. Mazzini lived here for a short time. World's End Passage, formerly 'The way between the pales,' afterwards 'World's End Lane,' is a short row of old cottages. Here died, in 1831, at the age of 111 years, Patrick Gibson, purser in the Navy, who was present at the taking of Quebec, in 1759. There is a portrait of Gibson, painted in 1831, by Macartan, in Greenwich Hospital.

We now arrive at the modern representatives of the Old Chelsea nurseries. Facing one another are Wimsett's (considerably enlarged after the closing of Cremorne) and Bull's (established in 1845). Veitch's 'Royal Exotic Nursery,' established in 1856, occupies the site of Knight's nursery, which dates from 1808. Mr. Joseph Knight was previously gardener to Mr. George Hibbert, of Clapham Common, who made a speciality of the collection of Cape plants.

Near Bull's nursery formerly stood an old inn called the Duke of Marlborough, occupied when Faulkner wrote, by the gate-keeper of the neighbouring turnpike.

Just before we reach Stanley Bridge is a timber-yard, formerly occupied by Ormson's Horticultural Works. The house near these premises was formerly called Dudmaston House. It was the residence of Mr. Poole, who built a chapel there, in which many famous preachers ministered. Dr. Raffles preached there his first sermon.

LITTLE CHELSEA AND FULHAM ROAD.

Crossing Stanley Bridge we pass the boundary line which separates Chelsea from Fulham, but in the days when all was open land between this spot and the village of Fulham, more than a mile off, an old house, Sandford Manor House, facing the creek, and still standing, was generally spoken of as in Chelsea. Tradition has long associated this house with Nell Gwynne. Mr. Peter Cunningham in his researches could find nothing to support this tradition, and has expressed his doubts as to its truth, but some probability has been given to it by the discovery in the garden, a few years back, of a plaster medallion of 'honest Nell.'

Here, too, it is believed, lived Joseph Addison. Addison had a country house, 'near Chelsea,' as early as 1710, for Swift in the Journal to Stella, records dining with him there on several occasions :

'Sept. 15th, 1710. We dined at a country house near Chelsea, where Mr. Addison often retires.'

'On the 18th I dined with Mr. Stratford at Mr. Addison's retirement near Chelsea.'

'On the 29th, I dined with Mr. Addison and Jervas the painter, at Mr. Addison's country place.'

Macaulay tells us that Addison enjoyed nothing so much as the quiet and seclusion of his villa at Chelsea. From this 'retirement' it was a pleasant stroll across fields to Holland House, then occupied by his friend the Countess of Warwick. Probably he gave up Sandford Manor House on his marriage with that lady in 1716.

The scene at this spot is now very different to what it was in Addison's time. The creek is now a dirty ditch, lined with ugly wharves and sheds. The once pleasant fields are now covered with huge gasometers, shrieking railway engines dash past constantly, and a wilderness of more or less dingy streets covers the farm-lands and gardens that lay between Chelsea and Holland House.

Passing Chelsea railway station we arrive at Stamford (formerly Standford) Bridge in the Fulham Road. Eastwards, beyond the grounds of St. Mark's

STAMFORD BRIDGE, FULHAM ROAD.

College, is Little Chelsea, the north side of which is now included in South Kensington.

'Hamilton's Survey,' corrected to 1717, does not mark any buildings in this district; this is an unaccountable omission, as it is beyond question that there were several important houses at Little Chelsea in the seventeenth century. Thus in 1636, Sir Francis Kynaston, unable to obtain possession of Chelsea College, moved his academy, the 'Museum Minervæ,' to Little Chelsey. In 1635 the Right Hon. Sir James Smith (probably the Junior Sheriff of London in 1672), built a house here; he died in 1681, and was buried in the old church. His widow continued to reside in the house until 1695, and four years later the estate was purchased from her heirs, the Bovey family, and the house was rebuilt or extensively altered by Anthony Ashley Cooper, third Earl of Shaftesbury, who had just succeeded to the title on the death of his father. (The Boveys had been resident in Chelsea for at least half a century. In the Papers of the Committee for the Advance of Money, we find Ursula Bovey, of Chelsea, assessed at £400 on August 24, 1643; ordered to be brought up in custody to pay her assessment, February 9, 1644; her son, Ralph Bovey, of Gray's Inn, to pay her assessment, or have it levied on his estate, April 2, 1645; and on January 13, 1646, a note that the amount had been paid.) Shaftesbury is first named in the parish rate-book in 1700. He had been educated by the celebrated John Locke, who was perhaps an occasional guest at Little Chelsea, but the generally received statement that

SHAFTESBURY HOUSE, LITTLE CHELSEA, FULHAM ROAD.

he wrote the greater part of his 'Essay on the Human Understanding' there is clearly wrong, as this notable book first appeared in 1690. Lord Shaftesbury was the intimate friend of Addison, another frequent guest, who is believed to have written several of his 'Spectators' in this house. Lord Shaftesbury himself is famous as the author of 'The Characteristics of Men, Manners, Opinions, and Times.' He suffered continually from asthma, and in 1706 the 'great smoak' drove him from Chelsea to Hampstead. He retained his house, at Chelsea, however, until 1710, and in the following year retired to Italy, and died at Naples in 1719. Some of his letters dated from Little Chelsea, 1708, are still extant.

Shaftesbury House was bought by Narcissus Luttrell, a famous collector of books, and horticulturist. Upon the former trait, Dr. Dibdin says :

'Nothing would seem to have escaped his lynx-like vigilance. Let the object be what it may (especially if it related to poetry), let the volume be great or small, or contain good, bad, or indifferent warblings of the muse, his invariable craving had stomach for all.'

Sir Walter Scott, too, in his edition of Dryden's works, says:

'The editor has been greatly assisted by free access to a valuable collection of the fugitive pieces of the reigns of Charles 2, James 2, William 3, and Queen Anne. This curious collection was made by Narcissus Luttrell, Esq., under whose name the editor usually quotes it. The industrious collector seems to have bought every political tract, of whatever merit, which was hawked through the streets in his time, marking carefully the price and the date of his purchase. This collection contains the earliest editions of many of our most excellent poems, bound up, according to the order of time, with the lowest trash of Grub Street.'

From September, 1678, to April, 1714, he kept a minute diary of the events of the time. The MS., in seventeen volumes, 8vo., was bequeathed to All Souls' College, Oxford, by his descendant, the Rev. Luttrell Wynne, and there it remained, practically unknown, until Macaulay informed the world that it had been of considerable use to him in the preparation of his history. From the terms in which he spoke of it, it was hoped that its publication would be of service to other historians, throwing those side-lights on contemporary events which make the diaries of Pepys, Evelyn, and others so valuable. Accordingly it was issued in six volumes in 185⁻, but it proved to be little more than a bare catalogue of such occurrences as found their way into general gossip.

Some years since a descendant contributed to the Royal Horticultural Society a paper on twenty-five varieties of pears cultivated by Narcissus Luttrell, at Chelsea, between the years 1712 and 1717.

From the register of burials at Chelsea, we obtain three notices relating to him and his family :

'1727. Narcissus, son of Narcissus Luttrell, Esq.'
'1732. Narcissus Lutttell, Esq. July 6.'
'1740. Francis Luttrell. Sept. 3.'

Hearne, in his 'Diary,' mentions the death of Narcissus Luttrell :

'August 13th, 1732.—About the beginning of July last the prints tell us that, after a tedious indisposition, died Narcissus Luttrell, Esq., of Little Chelsey, a gentleman possessed of a plentiful estate, and descended from the ancient family of the Luttrells of Dunstan Castle in Somersetshire.'

'August 14th.—The aforesaid Mr. Luttrell was well-known for his curious library, especially for the number and scarcity of English History and Antiquities, which he collected in a lucky hour at very reasonable rates ; books of that nature though they have always bore good prices being much cheaper then, than they have been of late years. But though he was so curious and diligent in collecting and amassing together, yet he affected to live so private as hardly to be known in private, and yet for all that he must be attended to his grave by Judges, and the first of his profession in the Law, to whom (such was the sordidness of his temper), he would not have given a meal of meat in his life. As a recommendation of his collection of books we are told it was present in that place where Mr. Lock and Lord Shaftesbury studied, whose principles, it may be, he imbibed. No doubt but it is a very extraordinary collection. In it are many MSS., which, however, he had not the spirit to communicate to the world, and 'twas mortification to him to see the world gratified with him without his assistance. An instance hereof is Leland, of whose works he had I am told a transcript of considerable age, and when I was publishing him, he was pressed more than once to communicate it (as I have lately heard) to no purpose. He hath left a son, who is likewise a bookish man.'

From the ¦Luttrells, Shaftesbury House passed to Mr. Serjeant Wynne, who died there in 1765. His son, Edward Wynne, also a barrister, and author of '¸Eunomus,' and other works, also died there in 1784. The house then became the property of his brother, the Rev. Luttrell Wynne, D.D., who alienated it to William Virtue. This last sold it to the parish of St. George's, Hanover Square, and by them it was converted into a workhouse. By an Act of Parliament it was declared to be in that parish so long as it was applied to that use.

Shaftesbury House remained almost in its original condition until it was entirely pulled down in 1856. Croker says :

> ' Until recently it was astonishing to find amid the rage for alterations and improvements, the formal old-fashioned shape of a trim garden of Queen Anne's time carefully preserved ; its antique summer houses respected, and the little infant leaden Hercules, which spouted water to cool the air from a serpent's throat still assuming its aquatic supremacy under the shade of a fine old medlar tree ; and all this, too, in the garden of a London Parish Workhouse ! Not less surprising was the interior. The grotesque workshop of the pauper artisans, said to have been Lord Shaftesbury's doing, and over which was his famous library, was then an apartment appropriated to a girls' school. On the basement story of the original house the embellished mouldings of a doorway carried the mind back to the days of Charles I. . . . Nor should the apartment then occupied by the intelligent master of the workhouse be overlooked. The panelling of the room, its chimney-piece, and the painting and frame work above it placed as completely in a chamber of the time of William III., and we only required a slight alteration in the furniture, and Lord Shaftesbury to enter to feel that we were in the presence of the author of the Characteristics. The stairway, too, with its spiral balusters, as seen through the doorway, retained its ancient air.'

A stone in the pavement before one of the summer-houses, engraved ' ANNO. DM. . 1635,' probably recorded the date of the original building. Shaftesbury House is minutely described in Croker's ' Walk from London to Fulham.'

Another famous house in Little Chelsea was that in which ' that pious admirable Christian and excellent Philosopher,' Robert Boyle lived. He was resident there as early as 1661, when Evelyn records that he ' went with that excellent person and philosopher, Sir Robert Murray, to visit Mr. Boyle at Chelsey, and saw divers effects of the Eliopile for weighing air.' A French scientist, M. de Monconys, also records a visit to him ' à un village nommé le petit Chelsey.' He gives a short account of his study :

'He has a very fine laboratory, where he makes all his extracts, and other operations, one of which he showed me with salt, which being put quite dry with gold leaves sixteen times thicker than that used by gilders into a crucible on a slow fire, even over a lighted candle, the salt calcined the gold so perfectly that water afterwards dissolved them both, and became impregnated with them in the same manner as with common salt. He possesses a very fine telescope, and two excellent microscopes which are larger than mine.'

Evelyn has a very crisp and vivid note :

'Glasses, potts, chymical and mathematical instruments, books and bundles of papers did so fill and crowd his bed-chamber, that there was but just room for a few chairs.'

Boyle's sister was Lady Ranelagh (mother of the future Paymaster of the Forces), for whom he had the greatest affection. Evelyn writing to William Wotton, some five years after his death, in January, 1691-2, says :

'Boyle lasted accordingly though not to a great yet to a competent age ; three score years, I think ; and to many more he might, I am persuaded, have arrived, had not his beloved sister, the Lady Viscountess Ranelagh, with whom he lived, a person of extraordinary talent and suitable to his religious and philosophical temper, died before him. But it was then that he began evidently to droop apace ; nor did he, I think, survive her above a fortnight. But of this last scene I can say little being unfortunately absent, and not knowing of the danger till it was past recovery.

'His funeral (at which I was present) was decent, and though without the least pomp, yet accompanied with a great appearance of persons of the best and noblest quality, beside his own relations.

'He lies interred (near his sister) in the chancel of St. Martin's Church ; the Lord Bishop of Salisbury preaching the funeral sermon with that eloquence natural to him on such and all other occasions.'

This bishop was the celebrated Burnet. There is a curious reference to his death in a letter of Sir Charles Lyttleton to Christopher, the first Viscount Hatton, January 9, 1692 :

'Mr. Robt Boyl was buried at St. Martin's, on Thursday, in ye same grave wth his sister Ranelagh. He was not sick above 3 houres, but s^d his heart was broke when she died. The B^p of Salisbury preached his funerall sermon, at wch there was a mighty crowd.

'There is an odd report goes that, when Lady Ranelagh lay dying, there was a flame broke out of one of ye chimneys, wch being observed by ye neighbours gave notice of it, and the chimney being looked into, there was no cause found for it in ye inside, yet appeared to flame for some time to those wthout ; and ye same thing happened when Mr. Boyl died ; but ye B^p, by ye way, mentioned nothing of it in his sermon, but abundance of ye flames of his charity.'

The same story was told of the death of Dr. Busby.

Boyle was brother to the Earl of Orrery, and at Dr. Whitaker's house at Little Chelsea, Boyle's nephew, the fourth earl, was born in 1676. This earl grew up to be a man of mark, and was called by Dr. Aldrich, 'the great ornament of Christ Church.' He wrote a comedy, 'As You Find It,' as well as some poetical efforts. An edition of the 'Epistles of Philaris' involved him in that famous controversy with Bentley, which Swift satirized in 'The Battle of the Books.' The Orrery was named after him by the inventor, and the earl himself is said to have improved it. He died in 1737.

Dr. Baldwin Hamey, an eminent physician, and friend of Dr. Harvey, came to Little Chelsea in 1661. But for his singular modesty he might have been a knight, Court physician to Charles II., and president of the College of Physicians. By his removal to Little Chelsea, his valuable library (bequeathed to the College of Physicians) escaped destruction in the great fire of 1662. Throughout the troubles of the Great Rebellion, although practising much among the Republican leaders, Hamey had been a staunch Royalist, and had sent several sums of money to the exiled Charles II. 'I have,' says Palmer, 'a receipt by me under King Charles II.'s own hand, all written by himself at Breda, in which for a blind he makes the money received of B.P.H., *i.e*, B.H.P.—Baldwin Hamey, Physician.' In Chelsea he is remembered for his benefactions to the old church, among which was the gift of the great bell which bore his name. In gratitude, Dr. Littleton, the rector, addressed some Latin verses to him, printed at the end of the first edition of his Latin Dictionary. His death is recorded in the register:

'1676. Dr. Baldwin Hamey. May 18.'

His portrait at the age of thirty-eight, painted by Vandyck, was presented to his college at Oxford by his great nephew, Ralph Palmer, who succeeded him in the house at Little Chelsea.

Ralph Palmer was married to Alice White, of the family of Dr. Francis White, Bishop of Ely. Their eldest daughter, Elizabeth, married John, second, but eldest surviving son of Sir Ralph Verney, first baronet, of Middle Claydon, Bucks. John Verney succeeded as second baronet, and in 1703 was created Baron Verney of Belturbet, and Viscount Fermanagh, in Ireland. The correspondence between the various members of these families is preserved among the Verney and Ingilby MSS., and contains many references, some of which have already been quoted, to Chelsea life in the first quarter of the eighteenth century. In 1706, we find Palmer writing to Sir Ralph Verney:

'We heartily wished you amongst us the other night at my chamber, where your sister Cave, Sir Thom., Mr. Cave and Mrs. Adams, and my she friends, etc., to the number of a score, assembled to hear some of the opera of Arsinœ and Camilla songs performed, where likewise Mr. Hadley, his son, lady and daughter, and Serjeant Cheshire were too.'

In 1720 we find him sending a silver candlestick, accompanied with a Latin letter, to Dr. King, rector of Chelsea, on the occasion of his birthday, for which Dr. King thanked him in another Latin letter. Among his correspondents we find Jonathan Richardson, the painter and connoisseur; Dr. Charlett, of Oxford University, etc.

Ralph Palmer died in January, 1716, and was buried on February 1. A tablet to his memory hangs in the old church.

Bowack (1709) tells us that ' at Little Chelsey stands a singular, handsome house, with a noble courtyard and good gardens, built by Mr. Mart, now inhabited by Sir John Cope, Bart., a gentleman of an ancient and honourable family, who formerly was eminent in the service of his country abroad, and for many years of late in parliament, till he voluntarily retired here, to end his days in peace.'

Mr. Mart is mentioned in the list of proprietors in the common pasture, 1713, as the owner of what was Evans' farm in 1647.

Sir John Cope is mentioned in a letter from John Verney to Sir Richard Verney, July 1, 1680 :

> ' Yesterday Shaftesbury (that is, the first earl) and the rest, to whom were added Sir John Cope and Sir Rowland Win and others to the number of 26 or 27, went again to Westminster with their information, but the grand jury were dismissed ere they came, by an hour, which makes some people think there is a false brother among them. 'Tis said Shaftesbury told the judges they did not according to the law to dismiss the grand jury as they did, and that Raymond stood up and answered, he thought he understood law as well as his lordship.'

A previous letter on June 30 explains the object of this deputation :

> ' On Saturday ten lords (Huntingdon, Gray, North, etc.), and ten commoners (Thos. Wherton, Thos. Thinn, Sir Scrope How, Lord Candish, Lord Russell, etc.), met at the Court of Requests, and designed at the King's Bench Bar to give an information to the grand jury of Middlesex, that the Duke of York was a Papist (and some say that they designed to accuse him as a traitor, for being reconciled to the Church of Rome, under an old statute, and they went to Jones about this, or some other point, who told them 'twas not law). But the judge having some private notice of their design called the grand jury and dismissed them for this term. They told the judges that many weighty matters lay before them; but the judges would not believe them, but dismissed them.'

Another letter from the same source says :

> ' There is no indictment brought against Lord Shaftesbury, and the town talks confidently that he must go out without bail. Sir John Cope is foreman of the grand jury, and Tom of 10,000 is his companion *cum multis aliis.*'

On June 19, 1690, ' Gallen, son of Sir John Cope, Bart.,' was baptized at the Old Church, and on February 8, 1720, ' John, son of Captain Gallen Cope.' Galen Cope was the fourth of seven sons, and was living at Chelsea at the time of his father's death in 1721. His brother Anthony has already been mentioned as the correspondent of Moses Goodyear, of Chelsea. It was another son of Sir John Cope who was beaten by the Young Pretender at Preston Pans in 1745.

Admiral Wishart, placed on the retired list in consequence of his Jacobite leanings, succeeded the Copes. He died in 1723, and on July 15, 1723, the following advertisement appeared in the *Daily Courant :*

> ' To be sold by auction, the household goods, plate, china ware, linen, &c., of Sir James Wishart, deceased, on Thursday, the 18th instant, at his late dwelling house at Little Chelsea. . . . N.B. A Coach and Chariot to be sold, and the house to let.'

The house was taken, apparently in the same year, by Admiral Sir John Balchen, who was lost in his ship, the *Victory*, in the Bay of Biscay, 1744.

The house was afterwards used as a private lunatic asylum, kept by a Mr. Duffield. Hither came Montagu Bacon in 1749, and was treated by Dr. Martyn, father of the Rev. Thomas Martyn, professor of Botany at Cambridge. Its site is now occupied by Odell's place.

In the curious pamphlet by Alexander Cruden (author of the Concordance), called ' The Adventures of Alexander the Corrector,' etc. (1753-4), we read :

> 'Mr. Duffield, Master of the Academy in Gloucester Street, and of the two great Chelsea Academies . . . at first consented to receive him, . . . but understanding that Alexander was to be the patient, he would by no means receive him . . . but recommended his nephew, Peter Inskip, one of his keepers or tutors at Chelsea, who had a private house there' (p. 3).
>
> 'The Corrector arrived at Inskip's house, two doors beyond the Three Jolly Butchers, in Little Chelsea, ten minutes after six by his clock, and lodged in his first floor—a neat, well-furnished apartment, that might have served a prince ; but it was made to serve as a prison for the Corrector, and he has been barbarously used in it by Inskip' (p. 9).
>
> Inskip's two brothers, 'one of whom is also a tutor in the Chelsea Academy, and the other keeps the King's Arms, an alehouse in Little Chelsea' (p. 10).

Edward Hyde, third Earl of Clarendon, died at his house at Little Chelsea April 1, 1723. He was the son of Henry, second Earl, a frequent visitor to Chelsea, whose diary has been quoted several times.

The name of Lochée is inseparably connected with Little Chelsea. About 1770, Louis Lochée, author of several works on fortification, opened a military academy there, laid out as a fortification. It would be interesting if we could find out who planned the ' fortifications ' of this academy. An obscure Chelsea architect, a Mr. Trought, exhibited ' A design calculated for a military gentleman with regular bastions in the angles of a square, in the Royal Academy, 1773.' The institution acquired a high reputation, and a large number of military men received their education in it. One of the first attempts at military ballooning was made there on October 16, 1784. This was the celebrated voyage by Blanchard, which Walpole tells us he called out to see. There is a coarse contemporary print of the event, with the following inscription :

> 'Grand ærostatic balloon, in which Mr. Blanchard, on Saturday, 16 October, 1784, ascended from the military academy at Little Chelsea, a fourth time into the atmosphere, accompanied by the ingenious Mr. Sheldon. At ten minutes after twelve the gallant adventurers, preceded by two small balloons as signals, after taking leave of their generous host, and a numerous circle of nobility and friends, arose with the most majestic grandeur, and, wafted by the prayers and plaudits of upwards of 400,000 spectators, in eight minutes were lost in æther. After a number of astonishing manœuvres and evolutions, the travellers made stop at Sunbury, where for the expediting machine, the gallant Sheldon (unwillingly) descended, and left his friend to pursue alone his journey through the trackless void, who, after passing over Guildford, Farnham, etc., about 3 o'clock in the afternoon, finding the day too far spent to cross the Channel to Brest, after hovering a

considerable time over Portsmouth, Isle of Wight, etc., alighted at Rumsey, near Southampton, and amidst universal acclamation finished, perhaps, the most extraordinary journey ever performed by a sublunary balloon. London, published by R. Wilkinson, No. 58, Cornhill, 16 October, 1784.'

The elder Lochée died in 1787, and was succeeded by his son, another Louis. He took part in the Flemish revolution in 1790, was taken prisoner by the Austrians, and eventually executed. His death is recorded in the *Gentleman's Magazine,* June, 1791:

'At Lisle, in Flanders, Lewis Lochée, Esq., late Lieutenant Colonel of the Belgic Lion, and formerly keeper of the Royal Military Academy at Chelsea.'

THE GOAT IN BOOTS, FULHAM.

The house, now called Hollywood House, is inhabited by Captain Nesbit, who some years ago found the entire skeleton of a horse in his garden, doubtless a relic of the Academy.

At the corner of Walnut-Tree Walk (now Redclyffe Gardens) stood Burleigh House, the residence of William Boscawen, translator of 'Horace,' and author of several works. He died there May 6, 1811. It afterwards became a ladies' school.

Going eastwards we come to Park Walk, named after Chelsea Park, of which it was the western boundary. This was once a pleasant avenue called Lover's Walk, and is so marked on Hamilton's Survey, but it lost its romance in the ridiculous name of 'Twopenny Walk.' In 1763, Francis Aliamet, a good engraver, son of the celebrated Jacques Aliamet, gives his address as 'near the Chapel, Chelsea' (Park Chapel?) in the catalogue of the Free Society of Artists. At the north end of Park Walk stands the Goat and Boots, a tavern built during the time of the Commonwealth. It was one of the houses which enjoyed the right of common 'for two cows and one heifer.' In 1663 it was known as the Goat simply, and it was still so called in the Verdict of the Court Leet, 1683. The sign has given rise to considerable discussion. Croker has ingeniously suggested that it is a corruption of a latter part of a Dutch legend: 'Mercurius is der Goden Boode' ('Mercury is the Messenger of the Gods'), commonly attached, says Croker, to post-houses in the early part of the seventeenth century. There is no ground, however, for supposing that the house was ever known as 'The Mercury.' It has also been suggested that the goat on the sign was booted in honour of that veteran goat that twice sailed round the Globe, once with Captain Wallis, and at last found an asylum in Greenwich Hospital. A third suggestion is that the sign was originally a satire on Welshmen. A writer in the *Craftsman*, June 17, 1738, mentions the Hog in Armour, and the Goat in Jackboots, as occurring on the signboards of Hampshire and Wales. Captain Grose, in his 'Essay on Caricature,' mentions the goat, leek, and hayboots as a standard joke against Welshmen. The original painting of the sign is attributed to Christopher Le Blon, who attempted to set up a tapestry factory in Chelsea Park, and George Morland, who is reputed to have repainted it in settlement of a tavern bill, is supposed to have given the goat its present attributes. The sign still hangs outside the house (recently rebuilt), but after the many repaintings it has undergone no trace of Morland's work now remains, except, perhaps, in the outline.

Passing Chelsea Park, the history of which has already been given, we arrive at the tavern called the Queen's Elm. The story of the great Lord Burghley sheltering with Queen Elizabeth during a shower of rain under a tree which stood here, and saying, 'Let this tree be henceforth known as the Queen's Elm,' is well known. The story may not be true, but the 'Queen's Tree' was recorded in the Parish Books as early as 1586, when one Bostocke planted an arbour round it at the expense of the parish. This 'arbour' appears to have been a ring of nine elms. Steele calls the spot 'The Nine Elms' in 1711, and we find 'The Nine Elms, Chelsea,' given as an address as late as 1805. The 'Queen's Elm' is mentioned in 1687, when the surveyors of the highway were amerced for not mending the road properly 'from the Queen's Elm to the Bridge, and from the Elm to Church Lane.' The Elm was also called 'The Cross Tree' (Hamilton's Survey), and the High Elm (Vestry Minutes, and Sir Hans Sloane, 1727).

Opposite is a Jewish burial-ground, laid out in 1816 (A.M., 5576), and near it a milestone, with the information that it is one and a half miles to London. It marks the site of the turnpike pulled down in 1848. Next to the burial-ground is the Chelsea Hospital for Women, founded 1871, a handsome red brick building erected in 1883. Hence to Charles Street was formerly a terrace known as York Place. Here lived and died Francis Hargreave, the editor of a ' Collection of State Trials,' in eleven folio volumes, published in 1781. Several of these houses were used for some years as an extension of the Consumption Hospital, and were pulled down for a fine new building erected in 1881, ' In Memoriam, Cordeliæ Reid.'

Passing Charles Street (now included in Arthur Street), where lived Sydenham Teast Edwards, F.L.S., a clever botanical draughtsman, who died in Barossa Place, Trafalgar Square, February 8, 1819, we come to Sydney Street, leading into the King's Road.

The new St. Luke's Church is situated in Sydney Street. The idea of building a new church for Chelsea was first mooted in 1751, when it was resolved at a vestry to appoint a committee to consider the present state of the church, and of the necessity of enlarging it, or building a new one. They resolved to repair the old one ' in the best and most frugal manner,' and as the estimate only amounted to £59 16s., it is evident that frugality was by no means lost sight of. Fifty years afterwards it was in such a state of decay that an expenditure of £1,862 was necessary for its thorough repair, and this outlay was met by the rate of one penny in the pound.

In 1806 it was resolved at a Vestry, that, ' considering the bad state of the present church, it not being large enough for the accommodation of this populous parish, and above all its distance from the most populous parts, that it be recommended, instead of repairing it, that measures be resorted to for erecting a new one in a more central spot.' This recommendation was rejected, and in the following year ' It was moved by A. Stephens, Esq., that the question of a new church be adjourned until the time of peace ; and upon this motion being seconded, the same was carried by a show of hands, upon which Mr. Stephens and the principal part of the majority who supported his motion, withdrew from the church, with acclamations of joy.' Possibly some of the joy arose from respect for the old building, and the desire to retain it as the parish church, but it is to be feared that most of it arose from the temporary escape from an addition to the rates. This respite lasted for some years. In 1815, the Archdeacon surveyed the church and desired its immediate reparation, concluding his order with ' a special recommendation to the parish of Chelsea to find some means of providing a more adequate accommodation for the inhabitants of this very large and populous parish.' Three years later it was decided to erect a new church without delay, a sum not exceeding £30,000, being required for the purpose. It was resolved that the

43

new burial-ground, for which an act had been obtained in 1810, was the most suitable spot for its erection.

The Act for building the new church was obtained in 1819 (59 George III., c. xxxv.), and the first stone was laid on October 12 of the year following, by the Hon. and Rev. Dr. Wellesley, rector, acting as proxy for his brother, the Duke of Wellington, who had received 'the King's commands to attend him

ST. LUKE'S CHURCH.

on public business that day at his palace in Pall Mall.' The building was finished in 1824, and consecrated on October 18 in that year.

The architect was Mr. James Savage (died March 7, 1851), and this church, undoubtedly his best work, is one of the most remarkable efforts of the band of architects who brought about the revival of the Gothic or Christian architecture at the beginning of the present century. In this respect the building will always retain a high architectural interest. It is built of Bath-stone, in the Perpendicular style, and consists of a nave and aisles with flying buttresses, a chancel and vestry at the east end, and a dignified and well-proportioned tower 142 feet high, rising from a species of narthex at the west end. On the whole, the exterior, though not without those shortcomings that generally accompany the ambitious efforts of second rate men, is imposing and well-proportioned. The interior calls for little remark, but the vaulted roof, groined throughout in stone, excited much interest at the date of its construction.

Among the other architects who sent designs to the committee were G. Julian, junr.; J. Cooper, and W. Tite, whose designs were exhibited at the Royal Academy in 1820.

The altar-piece, 'The Entombment of Christ,' is, perhaps, the best work that James Northcote, R.A., produced. It was presented by the British Institution. A copy of G. F. Watts' noble conception, 'Time, Death and Judgment,' was given to the church in 1888.

A bas-relief by Chantrey, to the memory of Colonel the Hon. Henry Cadogan, placed at first in the old church was transferred to the present building on its completion. Several members of the Cadogan family, including Charles Henry, Earl of Cadogan, who died in 1832; Honoria Louisa Countess Cadogan, died 1845, and Admiral the Right Hon. George, Earl Cadogan, died 1864. There are not many memorials in the church, but among them are tablets to the memory of General Wilford, died 1822; Luke Thomas Flood, died 1860; and the Rev. Charles Kingsley, M.A., rector of Chelsea, and father of the novelist, died 1860.

Among those buried in the cemetery were: Carlo Rovedino, an Italian bass singer, died 1822; Dr. John M'Leod, the explorer and companion of Sir Murray Maxwell, died 1820; Thomas Davey, the celebrated florist at King's Road, died 1833; William Blanchard, comedian, who lived in Camera Square, Chelsea, died 1835; 'Kingly' Egerton, another actor, died 1847.

Among the residents in Sydney Street we may notice: Dr. Biber, editor of 'John Bull,' and author of a life of Pestalozzi; Thomas Wright, the antiquary; and Henry Warren, the President of the Society of Painters in Water-Colour.

Chelsea Common or Heath, extended from Sydney Street on the west to Blacklands Lane (now Marlborough Road) on the east; Fulham Road was the northern boundary, and College Place the southern. The whole extent was about thirty acres. At the north-west corner were some gravel-pits and a large pond, the site of which is now occupied by the Onslow dwellings. Thus we have Pond Place, where Curtis the botanist died on July 7, 1799.

Certain old houses and farms had a right of pasture on this common, and there was a portion reserved for the poor. On Hamilton's Survey, 'the poor houses' were marked at the south-west corner. The following lists of the proprietors of common pasture are taken from Faulkner, and an undated MS. in the British Museum (Add. 15609, f. 28) :

Parsonage Ho., 6 cows 3 heifers.
    1647 Dr. Wilkinson.
    1663 Dr. Littleton.
    1674 Dr. Littleton.
    1713 Dr. King.
Shrewsbury House, 2 cows 1 heifer.
    1647 Earl of Devon.
    1663 J. Alston.
    1674 J. Alston.
    1713 Mr. Butler.
    ? But before 1723, Mr. Robert Butler.
Evans Farm, 6 cows 3 heifers.
    1647
    1663 J. Sanders.
    1674 John Bennet.
    1713 Mr. Mart.
    (Before 1723), Mr. Hull for Mr. Mart or Mr. Henry Newdike.
Two Cottages in Church Lane, 4 cows 2 heifers.
    1647 John Chaire.
    1663 Six Cottages in Church Lane, formerly two cottages, Albion Chaire.
    1674 A. Chaire.
    1713 J. Nicholas.
Two houses, one called 'The Dog,' the other Sir John Danvers, 2 cows 1 heifer.
    1647 Mr. Shugbury.
    1663 House lately called the sign of the Dog, Lombard Street, now called the Sun.
    1674 Ed. Harris.
    1713 Mr. Peacock.
    (Before 1723), Brian Wade for Mr. Hawes now R^d Peacock.

Four houses next the Dog, 6 cows 3 heifers.
    1647 Mr. Crouch.
    1663 Three Cottages near Watermn's Ct., C. Cretche.
    1674 G. Plucknett.
    1713 Valentine Arnold.
    (Before 1723), Mr. G. Bell for Mr. Arnold.
One Cottage, 2 cows 1 heifer.
    1647 Duke of Bucks.
    1663 Lindsey House, Earl of Lindsey.
    1674 Robt. Earl of Lindsey.
    1713 C. Bertie.
Sir A. Gorges, several tenements that have Common ; all generally disclosed for 3 acres of Lammas Land, over against Battersea Church, 6 cows 3 heifers.
    1647 Reynolds Farm.
    1663
    1674 C. Cheyne, Esq.
    1713 Sir H. Sloane.
Sir Edward Powell, one Cottage, 2 cows 1 heifer.
    1647 The Magpie Cheyne Walk.
    1663
    1674 J. Leverett.
    1713 John Herne.
    (Before 1723), Mr. H. Clarkson.
3 farms, one pulled down, in the Marquise's Yard, 2 cows 1 heifer.
    1647 Prince's Arms, Cheyne Row.
    1663
    1674 Elizabeth Preston.
    1713 E. Preston.
    (Before 1723), Benj. Stalwood, now Wm. Sloane.

James Luke's House. Church Lane, 2 cows 1 heifer.
    1647 The Goat, Little Chesea.
    1663
    1674 Jas., Lord Norris.
    1713 Thos. Wharton, Esq.
    (Before 1723), Mr. Sloane.

Among the Additional MSS. of the British Museum (15609, f. 28) there is a plan of the common marked out in various allotments. Its date is evidently between 1712 and 1732. Blackland's Lane is there called 'the Road from Mr. Whitfield's to the Pound.' This pound stood near the inn called the Cow and Calves, and is indicated in the plan. The common was under the care of a cow-keeper, whose business it was to mark the forty cows and twenty heifers, and drive them home at night. This survival of an ancient system undoubtedly dates back to the Saxon times; very similar customs still prevail in many German villages. The rules for the regulation of the common were given by Faulkner as follows:

		£	s.	d.
1.	All cattle to be marked with two letters, by a tar mark, under a penalty of	o	2	6
2.	The Bailiff refusing to mark shall forfeit	o	5	o
3.	To pay for marking yearly, per cow	o	o	4
4.	The Owners of Common may let their common to inhabitants in the parish of Chelsea, and no other.			

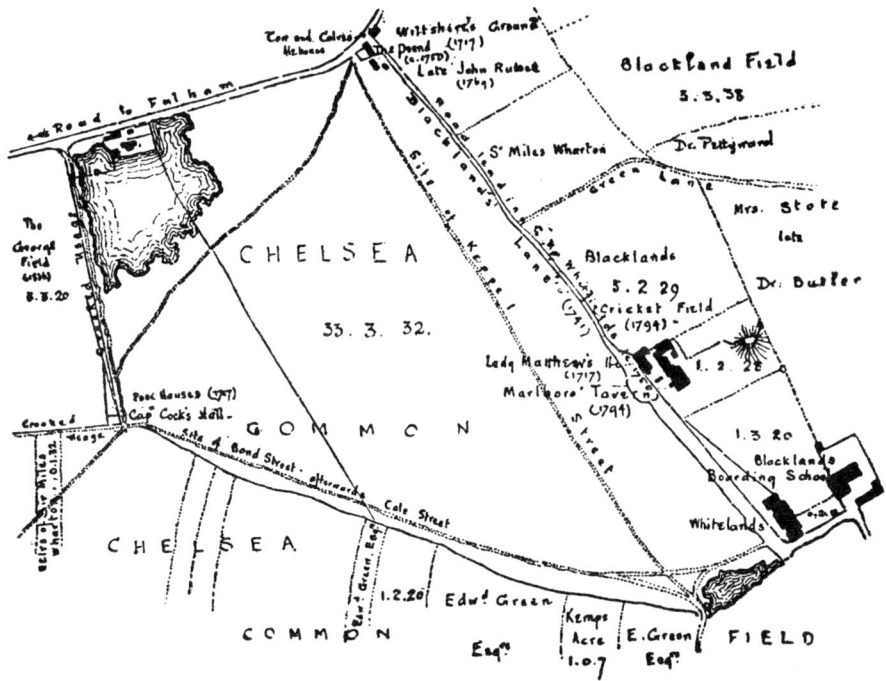

CHELSEA COMMON, FROM A PLAN OF THE MANOR OF CHELSEA, 1769.

In 1674, when the old church was repaired, the various persons who shared in the right of common, agreed that it should be enclosed and let for twenty-one years for the benefit of the church. This was done, and a lease of the common taken by George Hill and Francis Guildford. In 1695, it was again opened and applied to its original use until the beginning of the present century, when the proprietors agreed to let it on building leases, and an Act of Parliament was obtained to confirm their action.

Several reviews of troops were held on Chelsea Common between 1642 and 1649, the period of the Civil War, and here, too, in after years, the City Train Bands used to exercise.

Upon the site of this common we now find a network of streets, mostly narrow and squalid. Cale Street takes its name from Judith Cale, a benefactor to the parish, who left £6 18s. annually, to be given to six poor widows in money every Christmas Day, at the discretion of the minister and the church-wardens. In College Street is a church founded by the Irvingites. This was built about 1835, by the Rev. John Henry Owen, who had previously officiated at Park Chapel (1822 to 1834), and was therefore generally known as Owen's Chapel. Carlyle mentions a visit of Edward Irving to Cheyne Walk in October, 1834: 'A short, affectionate visit, the first and last.' Carlyle 'watched him till at the corner of Cook's Grounds he vanished, and they never saw him more.' Irving died at Glasgow in December of the same year. There was connected with this church, another Thomas Carlyle, whom Mrs. Carlyle, in one of her letters, calls 'that other angel.'

Whitehead's Grove, a good thoroughfare, named after an enterprising builder, who built most of these streets, leads at its western end into an irregular space still called Chelsea Common.

From College Street to Keppel Street was formerly a row of nine small houses looking upon green fields and nurseries, now occupied by Pelham Crescent, etc. This row was called Amelia Place, and at No. 7 John Philpot Curran, the Irish patriot, brilliant wit, and learned lawyer, serenely breathed his last on October 14, 1817. When John Banim, the Irish novelist came to England in 1822, he took lodgings in the same house 'to dream of his country,' as he said, 'with the halo of Curran's memory around him.'

The Admiral Keppel tavern was built in 1790, and had large tea-gardens in the rear. Croker has preserved the following rude distich, which was painted under the sign:

> 'Stop, brave boys, and quench your thirst;
> If you won't drink, your horses murst!'

The tavern stands on the boundary line which separates Chelsea from Kensington, and is rated in both parishes. In former times the boys beating the bounds on Ascension Day had to pass through the front door and clamber through a window at the back, an odd sight which many of the older inhabitants yet remember. The old house was rebuilt in 1856.

Marlborough Road and Marlborough Square of course take their name from the hero of Blenheim who is believed to have been a resident of Chelsea for some time. At the south end of Marlborough Road was an old house with plastered front, which bore the date 1705. This was, apparently, the house called 'Mr. Whitfield's' on a plan of Chelsea Common in the British Museum (15609, f. 28). It is supposed to have been occupied at one time by the great Duke of Marlborough; but, I have found no proof of such occupation. For many years it was in the occupation of Messrs. Scott, Cuthbertson and Co., and was partly used by them for their paper-staining works, and partly let out in tenements. It stood upon the Blacklands Estate, presented by the Earl Cadogan to the trustees of the Guinness Fund, and was demolished in 1890.

The boundary of Chelsea passes north of Walton Street, formerly June Street). This portion of the parish began to be laid out during the latter half of last century, and was called Hans Town in honour of Sir Hans Sloane, but is now more generally known as Upper Chelsea.

Lennox Gardens and Cadogan Square stand upon that portion of the estate which was until recently Prince's Cricket Ground, the scene of numerous famous, and withal, very fashionable matches. The whole of this district was known as 'Blakelands,' at least as early as 1544, when it already formed part of the manor, and was in the occupation of Sir William Paulet, Lord of St. John, afterwards Marquis of Winchester. Mr. J. R. S. Clifford has suggested, with much probability, that it took its name from the dark heath which, we may easily believe, covered the once open uncultivated lands. The nature of the soil, and the fact that the adjacent common was once called Chelsea Heath, favour the acceptance of this suggestion. On Hamilton's Survey only two houses are marked on this district—Blackland's House and Lady Matthews' House.

The close of land adjacent to Blackland's House is named on the map, 'Lord Cheyne's Lands,' and this special application of his name may, perhaps, be taken to indicate that it was in Blackland's House that the first Viscount Newhaven lived before he purchased the manor of Chelsea. Little is known of the history of the house. In his will (1698) Cheyne bequeathed this house to his son, the second Viscount Newhaven. In 1705 it was a French boarding-school, and in 1763, a Mrs. Mary Britain was buried from Blackland's School. The house was leased from the lord of the manor by Sir Francis Shuckburgh in 1820. This tenancy accounts for the name of the Shuckburgh Arms, at the north-west corner of what was formerly called Butterfly Alley. Sir Francis' lease terminated in 1884, but years before that date the lease had been transferred to Dr. Anderson, who converted the house into a private lunatic asylum. His lease was renewed by the Earl Cadogan in 1884. In 1890, when the earl generously gave the site, about one acre in extent, and valued at £40,000, to the Guinness Fund Trustees, he bought up the remainder of the lease of twelve years; Dr. Anderson then removed his asylum to Newlands House, Tooting Common.

The other house was inhabited by Lady Matthews in the reign of William III. Little or nothing is known about her. It is probably her daughter that is alluded to in one of Ralph Palmer's letters, June 15, 1708:

> 'Mr. Talbot (Bishop of Oxford's son) is stolen by the Lady Matthews' daughter, she being under 16, and worth 9 or 10,000*l.*'

We next hear of the house as ' The Marlborough Tavern,' with tea-gardens and a cricket-field, and it is so marked on Horwood's Map, 1794. This tavern disappeared when Cadogan Street was laid out; its western end cuts across

THE PAVILION, SOUTH FRONT.

the site of the tavern. Part of the site of the garden still remains at the rear of the Catholic church of St. Mary in this street.

In 1777 Mr. Holland took a lease of one hundred acres from Lord Cadogan, and laid out portions of the land for building purposes. He reserved twenty-one acres of the land for his own residence. The house he built (in 1780) is said to have been designed as a model for the Brighton Pavilion; it was a formal structure, of a tame, spiritless design in the classic taste, and the pavilion was built from another and more fanciful design. Mr. Holland's house, however, though sometimes called Holland House, was more generally and at length finally known as the Pavilion. Thus we have Pavilion Road in the near neighbourhood. The whole of the architect's designs for this building are in the British Museum (see 'Map Catalogue'). On them occurs the following notes:

> 'The house is built of Timber, cover'd with Large Welch Slates, with Dripping Eves. The outside is faced with weather Tyles, made in The New Forest, the price delivered in London £4 p^r Thousand, a Thousand will go as far as Twelve Hundred of Bricks, and there is no Doubt the Tyles will resist the Weather a longer time than Bricks, it was that circumstance which gave rise to the use of them some years ago at a Building on the Sea Shore in the New Forest constructed for Mr. Robert Drummond by Mr Holland.
>
> 'The Colonnade wood sanded to imitate Stone.'

The interior was handsomely furnished, and among the artistic treasures were busts of Pitt and Fox by Chantrey; a cast of Porson's head, taken after death, with some of the hair adhering to the plaster; a curious and valuable clock, contrived by Thwaites, which indicated the time on dials in various parts of the house; and two pictures by Fuseli—'The Vision of Lady Jane Grey before her Execution,' and 'A Scene from Lear.'

The gardens were planned by 'Capability' Brown, the famous gardener of the eighteenth century, who, disdaining all conventional rules, and relying entirely on Nature's plan, raised the art of gardening to a level it had never before reached. He is said to have answered a companion who was praising the beauty of a scene: 'Yes, only God Almighty and myself can produce such a scene as that.' This remark recalls the stupendous vanity of Sir Godfrey Kneller. At Chelsea he laid out an avenue of limes leading to the house, shrubberies, a lake and a small deer park. Taste was then favourable to the introduction of artificial ruins, a relic of which we may see at Virginia Water, and in the Pavilion Garden an ice-house was built of the stonework from the recently demolished palace of Cardinal Wolsey at Esher; the brickwork, too, was brought from some old houses pulled down at Westminster. It was designed to represent an ancient priory, and 'the appearance of age and decay,' we are told, was 'strikingly faithful.'

After Mr. Holland's death, the Pavilion was purchased by Mr. Peter Denys, and after his death, his widow, the Hon. Lady Charlotte Denys, continued to inhabit it. Their son George William, who became a baronet in 1813, was equerry to the Duke of Sussex.

The Pavilion was pulled down in 1879; the grounds were cleared, and laid out with squares and terraces of handsome houses, inhabited by people whose names are well-known in society. Among them we find, in Lennox Gardens,— Mr. E. Sherrard Kennedy, the artist (Walton House), whose home is a museum of objects of beauty, including many fine pieces of old tapestry, and an unrivalled collection of Grès-de-Flandres; Mr. Frank Lockwood, Q.C., M.P. (No. 26); the Marquis of Northampton (44); and his son the Earl Compton,

44

M.P. (51). In Cadogan Square,—Viscount Coke (13) ; Mr. C. Austen Leigh (35) ; Lord Balfour of Burleigh (47) ; Mr. Hans Sloane Stanley (49) ; Mr. F. W. Lawson, the artist who has already been mentioned (61) ; Lieut.-Col. W. H. Walrond, M.P. (65) ; Admiral Sir George Willes (73) ; and Lord Elcho, M.P. (62). In Pont Street,—Lord Lawrence (66) ; and Sir Charles Du Cane, K.C.M.G. (42).

'Snug Hans Place,' which is within the Chelsea boundary, has always been a 'quiet and respectable locality,' though its quiet has been greatly intruded

L. E. L.'S RESIDENCE IN HANS PLACE.

upon by the great increase of houses in this part. Letitia Elizabeth Landon was born at No. 25, and spent the greater part of her life here. She was educated in a well-known school kept at No. 22 by Miss Rowden, authoress of several works, who eventually became the Countess of St. Quentin. Among her many pupils whose names have found their way into the pages of history may be mentioned Miss Roberts, who wrote on India ; Lady Caroline Lamb, who stabbed herself with a pair of scissors for Lord Byron's sake ; Mrs. S. C.

Hall; Lady Bulwer; and Miss M. R. Mitford. Both these houses are now rebuilt. Miss Landon did most of her literary work in the seclusion of this square: 'The Improvisatrice,' 'The Troubadour,' 'The Golden Bracelet,' as well as her novels and many small poems were written in a little room—always littered over with scraps of paper—most simply furnished, a small dressing-table serving for writing-table.

She worked very hard indeed; so hard that she wrote to one of her friends, 'There is one conclusion at which I have arrived, that a horse in a mill has an easier life than an author. I am fairly fagged out of my life.' The quiet of her situation would therefore be the more agreeable to her, and she playfully exaggerates it to a correspondent who had written of the 'fascinations of Hans Place':

> 'Vivid must be the imagination that could discover them.
> Never hermit in his cell
> Where repose and silence dwell,
> Human shape and human word
> Never seen and never heard,
> had a life of duller calm than the indwellers of our square.'

Shelley passed a few of his feverish days in this retreat, and in recent times Sir Herbert Stewart (to whose memory a small granite fountain with bronze portrait in bas-relief has been erected), and Lady Lindsay of Balcarres have dwelt here.

One of the earliest residents of Hans Place was Francis Frederick Eckhardt, inventor and manufacturer, in Chelsea, of damask papers, hangings, etc. He gives Hans Place as his address in 1798. Charles Grant, Viscount de Vaux, another inventor, lived in 'Elizabeth Street, Hans Square,' in 1808.

To the east of the Pavilion were Catleugh's market gardens and nurseries. It was part of this ground that was taken to form Prince's Cricket Ground, but a small portion remained until 1877. The gardens were famous for their choice pines.

From Walton Street the boundary line runs along behind the north side of the houses in North Street, and across Sloane Street to the north of Lowndes Square, curving round slightly to the east of William Mews, whence it follows the old course of the Westbourne. Chelsea thus includes a portion of aristocratic Belgravia—Lowndes Square, Cadogan Place, and Pont Street.

The district which includes Sloane Street, Cadogan Place, Hans Place, and the neighbouring streets, was laid out by Mr. Holland of the Pavilion shortly after 1777, and called Hans Town. The American War is said to have interrupted the progress of the building during some years. In 1787 an Act of Parliament was obtained, appointing commissioners for the paving, lighting, etc., of the streets. This arrangement worked well for the district, which from the first assumed an aristocratic character.

A nursery ground, conducted by Messrs. Salisbury and Curtis, formerly occupied the site of Cadogan Place Gardens. These gardens, planned by Mr. Salisbury in 1807, were laid out and labelled on the Linnæan system in seventeen divisions, occupied about six acres, and formed, as we can imagine, a very agreeable promenade. Mr. Tate came into possession in 1820, entirely altered the original arrangement, and formed the garden into a public promenade. Lastly, Mr. Tuck occupied a portion of these gardens. Cadogan Place has still its connection with horticulture, as Messrs. Waterers' famous rhododendron show is held there annually. A cottage in these gardens was occupied for some years, until its demolition in 1890, by Mr. Felix Moscheles, the artist, and was the scene of many interesting literary and artistic re-unions.

Mrs. Jordan, the famous actress, of whom Romney painted several beautiful portraits, had her last London residence in Cadogan Place. Wilberforce, the abolitionist, died at No. 44, the residence of Mrs. Lucy Smith, in 1832. Chelsea House, the town residence of the Cadogan family, has already been mentioned, and among other present residents are the Marchioness of Queensberry, Major-General Freemantle, and the Hon. Evelyn Ashley.

Lowndes Square, another fashionable quarter, is just within the elbow of the boundary. On Hamilton's Survey (continued to 1717) this site is occupied by a 'Spring Garden,' a place of entertainment, well spoken of by Dr. King. On Rocque's Map, 1741-5, the district is marked 'Lowndes, Esq.' On Horwood's Map, 1792, we have 'The Rural Castle'; while in Thompson's, 1836, we have 'Lowndes Square' laid out, but unbuilt. Viscount Sherbrooke, better known perhaps as Sir Robert Lowe, and the Right Hon. Earl of Kimberly here have their town houses.

At No. 76, Sloane Street, lives the Right Hon. Sir Charles Dilke, Bart., descended from several old Puritan families—the Wentworths, Wiggestones, Vanes, Bradshaws, Stricklands, and Cawleys, famous in Elizabethan and Stuart times. Sir Charles was born in this house, and was the son of Sir Charles Wentworth Dilke, Bart., who had so much to do with the arrangements and conduct of the Great Exhibition of 1851.

Chelsea (including Kensington, Fulham, and Hammersmith) first became a Parliamentary borough in 1868, and on November 18 of that year, Sir Charles Dilke and Sir Henry Hoare were chosen its first representatives, both in the Liberal interest. During this period Sir Charles published his famous work, 'Greater Britain,' which has passed through so many editions, and has recently been rewritten under the title of 'Problems of Greater Britain.' He retained the representation of Chelsea until the election of 1886, when he was defeated by Mr. C. A. Whitmore, Conservative. During his parliamentary career, Sir Charles Dilke was one of the most valued members of his party, and generally looked upon as the future premier. In 1880 he became Under-Secretary for Foreign Affairs, and in 1883, President of the Local Government Board, with a seat in the Cabinet. He carried several Acts of Parliament—the Parliamentary and Municipal Registration Act, 1878, another in the same year extending the hours of polling, and the Diseases Prevention (Metropolis) Act, 1882. The Redistribution Bill of 1884-5 is generally understood to be entirely his work.

Sir Charles married, firstly, Katherine, daughter of Captain Arthur Gore Shiel, and, secondly, Emilia, widow of the Rev. Mark Pattison, Rector of Lincoln College, Oxford. The present Lady Dilke has taken a high position in contemporary literature, was for some years art critic of the Academy, and has now found a useful sphere in the organization of female labour, and the formation of women's trades unions.

Among present and past residents in Sloane Street are Robert Bisset, LL.D. (died 1805), who kept an academy there; Charles Bentley, water-colour artist; the Right Hon. Charles Pelham Villiers, M.P.; Lord Alwyne Compton; Mr. G. G. Adams, sculptor; and Miss M. Brooks; Mr. A. Ossani, Mr. O. S. Schoelderer, and J. B. Burgess, A.R.A., artists.

Near Sloane Square stands Holy Trinity Church, the parish church of Upper Chelsea, built 1889-90, from the designs of the late J. D. Sedding, F.R.I.B.A. It occupies the site of another church, built 1828-30, from the design of Mr. Savage, architect, of St. Luke's, Chelsea. As a piece of architecture the older building was a mélange of Gothic items of various periods, and was very adversely criticised at the time of its erection. The Rev. H. Blunt, M.A., curate of St. Luke's, was the first rector.

Almost the whole of Lower Sloane Street and George Street, with Chelsea Market, has been removed, and their sites are now occupied by Sloane Gardens, handsome red brick houses built in the prevailing style.

THE OLD BUN-HOUSE.

Grosvenor Row was once known over a wide area for its famous bun-house. It was really in Pimlico, just beyond the Chelsea boundary; but as Pimlico was hardly in existence in the days of 'Chelsea' buns, and as the bun-house is closely associated with Old Chelsea, some notice of it cannot be omitted.

Dean Swift is, perhaps, the earliest writer who mentions the buns. In his Journal to Stella, 1712, he writes :

'Pray are not they fine buns sold here in our town ? Was it not r-r-r-r-r-rare Chelsea buns ? I bought one in my walk.' Evidently they were already famous, and attracted crowds to Chelsea fields at holiday times, for elsewhere in the Journal he tells how he was stopped by a crowd of 'boys and wenches, buzzing about the cake-shops like fairs. There had the fools let out their shops two yards forward into the streets, all spread with great cakes frothed with sugar, and stuck with streamers of tinsel.'

The buns were famous for their 'delicate flavour, lightness, and richness,' or as a local rhymer put it :

'O flour of the ovens ! a zephyr in paste !
Fragrant as honey, and sweeter in taste !
*   *   *   *   *   *
As flaky and white, as if baked by the light,
As the flesh of an infant, soft, doughy, and slight.'

Such a triumph of the baker's art certainly deserved the patronage of the highest, and so the poet goes on :

'Prelates and princes, and lieges, and kings,
Hail for the bellman, who tinkles and sings,
Bouche of the highest and lowliest ones,
·*   *   *   *   *   *
There's a charm in the sound which nobody shuns,
Of "smoking hot, piping hot, Chelsea buns !"'

Sir Richard Philips (1820), who tells us that for ten years he never passed the bun-house without filling his pockets, goes on to say :

'The present proprietor told me, with exultation, that George II. had often been a customer of the shop ; that the present King, when Prince George, and often during his reign, had stopped and purchased his buns ; and that the Queen, and all the Princes and Princesses, had been among his occasional customers.'

His Majesty George III. must have delighted in them very particularly, as he presented the proprietor with a half gallon mug in silver with five guineas in it. This mug was, doubtless, a prominent object in the museum of curiosities which existed there in a sort of rivalry to that at Don Saltero's. The objects were chiefly historical, and included two leaden figures four feet high of the British Grenadiers, presenting arms, in the costume of 1745 ; a bottle conjurer contemporary with its invention ; a plaster figure of 'Butcher' William, Duke of Cumberland ; portraits of George III. and his Queen ; a model of the bun-house ; and on the grounds which extended to where Graham Street, West, now stands were some grotto works. Grottoes were the fashionable rage of the first half of the eighteenth century. The most

THE OLD BUN-HOUSE.

famous, of course, was Pope's at Twickenham, but there was another almost as well known at Walpole House, Chelsea, Even now in the gardens of some old Chelsea taverns, strange, uncouth-looking dens are to be seen—which, by courtesy, may be called grottoes—the relics of a bygone craze.

Royal favour, probably, had a good deal to do with the reputation of the Chelsea buns. The swarms of people who flocked to the Five Fields at

Richard Hand

the Oldest Original Chelsey Bunn Baker

at the *Kings Arms*, at Chelsey

Remov'd from y Old Original Chelsey Bunnhouse

N.B. Who has the Honour to Serve the

Royal Family

REDUCED FACSIMILE OF AN OLD ADVERTISEMENT.

holiday times, particularly Good Fridays, from four in the morning onwards is nowadays almost incredible. Bryan says :

> 'From my own personal observation I should say, provided the weather was favourable, there were generally on Good Fridays nearly 200,000 people collected in the immediate neighbourhood. It was a fair to all intents and purposes, In the "Five Fields" there were drinking booths, swings, gingerbread stalls, nine-pins being played, gaming, and all the other vicious "entertainments," which disgraced the metropolis in former times.'

As late as 1829, he tells us, at least 240,000 buns were sold on Good Friday. Thus we can quite understand that this famous bun-house had afforded an ample competency to four generations of the same family—the Hands. One of these had held a commission in the Staffordshire Militia, and was jocularly known as Captain Bun. He was an eccentric character, wore a long dressing-gown and Turkish fez, and was well known throughout the district. After his death the property is said to have reverted to the crown.

The building materials and the museum were sold by auction on April 18, 1839. The grenadiers sold for £4 10s.; the figure of the Duke of Cumberland, 2 guineas; a portrait of 'Aurungzabe, Emperor of Persia,' 4 guineas; a painting of the interior of the bun-house, with the king and queen seated, in a dirty, tattered condition, £2 10s.; a model of the bun-house, with moving figures, 19s.; a paper model of St. Mary's Radclyffe, 2 guineas. The leaden figures of the grenadiers were afterwards in the possession of Mr. Hayes, of Eaton Place.

Separated from 'The old original Chelsea Bunhouse' by one house (a boys' school) was a more modern rival, which displayed its title on a board: 'This is the old Oakley Bunhouse.' No. 60, Pimlico Road, occupies the site of the former; No. 52, of the latter.

'The Old Original,' with its colonnade over the footway 52 feet long, was a picturesque building similar to the Pantiles at Tunbridge Wells. It disappeared in 1839, and although another bun-house took its place, the fashion had died out, and it has now no representative. All the open fields were being rapidly built upon, and the annual merry-makings became an impossibility. A writer in the *Penny Magazine* (1844) says :

> 'The Chelsea meadows are now covered with bricks, either making or drying, or built up into houses. The favourite Willow Walk, which led towards Chelsea from the Millbank, near the Penitentiary, has only one solitary dying willow left. The far-famed Chelsea bun-houses have stepped back from the road where they formerly stood ; they appear now as confectioners' shops in the line of houses forming the street, and the crowds who used to throng to them on Good Friday before the sun himself was up, are no longer to be seen there.'

Opposite the Bun-houses was Stromboli House and gardens, which appears in the old maps as 'Strumbelo,' 'Strumbels,' etc. It was a popular place of entertainment about 1788, a humble imitation of Ranelagh Gardens. The old house, with an inscription on stone, still exists, and is converted into shops.

THE CHELSEA WATER-WORKS.

Like the 'Chelsea Bun-House,' these works were outside the boundary, and in the parish of St. George, Hanover Square. As the western suburbs grew the old water supply was found insufficient, and in 1723, the Chelsea Water-works Company was incorporated by Act of Parliament (8 George I., c. 26) to meet the demand. An engine-house was built with the materials of

NEW FIRE ENGINE, CHELSEA WATER-WORKS, 1780.

JENNY WHIM'S BRIDGE, CHELSEA WATER-WORKS, 1752.

the old church of St. Martin's-in-the-Fields (pulled down in 1721) alongside a canal, now called the Belgrave Basin; and two reservoirs were formed, one in Hyde Park (removed 1828), where the sunken flower-garden now is, and the other in St. James's Park.

The undertaking was for a long time unprofitable; no dividend was declared for forty years. Nevertheless this company has a distinguished record in the efforts to improve the water supply of London. In 1746 the first iron main pipes were laid between the engine-house and Hyde Park; its two atmospheric engines, erected by Wyse, and the engine constructed by Boulton and Watt, were objects of interest and curiosity; their engineer, Mr. Simpson, has the credit of leading the way in the process of filtration on a large scale. In 1825, 1826, and 1827, he made many experiments, which resulted in the formation of a filter one acre in extent in 1829. This was successful in its operation, and indeed little improvement has since been found possible in the system. In 1810 the company moved a little westward, to a piece of land about seven acres in extent, bounded by the Westbourne rivulet.

During the years 1811-1817 the company carried on a ruinous competition with the Grand Junction and West Middlesex Water-works Company, which was at length settled by a division of districts, the Chelsea Company retaining the right of supply only to those parishes surrounding its works.

The Chelsea Water-works are now at Kingston and West Moulsey, where they are able to obtain a purer supply. Those at Chelsea were not wanting in picturesque qualities, and there are several sketches and prints of the view from the bridge near the engine-house. Boydell's engraving (1789) is one of the most interesting.

KENSAL TOWN.

Besides Chelsea Proper there is a parcel of land, nearly 140 acres in extent, lying to the north of Kensington, which belongs to this parish. How it first became connected with Chelsea cannot be made out, but I am very strongly inclined to agree with the Rev. W. J. Loftie, who, in his recent History of Kensington asserts that it is the land mentioned in Edward the Confessor's Charter, in these words:

> 'Besides, together with this manor (as a free gift), every third tree and every third horse-load of fruits grown in the neighbouring wood of Kyngesbyrig, which, as in ancient times, was confirmed by law.'

Faulkner, Davis, and others have assumed that ' Knightsbridge ' is merely a corruption of ' Kyngesbyrig,' and that the wood in question was therefore adjacent to Chelsea. The assumption was plausible, and fitted in very conveniently with local circumstances, but there are weighty reasons for dissenting from it. In the first place Knightsbridge itself is a Saxon name, and not a corrupt form. We find mention of a ' Cnihtabryge ' near Radnor in

SITE OF KENSAL TOWN IN 1836.

the year 774, and of a ' Cnihta bryc ' near Patney, in Wiltshire, in the year 963. Faulkner himself quotes an early charter (but does not give the date) of Herebert, Abbot of Westminster, in which Knightsbridge, ' in loco qui dicitur Gara,' is called ' Cnightebriga ' ('History of Kensington,' 1820, page 444). Secondly, there is a place called Kingsbury to this day, about four miles from

Kensal Town. This ' Cyngesbyrig' is mentioned in two Anglo-Saxon charters, and its wood probably extended for miles around. Traces of its extent are to be found in the names Kingsholt and Wormholt.

In the Domesday Book we read :

> ' In the Hundred.of Gare., William the Chamberlain holds two hides and a half, under the Abbot of St. Peter's in Chingesberie. . . .   This land belonged to Aluuin' horne theyn of the King Edward.'

' Aluuin horne ' was probably the Wluuene already mentioned.

In the possessions of Robert de Woodhouse in the eighteenth year of Edward III., ' Kyngesholt ' (which up to the present has been identified with the supposed wood at Knightsbridge) is bracketed with Willesdon, implying that these were neighbouring places, so that it seems fairly clear that Kensal Town is the modern representative of those possessions held by the Abbey of Westminster as of the Manor of Chelsea.

The greater portion of Kensal Town is included in the manor of Malurees, or Malorees, belonging to All Souls College, Oxford. The history of this manor was briefly worked out by Lysons (Environs, III., 617, 618). From the title-deeds belonging to the Hon. T. F. Wenman, LL.D., he found that William Northwall released this manor to Bartholomew, Lord Burghershe in 1354. In the same year Lord Burghershe granted it to John Peeche, citizen and clothier, who died 1379, when he bequeathed it to his son Sir William Pecche (Escheats 3 R. II., n. 54). In 1412 a John Pecche granted the reversion of it to Elias Davy—it had been previously granted to William Constantyn and his wife. At length the manor was conveyed by William Crowmere and others to Thomas Chichele and others, who surrendered it to Henry VI., by whom it was granted to All Souls (Title-deeds belonging to the College).

In 1543, when the Ecclesiastical Survey was made, the college received a yearly rent of £13 6s. 8d. from William Cade for the manor of Malleries, and two messuages in Harleston and Willesdon.

The portion of the district belonging to the manor of Chelsea is described in the ' Perticuler booke of the Chelsey Manor,' 1544 :

> ' De Henrico White ar° p firm cujusdm pastur in padington sepalit° existen infra iiij°ʳ clauss unde vn claus voc *Darkingby Johes*, al voc *Homefield*, ter voc *balserfield*, et quart voc *bandilandes*, que quidem pastur ac ptn Wellmˢ Person nup tenint ad firma sic dimiss pd henr. white, p indeñ. Wi. Sande milᶜ· Dni. Sandes et Dne Margarie uxor eius dat xxxiij° die febr a° xvij° H. viij° Heñd a festo Anunc 9ᵈ erit in H° dno 1527 p termino xxjᵘˢ annorr ex tunc pn sequen et plena complerd iiijˡⁱ.'

The term ' bandilandes ' also occurs as a field-name in Fulham.

None of these field-names have been preserved. In 1694 Dr. King gives their names as follows :

1. A ground lying on the west side of the Common, called by the name   *Acres.*
of the Mead, supposed to be demised to Mr. Fowks of Gray's Inn   32
2. The *Wood* ground called by the name of Bushfield, held by Dr.
Rogers 16
3. The Barn Field, held by the same Dr. Rogers 22
4. The Four Hills, part whereof is demised by All Souls College to the
said Dr. Rogers, and other part thereof to Madam Nelthorp ... 64

        134

Dr. King adds the note :

    " This account falls short of my late Lord Cheyne's given in to me,   *Acres.*
    which made out the grounds... 156

    The Rev. Mr. Heber, rector of the parish, caused the lands to be surveyed, and an accurate map to be taken in 1767. At this date the land was divided into nine portions, the total rather more than the estimate of Dr. King :

					Acres.	*Roods.*	*Perches.*
1. Mr. Godfrey ...	...	Plow Field	...	...	23	1	21
2. ,, ,, ...	...	Cutler's Field	...	...	21	1	10
3. ., ,, ...	...	Barn Field	...	...	23	3	32
4. ,, ,, ...	...	Twelve Acres	...	...	12	3	39
5. ,, ,, ...	...	Another Ditto	...	...	15	2	15
6. Mr. Liffe ...	...	The Slip	...	...	2	2	31
7. Ladies of the Manor	...	Another Ditto	...	...	4	2	6
8. Mrs. Partridge ⎰		Thirty Acres	...	...	⎰ 7	0	12
9. ,, ,, ⎱					⎱ 26	2	2
					137	3	8

Richardson's Survey, 1769, also gives these divisions and owners, and names the district Chelsea Reach.

In 1795 an Act of Parliament was obtained for the construction of the Paddington Canal, and it passes through this portion of Chelsea parish between the Harrow and Kensal Roads. The Canal was opened with an aquatic procession on July 10, 1801. Thompson's Map, 1836, on which also this district is called Chelsea Reach, shows it as still consisting of the nine fields above given. At the west end of the Harrow Road were Agnes Cottage, a Tea Garden, and two or three small houses called Sander's Place. No other building is marked.

The whole of this district is now closely built over and occupied by a dense population, mainly of the working class. All to the north of the canal belongs to the British Land Association, and is known as the Queen's Park Estate.

SUPPLEMENT.

————••————

CORRECTIONS AND ADDITIONS.

Page 32. Delete the words 'by some . . . made out.' (See p. 87.)

Page 37. 'Coxe's Close,' on the map, should be placed north of the roadway.

Page 40. For 'M. de Puysieulx' read 'M. de la Boderie.'

Page 51. For 'Sunbury' read 'West Moulsey.'

Page 71. For 'Lord Edmund and Lord John Bray' read 'Edmund, Lord Bray, and John, Lord Bray.' The name is also written 'Braye' and 'Braie.'

ACCOUNT OF THE FUNERAL OF JOHN, LORD BRAY, FROM THE ORIGINAL IN THE HERALDS' COLLEGE.

'The 'ntyrement and buryall of the Right honable John Lord Braye, who depted this liefe within the late Blackfreyers in London, on Thurs-daye the 18. of Novembre at 3 of the clocke in the aftrenone, 1557, An. 4 & 5 Phi. & Mar. and was buried at Chelseye in the myddest of the hyghe chauncell there, with his father and grandfather undre one highe tombe there

'Itm, he lefte behind hym his wiefe Anne, daughtre to Frauncys Erl of Shrewisburye, then lyvinge, by whom he had childe, and so died without issue, and made no will, but comytted thordre of all things to his mother, Dame Jane Braye, late wife to Edmond Lorde Braye.

'Itm, after the bodye was colde hyt was bowellid, cered, and coffend, and browght into the greate chambre, where it was leyd undre a table covered with a large pawle of blacke unwatered chamblett, with a whyte crosse of the lyke, with 6 schocheons of his arms and his wiefe, wrought on Buckeram ; set thereon a crosse, 2 tapres and 4 other, al the which still burned duringe his abode there, with contynewall watche, which was till 'Tuesdaye the 23 of Novembre, about 8 of the clocke in the mornynge, that al was in a readyness, at which time he was conveyed to Chelseye as followeth.—Fyrst, the crosse, and on eyther side the 2 whyte branches borne by 2 Clerks—then 24 Clerks and 8 prysts ; —then Edward Merlyon, his hood on his head, bearing the Standerde ;—after hym Sʳ Richard Wheytley and Sʳ Richard Harrys, chapleyns, in theyre gownes and typpets ;— then Thomas Udall with the bannʳ of Armes ;—after hym Rudge Dragon, with the helme and creste ;—then Rychemonde, with the cote of armes ;—and after hym Garter ;—then the corpse as afore borne by 6 of his men, viz, Christopher Banks, George Vaux, George Stadley, Alexander Morley, Davye Morgan, and John Lackye ; and on thone syde went Francis Sawnders with the bannʳ of the trynyteye, and on thother syde Tryamor Smyth, with St. George, bothe of them havinge ther hoodes on theyre heads—and along on both sydes were 18 staffe torchys, carried by 18 poore men in black gownes. Then next aftre the corpse as chiefe morner, went Sʳ George Broke, Knight of the Garter, Lorde Cobham; —after hym his son Mʳ Thomas Broke, and Mʳ Edmond Verney, then Mʳ John Broke, and Mʳ Thomas Lyefylde, and last Mʳ Edmonde Bray and Mʳ Halshe, and aftre them all other comers, in which ordre they proceaded to the Bridge at the Blackfreers, where was 2 greate barges coverd with black, garnyshed with scoocheons, thone for the morners and gentlemen, thother for the body, quere, hatchments, and other. Where all things placed they rowyd uppe tyll they cam to Chelseye (alwaies that with the bodye afore thother) where they landed, and proceaded as afore tyll they cam to the Churche, where at the dore the bodye was recefyd, and then conveied into the quere, where in the myddest it was sett upon Tressles, with dowble and barriers, stoles and Quyssheons for the morners covered with blacke, garnyshed with scoctscheons and in lyke manner was the chauncel and quere hangyd and garnishyd, and at every corner of the inner barryers stode a highe standing candle stycke gylte, with a great mayne tapre thereon, and on eche two Scoocheons of his armes. Then the bodye placed with the hatchements sett thereon, and all other things in ordre, Richemonde herald bade the prayer as followeth : " For the Soule of the Right honable Sʳ John Braye, Knight, late Lord Braye, of your charytie say a pr. nr." which he bade at other tymes accostomyed, and then dyridge began, which ended, masse of requiem began durynge which tyme at the syde awltre were dyverse Masses seid, and at magnificat ; benedictus ; aftre the Gospell, and at libera me the person censyd the corps.

'Then at the offerynge, Mʳ Garter; Rychemonde, and Rudge Dragon proceaded uppe before the chiefe morner, thother 6 morners following him, where all onely he, offeryd the massepennye, a peece of golde and returnyd to his place. Then Mʳ Garter at thend of these, delyvered the cote of armes to Mʳ Thomas Cobham and Mʳ Verney, who, with Rychemonde before them, offeryd the same, which Rudge Dragon at the prysts hands received, and placed on the awltre, and so they returnyd, goinge uppe the north ile, and returninge down the south ile. Then Mʳ Garter d d the target to Mʳ John Cobham and Mʳ Lyefylde who with Roudge Dragon before them in lyke ordre, offeryd the same, which Rychemonde placed on the awltre, and returnyd ; Then Mʳ Garter d d the swerde to Mʳ Braye and Mʳ Halshe, who with Rychemonde before them likewise offeryd the same, the hylte forwarde, which Roudge-Dragon placed on the awltre, and thelme and creste, which Rychemond placed on the awltre and so they returnyd to theyre places—and then the Lord Chiefe morner alone, with Rychemond afore him, proceaded uppe and offeryd for himselfe, and after returnyd, and took hys place. Then Mʳ Thomas Cobham, and Mʳ Verney offered for themselfs and returnyd to theyre places. And aftre them thother 4 morners offeryd likewise for themselfs, 2 after 2,—and then all gentlemen and other that wolde : which offering fynished, the sermon began by Father Peryn, a black freer ; whose anthem was " Scio quia resurget in resurrectione in novissimo die" whereupfon he declaryd how Chryste raised Lazarus from deathe, seying howe he was a gentleman given to chyvalrie for the welthe of hys country, and so he seid that noble man which there laye deade was, in whose commendacion amonge many other thyngs, he fynished his sermonde, which don, mass proceaded till St. John's Gospell, that the bannʳ and standarde were offeryd, and aftre the body buryed, in which meane tyme et libera me, the morners departed to theyre botts, and so to London to hys seid howse to dynnr, where they and other dyned, which ended, every man depted at theyre pleasure. And the morrowe the hatchments and banners were sett upp in the chauncell at Chelsey accordinglie.'

'*The Paynter's Chardge at the seid Buryall of the Lord Braye.*

						s. a.
'Itm for hys standarde whys his crest of the Lyon between two wyngs, powdered with the dunne croppe earyd connye and the brake, and his woorde "Sera comme a Dieu plaira"'			...	...	Pryce	33 4
A banner and armes, pryce ...	...	...	...	...	...	26 8
Two banners of Seynts	...	...	...	...	...	40 0
A coote of armes	...	...	...	...	...	33 4

46

						s.	d.
A creste, carved and kylte ...	...	...	...	...	...	10	0
The mantels of blacke velvet, with gylte knopps and sylke tassels					...	13	4
A target ...	...	...	...	...	...	10	0
Six scoocheons in buckeram		...	...	...	...	10	0
Two doz in mettal at 15ᵈ the pece		...	...	...	...	30	0
Four doz in cooler at 10ᵈ the pece		...	...	...	...	40	0
For 5 iron brasses ...	...	...	...	...	...	10	0
Four black staves ...	...	...	...	...	...	4	0

Sum £13 os. 8d.'

Page 74. The statement that the More vault is now quite empty was given by the author upon what he regarded as the highest authority. It has since transpired that his informant was mistaken. The present condition of the vault is unknown to the church authorities, and Father Morris has recently written a paper, in which he strongly contends that the body of Sir Thomas More was reinterred at Chelsea Old Church.

Page 98. For ' Sandley ' read ' Sandby.'

Page 101. For ' Mrs. Schrieber ' read ' Lady Charlotte Schreiber.'

Page 137, line 23. For ' about ' read ' above.'

Page 159. Lord Lyndhurst was the son, not the nephew, of Copley.

Page 160. For ' Glynn ' read ' Glyn.'

Page 174. For ' 1832 ' read ' 1752.'

Page 176. Mrs. Gaskell, the novelist, was born in Lindsey Place, 1810. She was the daughter of a Mr. Stevenson, Unitarian minister.

Page 176. Mr. Crossley, Q.C., who died in 1892, lived at Belle Vue Lodge, 91, Cheyne Walk, a large house which was formerly occupied as a Naval and Military Academy. There is a good lithographed view of it by W. L. Walton.

Belle Vue Cottage is 104, Cheyne Walk, and is occupied by an old Chelsea family named Greaves. The pictures and etchings of old Chelsea, by Messrs. Walter and Henry Greaves, have been mentioned in the course of this work. These artists, too, have carried out the decoration of the Streatham Town Hall, one room entirely with Chelsea scenes and subjects.

Page 194. For ' Trelawney ' read ' Trelawny.'

Page 195. The ' ingenious artist ' who drew (on stone) the figures discovered in Winchester House was Miss Gulston.

For ' Lady ' North read ' Mrs. ' North.

Page 212. Fielding was the brother, not the son, of the novelist.

Page 213. Carlton House is No. 15, Cheyne Walk, and is now occupied by the Right Hon. L. H. Courtney, M.P.

Cecil Lawson's initials are scratched on one of the windows.

Page 234. The site of Robartes House is now (1892) being covered with 'high-class flats.'

Page 235. For 'Marquetel' read 'Marguetel.'

Page 241. The title 'Ormond House' should appear on page 240.

Page 253. For 'Mr.' read 'Sir W.' Tite.

Page 279, line 3. After 'St. Paul's' read 'the old East India House, and.'

Page 282. For 'balloque' read 'belloque.'

Page 291. For 'Colludon' read 'Colladon.'

Page 302. For 'Howard' read 'Horwood.'

Page 304. Delete the reference to Addison.

Page 320. Read 'James' for 'John Fuge.' The lithographs mentioned were drawn, after the death of Mr. Fuge, by H. Warren, from the former's water-colour drawings, which are still in the possession of his family. They were published by Mr. G. F. Fuge, of Sloane Square.

Page 348. For 'Sir' read 'Mr.' Robert Lowe.

For 'Kimberly' read 'Kimberley.'

Page 360, line 14. Insert 'no' after 'had.'

Page 9. Delete the reference to Bagnigge Wells.

1538, July 18 and 25. Despatches of M. de Castillon, Ambassador from France, dated from Chelsey. (Reports of the Dep. Keeper of the Records.)

1587-8, Jan. 26. Chelsea. Letter from Margaret, Countess of Cumberland, to the Earl of Rutland (Rutland Papers). Henry Constable addressed a sonnet 'To the Countesses of Cumberland and Warwick, Sisters,' *circa* 1590. They were daughters of Francis, Earl of Bedford. The former died in 1604, the latter in 1616.

In an extract 'from Dugdale's *Baronage*, with additions and corrections from Public Records,' by George Baker, in his 'History and Antiquities of Northamptonshire,' the family of Fenés—which, according to Dugdale, is the usual form of the name in England (there being no equivalent in the Italian nor in the Northern languages for Ph, used by the Breton branch of Phenés, as in Pharamond, Dauphin, Stephen, Στέφανος, it being the Greek Φ, Phi ; or the Phœnician ᓄ, Phe ; the only approach to which is the Gothic Ⱪ, Fe ; the Norse = Norman ᚱ, Feu ; and the Anglo-Saxon Ⱪ, F), is traced from Robert, High Constable of France, son of John, of Mortock, in the Co. of Somerset ; Clopham, in the Co. of Surrey ; and Wendovre, in the Co. of Bucks, who was attainted for adherence to the French King, in 14 Edward III., back to Ingelram, who was slain at Acon. . . . and who married Sibilla, daughter and heiress of Faramus (Pharamus), nephew of

Queen Maud, wife of King Stephen, and who was ruler of that King's household; and to whose grandson, also named Ingelram, were transferred, in 33 Henry III. (1249), the lands, lordship, and homage (by the King's command) in Northamptonshire, of the Earl of Ghisnes. William, son of the last-named Ingelram, proved his right to the feudal service of Sir Philip de Montgomery in 21 Edward I. (1293). In formal documents the Fenes = Phenés approached their ancient style as far as possible by spelling the Greek Phi. 'Fi,' signing as Fi-enes, Fyens, and Fenys. On the Breton branch (ancient lords of lands of Ancenis and Sa-venay, Sa-phenés, from Pharamus de Sarphenés) finally leaving the S.E. Departments, near the mouth of the Loire, where their arms and crest abound in the public monuments, and seeking refuge in Flanders and the British Islands, after the Revocation of the Edict of Nantes, the Ph was again abandoned in England, the name abbreviated, and the accent, which (from not being understood in England) had been taken for the upper part of an L and transformed into L by some writers, and by others had been looked on as marking an abbreviation, who inserted an N, again restored; the signatures being Fene, Fenée, and more usually Fené, as shown in Miss Florence Layard's extracts of Huguenot names lately published by the Huguenot Society, of which society Dr. Phené, LL.D., F.S.A., was one of the original founders. In Southern France and in Italy the phonetic pronunciation was preserved by Venay. Finet, and Vinet. The family is traced, in Dugdale's *Baronage*, by its intermarriages into the princely family of Condé; the Counts Boloin, Ponthieu, Chatillon, and Monceaux; the Lords Dacres; the Lady of Coupland in Maine; the Earls of Hereford, Lincoln, Essex, March, and Flanders; Viscount Wimbledon, Lord John Zouche, Viscount Banning; Sir Henry Baker, Sir Arthur Throkmorton, Sir Thomas Wykham, Sir Richard Harcourt of Stanton Harcourt, Sir John Danvers, Sir William Barentine, Sir William Farmour, Sir William Kingsmill, Sir Francis Boynton, Sir Walter Erle, Sir Charles Wolseley, Sir John Twisleton, Sir John Elyot, etc.

Richard, son of Roger, son of Sir William Fi-enes, was made Lord Dacre on November 7, 37 Henry VI., whose descendant, Gregory Fenes, Lord Dacre, was buried at Chelsea, 1594 (36 Elizabeth), where the Phenés = Fenés were then located, and have been holders of land in Chelsea since then to this day.

His sister Margaret was adjudged with the consent of King James to possess and to transmit the title of Barons Dacres to her children and their descendants, one of whom, Thomas, was in 22 Charles II. made Earl of Sussex.

James, the second son of Sir William Fenés, was, in 25 Henry VI., made Lord Say and Sele, and appointed Lord Chamberlain; and a descendant of his married the daughter of Sir John Danvers. And Sir Richard Fenés, his descendant, was confirmed by King James I. Lord Say and Sele, and the title to his descendants.

(Kindly communicated by Dr. Phené, F.S.A.)

1627, Mar. 29. Letter dated from Chelsea by Sir John Borlase. (Dom. St. Papers, Chs. I., lviij.)

1630, Dec. 13. Will of Dr. John Donne,—' Item I give to my son George that Annuyte of Fortye Pounds yearelie for the payment of wch my hono^rable frend Sr John Dãvers of Chelsey, Knighte hath some yeares since accepted from me Firste Twoe Hundred Poundes and after One hundred Marckes, of wch Annuytye thoughe there be as yett noe assurance yett there remayne wth me Bondes for those severall Sommes. And Sr John Dãvers will uppon requeste make either such assurance or repaye the moneye as he hathe always promised me. Proved 5 Ap. 1631.'

1636. See p. 102. Lady Vanlore was Jacoba or Jacomina, daughter of Henry Teighbot, of London, merchant Stranger, and wife of Sir Peter Vanlore, kt., Dutch merchant, naturalised by Act of Parliament. Lady Mary Powell was their 4th d., born *c.* 1586, m. Sir Edward Powell, kt. and bart., of Chelsea and Pengathley, co. Hereford. Maria, d. of Sir P. Vanlore of Tilehurst, bart., son of Sir Peter V., kt., married Henry Alexander, Earl of Stirling, and d., s.p., 1650.

1640, Nov. 11. Document dated from Chelsea by Sir Peter Osborne, Deputy Governor of Guernsey (Dom. St. P., cccclxxj., 35). 1641, Aug. 4. Letters &c. of the Same.

1643, May 2. Marriage License of Matthias Browne, of Chelsea (son of Matthias Browne the elder), about 21, and Mary Gorges, of Chelsea, about 20, widow of Mr. [Arthur] Gorges, late of Chelsea (Chester).

Proceedings of the Committee for the Advance of Money :

1644. Lady Mary Powell, Chelsea. May 15,—assessed at 300*l.* 1646, Oct. 16,—Ordered to pay up ½ forthwith. Oct. 21, Chelsea, Sir John Danvers to the Committee,—The enclosed petition will be verified on oath, both of the lady petitioning, and of Mr. Crompton, executor to Lady Vanlore. Being a trustee for Lady Powell, and having observed her and Mr. Crompton's fidelity to Parliament through the wars, I beg favour for her, as she has suffered 'afflictions unexpressible.' Crompton has also shown good affection to serve Parliament. Nov. 11,—Having paid 100*l.* she is to be heard about her assessment, any former order to the contrary notwithstanding. 1651, Apr. 29,—Information that she and Mr. Crompton in 1643, sent 500*l.* to the king at Oxford to aid him in the war, and held correspondence with the enemy.

1644. Nicholas Harman, Chelsea. May 22,—Assessed at 500*l.* 1646, July 24,— Having paid up ½ and made affidavit that 100*l.* is his proportion, order that 150*l.* be repaid him, and the sequestration be taken off his estate.

1645. Sept. 1.—Information that Mr. Puleston, of Chelsea and the Middle Temple, owes Thomas Edwards of Shrewsbury, 500*l.*

1645. Lady Grissel Poynts, Chelsea. Feb. 14,—Assessed at 300*l.* Feb. 16,— Discharged further attendance.

Extract from the Pedigree of Lee :

Francis Hy. Lee   +   Anne
 s. & h. of Hy. L. (s. of Sr Robt. L., kt.) 1st.   d. of Sr Jno. St. John, of Lydiard Tregooze,
 bt., and Eleanor, 4th. d. of Sr R^d Wortley,   co. Wilts, Kt. by Lucia, d. & h. of Sir
 of Wortley, Kt. (m. 2, Ed^d Ratcliffe, 6th. E.   Walt. Hungerford, of Farley Castle, co.
 of Sussex ; 3, Robt. Rich, 2nd. E. of War-   Wilts, Kt.
 wick ; 4, Ed. Montague, 2nd. E. of Man-   m. 2 Hy. Wilmot, 2nd. E. of Rochester,
 chester) b. 28 Feb. 1615 ; succ. as 2nd.   mother of Wm. 3rd. Earl, the poet ; bu.
 Bt. 1631 ; lived at Chelsea, co. Midd., d.   at Spelsbury.
 1639, bu. at Spelsbury.

Hy. L., s. & h.   +   Anne
 b. 21 Nov. 1637, succ. as 2^d bt., 1639 ;   eld. d. & co-h. of Sr Jno Danvers of
 M.P. for Malmesbury, in Parl. of 18 Mar.   Chelsea.
 1658 ; bu. Spelsbury 1659.   m. 1655.
      d. 1659.

Eleanor L., bap. 1658 ;	+	Ja^s, son of Montague	Thos, eld. s. & h. of	+	Anne L., bap. 1659 ;
co-h. of father ; m.		Bertie, 2nd. E. of	Philip, 4th. Baron		co-h. of father ; m.
1671 ; d. 1691 ; bu. at		Lindsey, by wife,	Wharton (cr. E. &		1673 : d. without issue ;
Rycott.		Bridget Wray.	M.). by Jane, d. &		bu. Waddesdon, co.
		Cr. E. of Abingdon,	h. of Arthur Good-		Bucks, 10 Nov. 1685.
		30 Nov. 1682, d. 22	win, of Upp. Win-		
		May 1699, æt 46.	chendon, co. Bucks.		
		bu. Rycott, Oxon.	d. Ap. 12, 1715.		

1671. Among the Epigrams of Richard Flecknoe is one ' To the Duchess of
      Monmouth.'

1672. Sept. 11. Marriage License of Isaac Alston of Chelsea, bachelor, about
      21, and Mrs. Mary Seale, of St. Dunstan's in the West, spinster,
      about 21 (Chester).

168$\frac{8}{9}$ Mar. 12. Extract from a News letter,—' Lady Paulina Montagu, daughter
      of the Earl of Sandwich, died this week at Chelsea, of a con-
      sumption.' (Fleming MSS.)

1690. The New Poems of Tom D'Urfey contain, ' To the Right Hon. the Earl
      of Radnor, on his Marriage,' etc. ' Epithalamy on the Marriage
      of the Right Hon. the Lady Essex Roberts.' ' An Elegy on the
      Death of that true perfection of Beauty and Goodness, the Lady
      Essex Spicket, who dyed of the small pox immediately after
      marriage.'

1714, Aug. 16. Edward Fowler, Bp. of Gloucester, died at Little Chelsea
      (Croker). See page 239. Buried at Hendon (Thorne).

1716. Peers, etc., summoned to his Majesty,—' The Bishop of Winchester,
      Lady Radnor, Lady Ketley, the Countess of Lindsey,' all of
      Chelsea (Coke MSS.).

$17\frac{19}{20}$, Feb. 16. Marriage License of Thomas Blow, bachelor, 40, and Mary Butler, spinster, 23, both of Chelsea (Chester).

1722. April. Dyed Mr. Robethon, one of his Majesty's private Secretarys for the affairs of Hanover, at Chelsea (Mawson's Obits.).

$172\frac{3}{4}$, Feb. 8. Dyed in his house in Chelsea, Sr John Humble, paymaster to several of the Lotteries (Mawson's Obits.).

1725, Aug. 25. Dyed at Chelsea, the Honble Mrs. Elizabeth Molesworth, Daughter to Dr. Welwood (Mawson's Obits.).

1729, Nov. 16. Died at his house at Chelsea, Mr. Abel Boyer, author of the French Dictionary, and the life of Queen Anne, and the Political State of Great Britain (*Monthly Chronicle*).

1752, Dec. 17. Mignonette first grown in the Botanic Garden, Chelsea (Blunt, A Chelsea Calendar).

1778, Oct. John James Masquerier, artist, born at Chelsea (Redgrave).

1790, Oct. 16 and Nov. 1. Specification by Joanna Hempel, of the King's Private Road, Chelsea, of an invention of filters (Cl. Roll, 30 Geo. II., p. 8, n. 8).

1801, Mar. 15. Samuel Rudder, author of a History of Cirencester, died at Chelsea (*Gent. Mag.*).

1807. The first Gaelic New Testament, printed in England, executed at Chelsea (Cotton).

Lineage of the Elers of Chelsea :

Peter Elers: of an ancient German Baronial family, settled in England on accession of George I.

Peter Elers, of Chelsea, d. 1753; bu. in West- + Dorothy, youngest da. of Peter Carew, of minster Abbey. Carew Castle, Pembrokeshire; d. 1785.

Ann, b. 1717; m. Wm. Posten. George, of Chelsea, d. 1784; + Mary, d. of Peter Chavon. bu. at Chelsea.

Carew, b. 1755; d. 1821; + Susanna, d. of Wm. Peter, Rector of Rishangles, Charlotte. bu. at Chelsea. Yarrow. Suffolk.

Carew Thomas, b. 1790; Rector of Rishangles, Suffolk. William, of Old-bury, Kent. George, of Crowcombe. Elizabeth. Caroline. Sophia. Mary.

Shaftesbury House. 'The lodge at the entrance . . . is peculiar, the gate being of old wrought iron. . . . The stone steps are old times, they are wide and much worn ; a low wall flanks either side, and on the right downwards are steps of narrower dimensions leading to the underground apartments. . . . The Hall is panelled in, so as to form a passage, but this is a modern innovation ; there can be no doubt of its having been in Lord Shaftesbury's time a good-sized hall ; the banisters and supporters of the very handsome staircase are in admirable preservation, delicately rather than richly carved in oak. What remains of the old house is chopped up, as it were, into small apartments ; but there are rich and varied indications of the light of other days to illumine the whole. Over several of the doors are strips of paintings, which as well as can be seen through thick varnish, are the productions of no feeble pencil. . . . Some of the rooms retain an antique air.' (Mrs. S. C. Hall, 'Pilgrimages to English Shrines.')

Danvers House. John Schurman, assistant of Nicholas Stone, sculptor, carved two shepherds sitting, two sphinxes, and Hercules and Antæus, for Sir John Danvers' garden at Chelsea, at the rate of sixteen pounds (Walpole, Anec. II. 40).

Recent Demolitions. Whiteland's House, King's Road, pulled down 1890, re-built 1891. A handsome gateway of beaten iron has been preserved and re-erected at the entrance. (See p. 319.)

Lordship Place, early eighteenth century houses, pulled down 1891-2.

Lawrence Street, west side, houses on site of porcelain factory, and others, including the vaulted passage to Augusta Court, mentioned on p. 85, pulled down 1891-2.

Old houses in Church Street, built 1679, pulled down 1891 ; 'Rectory Chambers' erected on site 1891-2.

The early demolition of the Turk's Row group of tenements is proposed (Feb., 1892).

APPENDIX I.

RECTORS OF CHELSEA.

1. Sir Robert de Staundone. The first recorded rector. He is mentioned in the will of his brother, Gerard de Staundone, Rector of Styvenach : ' To Peter de Batlesfeld houses in the lane and parish of S. Martin Ogar de Candilwyk-strate for life, subject to a payment of five marks annually to Sir Robert de Staundone, Rector of Chelchehuth ; remainder to the said Robert for life ' (February 2, 1314, 1315). See R. R. Sharpe, ' Col. of Wills proved in the Court of Husting, London,' Vol. I., p. 250.

2. Roger de Berners. Instituted by the king (Pal. 9, Ed. II., p. 2), May 1, 1316 ; on December 30, 1324, he was appointed one of the Bishop of London's proctors before the Justices of the King's Bench in cases of clergy accused.

3. Nicholas de Hosbound. Instituted by Edward III. in 1339.

4. Martyn de Moulish. Also instituted by Edward III. (Pal. 22, Ed. III., p. 2) September 1, 1348.

The following twenty rectors were appointed by the Abbot and Convent of Westminster :

5. William Palmer, 1368. He resigned the same year. A William Palmer was instituted Rector of St. Alphege, London, in 1397, and died in 1400.

6. Thomas de Preston, 1368 ; resigned the same year. A Thomas Preston was Rector of St. Margaret, Lothbury, in 1393.

7. John Basset, 1368 ; he resigned in 1371 ; Rector of Chadwell, Essex, 1389 ; died, 1399.

8. John de Stansted, Rector of Stanway, Essex, instituted Rector of Chelsea, 1371 ; exchanged with Rector of Copford, Essex, 1372.

9. John de Foydon, or Foxden, Rector of Copford, Essex (1370) ; instituted Rector of Chelsea, November 25, 1372.

10. Ric. Mockynton, August 5, 1385 ; resigned in the same year.

11. Ric. Everden, 1385; resigned.

12. J. Beaugraunt, October 25, 1388; resigned.

13. J. Bishop, November 4, 1392; resigned, 1394; Rector of Thistley-cum-Maningtree, Essex, 1440; died, 1445.

14. Robert Onum, March 4, 1394.

15. John Balsham, June 25, 1394.

16. Joh. Scarburgh, March 26, 1433; resigned the same year; Rector of Duddinghurst, 1436; Wareley Magna, 1437; East Dommiland, 1438; Roding Alta, 1465.

17. Gafr. Medewe, Rector of Farnham, Essex, 1427; Buckland, Hertfordshire, 1433, and of Chelsea the same year; resigned in 1435.

18. Alex. Brown, August 31, 1435; resigned in 1442; Rector of St. Ethelburgh, London, 1447.

19. Tho. Boleyn, LL.B., July 15, 1442; Prebendary of Portpool, London, 1447; died, 1451.

20. William Walesby, Dean of St. Stephen's, Westminster, 1446; appointed keeper of the clock and tower called the Clock House at Westminster by Henry VI., with wages of sixpence a day; resigned the rectory of Chelsea in 1450.

21. William Lilly, October 16, 1450; resigned the following year and became Rector of St. Mary, Somerset, London.

22. Tho. Chalers, November 2, 1451; died the same year.

23. Will. Fidcon, December 8, 1451; resigned in 1454.

24. John Pennant, July 11, 1454; resigned the following year.

25. Will. Hebbing, Rector of Waltham Parva, Essex (1432); Rector of Stanmore Magna, Middlesex (1438); instituted Rector of Chelsea, March 3, 1455; resigned the following year; Vicar of West Ham, Essex, 1460; Vicar of Standon, Hertfordshire, and Rector of Keldon Hatch, Essex, 1464; died, 1466.

26. Will. Massanger, October 18, 1456; died, 1469.

27. Will. Mille, January 26, 1469; resigned, 1481.

28. Joh. Mardelaye, July 30, 1481; resigned, 1486.

29. Thos. Machey, M.A., October 31, 1486; resigned, 1492; subsequently Vicar of Ruislip, Middlesex, which he resigned in 1497.

30. Geo. Percy, alias Gard, Vicar of Rainham, Essex (September 28, 1482), resigned March, 1483; Vicar of Ruislip, February, 1483; Rector of Chelsea, June 6, 1492; resigned, 1500 (?); resigned vicarage of South Bemflete, 1506.

31. Will. Ingelard; resigned.

32. Robert Tunstall, September 26, 1502 ; resigned following year.

33. Thomas Laworth, December 16, 1503.

34. Robert Dandie ; resigned, 1530.

35. John Larke, Rector of St. Ethelburgh, London, 1504 ; presented to rectory of Woodford, Essex, January 18, 1526, by Sir Thomas More ; and to that of Chelsea, March 29, 1530, by the same ; executed at Tyburn, March 7, 1544, for denying the King's supremacy.

36. Robert Richardson, born about 1500 ; entered his noviciate at Abbey of Cambuskenneth, 1519 ; went to Paris, $152\frac{2}{3}$; introduced to Thos. Cromwell by Walter Cromer, one of the King's physicians ; entered the service of Henry VIII. as political agent and preacher ; at Rome, 1535 ; preached at Paul's Cross, November, 1536 ; prisoner at Dieppe, 1543 ; released on April 3 of that year, and spent from June to November in an evangelical tour in Scotland ; instituted as Rector of Chelsea, March 19, 1544, on attainder and execution of John Larke. (The following occurs in the Acts of the Privy Council,—At Westminster the xv[th] July (1546),—'Sir Robert Richardson, parson of Chelsith, who had remayned in the custodie of the Bishop of London, for his light behaviour in matters of religion repenting his former lewdness was, with a good lesson and submission, dismissed and put to libertie.'—New Series, Vol. I., p 485.) Rector of St. Martin, Ironmonger Lane, 1550 (resigned 1553) ; ejected from the rectory of Chelsea, for being a married priest, by Mary, 1554 (there is an account of his public sermon of recantation in Machyn's Diary) ; re-instituted by Elizabeth, 1559 ; Rector of Hanworth, Middlesex, 1562 (patrons, Francis Newdigate and Anna, Duchess of Somerset) ; resigned his living at Chelsea, February 8, 1569 ; Vicar of Chigwell, Essex, 1570 ; died, 1573. (Many of these particulars were kindly communicated by Mr. C. Davis Sherborn, and for permission to use them I am indebted to R. B. Stuart, Esq., of Glasgow College.)

37. Jac. Proctor, presented January 15, 1554, by Mary on the ejectment of Robert Richardson ; died the same year.

38. Ric. Myers, presented August 8, 1554 ; died, 1558.

39. Matt. Myers, presented October 8, 1558.

40. Joh. Churchman, presented by Ann, Duchess of Somerset, February 8, 1569. The following baptisms occur in the Chelsea Register,—Winifred Churchman, June 19, 1568 ; 'Tyberia Churchman, filia Joh[is] Churchman hujus ecclesiæ Rectoris, 17 die Februarii, 1573.'

41. Thos. Brown, D.D., presented June 7, 1574 ; Rector, St. Mary, Colchester, 1558-1562 ; Vicar of Easter-bona, 1559-1565 ; Rector of Dunton,

1564; Rector of St. Leonard, Foster Lane, 1567-1574; Rector of Chelsea, 1574. In the Chelsea register is found, 'Gabriel the son of Thomas Browne, Parson, 3d April, 1576; died May 3rd, 1585, and is buried in the cloisters at Westminster Abbey.'

42. Ric. Warde, Vicar of Epping, 1554; deprived, 1556; cofferer to Queen Elizabeth; presented June 18, 1585; his wife Catherine was buried at Chelsea, December 16, 1605: married the second time to Elizabeth Fisher, in the old church, on January 2, 1607. Among the baptisms we find, 'Elizabetha, fil. Ric. Warde, Rectoris, December 26, 1607'; and 'Prudencia, fil. Rich. Warde, Rectoris, November 1, 1609.' He was buried at Chelsea, September 2, 1615. By his will he bequeathed £15 for the poor of the parish, and for the repair of the lead on the church.

43. George Hamden, M.A., presented by the Earl and Countess of Nottingham, December 2, 1615. Among the baptisms is 'John, son of George Hamden, Doctor of Divinity, and Parson of this church, December 16th, 1619.' Died 1632.

44. Samuel Wilkinson, D.D., presented by Edward Barton, December 4, 1632. Among the Chelsea baptisms is 'Dorothy, daughter of Mr. Samuel Wilkinson, Parson, March 16th, 1637.' Provost of Chelsea College, 1645; collated to the prebend of Neasdon in 1668; died the following year, and was buried at Chelsea, January 7, 1669.

45. Adam Littleton, D.D., born November 8, 1627, presented by Charles Cheyne (afterwards Viscount Newhaven), Lord of the Manor, February 3, 1669; married the daughter of Richard Guildford, Esquire, of Chelsea (she survived her husband four years, and was buried in the old church, November 14, 1698); received a grant from Charles II. to succeed Dr. Busby as Head-Master of Westminster School; appointed one of the Royal Chaplains; he died in 1694, and was buried at Chelsea.

46. John King, D.D., born 1652; Dean of York; married (secondly) Elizabeth, daughter of Joseph Aris, of Adstone, Northamptonshire, and widow of the Rev. John Eston, by whom he had seven children; through her he acquired the patronage of Pertenhall; he presented this living to the Rev. Mr. Cheyne, on receiving the presentation from Viscount Cheyne to the Rectory of Chelsea, 1694. In the Chelsea Register we find, 'John, son of the Rev. John King, Rector, Aug. 5, 1696'; 'Joseph, son of John King, Rector, Jan. 23, 1698'; 'William, son of Dr. John King, October 6th, 1700'; 'Eulalia, daughter of Dr. John King, August 4th, 1703.' He died in 1732, and was buried at Pertenhall.

47. Sloane Elsmere, D.D., presented by Sir Hans Sloane, Bart., August 3, 1732; died at Chelsea 1766.

48. Reginald Heber, M.A., presented December 5, 1766.

49. Thomas Drake, D.D., Rector of Malpas, Cheshire; exchanged with Heber, August 4, 1770.

50. W. B. Cadogan, M.A., presented May 28, 1775; died 1797.

51. Charles Sturgess, M.A., presented May 1, 1797.

52. Hon. and Rev. Valerian Wellesley, D.D., presented August 17, 1805.

53. Rev. W. Lockwood, M.A.

54. Rev. Charles Kingsley, M.A., died 1860.

55. Rev. Gerald A. Blunt, M.A., 1860.

WHITELAND'S COLLEGE, KING'S ROAD, 1889.

APPENDIX II.

———••———

LIST OF THE INSCRIPTIONS IN CHELSEA OLD CHURCH.

Sir Thomas More and Joanna his first wife.   See p. 72.
Lady Jane Guyldeforde, Duchess of Northumberland.   See p. 75.
R. Gervoise, sone of the Sheriff of London.   See p. 76.
Thomas Hungerford.   See p. 76.
Thomas Lawrence.   See p. 77.
Gregory Fynes, Lord Dacre of the South, and Anne Sackville, his wife.
See p. 77.

Catharine, d. of John, Duke of Northumberland, & wife of Henry Hastings,
Earl of Huntingdon.   See p. 76.

Sarah, d. of Thos. Lawrence, and wife of Richard Colville of Newton, Isle
of Ely.   See p. 77.

Sir Robert Stanley, Kt., Ferdinando, his son, and Henrietta Maria, his
daughter.   See p. 79.

Sir John Lawrence.   See p. 77.

Humphrey Peshall of Halney, Hales Owen, and Mary, d. of Richard Blount
of Rasley, his wife.   See p. 83.

Elizabeth, d. of Sir Theodore Mayerne, and wife of Pierre Marquis de
Caumont.   See p. 79.

Henry Lawrence, youngest son of Sir John; d. Oct. 14: 1666, æt. 29.
Black marble slab on floor of Lawrence Chapel.

Arthur, son of Sir Arthur Gorges, Kt.; d. April 8: 1668; m. Dame Mary,
d. and co-heir of Paul, Lord Viscount Bayning.   Black marble slab in S.
aisle.

Richard Munden; d. 1672.   Stone in north side of churchyard.

James, son of Matthew Buck; d. Dec. 21: 1680, æt. 62; and Mary his
wife.   Also, Elizabeth, d. of Humphrey Rogers of Richmond, Surrey, his

second wife; d. Nov. 23: 1674, æt. 50. Black marble tablet on wall of N. aisle, on the r. of the Cheyne monument.

Richard Guilford; d. Nov. 16: 1680, æt. 66 yrs. Abigail, d. of John Wood, co. York, his 1st wife; and Elizabeth, d. of Roger Friend, of Lambeth, his second wife. Marble tablet on wall of N. aisle, to the r. of the Cheyne monument.

Frances, 2nd d. of Sir John Laurence; d. Nov. 8: 1685, æt. 70 yrs.

Anne, only d. of Edward Chamberlayne, LL.D., wife of Sir John Spragg, Kt., d. Oct. 30: 1691. Slab on S. outer wall, to r. of the old doorway.

Peregrine Clifford Chamberlayne, R.N., eldest son of Edward Chamberlayne, LL.D.; d. Nov. 6: 1691. Marble tablet on S. outer wall, to l. of the old doorway.

Samuel Forest; d. 1692. Stone on N. side of the churchyard.

Edward, son of Edward Chamberlayne, LL.D.; d. May 14: 1697. Oblong tablet (erected by his father) on S. outer wall, above the old doorway.

Jane, d. of William, Duke of Newcastle, and wife of Charles Cheyne. See p. 79.

Baldwin Hamey, M.D.; d. 1676, æt. 76. Slab on a pillar near the Gervoise arch. See p. 83.

Adam Littleton, S.T.P., Rector of Chelsea; d. June 30: 1694, æt. 67. Square marble tablet [the inscription re-cut, and 'incolis' altered to 'inootis'] on N. wall of the lower chancel.

Charles Cheyne, Viscount Newhaven. See p. 81.

Hester Hill; d. 1699. Marble tablet in the belfry, near the West entrance.

Christopher Cratford; d. 1702. Stone on N. side of the churchyard.

Edward Chamberlayne, LL.D. See p. 81.

Sarah, only d. of Richard Clifford, wife of Edward Chamberlayne, LL.D.; d. Dec. 17: 1703, æt. 69 yrs. 3 m. Large stone slab on S. outer wall, to the E. of the large window.

Flora Butts; d. 1704. Stone on N. side of the churchyard.

John, second son of David Pennant, of Bingham, co. Flint; d. June 5: 1709, æt. 69. Stone (erected by his wife) on N. side of churchyard.

William Clarkson; d. 1712. Marble tablet in the belfry, W. entrance.

Robert Butler; d. 1712. Stone on N. side of churchyard.

Sir William Milman; d. Sept. 3: 1713, æt. 64. Tablet on S. wall of the More Chapel.

Ralph Palmer; d. Feb. 1: 1715, æt. 80, and Alice, his wife; d. Sept. 14: 1708, æt. 75. Slab on a pillar near the Gervoise arch, below inscription to Baldwin Hamey.

Mary, d. of Bartholomew Smith, of the Soke, Winchester, m. 1st. John Wyburnd of Cawkwall, Kent, 2nd., George Bolney, of Bolney; d. 1716, æt. 88.

Jennett, wife of Alexander Hamilton: d. Sept. 9: 1716; and Alexander Hamilton, d. Nov. 30: 1724, æt. 72. Marble tablet, on the wall of N. aisle, near Cheyne monument.

Henry Raper; d. May 11: 1789; and Katharine, his wife; d. Nov. 12: 1823. Marble sarcophagus on the wall of N. aisle.

Sir John Munden; d. 1679.

Ann, d. of Thomas Lowfield; d. Dec. 25: 1720.

Ann, d. of Hugh Stafford, of Pynes, co. Devon; d. July 30: 1722, æt. 18; and Hugh, only son of the same; d. Apr. 29: 1729, æt. 23. Tablet on N. wall of lower chancel.

Anne, widow of Thomas Wakelin, of York Buildings, Westminster, Apothecary; d. Sept. 17: 1722, æt. 44. Marble tablet in S. aisle to r. of W. entrance.

Thomas Putland; d. 1723. Stone in floor of lower chancel.

Thomas Hurd, Post Captain and Hydrographer in the R.N.; d. Apr. 29: 1723. Plain marble slab on E. wall of lower chancel.

John Chamberlayne, F.R.S.; d. Nov. 2: 1723, æt. 57. Small marble tablet on S. outer wall, above tablet to P. C. Chamberlayne.

Thomas Bowes, M.D. and F.R.S.; d. 1723. Marble tablet on outer wall of the vestry.

Mrs. Methuen; d. 1723. Marble tablet on outer wall of the vestry.

Ann, wife of Capt. Richard Culliford; d. Sept. 8: 1726, æt. 67.

Clayton Milbourne; d. 1726. Stone on N. side of the churchyard.

Andrew Churchill; d. 1731. Stone on N. side of the churchyard.

William Moncrieff, Prof. of Humanity at St. Andrews; d. 1732. Marble tablet on outer wall of the vestry.

Maria, d. of William Buckby, Serjeant at Law; d. 1728. Tablet on N. wall of upper chancel.

Brigadier Jean Antoine Cavalier, Leader of the Camisards; d. 1740. Stone on N. side of the churchyard (mentioned by Faulkner, but now missing).

Alexander Reid; d. 1743, On N. side of the churchyard.

Anna Maria Powell, wife of Capt. Dawley Sutton; d. 1745. Marble tablet in belfry, W. entrance.

Henry Lussan, J.P. co. Monmouth; d. 1750.

Edward Stanley, of Dalgarth, co. Cumberland; d. July 23: 1751, æt. 61. Tablet on N. wall of lower chancel.

Henry Powell; d. Dec. 8: 1752, æt. 77; Elizabeth, his wife; d. Apr. 28:

1726 ; and Elizabeth their daughter ; d. (unmarried) Apr. 23 : 1774, æt. 62. Slab on the W. side of a pillar, near the Gervoise arch.

Sir Hans Sloane, Bt., and Elizabeth, his wife. See p. 81.

Joanna Rhodes ; d. 1753. Stone on N. side of the churchyard.

Sarah Eyre ; d. 1755. Stone on N. side of the churchyard.

Anne Skinner ; d. 1756. Slab on the N. wall of upper chancel.

Margaret, wife of Henry Hewitt ; d. Jan. 17 : 1762, æt. 58. Henry Hewitt ; d. May 27 : 1771, æt. 75. Marble tablet in Laurence Chapel.

John Hutchins, of Chelsea ; d. Feb. 8 : 1762, æt. 67. Elizabeth, his wife ; d. Dec. 7 : 1762, æt. 64. Flat stone in the middle aisle.

Francis Thomas, Director of the Porcelain Factory ; d. 1770. Flat stone in S. aisle.

Philip Miller, Curator of the Apothecaries' Garden. See p. 83.

Agnes Smith ; d. 1773. Stone on N. side of the churchyard.

Mary Emilia Williams ; d. 1774. Stone on N. side of the churchyard.

Martha, widow of Col. John Cottrell ; d. 1778. Stone on N. side of the churchyard.

William Rush ; d. 1779. Stone on N. side of the churchyard.

Charity, wife of Nicholas Adams ; d. Aug. 1 : 1781, æt. 32. Nicholas Adams, d. June 7 : 1787, æt. 78. On outer vestry-wall, near the door.

Lucy Wilton, wife of —— Smith ; d. Aug. 22 : 1781, æt. 33. Ann Wilton ; d. Mar. 10 : 1781, æt. 23. Two urns in white marble, designed by their father, Joseph Wilton, R.A., sculptor, in E. wall of upper chancel.

William Hart, of Stapleton, co. Gloucester (father-in-law of Sir Francis Milman, Bart.) ; d. Jan. 13 : 1785, æt. 85. George Hart ; d. Sept. 19 : 1791, æt. 86 yrs. John Dyer Milman ; d. Dec. 5 : 1786, æt. 2 yrs. 10 m.; Francis Sophia Milman ; d. Dec. 11 : 1786, æt. 11 m.; and Charles Dyer Milman ; d. Aug. 25 : 1790, æt. 7 m., Children of Sir Francis Milman, Bart. Tablet on S. wall of More Chapel.

Maj. Gen. Henderson, 13th Foot ; d. 1787. Stone on N. side of the churchyard.

Nicholas Ray ; d. 1788. Stone in floor of lower chancel.

Mary Hall Stanton, of Barbadoes ; d. 1789. Stone on N. side of the churchyard.

Charlwood Lawton ; d. 1790. Stone on N. side of the churchyard.

Ludar Lang ; d. 1791. Flat stone in the floor of More Chapel.

Mary Haynes ; d. 1791. Stone on N. side of churchyard.

Mary, wife of Edward Read ; d. Jan. 21 : 1792. Edward Read ; d. Apr. 2 : 1812, æt. 82. Marble tablet in Laurence Chapel.

Richard Lamborne; d. 1793. Flat stone in the floor of More Chapel.

Martha, wife of John Denyer; d. Jan. 18: 1795, æt. 64. John Denyer; d. Jan. 6: 1806, æt. 76. E. Dennis Denyer, their only daughter; d. Apr. 6: 1828, æt. 58. Plain marble slab on E. wall of lower chancel.

Marianne; d. Nov. 1795, æt. 4 m.; George; d. Nov. 1795, æt. 6 yrs.; John; d. Jan. 1796, æt. 3 yrs.; Children of George Hay Drummond, Prebendary of York, and Elizabeth Margaret, his wife. Oval tablet in lower chancel.

Benjamin Dodd; d. Nov. 10: 1796, æt. 70 yrs.

William J. Tullock, of Turnham Green; d. 1796. Stone on N. side of churchyard.

Sarah, wife of James Hovell; d. Nov. 22: 1798, æt. 48. James Hovell; d. Feb. 2: 1810, æt. 64. On N. wall of lower chancel.

Matthew Squire, Rear Admiral of the Red; d. Jan. 22: 1800, æt. 55.

Capt. William Daniell, R.N.; d. Feb. 21: 1800, æt. 61. Marble tablet in S. aisle, to r. of W. entrance.

Thomas Simpkin; d. Dec. 27: 1801, æt. 53. Elizabeth Simpkin; d. Jan. 12: 1826, æt. 77.

David Heatley, Agent Victualler to the Mediterranean Fleet; d. 1803.

Henry Sampson Woodfall, printer; d. Dec. 12: 1805, æt. 66. Stone in N.E. corner of churchyard removed, commemorating the original, to make room for the Miller obelisk, and now missing.

Anna Bridge; d. Dec. 6: 1807, æt. 80. Marble tablet in lower chancel.

Montague, son of Rev. John Rush, and Honour, his wife; d. Feb. 13: 1808, æt. 14 days. Oval tablet of white marble on N. wall of upper chancel, to r. of Hungerford monument.

T. W. Reid; d. Dec. 26: 1810, æt. 6 yrs.; J. A. Reid; d. Apr. 21: 1813, æt. 21; sons of Mr. Reid, Surgeon. Thomas Ranby Reid; d. Aug. 19: 1819, æt. 54. On N. outer wall of Laurence Chapel.

Sarah, wife of William Collins; d. Aug. 11: 1811. William Collins; d. Sept. 10: 1828, æt. 72. Marble tablet in S. aisle, to r. of W. entrance.

Henry, son of Rev. John Rush; d. Mar. 12: 1812, æt. 21 days. Small oval tablet in white marble on N. wall of upper chancel, to r. of the Hungerford monument.

Matilda Susan, d. of William Wylly, Attorney General at Bahama, wife of Capt. Chambers, R.N.; d. Feb. 1: 1813, æt. 24. In S. aisle to r. of W. entrance.

Jane Hill; d. May 28: 1813, æt. 72. Edward Hill; d. Dec. 23: 1816, æt. 77. On the outer vestry-wall, near the door.

Honour Chambers, wife of Rev. John Rush; d. Oct. 1814, æt. 37. George Lee, son of Rev. John and Honour Rush; d. Nov. 28: 1814, æt. 12 weeks 3 d. Oval tablet in white marble on N. wall of upper chancel, to r. of the Hungerford monument.

Jane, d. of the Rev. John Baker, M.A., of Ilchester, co. Somerset, wife of Capt. William Toovey, and secondly of the Rev. Montague Rush; d. Aug. 31: 1815, æt. 71. White marble tablet on S. wall of upper chancel, above the Mayerne tablet.

Maj.-Gen. John Brown; d. Mar. 20: 1816, æt. 68. Marble tablet in S. aisle, to r. of W. entrance.

Eliza Chambers, sister of Honour Rush; d. Mar. 2: 1818, æt. 33. Oval tablet in white marble on N. wall of upper chancel, to r. of the Hungerford monument.

Sydenham Teast Edwards, F.L.S., etc.; d. Feb. 8: 1819, æt. 50. Marble tablet in S. aisle, on r. of W. entrance.

John Ludlow; d. Jan. 27: 1820, æt. 22. On outer wall of the vestry, near the door.

Elizabeth, widow of Thomas Tyndale, of North Cerney, co. Gloucester; d. Mar. 23: 1821, æt. 87. Marble medallion, supported by angels (Rossi, sculptor), on S. outer wall, under slab to Dr. Chamberlayne.

Catharine, wife of Rev. Thomas Mahon, Rector of Newport Pral., co. Mayo; d. Apr. 27: 1822, æt. 20. Marble tablet on wall of the S. aisle.

Catherine Long; d. July 11: 1822, æt. 56. Marble tablet on the outer wall of the vestry.

Edward Hall, Surveyor and Architect to the Navy Board; d. Nov. 22: 1823, æt. 58. Plain marble slab on E. wall of lower chancel.

Isabell Margarett Claremont; d. Sept. 15: 1824, æt. 14. Marble tablet to r. of W. entrance.

Henry Cooper, barrister; d. Sept. 19: 1824, æt. 41.

Frederica, wife of Capt. Hurd, Grenadier Guards; d. Dec. 18: 1824. Plain marble slab on E. wall of lower chancel.

Thomas Long; d. Oct. 29: 1827, æt. 66. Marble tablet on outer wall of vestry.

Mary Anne Alice, sister of Lucy Smith, wife of Charles Bayley, H.E.I.C.; d. Feb. 17: 1828, æt. 45. Marble tablet, ornamented (erected by Joseph Wilton), to l. of W. entrance.

Maria, eldest d. of Capt. John Maude, R.N., wife of J. C. Hyde, surgeon, of Queen's Elm; d. Oct. 4: 1831, æt. 46.

Rev. Edmund, son of John Staunton, of Longridge, co. Warwick ; d. Sept. 16 : 1835, æt. 58.

John Beech ; d. Nov. 8 : 1836, æt. 80.   Sarah, his wife ; d. Nov. 16 : 1839, æt. 78.

Jane, eldest d. of Rev. Montague Rush, of Heckfield, wife of Col. Tyndale, of the Life Guards ; d. Sept. 25 : 1842, æt. 72.   Marble tablet.

Rev. John Rush, LL.B., Rector of Hartwell-cum-Hampden, Bucks, and Incumbent of the Old Church at Chelsea ; d. June 4 : 1855, æt. 85.   Marble tablet.

Rev. Richard Wilson, D.D. ; born Dec. 29, 1798 ; d. Oct. 9, 1879.   Marble tablet, with portrait medallion, ' erected as a tribute of respect by the inhabitants of this district to commemorate the gratuitous services rendered by the late Dr. Wilson, in officiating for a number of years as Sunday evening lecturer in this church.   He had filled, among other offices, those of Fellow of St. John's College, Cambridge, Dean of the College of Preceptors, and was an accomplished Hebrew scholar ; and to his humility as a minister of the Gospel there was united a kind and genial bearing to all who knew him.'

ENTRANCE TO THE ROTUNDA, RANELAGH GARDENS.

APPENDIX III.

CHELSEA CHARITIES.

1582. *John Lyon.*

> One-twentieth part of the clear yearly income arising from his estate to be applied towards defraying the expenses of maintaining that portion of the Harrow Road, situate in the parish of Chelsea.

1595. *Anne, Lady Dacre.*

> Two in-pensioners, one man and one woman, at Emanuel Hospital, with annual stipend of 20*l.* and 3 tons of coal.
>
> One male out-pensioner, at 10*l.* per annum.
>
> Candidates must be single, of good character, Protestant in religion, not possessed of goods exceeding 200*l.* in value, or of more than 10*l.* per annum income, and not less than 56 years of age.
>
> Vacancies among the in-pensioners are filled up from the out-pensioners.
>
> [The continuance of this bequest is subject to the maintenance in good repair of the Dacre tomb in Chelsea Old Church.]

1597. *Edward Page.*

> Interest on 10*l.* to be distributed annually to the poor. [Obsolete; see p. 105.]

1600 (*c.*). *John Powell.*

> Interest on 10*l.* annually. [Obsolete.]

1604. *Thomas Young.*

> 20*s.* per annum to the poor. [Obsolete.]

Ante ⎱ *Thomas Evans.*
1620. ⎰ *Lady Anne Harrington.*

> Interest on 20*l.* to be annually distributed to the poor. [Obsolete.]

1630. *Madam Dudley Gorges, Lady Lane.*

> 20*s.* annually to the poor in consideration of being granted permission to enclose acres of Lammas Land. [Obsolete; see p. 41.]

Prout } *Mrs. Child.*
1634. }   1*l.* to the poor.
1645. *Lady Stonor.*
    20*s.* annually to be spent in bread for the poor. [Obsolete.]
1653. *William Preston, of 'The Feathers' tavern, Cheyne Walk.*
    20*s.* to be distributed to the poor.
1654. *Christopher Plucknett.*
    20*s.* annually, chargeable upon his estate, called Hanger and Town
        Mead, Fulham, to be spent in bread in January. [Obsolete.]
    Faulkner says (ii. 108), 'This land is now (1829) the property or
        Mr. Bolton, from whom the rent-charge is annually received.'
1657. *Henry Ashton.*
    40*l.* to be lent on bond, free of interest, to 8 poor tradesmen in sums
        of 5*l.* for two years. Then to be called in and lent out again
        in the same way. [Obsolete.]
1662. *James Leverett.*
    Rent charge of 14*l.* per annum upon the 'Magpie [and Stump]'
        tavern, 37 (formerly 34) Cheyne Walk; 10*l.* paid quarterly to
        poor housekeepers and inhabitants of Great Chelsea; 4*l.* to the
        Churchwardens, Overseers, Constables & Clerk of the Parish for
        an annual dinner at the Magpie.
    [Paid by the stewards of the Earl Cadogan.]
1663. *Edward Cheyne.*
    Rent charge of 6*s.* per annum on a house in Cox's Close, to be given
        in bread annually on March 10th, in commemoration of testator's
        deliverance from fire on that day.
    [This bequest lapsed for 82 years, but by the exertions of Mr. R.
        Chambers was recovered in 1835, and all arrears were paid up
        by the then Earl of Cadogan. These amounted to £26 12s. 9d.,
        which sum was invested in 3 per cent. Consols, and the interest is
        now added to the original bequest. The rent-charge is paid by
        the stewards of the Earl Cadogan.]
1679. *William Ashburnham.* (See p. 69.)
    The custom of ringing appears to have been discontinued about 1825.
1680. *Richard Guildford.*
    Rent charge of 10*l.* per annum on four tenements in Horse Shoe
        Court (formerly 'Sword and Buckler Court'), Ludgate Hill, dis-
        tributed on Dec. 5th, as follows,—
        8 poor women and 8 poor men, parishioners, 10*s.* each.

1680. *Richard Guildford* (continued).

> To the Minister for a Sermon, 1*l*. 1*s*. 6*d*.
>
> To the Clerk, 2*s*. 6*d*.
>
> To the ringers (or to the poor if they do not ring), 5*s*.
>
> To the Ministers, Churchwardens, and Overseers, for a dish of meat and drink, 11*s*.
>
> [This bequest lapses and goes to the parish of Lambeth if not fulfilled annually on December 5.]

1703. *Edward Chamberlayne* (continued by his son).

1723. *John Chamberlayne*.

> Rent charge of 10*l*. per annum on No. 11 (formerly 62 and previously 59) Church Street, due at Lady Day free from all deductions except Income Tax.
>
> For free education of 5 poor boys, 5*l*.
>
> For apprenticeship of one poor boy to some handicraft or trade (originally that of waterman), 5*l*.
>
> [By scheme approved by Charity Commissioners, January 27, 1888, the latter sum may be applied to promoting the technical education of Chelsea boys, present or past exhibitioners in the United Westminster Schools.]

1704. *William Mart*.

> 10*l*. to be distributed to the poor.

1705. *William Petyt*. (See p. 105.)

1709. *Mrs. Cranenburg*.

> 5*l*. to the Charity School; 5*l*. to the poor.

1716 and 1727 } *Mrs. Vincent*.

> 2*l*. to the poor in each year.

1717. *Judith Cale*.

> Interest on 230*l*. invested in $2\frac{3}{4}$ p.c. Consols, paid annually on Christmas Day to six poor widows.

Francis Robartes.

> 5*l*. to the Charity School.
>
> 5*l*. to the poor.
>
> [Obsolete.]

1722. —— *Clarkson*.

> 20*s*. per annum to the Charity School.

Thomas Bromwich.

> 20*s*. per annum to the Charity School.

1722. *Thomas Stewart.*

Bequeathed 100*l.* for an altar-piece for the old Church. [This does not appear to have been used.]

Also, 50*l.* for an annual sermon on Psalm l. 14-15.

Faulkner quotes the following from a letter of Thomas Martyn, May 19, 1810: 'Dr. King never having laid out Mr. Steward's fifty pounds, the charge of paying the interest devolved upon his two surviving daughters; upon their death and my father's it devolved upon me, as my mother's heir, and Mr. King as my aunt's executor. That there might be an end to it, our connection with Chelsea being dissolved, I purchased 100*l.* in the 3 per Cents., which were then about 57, with the consent of Mr. Sturgess and the churchwardens.'

[This £100 stock is now in 2¾ per cent. Consols. If the sermon were omitted the dividend was to go to the Boys' Charity School.]

1727. *Richard Willis, Bishop of Winchester.*

20*l.* to the poor.

Lord Peterborough.

10*l.* 10*s.* to the poor.

1728. *Gertrude, Lady Cheyne.*

10*l.* to the poor.

Mrs. Perkins.

5*l.* to the poor.

1734. *Sir Robert Walpole* gave 50*l.* towards building the workhouse.

1766. *Charles Larchin.*

20*l.* to the Charity School.   (See p. 115.)

Rev. Sloane Elsmere, D.D.

Sermons to be published for the sole benefit of the 'Charity Girls' School'; they produced 115*l.* 18*s.* 4*d.*   (See p. 115.)

1771. *Henry Hewett.*

50*l.* to the Charity School.   (See p. 115.)

1772. *Stephen Fox.*

200*l.* to the Charity School.

1782. *William Jousselin.*

30*l.* to the Charity School.

George Beck.

20*l.* to the Charity School.

1788. *Peter Cornud* (or *Cornude*).

10*l.* to the Charity School.

1788. *David Rice.*

10*l.* to the Sunday Schools.

1790. *John Franklin.*

Interest on 100*l.* in 2¾ p.c. Consols, for bread to be distributed annually in the months of December and January.

1791. *Mary Franklin.*

5*l.* to the Charity School.

Sarah Coggs.

40*l.* to the Charity School.

1798. *Samuel Hunton.*

Interest on 176*l.* in 2¾ p.c. Consols, for bread and coals to be distributed to poor widows and those of large families some time before Christmas.

1805. *Martha Burnsall.*

50*l.* and a house and premises in South Street, Hanover Square. Invested as 300*l.* in 5 p.c. Navy Stock, now 315*l.* in 2¾ p.c. Consols. To be distributed annually for the benefit of poor decayed housekeepers.

1812. *Catherine Abbott.*

Interest on 272*l.* 4*s.* 3*d.* in 2¾ p.c. Consols, to be distributed annually on January 1st, to six poor old decayed women.

Henry Hailstone.

50*s.* per annum for 21 years, to be annually distributed to the poor on Christmas Day.

1813. *John Gregory.*

21*l.*, to which the churchwardens added 2*l.* 14*s.* 6*d.* and purchased therewith 25*l.* in Navy 5 per cents. Now 26*l.* 5*s.* in 2¾ p.c. Consols. Distributed annually in bread to poor parishioners on Dec. 18th.

1822. *John Long.*

Interest on 118*l.* 17*s.* 5*d.* in 2¾ p.c. Consols, to be distributed to the poor in bread, annually on Jan. 14.

1824. *Elizabeth Dennis Denyer.*

Annual sum of 192*l.* 14*s.* 5*d.* arising from 2¾ p.c. Consols.

To 4 poor spinsters, parishioners, not under 60 years of age, of good character, constant at a place of worship (when able), who have never been beggars, 7*l.* each.

To 4 poor spinsters of same description 11*l.* 12*s.* 6*d.* each. (This part of the income, arising from a portion of the estate which

49

1824. *Elizabeth Dennis Denyer* (continued).

   fell to the Crown, and was allowed to charity upon petition, is called the King's Bounty.)

   By Mrs. Denyer's will the interest of the money placed in trust was, upon the death of her last annuitant, to be divided equally among 7 poor spinsters as described above. This now amounts to 119*l*.

   These gifts are annually distributed upon one of the first six days of January.

1827. *Thomas Morrison.*

   He left considerable property for the benefit of decayed house-keepers, etc., but it was not recovered on account of an alleged informality in the will.

   Mrs. Norman.

   Interest on 112*l*. 4*s*. in 2¾ p.c. Consols, to be annually distributed in coals, during the last week of January, to poor residents.

1828. *Elizabeth Smith.*

   Interest on 450*l*. in 2¾ p.c. Consols, applied as follows,—

   To the minister for a sermon on August 8th, 2*l*. 2*s*.

   To the Clerk, 1*l*. 1*s*.

   To the Parish Charity Schools for Boys and Girls, 2*l*. 2*s*.

   For Bread to be distributed to poor parishioners on August 8th, 7*l*. 2*s*. 4*d*.

1832. *Anne Sammon.*

   Interest on 210*l*. in 2¾ p.c. Consols, to be distributed annually in bread and coals on Dec. 24th.

1833. *William Gibbs.*

   Interest on 630*l*. in 2¾ p.c. Consols, to be divided equally between 18 poor men and 18 poor women. parishioners, above 60 years of age, who have not at any time been maintained in the Workhouse.

1847. *Charles Hatchett.*

   Interest on 112*l*. 7*s*. 2*d*. in 2¾ p.c. Consols, to be distributed annually in bread on Jan. 2nd to poor parishioners.

1849. *Luke Thomas Flood.*

   Interest on 1500*l*., 3 p.c. Bank Annuities, now 1534*l*. 10*s*. 6*d*. India 3 p.c., to be distributed annually as follows,—

      To the Clergyman for examining the Boys and Girls of the Parochial Schools, in the knowledge of the Church Catechism, and for a Sermon, 2*l*.

      To the most deserving boy and girl in the above examination, 1*l*. each.

1849. *Luke Thomas Flood* (continued).

> To the most punctual boy and girl in attendance at the above schools, 1*l.* each.
>
> To 7 girls and 8 boys, for singing Luther's hymn at the said Sermon, 1*s.* each.
>
> To the Organist who accompanies and plays the Dead March in 'Saul,' 1*l.* 10*s.*
>
> To the Master and Mistress who attend the said service, 10*s.* each.
>
> To the Clerk, 10*s.*
>
> To apprenticeships, 18*l.*
>
> For clothing children so apprenticed, 10*l.*
>
> For payment of Income Tax or for bread, 8*l.* 5*s.* 8*d.*

Interest on 1000*l.* in 3 p.c. Reduced Bank Annuities (now 1023*l.* India 3 p.c.) to be applied on Jan. 13th annually as follows,—

> To one deserving poor man, of 60 years or upwards, parishioner and householder, 15*l.*
>
> To one deserving poor woman under same conditions, 15*l.*

Interest on 100*l.* in 3 p.c. Consols, now 103*l.* 1*s.* 8*d.* India 3 p.c., as follows

> To be divided among the Vestry Room keeper, pew-openers, etc., employed on Jan. 13th, 1*l.* 10*s.*
>
> Towards the repair of the tomb or monument of the testator, 1*l.* 10*s.*
>
> Balance in bread, 1*s.* 8*d.*

Interest on 400*l.* Consols, now 412*l.* 6*s.* 9*d.* India 3 p.c. as follows,—

> For a repast to the Trustees, Clergymen, etc., not exceeding nine in number, 9*l.*
>
> For the same to the Teachers, Church Keeper, Pew Openers, Beadle, etc., 3*l.*
>
> Balance in bread, 7*s.* 4*d.*

1850. *Washington Cornelius Winter Ashfield* (otherwise *Washington Cornelius Ashfield*, otherwise *Washington Cornelius Winter*).

> Interest on 1000*l.* in 2¾ p.c. Consols to be divided annually on Dec. 21st, equally between 30 poor widows, housekeepers of at least ten years standing.

1853. *Mrs. Mary Carey.*

> 150*l.* for the poor of Upper Chelsea.

1856. *Mrs. Sabina Stirling Burgess.*

> 100*l.* in 3 p.c. for the poor of Upper Chelsea.

1857. *Sophia Forbes.*

Interest on 207*l.* 5*s.* 1*d.* in 2¾ p.c. Consols, to keep in repair the vault and monument of Testatrix in the Churchyard of St. Luke's Church : at the end of every 4 years the surplus is to be divided between the poor of the parish not in receipt of parochial relief.

1860. *Frederica Temple.*

5*l.* annually during the incumbency of the Rev. W. Niven to the charities of St. Saviour's Church.

1861. *Frances Elizabeth Eggleton.*

Interest on 200*l.* in 2¾ p.c. Consols to be distributed annually on Christmas Eve as follows,—

A shoulder of mutton, 7 to 8 lbs., and 4 lbs. of bread to 20 poor persons, married and having a family.

The surplus (if any) to be spent in wine for the Rector and Churchwardens.

Miss Philadelphia Catherine Roberdeau.

Various sums amounting to about 500*l.* to the Chelsea charities.

1862. *Charles Rawlings.*

Interest on 419*l.* 7*s.* 4*d.*, India 5 p.c. Stock, now India 3½ p.c., to be annually divided in the week preceding Christmas Day, equally between 4 poor housekeepers of the parish.

Mary Rogers.

Interest on 290*l.* 6*s.* 5*d.* in 2¾ p.c. Consols, to be distributed annually on Dec. 21st, in blankets and coals for aged poor parishioners.

1865. *Mrs. Sarah Handford.*

50*l.* to the Parochial Schools.

Miss Jemima Bennett.

540*l.* among the various Chelsea charities.

1866. *Miss Chittock.*

10*l.* to the Park Chapel Schools.

1867. *Miss Harriett Burrard.*

500*l.* to St. Luke's Parish Schools.

1877. *George Wood.*

Interest on 1062*l.* 8*s.* 4*d.* Consolidated 3 p.c. Annuities (now 1055*l.* 16*s.* 4*d.* India 3 p.c.), to be distributed half-yearly amongst the poor of the parish, irrespective of clime or creed.

1882. *Ann Hill.*

Interest on 900*l.* Consols, to be distributed annually in the first week of January, equally between 3 widows and 3 spinsters, parishioners.

APPENDIX IV.

BIBLIOGRAPHY.

Works marked (C) *are in the Chelsea Public Library.*

Acts of Parliament.

Act for repairing the roads in the parishes of Kensington, Chelsea, and Fulham. Ao. 12 Geo. I.

Act for enlarging term and powers of the above. Ao. 8 Geo. II.

Act for the better regulation of buildings and preventing fires in the cities of London and Westminster, the parishes of . . . St. Luke, Chelsea, etc. Ao. 14 Geo. III., cap. 78.

Act for building a new church in the parish of St. Luke, Chelsea. 1819.

Chelsea Rectory Act, 1825.

Act for Collecting the Poor's Rate, etc., of the Parish of St. Luke, Chelsea. With the Bye-Laws made by the Committee Men. 1826. (C)

Act for the Administration of the Poor Laws, in the parish of St. Luke, Chelsea, etc., and relating to the Highways of the said parish. Ao. 4 & 5. Vic. c. 17.

Act for the better paving, lighting, cleansing, etc., the parish of Chelsea, exclusive of Hans Town. Ao. 8 & 9 Vic., cap. cxliij.

Chelsea Rectory Act, 1870.

Alfordus (otherwise Michael Griffiths).

Fides Regia Britannica. Leodii, 1663, fol.

Allen, Thomas.

History and Antiquities of London. London, 1827-29, 8vo.

Ambulator, The. London, 1787, etc., 12mo.

Anderson, J. P.

Life of D. G. Rossetti. London, 1887, 8vo.

Anonymous.

Chelsea Book Series [Tracts by the Minister of Park Chapel]. London, 1873, etc., 32mo.

Anonymous (*continued*).

  Chelsea College. A Briefe declaration of the reasons that induced King James and the State to erect a College of Divines and other learned men at Chelsey. 1645, 4to.

  Chelsea College [Hospital]. Case of the agents for the out-pensioners. [London, 1755?], s. sh. fol.

  Chelsea Householder, The. A Novel. London, 1882, 8vo.

  Chelsea Monarch, The, or money rules all. London, 1731, folio.

  Gwynne, Nell. Memoirs of the Life of Eleanor Gwynn. London, 1752, 8vo.

  Handbook of the Antiquities, etc., of Chelsea. London, 1841, 12mo.

  Parochial Pickings [chiefly consisting of animadversions on the capabilities of the medical officer of the parish]. London, 1831, 8vo.

  St. Luke's Church. An Account of the erection of the New Parish Church. London, 1824, 8vo.

  Trial of all the prisoners at the late Chelsea Sessions [satirical; parochia affairs]. Chelsea, 1822, 4to.

Barham, Henry.

  An Essay upon the Silkworm. London, 1719, 8vo.

  The Produce of India, etc., produced in England. London, 1720, 8vo.

Birch, W. de Grey.

  Cartularium Saxonicum. London, 1883, *et seq.*, 4to.

Blunt, Rev. Gerald (ed.).

  A Chelsea Calendar, Christmas, 1888. London (pp. 50), 1888, 4to. (c)

Brayley, E. W., etc.

  London and Middlesex (5 vols.). London, 1810-16. (c)

Brayley, E. W., and Britton, J., etc.

  Beauties of England and Wales (18 vols.). London, 1801-15, 8vo.

Bryan, George.

  Chelsea in the Olden and Present Times. Chelsea, 1869, 8vo. (c)

Bumpus, T. F.

  London Churches. London, 1881, etc., 8vo.

Burgess, Rev. Richard.

  Sermon on the Death of the Rev. Henry Blunt, A.M. London, 1843, 8vo.

Burleigh Papers.

Burroughs, J.

  Fresh Fields. London, 1885. (c)

Burt, Isabella.

  Historical Notices of Chelsea, etc. London, 1871, 8vo. (c)

Butler, Rev. Weeden.
    Philanthropy, Religion, and Loyalty. A Sermon. London, 1798, 8vo.
    Sermon preached before the Chelsea Armed Association. Chelsea, 1799, 8vo.
    Correspondence of. MSS. Additional, British Museum, n. 27577-8.
Butler, Rev. Weeden, jun.
    Bagatelles. London, 1795, 8vo.
C., E. M.
    Moravians in England, The. 4to. (c)
Carlyle, Jane Welsh.
    Letters and Memorials of (ed. Froude, 3 vols.). London, 1883, 8vo. (c)
Carlyle, Thomas.
    Reminiscences (ed. Froude, 2 vols.). London, 1881, 8vo. (c)
Carter, Mrs. Elizabeth.
    Letters to Mrs. Montagu (ed. M. Pennington). London, 1817, 8vo.
    Memoirs, by M. Pennington (2 vols.). London, 1808, 8vo.
    Poems on Several Occasions. London, 1789, 12mo.
Cecil, Rev. Richard.
    Discourses and Memoir of the Hon. W. B. Cadogan, M.A. London, 1798, 8vo.
    Memoir of the Hon. and Rev. W. B. Cadogan, M.A. London, 1822, 8vo.
Chaffers, William.
    Marks and Monograms on Pottery. London, 1886, 8vo. (c)
Chester, Col. Joseph Lemuel.
    London Marriage Licenses. London, 1887, 4to.
    Westminster Registers. London, 1876, 4to.
Clarendon Papers (ed. W. Macray). Oxford, 1869, *et seq.*, 8vo.
Clifford, J. R. S. ('Quiz').
    Various Articles on Chelsea History published in the *West Middlesex Advertiser*.
Collier, J.
    Ecclesiastical History of Great Britain (2 vols.). London, 1708-14, fol.
Collins, Arthur.
    Letters and Memorials of State (2 vols.). London, 1746, fol.
Court and Times of Charles I. London, 8vo.
Croker, T. C.
    Walk from London to Fulham. London, 1860, 8vo. (c)

Originally published in *Fraser's Magazine*, 1845.

Cross, J. W.
> Life of George Eliot.   London, 1886, 8vo.

Cruden, Alexander.
> Adventures of Alexander the Corrector, &c. (3 parts and appendix).
> London, 1753-4, 8vo.

Cunningham, Peter.
> Handbook for London (2 vols.).   London, 1849, 8vo.

Danvers, Sir John, Bart.
> Notes on the Case of Sir John Danvers's Settlement.   London (?),
> 1691 (?), s. sh. fol.

D'Arblay, Mme. (Fanny Burney).
> Diary of (ed. Charlotte Barrett, 7 vols.).   London, 1842-6, 8vo.
> Memoir of Dr. Burney.   London, 1832, 8vo.

Darley, Rev. John.
> The Glory of Chelsea College revived.   London, 1662, 4to.

Davies, Rev. R. H.
> Chelsea Old Church.   A Lecture.   Chelsea, 1887, 24mo.   (c)

Davis, H. G.
> Memorials of Knightsbridge.   London, 1859, 12mo.   (c)

De Dominiceti, Bartholomew.
> Address.   London, 1782, 8vo.   (c)
> A plan for extending the use of artificial water baths.   London,
> 1771, 12mo.   (c)

Dibdin, Charles.
> The Chelsea Pensioner ; Comic Opera.   London, 1779, 8vo.

Dilke, Sir Charles Wentworth, Bart.
> Old Chelsea.   A Lecture.   1st edition, Chelsea, 1886, 8vo.
>   ,,   ,,   ,,   2nd edition, Chelsea, 1888, 8vo.   (c)

Don Saltero's Coffee House.
> Catalogue of the Rarities.   Various editions, 12mo.   (c)

Dugdale, Sir William.
> Baronage of England (2 vols.).   London, 1675-6, fol.

D'Urfey, Thomas.
> New Poems.   London, 1690, 8vo.

Dyce, Rev. Alexander (editor for Shakspere Society).
> Sir Thomas More.   A Play.   London, 1844, 8vo.

Elmes, James.
> Topographical Dictionary of London.   London, 1831, 8vo.

Elsmere, Rev. Sloane.
> Sermons (2 vols.).   London, 1769, 8vo.   (c)

Emerson, G. R.
> Excursionists' Guide to Environs of London.   London, 1867, 8vo.

Evelyn, John.
> Diary and Correspondence (4 vols., ed. Bray).   London, 1881-6, 8vo.   (c)

Faulkner, Thomas.
> History and Description of Chelsea Hospital.   London, 1805, 12mo.   (c)
>> The MS. of this work is now in the Chelsea Free Library.

> History of Chelsea.   1st edition, 1 vol., London, 1810, 8vo.   (c)
> ,,   ,,   2nd edition, 2 vols., London, 1829, 8vo.   (c)
>> There is a copy of this 2nd edition inlaid to 4to., and extended to 4 vols., with extra portraits, views, autographs, etc., the collection of the late Mr. W. Mayer, of Liverpool, in the Chelsea Free Library.

> Papers in *Gentleman's Magazine*, 1832.
> ,,   *Illustrated Polytechnic Review*, 1843.

Field, H.
> Memoirs of the Botanic Gardens at Chelsea.   London, 1820, 8vo.   (c)
> ,,   ,,   ,,   ,,   ,,   Revised and continued by
>> R. H. Semple.   London, 1878, 8vo.   (c)

Flecknoe, Richard.
> Epigrams of all Sorts.   London, 1671, 8vo.

Froude, J. Anthony.
> Thomas Carlyle: A History of his Life in London (2 vols.).   London, 1890, 8vo.   (c)

Gaskell, Frederick.
> List of Chelsea Charities.   Chelsea, 1849, 12mo.

Gleig, Rev. G. R.
> Chelsea Hospital and its Traditions.   London, 1857, 8vo.   (c)
> Chelsea Pensioner, The.   A Novel.   London, 1831, 8vo.
> Veterans of Chelsea Hospital.   London, 1857, 8vo.   (c)

Goode, Rev. Wm.
> Sermon on the Death of the Hon. and Rev. W. B. Cadogan, A.M.
>> London, 1797, 8vo.

Gosse, E. W.
> Life of Cecil Lawson.   London, 1883, 4to.   (c)

Haddan, A. W., and W. Stubbs (editors).
> Councils and Ecclesiastical Documents relating to Great Britain and Ireland (3 vols. in 4).   London, 1869-78, 4to.   (c)

Hall, Mrs. S. C.
> Forlorn Hope, The.   A Chelsea Story.   London (no date), 4to.   (c)
> Pilgrimage to English Shrines.   London, 1850, 4to.

Hanway, Jonas (?).
    Reasons for Opening the Maritime School, Chelsea. London, 1779. (c)
    Rules and Regulations of the Maritime School. [London, 1781,] 12mo.
Hare, A. J.
    Walks in London. London, 1883, 8vo.
Hartlib, Samuel.
    The Reformed Spiritual Husbandman. London, 1652, 4to.
Hassell, J.
    Excursions on the Thames. London, 1823, 12mo. (c)
Hastings, Selina, Countess of Huntingdon.
    Life and Times. London, 1844, 8vo.
Haynes.
    Accurate Survey of the Botanic Gardens, Chelsea. London, *circa* 1751.
Hughson, David.
    London (6 vols.). London, 1805-9, 8vo.
    Walks through London. London, 1817, 12mo.
Hunt, J. H. Leigh.
    Autobiography. London, 1850, 8vo. (c)
Hurdis, James.
    Sir Thomas More. A Tragedy. London, 1792, 8vo.
Hutt, G. (editor).
    Papers Illustrating the Origin and Early History of Chelsea Hospital.
        London, 1872, 8vo. (c)
Hutton, Laurence.
    Literary Landmarks of London. London, 1885, 8vo. (c)
Irving, J.
    Some Account of the Family of Smollett. Dumbarton, 1859, 4to.
Jewitt, Llewellyn.
    Ceramic Art of Great Britain. 1st edition, London, 1877, 4to.
       ,,   ,,   ,,   ,,   2nd edition, London, 1883, 4to. (c)
Kemble.
    Codex Diplomaticus ævi Saxonicum (6 vols.). London, 1839-48, 8vo.
King, Rev. John, Rector of Chelsea.
    Sermon at the Funeral of Sir Willoughby Chamberlain. London,
        1697, 4to.
    Manuscripts :
        Supplement and Remarks on Life of Sir Thomas More.
        Letter designed for Mr. Hearne respecting Sir Thos. More's House
          at Chelsea.
            For another copy see *Notes and Queries*, 2nd series, ii. 324.

King, Rev. John.   Manuscripts (*continued*).

    A Copy of the Dean of N.'s Letter to Mr. Chamberlayne.

    Epitaphs, Riddles, Verses on Various Persons.

The above are in the British Museum.

    Account of Chelsea.

In the Rectory Library.

Kingsley, Rev. Henry.

    The Hillyars and the Burtons.   A Novel.   3 vols.   London and Cambridge, 1865, 8vo.   (c)

Republished in the *West London Press.*

Knaggs, Rev. Thos.

    Sermon at Funeral of Mrs. Elizabeth Roberts.   London, 1710, 8vo.   (c)

Knight, Charles (editor).

    London (6 vols.).   London, 1841-44, 8vo.   (c)

    ,,   Revised by Walford.   London [1875-77], 8vo.

Kruse, P.

    Efforts made by the Inhabitants of Chelsea to give efficiency to the Act of Parliament passed for their benefit.   Chelsea, 1822, 12mo.   (c)

    Further Statement on the same subject.   Chelsea, 1823, 12mo.

Larwood, J., and J. C. Hotten.

    History of Signboards.   London, 1867, 4to.

L'Estrange, A. G.

    The Village of Palaces (2 vols.).   London, 1880, 8vo.   (c)

Littleton, Rev. Adam.

    Sermon at Funeral of Mrs. Mary Alston.   London, 1671, 4to.

    Sermon at Funeral of Lady Jane Cheyne.   London, 1669, 4to.

Loftie, Rev. W. J.

    History of London (3 vols.).   London, 1883-4, 8vo.   (c)

Luttrell, Narcissus.

    Briefe Historical Narration of State Affairs.   Oxford, 1857, 8vo.

Lysons, Rev. Daniel.

    Environs of London.   London, 1795, etc., fol.

    Supplement.   London, 1811, fol.

Macquoid, Katherine S.

    The Little Hospital by the River, 1877.

    The Little Hospital in Cheyne Walk, 1882.

Two papers in *Macmillan's Magazine.*

Magna Britannia (6 vols.).   London, 1720-31, 4to.

Maitland, William.

    History of London.   1st edition, London, 1739, fol.

Maitland, William (*continued*).
> History of London, continued to 1772, by Rev. J. Entick (3 vols.).
> > London, 1772, fol.

[Manning, Anne.]
> Chelsea Bun-House, The.   London, 1855, 8vo.   (c)
> Household of Sir Thomas More, The.   London, 1860, 8vo.   (c)

Marryatt, Joseph.
> Pottery and Porcelain.   3rd edition, London, 1868, 8vo.

Martin, Benjamin Ellis.
> Old Chelsea.   London, 1889, 8vo.   (c)
> > Originally published in the *Century Magazine*, 1886.

Martyn, Thos.
> Account of an Aurora Australis seen at Chelsea, 1738-9.
> Account of an Earthquake felt in London, 1749-50.

Matthew Paris.
> Chronica Majora (ed. Luard).   London, 1872, etc., 4to.

Metcalfe, Walter C.
> Book of Knights, London, 1885, 8vo.

Meteyard, Eliza.
> Life of Joshua Wedgwood (2 vols.).   London, 1865-6, 8vo.

Mogg, E.
> London in Miniature.   London, 1820.   (c)

More, Sir Thomas.
> Various lives of ; among others :
> > Cayley, A. (2 vols.).   London, 1808, 4to.   (c)
> > Hoddesdon, J.   London, 1652.   (c)
> > Macintosh, Sir J.   1831.   (c)
> > More, Cresacre (ed. Hunter).   London, 1828, 8vo.   (c)
> > Roper, William (ed. Lumby).   1888.   (c)

Munk, Wm.
> Roll of the College of Physicians of London.   London, 1878, 8vo.

Murray, J. F.
> Picturesque Tour of the River Thames.   London, 1853.   (c)
> Environs of London.   London, 1842, 8vo.

Newcourt, Richard.
> Repertorium Ecclesiasticum Parochiale Londinense (2 vols.).   London,
> > 1708-10, fol.

Nicholas.
> Testamenta Vetusta.   London, 1826, 4to.

Nicholls, J. G.
    Correspondence of Bishop Atterbury (5 vols.).
    Progresses of Queen Elizabeth (3 vols.). London, 1788-1805 4to.
Nightingale, James E.
    Contributions towards the History of Early English Porcelain. 1881. (c)
Norden, J.
    Speculum Britanniæ. London, 1724, fol.
O'Driscoll, J.
    Memoir of D. Maclise, R.A. London, 1871, 8vo
Partington, C. F. (editor).
    National History and Views of London and its Environs (2 vols.).
        London, 1834.
Pepys, Samuel.
    Diary and Correspondence (ed. Braybrooke), with additional notes by M.
        Bright. London, 1875-79, 8vo.
Periodical Publications :
    Local Press :
        West Middlesex Advertiser.
        West London Press (formerly Chelsea News).
        Chelsea Herald. Extinct.
        Chelsea Gazette. Contained parochial reports, etc. Nos. 1-8, all
            published. Chelsea, 1822, 12mo.
        Chelsea Magazine. Published by the Chelsea Athenæum, but none of
            the papers relate to Chelsea history. London, 1861, 8vo.
        Parish Magazine.
        Old Church Magazine.
        Park Chapel Magazine.
        St. Mark's Magazine.
        St. Saviour's Magazine.
        Whiteland's Annual.
    Antiquarian, artistic, and other publications :
        The Gentleman's Magazine.
        The Monthly Magazine.
        Notes and Queries.
        The Herald and Genealogist.
        The Antiquary.
        London and Middlesex Note-Book.
                The above for general information.
        The Art Journal.
        The Portfolio.

Antiquarian, artistic, and other publications (*continued*).
    The Magazine of Art.
    The Artist.
        For biographies of artists, etc.
    The Architect.
    The Builder.
        For accounts and illustrations of new buildings, etc.

Phené, J. S.
    Les Huguenots.
    Old London. Old Chelsea.
        Papers read before learned Societies.

Phillips, Sir Richard.
    A Morning's Walk from London to Kew. London, 1820, 8vo. (c)
        Originally published in the *Monthly Magazine.*

Redgrave, Samuel.
    Dictionary of English Artists. London, 1878, 8vo.

Remembrancia of the City of London (ed. Overall). London, 1878, 8vo.
        Several references to Chelsea fisheries, etc.

Reports :
    Chelsea Charities, by C. Lahee, Clerk to the Vestry. Chelsea, 1863-67, fol.
      ,,   ,,   revised to December, 1890, by Thos. Holland, Clerk.
        Chelsea, 1890, 8vo. (c)
    Chelsea Parish. General Bills of all the Christenings and Burials.
        [London, 1778-89,] fol.
    Chelsea Vestry. Annual Reports. Chelsea, 1855, *et seq.*, 8vo.
    Committee of the Bank for Savings for Chelsea. Chelsea, 1819, *et seq.*, 8vo.
    Hospital for Consumption.
    Hospital for Women.
    Ophthalmic Institution, York Hospital. First Annual Report. London,
        1819, 8vo.
    Royal Asylum for Destitute Females, 1822, *et seq.*
    Victoria Hospital for Children (Pharmacopœia). London, 1884, 8vo.

Richardson, T.
    Survey of the Manor of Chelsea. London, 1769, roll. (British Museum.)

Rocque.
    Survey of the cities of London and Westminster, etc., 1748. (c)

Rye, Walter.
    Notes on the Monuments, etc., in Chelsea Old Church.
    The Lawrences of Iver and Chelsea.
        Two papers in the *Herald and Genealogist.*

Schroeder, H. B.
    Chelsea Quarters ; a Ballad. London, 1790 (?), fol.

Sharpe, R. R.
>   Calendar of Wills, Court of Husting (2 vols.).   London, 1889-91, fol.

Shepherd, Samuel.
>   Spring Buds; Poems.   London, 1844, 12mo.

Smith, Thomas.
>   Handbook for Visitors to the Royal Hospital.   London, 1851, 12mo.

Smith, Thomas Tunstall.
>   Sermons preached at Chelsea, 1842.   (c)

Spenser, Edmund.
>   Daphnaïda, 1596.

State Papers, etc. :
>   Acts of the Privy Council.
>   Calendar of Ancient Deeds.
>   Calendar of Patent Rolls.
>   Calendar of the Proceedings of the Committee for Advance of Money.
>   Calendar of the Proceedings of the Committee for Compounding.
>   Calendar of State Papers.   (c)
>   Chelsea Hospital.   Further Papers presented to the House of Commons relating to the Building of a New Infirmary.   1809.
>   Domesday Book.   Illustrated by R. Kelham.   London, 1788, 8vo. (2 vols., 1811-16).
>   Domesday Book.   Facsimile and translation of portion relating to Middlesex, by Harrison.   1876.   (c)
>   Holy Trinity Church, Sloane Street.   Papers relating to the building and negotiations with the Ecclesiastical Commissioners.   London, 1834, 8vo.
>   Home Office Papers.
>   Inquisitiones Post Mortem.
>   Journals of the House of Commons.
>   Letters and Papers of the reign of Henry VIII.
>   Originalia et Memoranda.
>   Reports of the Deputy-Keeper of the Records.
>   Reports of the Historical Manuscripts Commission.
>   Rotuli Curia Regis.
>   Rotuli Hundredorum.
>   Taxatus Ecclesiastica, etc., *circa* 1291.
>   Treasury Papers.

Steele, Sir Richard.
>   Epistolary Correspondence.   London, 1787, 8vo.
>   Life of, by G. A. Aitken (2 vols.).   London, 1889, 4to.   (c)

Stephen, Leslie (editor).
    Dictionary of National Biography. London, 1885, *et seq.*, 8vo. (c)
Strickland, Agnes.
    Lives of the Queens of England (8 vols.). London, 1840-48, 8vo. (c)
Swift, Patrick.
    Correspondence. London, 1741, 8vo.
    Journal to Stella. (See works by Scott.) London, 1883-4, 19 vols., 8vo. (c)
'Theophilus.'
    Chelsea in 1838, an Essay in Rhyme (2 parts). Chelsea, 1838, 8vo.
Thombury, V., and E. Walford.
    Old and New London (6 vols.). London (no date), 4to. (c)
Thorne, James.
    Rambles by Rivers (2 vols.) London, 1847-9, 12mo.
Thorpe, Benjamin.
    Diplomatarum Anglicum ævi Saxonicum. London, 1865, 8vo.
Timbs, John.
    Curiosities of London. 1855. (c)
    Chelsea China, article in *Leisure Hour*, 1867.
Transactions of Learned Societies, etc. :
    Archæologia.
    Camden Society Publications. (c)
    Chetham Society Publications.
    Harleian Society Publications.
    Historical Society Publications.
    Journal of the Archæological Institute.
    Journal of the British Archæological Association.
    London and Middlesex Archæological Society.
    Surtees Society Publications.
Trotter, Wm. E.
    Select Illustrated Topography. London, 1839. (c)
Tymms, Samuel.
    Compendium, etc., of Middlesex, London, and Westminster. No date.
Wakefield, Priscilla.
    Perambulations in London. London, 1814, 12mo.
Walpole, Horace, Earl of Oxford.
    Anecdotes of Painting (ed. Wornum, 3 vols.). London, 1849, 8vo.
    Letters (ed. Cunningham, 9 vols.). London, 1891, 8vo.
Warmstry, Thomas.
    The Baptized Turk. London, 1658, 8vo.

Weever, John.
  Ancient Funeral Monuments. London, 1631, fol.
Wild, C. R.
  History of the Royal Society. London, 1848, 8vo.
Whitelocke, R. H.
  Memoirs of Bulstrode Whitelock. London, 1860, 8vo.
Williams, Folkestone.
  Memoirs and Correspondence of F. Atterbury, Bishop of Rochester.
    London, 1869, 8vo.
Woodman, John.
  A Scheme to pay the Out-pensioners of Chelsea. London, 1740, 8vo.
  The Ratcatcher of Chelsea College. London, 1740, 8vo.

MANUSCRIPTS.

Additional, British Museum :
    5752. Payments for Royal Hospital.
    5853. Notes on Chelsea Church.
    5940. Reports upon the Out-Pensioners at Chelsea, 1711-13.
    8979. Notes on Chelsea Old Church.
    11506. (Scudamore Papers.)   Several letters relating to Sir John Danvers,
      Sir Arthur Gorges, etc.
    15609. Several Papers relating to Chelsea.
    27276. Walk through the British Museum, by Rev. Weeden Butler. 1767.
Additional Charters :
    16153. Mortgage of Marquis of Winchester's House. 1572.
Ashmolean, Oxford :
    857, 91. Warrant by Earl of Shrewsbury. Chelsey, Dec. 4, 1584.
    857, 159. Narrative of the Procession of the Lord Mayor and the Citizens
      to Chelsea, 160.
    1729, 4. Letter of Katherine Parr to Admiral Seymour, from Chelsey.
Bodleian :
    Coll. et Aul. Omn. An. cclix., 75. Charter of Foundation of Chelsea
        Hospital.
    Rawlinson, 341, 30. Inventory of Pictures, etc. at Buckingham House,
        Chelsey.
        381, 32. Assignment of a Pew in Chelsey Church, 1685.

Bodleian (*continued*).

    Tanner, cxlij. Will of Dr. Sutcliffe, copy, and paper concerning the same.
        Decree in Chancery concerning Chelsey College.
        Several letters on the state of Chelsey College.
        Petition of the Regent and Professors of the Museum
            Minervæ.
        ccxc. Letters upon Chelsea Hospital.

Cottonian (British Museum) :

    Aug. ii. 26-27. Charter of Offa of Mercia, 787.

    Faust. A. iii., f. 108*b*. Charter of Edward the Confessor printed in Hickes,
        Thesaurus (i., p. 158).

    Vesp. A. xiv., 147-151. Acts of the Council of Celchyth, 815. Revised
        version in Spelman and Wilkins.

Devonshire, Duke of. Household Books for Chelsea.

Harleian, British Museum :

    284, 76. Letter from John Dudley, Duke of Northumberland, Chelsey.

    376, 53 and 55. Letters of Muys de Holy, Chelsey, 7 Mart. 1630. s.n. and
        3 Julij, st. n., A.D. 1630.

    570. Norden's 'Speculum Britanniæ.'

    1096. Pedigree of Lawrence.

    1583, n. 128. Letter from Jaques Bruneau, Spanish Minister, dated Chelsi,
        7 de Fbre, 1625.

    1711. Said to contain a reference to Sir John Danvers' Estate in Chelsea.

    6281. Reference to Manor of Chelsea.

    6853, n. 88. 'Rentall of Lands belonging to Manor of Chelsey.'
        f. 202. 'Notes of [Gilbert] Earle of Shrewsbury's Answ[er] in the cause
            Breton against Shrewsbury.'

    7368. 'S[r] Tho[s] More—a play,' c. 1590.

Lansdowne (British Museum) :

    2, v. 'Particuler of Chelsey Manor.'

    85. Contains two papers relating to the Manor.

    289. Paper on Chelsea China Factory, by N. Sprimont (?).

    949. Will of Hugh, Bishop of Exeter.

Sloane (British Museum) :

    Note relating to Danvers House.

    The above list does not pretend to be exhaustive, but consists of the more important works which the author has found useful in the preparation of the present volume.

INDEX.

51—2

Elliot Stock, Paternoster Row, London.